The first edition of this book was written by Edward de la Billière, Keith Carter and Charlie Loram. The second edition was updated and partly rewritten by Chris Scott with additional research by Lucy Ridout. The third was updated by Jim Manthorpe, the fourth by Stuart Greig and the fifth by Henry Stedman.

BRADLEY MAYHEW updated this sixth edition. He is a British travel writer specialising in the mountains of Asia. He's the co-author of numerous Lonely Planet guides: *Trekking in the Nepal Himalaya*, *Nepal*, *India*, *Bhutan*, *Central Asia* and many others. He is also the co-author of Wilderness Press's *Top Trails: Yellowstone & Grand Teton National Parks* and starred in a ten-part documentary for European channel *Arte* on Europe's Most Beautiful Long Distance Trails.

Authors

Pennine Way First edition: 2006; **this sixth edition: 2023**

Publisher Trailblazer Publications
The Old Manse, Tower Rd, Hindhead, Surrey, GU26 6SU, UK
info@trailblazer-guides.com, trailblazer-guides.com

British Library Cataloguing in Publication Data
A catalogue record for this book is available from the British Library

ISBN 978-1-912716-33-3

© Trailblazer 2004, 2008, 2011, 2014, 2019, 2023: Text and maps

Series editor: Anna Jacomb-Hood   **Editing & layout**: Nicky Slade
Cartography & illustrations (pp67-70): Nick Hill   **Proofreading**: Jane Thomas
Index: Anna Jacomb-Hood   **Photographs (flora)**: © Bryn Thomas
All other photographs: © Bradley Mayhew (unless otherwise indicated)

The maps in this guide were prepared from out-of-Crown-
copyright Ordnance Survey maps amended and updated by Trailblazer.

Acknowledgements

FROM BRADLEY: Thanks to all the hikers I met on the trail and the numerous people who
answered my endlessly detailed questions. Special thanks to Chris and Corinne Dickson,
who put me up, fed me and revitalised me for the second half of the walk. Cheers to Keith
Down for his updates on the trail. At Trailblazer, thanks to: Nicky Slade for editing and layout, Jane Thomas for proofreading, Nick Hill for the maps and Anna Jacomb-Hood for the
index. I'd also like to thank all those readers who wrote in with comments and suggestions,
in particular Stuart Blackburne, Kevin Blick, Mick Brewster, Jonathan Brown, Dave Carroll,
Iain Chippendale, James Connolly, Mike Cowley, Keith Down, Bill Gallon (Chairman of the
Pennine Way Association), Harry Giles, Stuart Greig, Simon Hall, Mats Heder, Nichola
Hele, Paul Higinbotham, Tony Hufton, Muck Moses, Jolyon Neely, William O'Neill, Lee
Richardson, Chris Sainty, Mick Scarfe, Peter Steward, Ursula Studer, Simon and Sylvia,
John Smithson, Chris Taylor, Jane Taylor, Andrew Welsh, Vinny Whalley and Willemijn W.

A request

The authors and publisher have tried to ensure that this guide is as accurate and up to date
as possible. However, things change even on these well-worn routes. If you notice any
changes or omissions that should be included in the next edition of this guide, please email
us (⌨ info@trailblazer-guides.com) or write to us (address above). Those persons making
a significant contribution will be rewarded with a free copy of the next edition.

Warning: hillwalking can be dangerous

Please read the notes on when to go (pp13-16) and outdoor safety (pp78-80). Every effort
has been made by the author and publisher to ensure that the information contained herein
is as accurate and up to date as possible. However, they are unable to accept responsibility
for any inconvenience, loss or injury sustained by anyone as a result of the advice and information given in this guide.

Photos – Front cover: Climbing towards Great Shunner Fell from Hardraw.
This page: Hikers descending from Malham Cove.   **Previous page**: Looking back at
Walshaw Dean reservoirs, en route to Top Withins (see p120).   **Overleaf**: Flagstone
Pennine Way winding across the magnificent emptiness of Great Shunner Fell (see p171).

Updated information will be available on: ⌨ www.trailblazer-guides.com

Printed in China; print production by D'Print (☎ +65-6581 3832), Singapore

Pennine Way

138 large-scale maps & guides to 57 towns and villages

PLANNING – PLACES TO STAY – PLACES TO EAT

EDALE TO KIRK YETHOLM

STUART GREIG &
BRADLEY MAYHEW

TRAILBLAZER PUBLICATIONS

INTRODUCTION

About the Pennine Way

PART 1: PLANNING YOUR WALK

Practical information for the walker

Budgeting 32

Itineraries

What to take

Getting to and from the Pennine Way

PART 2: THE ENVIRONMENT & NATURE

Conserving the Pennines 60

Flora and fauna

PART 3: MINIMUM IMPACT WALKING & OUTDOOR SAFETY

Minimum impact walking

Outdoor safety

Contents

PART 4: ROUTE GUIDE & MAPS

Contents

ABOUT THIS BOOK

This guidebook contains all the information you need. The hard work has been done for you so you can plan your trip without having to consult numerous websites and other books and maps. When you're ready to go, there's comprehensive public transport information to get you to and from the trail and detailed maps (1:20,000) to help you find your way along it.

● Where to stay – from wild camping to B&Bs, hostels and hotels

● Walking companies if you want an organised tour and baggage-transfer services if you just want your luggage carried

● Itineraries for all levels of walkers

● Answers to all your questions: when is the best time to walk, how hard is it, what to pack and the approximate cost of the trip

● Walking times in both directions; GPS waypoints as a back-up to navigation

● Availability and opening times of cafés, pubs, tea-shops, restaurants, and shops/supermarkets along the route

● Rail, bus and taxi information for the towns and villages on or near the Way

● Street maps of the main towns and villages

● Historical, cultural and geographical background information

POST COVID NOTE

This edition of the guide was researched after the Covid pandemic but is liable to more change than usual. Some of the hotels, cafés, pubs, restaurants and tourist attractions may not survive the further hardships caused by rising fuel prices, inflation and staff shortages. Do forgive us where your experience on the ground contradicts what is written in the book; please email us – info@trailblazer-guides.com so we can add your information to the updates page on the website.

❏ MINIMUM IMPACT FOR MAXIMUM INSIGHT

Nature's peace will flow into you as the sunshine flows into trees. The winds will blow their freshness into you and storms their energy, while cares will drop off like autumn leaves. **John Muir** (one of the world's first and most influential environmentalists, born in 1838)

Why is walking in wild and solitary places so satisfying? Partly it is the sheer physical pleasure: sometimes pitting one's strength against the elements and the lie of the land. The beauty and wonder of the natural world and the fresh air restore our sense of proportion and the stresses and strains of everyday life slip away. Whatever the character of the countryside, walking in it benefits us mentally and physically, inducing a sense of well-being, an enrichment of life and an enhanced awareness of what lies around us. All this the countryside gives us and the least we can do is to safeguard it by supporting rural economies, local businesses, and low-impact methods of farming and land-management, and by using environmentally sensitive forms of transport – walking being pre-eminent.

INTRODUCTION

The Pennine Way is the grand-daddy of all the UK National Trails and although its 268-mile (431km) length doesn't qualify it as the longest trail (that honour goes to the mammoth 636-mile long South-West Coast Path), it was the first and is probably the best known of

As well as physical fitness... above all else a Pennine Wayfarer needs a positive mental attitude.

all the National Trails. Surprisingly, it is almost equally loved and loathed by those who walk it and it is certainly a challenge however you decide to tackle it.

As well as physical fitness, determination and an ability to smile in the face of a howling wind, above all else a Pennine Wayfarer needs a positive mental attitude. There will be times when you just want to throw in the towel, catch the next train or bus home and never return to the moors again, but you must overcome these moments of weakness if you want to reach Scotland and the Border Hotel.

As you progress, the walking gets easier as you become fitter, the scenery is diverse and engaging and there's always something of interest to see, including an incredible variety of plants and wildlife and some of the best walking on offer in the UK.

The path begins in the Peak District, in the heart of England and cunningly weaves between the old industrial centres of Manchester, Huddersfield, Halifax and Burnley. By sticking as much as possible

Looking back towards Edale from Swine's Back Tor, near Kinder Scout. The fine moorland scenery starts on Day 1, after the ascent from Edale up Jacob's Ladder.

Above: The Old Nag's Head, the pub in Edale that marks the start of the Pennine Way (see p86).

to the high heather moors between these conurbations it visits Stoodley Pike monument and Top Withins, thought by some to be Wuthering Heights from Emily Brontë's novel.

The path soon leaves the gritstone of the Southern Pennines behind and the rocks become light grey as you enter limestone country through the Airedale Gap and into Malham, the home of the incredible natural amphitheatre of Malham Cove. A tough day over Fountains Fell and Pen-y-ghent brings you to Horton-in-Ribblesdale, the start and finish of the Yorkshire Three Peaks walk. The Way visits the iconic Yorkshire Dales of Wensleydale and Swaledale and traverses Great Shunner Fell between them. After a quick stop at the highest pub in Great Britain (Tan Hill Inn) you reach the halfway point at Baldersdale. Now your muscles are like steel wires, you hardly feel the weight of your rucksack and your sights are firmly set on Scotland.

Possibly the best day walk anywhere in the country starts at Middleton-in-Teesdale, taking in three incredible waterfalls and the stunning glacial valley of High Cup followed, the next day, by the highest point on the walk over Cross Fell (2930ft/893m).

Below: High Cup Nick is one of the most impressive sights of the walk (see p199).

Beyond this, you spend a day walking the best section of Hadrian's Wall, before plunging into the forests of Wark and Redesdale, emerging into the town of Bellingham, the last proper outpost of civilisation before the end.

Technically you've left the Pennines behind now, as you pass through Byrness and over the rolling green mountains of the Cheviot range for the last marathon section into Kirk Yetholm.

You may arrive at the Border Hotel a different person – the walk has certainly had a profound effect on many of the people who have walked it (see the Personal Experience boxes throughout this book), but even if not, you've completed one of the planet's great walks. And if you've managed to do it without getting rained on, you really are one in a million!

About the Pennine Way

HISTORY

Anyone walking the Pennine Way today owes a debt of thanks to the journalist Tom Stephenson. When he first proposed 'a long green trail' in 1935 there were no official long-distance footpaths in the UK. He first described 'a Pennine Way from the Peaks to the Cheviots' in an article in the *Daily Herald* in June

> **When Tom Stephenson first proposed 'a long green trail' in 1935 there were no official long-distance footpaths in the UK**

of that year, in response to a letter from two American ramblers who were looking for suggestions on walks to do in England. America, he said, already had two incredible treks: the 2000-mile (3200km) long Appalachian Trail in the east

and the even longer, 2500-mile (4000km) John Muir Trail up the western side of the country. Albeit on a smaller scale, he suggested there was no reason why England couldn't produce a walk to compare with these enterprises.

It took 30 years of wrangling, negotiation, compromise and even conflict to agree a 256-mile* (412km) route from Edale, along almost the exact route proposed by Stephenson, to Kirk Yetholm in Scotland. The Pennine Way was finally opened at an official ceremony on Malham Moor on 24th April 1965. Like many 'official' openings, then and now, the path had been in common use for a while before this ceremony took place, with walkers using a pamphlet from the Ramblers' Association (as it was called at the time) to follow the route (see box p28-9). However, it wasn't until 1969 that the first official Pennine Way guide-book was published, by HMSO, written of course by Tom himself.

The original premise of a natural path, ie 'no concrete or asphalt', meant a much tougher walk for the first Pennine Wayfarers, as much of the path crossed terrain that tended to hold water, not least the dreaded peat bogs! As more and more feet churned the delicate peat into an ever-widening black morass, slabs were laid over the worst of the erosion to protect the environment and, as a result, walkers benefited from certain navigation and dry feet in places where previously neither was guaranteed. The Pennine Way was just the first of many, so if you walk any of the country's long-distance paths (official or otherwise), doff your cap and raise a glass to Tom Stephenson; surely the father of long-distance walking in the UK.

HOW DIFFICULT IS THE PENNINE WAY?

This book is not intended to mislead, so be prepared for a tough walk, especially if you plan to walk the Way in one go! There are only a few demanding days

---

❏ ALFRED WAINWRIGHT AND THE PENNINE WAY

Alfred Wainwright is best known for his Coast to Coast Path from St Bees to Robin Hood's Bay although he is also closely associated with the Pennine Way. It is he you must thank for the tradition that still persists: that anyone who completes the Way is rewarded with a half-pint of beer in the Border Hotel in Kirk Yetholm. Between 1968 and 1979 this was a full pint, paid for by the man himself, and it was costing him a small fortune – by his death it is estimate he had shelled out over £15,000 in free beer. Today Hadrian's Wall Brewery sponsors the beer and the accompanying free certificate.

Wainwright famously hated the Pennine Way, likening the bliss of finishing with that felt when you stop banging your head on a wall. He suffered from terrible weather and fell victim to the notorious peat bogs on Black Hill (now tamed) and was mightily relieved to be rescued by a companion and a Park Ranger who happened to be passing close by at the time. Thankfully the popularity of the walk has not been unduly affected by his words – perhaps it's the lure of that glass of beer at the end?

---

* Now 253 miles (407.5km) or 268 miles (431km) including optional side routes.

that you can't break down into smaller chunks, but the real challenge is walking day after day for over two weeks. The single most effective thing you can do to maximise your chances of both finishing and enjoying the trail is to figure in the occasional half-day off. (The others include having comfortable boots and keeping your pack as light as you can possibly make it.) If you could guarantee good weather for those two or three weeks, that would also reduce the difficulty of the Way,

The ruins of Top Withins (see p120), believed to be the inspiration and setting for the Earnshaws' house in Emily Brontë's *Wuthering Heights*.

but this is England and on the high moors you really can experience all four seasons in one day. The combination of zero visibility, high winds and a wet tent can temporarily sap the spirits, but fear not, the weather always changes.

Over recent years the waymarking has improved and slabs across some of the expanses of peat have made navigation easier,

Over the course of the Pennine Way you will climb approximately 40,000ft (12,000m)

but there are still wild and remote sections where navigation skills are required, so the ability to read a map and use a GPS or compass is essential. Half the Pennine Way is on open moorland and a quarter on rough grazing; only a tenth passes through forest, woodland or along riverbanks.

Over the course of the Pennine Way you will climb approximately 40,000ft (12,000m), but don't be put off, there are very few steep gradients and even the most serious sufferer of vertigo is unlikely to be troubled. There are about 230 miles (369.5km) on slopes of less than 10°, 20 miles (32km) on slopes of 10-15°, and only 3½ miles (6km) on steep slopes of more than 15°. However, if you can read a map and comfortably walk at least 12 miles (19km) in a day you should manage it; just don't expect every day to be a walk in the park.

'Nothing in life worth having comes easy', or so the saying goes and this applies to the Pennine Way. Many experienced and hill-hardened walkers leave Edale and never finish; but those who do can stand proud and claim to have walked one of the toughest paths in Britain.

The charming canal-side town of Hebden Bridge is one of the man-made highlights of the walk and a great place to take a day off.

INTRODUCTION

HOW LONG DO YOU NEED?

However long you take, you're unlikely to complete the Pennine Way faster than John Kelly did in 2021. The current record holder completed the route in 2 days, 10 hours and 4 minutes, running without sleep and with only one hour's rest. Most mortals average 17 days and even that schedule has some long days of well over 20 miles (32km) in it. Trying to fit the Pennine Way into a 14-day holiday is another order of magnitude, with many more challenging days, and would be a step too far for most walkers. A relaxed schedule with a couple of rest days will require 19-21 days.

Most mortals average 17 days and even that schedule has some long days of well over 20 miles (32km)

See pp39-41 for some suggested itineraries covering different walking speeds

Whichever schedule you choose, or have imposed upon you, there are going to be some long days that can only be broken by the flexibility of wild camping (see pp19-20), or by negotiation with B&B owners or taxi drivers for collection from the path and a return the next morning. The final 25½-mile (41km) marathon stage from Byrness to Kirk Yetholm is a prime example of this.

❏ DOING THE WALK IN SEVERAL STAGES

I first walked the Pennine Way in 2010 over 17 glorious days in May and it's an experience I will never forget; the accomplishment of a dream I'd had for almost 10 years. It's a long walk! Forgive the statement of the obvious, but few people (including myself) who set out on this endeavour have ever walked such a distance in one go before. It is a supreme test of both physical fitness and mental fortitude and many walkers fail to reach their goal in Kirk Yetholm. Many more just don't have the time to allocate the best part of three weeks to this challenge.

An alternative approach is to walk the Way in stages, breaking the route down into manageable chunks and completing it over one, two or even several years. On my 2010 walk I met a couple who spent one long weekend every year doing a stage of the walk. They were eight years in, with two more to go! For my update I was forced, through circumstances, to break the walk down into several short stages and as I was typically walking alone, I used a car, in conjunction with public transport to shuttle back and forth along the length of the track to complete these linear stages.

Trains alone can be used as far as the Roman Wall, with Bardon Mill station, on the Newcastle–Carlisle line, being two miles from Rapishaw Gap where the Pennine Way leaves the Wall and strikes out north towards Scotland. Beyond this point you will need to rely on a combination of buses and trains to complete your journey.

Between Edale and Bardon Mill there are stations at regular intervals, sometimes right on the Pennine Way, sometimes a two- or three-mile diversion away, but there are enough to provide a degree of flexibility into your stage lengths. I often used a car to drive to one station, park there, catch a train to a station further south and then walk for three or four days back to the car, but I could have managed with just trains alone.

I hope this information, along with the transport maps on p54 and p55, may provide inspiration for anyone who feels that the Pennine Way is out of their reach, for whatever reason. **Stuart Greig** (who updated the fourth edition of this guide)

In Swaledale; looking across the River Swale to the Pennine Way. The section through Swaledale from Thwaite or Muker to Keld is one to linger over,

When to go

SEASONS

The **main walking season** in the UK is from Easter (late March/April) to October; in terms of weather and lack of crowds the best months in which to do the Way are May, June and September.

Spring

In the UK, **March** can produce some of the most wintery conditions we experience, especially on the high hills. It may just as easily deliver wonderfully fresh sunny days though; so the best advice we can give is to hope for the best – but prepare for the worst!

> In terms of weather and the lack of crowds the best months in which to do the Way are May, June and September.

The month of **April** is one of the most unpredictable for walkers. The weather can be warm and sunny, though blustery days with showers are more typical; there is a good chance that snow will still be lying on the higher tops. On the plus side, hills are beginning to return to green, there won't be many other walkers about, there will be plenty of wild flowers and the birdsong will be at its best.

By **May** the weather has improved significantly and this is often the driest month of the year, with temperatures at just the right level for walking; not too hot, but

There are some wonderful places to camp along the Way. Note that in England you should get the permission of the landowner before you can camp anywhere but see pp19-20.

warm enough to bask in the sun at lunchtime. The long school summer break is still weeks away so the path will be quiet, wild flowers are out in their full glory and the daylight will outlast your stamina. A lot of facilities and many campsites open at Easter for the season.

Summer
Of the summer months, **June** probably has the most consistent walking weather and will be much quieter than **late July** and **August** when the UK schools finish

---

❏ FESTIVALS AND ANNUAL EVENTS ALONG THE PENNINE WAY

January to March
● **Montane Spine Race** (🖳 thespinerace.com) Held each January, this is Britain's longest non-stop foot race and competitors must complete all 268 miles of the Pennine Way, in winter, in under 7 days. The 2022 winner, Eoin Keith, finished in an incredible 92 hours 40 mins – yet even this wasn't enough to beat the previous event's (2020) record time of 87 hours 54 minutes, set by John Kelly.

April to July
● **Yorkshire Three Peaks Challenge** (🖳 threepeakschallenge.uk/yorkshire-three-peaks-challenge, see box p159) Now held one or two weekends a month between April and October in the area around Horton-in-Ribblesdale.
● **Fellsman Hike** (🖳 fellsman.org.uk) A 60-mile high-level traverse from Ingleton to Threshfield via Dodd Fell (see Map 53) held for over 50 years across two days in April or May. The event challenges the competitors' navigational skills and fitness.
● **Swaledale Arts Festival** (🖳 swalefestival.org) Brass bands, jazz, classical and various art and walking events; held over two weeks from late May to early June.
● **Yetholm Festival Week** (🖳 www.yetholmonline.org/festival-week.html) Equestrian festival in the second week of June with a rideout, games and a dance.
● **Edale Country Day** (🖳 edalecountryday.org.uk) Wacky races, wood turning, sheep shearing, morris dancers, brass bands and maypole dancing; held in June.
● **Twice Brewed Roman Wall Show** (www.facebook.com/RomanWallShow/) Sheep, shepherds and dog show on the second Saturday in June.
● **Malham Show** (🖳 malhamshow.co.uk) Agricultural show and other events, including falconry displays, held in late August.

August and September
● **Middleton Carnival** (🖳 www.facebook.com/middletoncarnival) is held in Middleton-in-Teesdale on the first Saturday in August.
● **Gargrave Show** (🖳 gargraveshow.org.uk) Over a century old, an agricultural show featuring prize cattle and sheepdog trials; mid August.
● **Dufton Agricultural Show** (🖳 duftonshow.co.uk) Agricultural show and sheepdog trials; last Saturday in August.
● **Bellingham Show & Country Festival** (🖳 bellinghamshow.co.uk) Last Saturday in August; expect country events, wrestling, tug-of-war, real ales and lots of live music.
● **Bowes Agricultural Show** (🖳 bowesshow.org.uk) A traditional English agricultural and farming show, held in early to mid September.
● **Three Peaks Cyclocross** (🖳 3peakscyclocross.org.uk) Held on the last Sunday in September and using the path from Pen-y-ghent to Horton; perhaps a day to avoid doing this stage of the Pennine Way.
● **Hardraw Scar Brass Band Festival** Near Hardraw Falls, on the second Sunday in September. Running annually from 1884 until 2019 it is hoped it will resume soon.

for the long summer holiday. Tourist numbers boom and places such as Haworth, Malham and the Yorkshire Dales become bustling hives of colourful waterproofs, traffic blocks the lanes and accommodation becomes scarce. Just because it's summer, don't expect constant sun; there's typically as much rain in August as there is in March, it's just warmer rain.

Autumn

Schools resume in early **September** and quiet returns to many places along the Way. Autumn colours make the rare woodland sections a sheer delight, but even the hills display a pleasant coppery hue as bracken dies back and the heather loses its purple flowers. The path is quieter with fewer tourists, but also because the weather becomes more unpredictable; you may well get some wonderfully warm, calm days, but you'll also get more windy and rainy days.

Expect similar conditions in **October** and **November**, with most days being wet and windy and with rare gems in between where the sun shines and the wind relents. Underfoot conditions begin to deteriorate; more rain means the ground becomes soaked and lowland pastures and high Pennine plateaus alike become wet and muddy.

Winter

According to the Christmas cards and Charles Dickens, winter is a month of cold, frosty mornings

Dropping down off the summit of Pen-y-ghent (see p155; © H.Stedman).

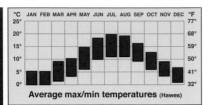

Average max/min temperatures (Hawes)

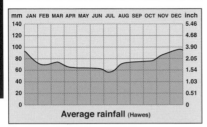

Average rainfall (Hawes)

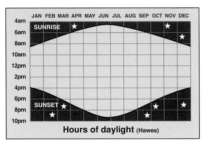

Hours of daylight (Hawes)

and snow-draped hills. You will get a scattering of wonderful clear winter days between December and the end of February, but they will be surrounded by windy, rainy days. Even snow, which, once fallen can add a magical element to the hills, can be disorientating and dangerous if it's falling heavily enough in high places.

As well as the days being much shorter, many B&Bs and guesthouse owners close up to go on their annual holiday and hostels bunkhouses and campsites close for long periods; even some shops close over the winter. Pubs also cut back their hours. As a result, you may struggle to complete the long stages in daylight and that brings its own problems and risks. You will need to carry more equipment too as you don't want to be caught out climbing Pen-y-ghent in snow and ice without crampons. This will mean your pack is heavier and therefore your speed will drop.

TEMPERATURE, RAINFALL AND DAYLIGHT HOURS

These days the Pennines are certainly less wet than their reputation suggests and if you pick your time of year you can minimise your chances of spending days encased in a waterproof shell. There is no 'right time' of the year to avoid the weather though; if there's anything predictable about the English weather, it's how unpredictable it will be. The charts above can only provide a rough guide.

Between late April and early September the daylight hours will usually exceed the hours you need to or, indeed, wish to walk along the Way. Outside this period though, careful note should be taken of the daylight available to you; leave early and finish early is a good approach to adopt, leaving time in the afternoon as a backup in case of problems or an injury that slows you down.

The hours of daylight chart gives the sunrise and sunset times for the middle of each month at Hawes, a town about halfway along the Pennine Way which gives a reasonably accurate picture for daylight for the whole trail.

Depending on the weather you can get a further 30-45 minutes of usable twilight after sunset. By this time you should be nearly done anyway, following a clear path to a village bathed in warm lamplight.

Above, left: Stoodley Pike (p114), on the hills above Hebden Bridge. **Above, right**: Eroded lime-stone of Malham Cove (Map 41), once an ancient waterfall and a geological highlight of the Way, during characteristically changeable weather. **Below, left**: As well as numerous sheep, you may see foxes or even cubs. **Right**: Approaching the impressive limestone amphitheatre of Malham Cove. **Bottom**: Idyllic Swaledale from the hillside trail between Thwaite and Keld (Maps 61-2).

Above: High Force (see p202) on the River Tees. **Top**: Descending from Dodd Fell into Hawes and the charms of Wensleydale. **Right**: Coming down from Great Shunner Fell into beautiful Swaledale, one of the loveliest dales along the walk; Hawes to Tan Hill section.

Above: Dramatic escarpment of Walltown Crags, (Map 102) where the Pennine Way joins the Hadrian's Wall Path for half a day passing still-impressive ramparts, turrets and garrisons, with several museums and forts just a short detour away. **Left**: Hikers descending through photogenic Sycamore Gap (Map 105). **Bottom**: Vindolanda Roman Fort (p240) is well worth visiting; exhibits in the excellent museum include well preserved daily objects such as shoes and even a Roman toilet seat (**below**).

Practical information for the walker

ROUTE FINDING

Despite the improvement in waymarks and the many helpful and photogenic wooden signposts, there are still plenty of places where you
will stand and think, 'Where's the path gone?' Fortunately, on some
open moorlands the presence of slabbed causeways not only makes
for easy going across the mire but also acts as an easy-to-follow trail,
even in zero visibility. However, the ability to read a map is the single
most-important skill you can acquire before setting out on the Pennine
Way. The ability to use a compass or a GPS is the next.

    There are sections of the route that are only ever walked by
Pennine Wayfarers, so you can't always rely on someone else coming along to help you out. The Pennine Way is very long and the relatively small number of walkers means that, unlike other national
trails, you can't simply follow the flow of folk leaving the town or
village in the morning. You have to rely on yourself. In many cases
there will be a visible path on the ground, made by walkers who have
come before you. This may be as subtle as footprints in the early
morning dew, a path of flattened grass across a field, or a track as
obvious as a wide scar in a peat moor; all of which may help in route
finding. The further north you get, the less often these worn paths
occur as the number of Pennine Wayfarers diminishes and you
become the trailblazer rather than the follower.

ELECTRONIC NAVIGATION AIDS AND MAPPING APPS

*I never carried a compass, preferring to rely on a good sense of direction ... I
never bothered to understand how a compass works or what it is supposed to do
... To me a compass is a gadget, and I don't get on well with gadgets of any sort.*
        Alfred Wainwright

While Wainwright's acolytes may scoff, other walkers will accept
GPS technology as a well-established navigational aid. With a clear
view of the sky, a **GPS receiver** will establish your position as well
as elevation in a variety of formats, including the British OS grid
system, anywhere on earth to an accuracy of within a few metres.
Most **smartphones** have a GPS receiver built in and can receive a
GPS signal from space as well as estimate its position often as accurately using mobile data signals from hilltop masts. These signals are
two different things: GPS comes free from American, Russian or

European satellites and is everywhere all the time but works best outdoors. Much stronger 4- or 5G mobile signals beam off towers up to 40 miles away and are what you pay the phone company for.

Accessing an online map with mobile data (internet via your phone signal, not wi-fi), your position can be pinpointed with great accuracy. But with no signal – as is the case in Britain's remoter upland locales – your phone will use GPS to display your position as a dot on the screen. Except that, *unless you import a map into your phone's internal storage* (which may require an app and even a small financial outlay) without a signal, the kilobit-sized 'tiles' which make up a **zoomable online map** cannot be downloaded. The internet browser's cache may retain a few tiles until the signal resumes or until you walk off that tile's coverage. Much will depend on your service provider.

The best way to use your mobile as an accurate navigation aid is to download a **mapping app** plus **maps** covering the route (see box p50). That will work with GPS where there is no phone signal. Then download and install a **Pennine Way tracklog** into this app and, ideally, your on-screen location dot will be pulsing right on that track as you walk along. Alternatively, if the maps in the mapping app you install already has the Pennine Way on it (eg OS maps, p50) you wouldn't need to also install a Pennine Way tracklog.

Unless you happen to own one with a decent sized colour screen, there's little benefit in buying a **handheld GPS** device except that *with decent maps installed*, you can be certain of establishing your location against a map anytime, any place, any where.

Using GPS with this book – tracklog and waypoints

A **tracklog** is a continuous winding line marking the walk from end to end, displayed on your screen; all you have to do is keep on that line. If you lose it on the screen you can zoom out until it reappears and walk towards it. A tracklog can be traced with a mouse off a digital map, or recorded live using a GPS enabled device. When recorded live, tracklogs are actually hundreds of waypoints separated by intervals of either time or more usefully distance (say, around 10 metres). Some smartphones or mapping apps can't display a tracklog with over 500 points so they get truncated into fewer straight lines, resulting in some loss in precision.

Where a tracklog is a continuous line, **waypoints** are single points like cairns. This book identifies key waypoints on the route maps; these waypoints correlate to the list on pp275-84 which gives the grid reference and description. You can download the complete list as a GPS-readable .gpx file of grid references (but with no descriptions) from 💻 trailblazer-guides.com. For these waypoints we've now also listed the three-word geocode used by **what3words** (see pp273-4; 💻 what3words.com) which could be useful in an emergency.

One thing must be understood however: **treating GPS as a complete replacement for maps, a compass and common sense is a big mistake**. Every electronic device is susceptible to battery failure or some electronic malfunction that might leave you in the dark. It's worth repeating that most people who've ever walked the Pennine Way did so without GPS.

ACCOMMODATION

There is no shortage of accommodation along the Pennine Way and the options increase if you're prepared to walk a mile or two off the path, although this is rarely an absolute necessity. Many of the towns and villages on the Way are situated in popular walking areas and have an abundance of walker-friendly establishments, including hotels, B&Bs, hostels, bunkhouses and campsites.

If you plan on walking in the high season (between mid July and early September), however, you are well advised to book B&B and pub accommodation several weeks in advance, especially if your stay coincides with a weekend or bank holiday as accommodation, even in a town with many options, can fill up quickly upon the announcement of a weekend of decent weather.

Camping

If you're doing the Pennine Way on a budget you may be considering using campsites for your evening stops. Be aware that facilities at campsites vary wildly between locations and you may just as easily find yourself directed towards a field already occupied by sheep, as pitching on the manicured lawn of a modern, fully equipped 'glamping' site. You may also be letting yourself in for the worst of both worlds – you lack the freedom and exhilaration of sleeping out in the wilds (see below) and the negligible soundproofing of close-packed tents means a rowdy group can ruin your evening.

As long as you avoid packed campsites, the flexibility offered by this approach can pay dividends; there's no need to book accommodation, you can change plans on a whim, or depending on the weather, and you can treat yourself to a more comfortable option whenever it's available. The only real advantages to campsites over wild camping are the perceived sense of security, the hot shower and toilets, access to wi-fi and phone charging, and the probable availability of a nearby pub for an evening meal. This last also means that you may be able to dispense with carrying food other than emergency rations.

Wild camping (See also box p39) Of all the national trails in England, the Pennine Way probably offers the best chance to wild camp along much of its length. Huge sections of the route are on high ground beyond the last farm wall or fence and there are plenty of inconspicuous places to pitch a small tent.

Wild camping offers the ultimate outdoor experience in this country, especially in the warm summer months; what could be better than sitting and watching the sun set behind the hills with your warm brew, or a wee dram, in hand? Perhaps, an early start to watch the sun rise? It also allows you to avoid the sometimes unnecessary diversion into town for accommodation, usually downhill with the inevitable uphill slog to return to the path in the morning.

The major difficulties with finding a good wild camping spot on the Pennine Way is the availability of water (often unappealingly peaty brown up on the moors) and the general sogginess and lumpiness of the land (again, especially on the moors). Finding protection from the wind can also be tricky.

Officially, in England and Wales, you need to seek the permission of the landowner before you can camp anywhere, but this is typically impractical and often impossible. An acceptable compromise, often shared by landowners, can be achieved by following these simple rules:

● Camp late or out of sight of nearby buildings and leave early
● Camp in small groups of no more than two or three tents
● Never make open fires
● Bury or pack out your toilet waste (see pp75-6)
● Leave no trace of your camp.

If you are spotted by a landowner, as long as you clearly look like a walker in transit they probably won't shoot you but, if they ask you to move on, you must comply. This is most likely to happen when crossing a grouse estate. Bedding down late and leaving early should reduce the chances of such a confrontation. Avoid camping beside a gate that is obviously well used to avoid inconveniencing a farmer coming and going from the hills.

In the Pennines there are some **wild camping black spots**: one is Kinder Scout, the first day out of Edale. Because of the high peat-fire risk during very dry and always busy summers it's not unknown for rangers to set out in the evening to harry wild campers. Spare the hassle and save your wild nights until you're over the Snake Pass, if not the A62. Ever busy Hadrian's Wall is also a place you must not even consider pitching a tent, as wild camping is strictly forbidden here to protect the as-yet unexcavated archaeological remains.

Camping barns, bunkhouses and hostels
For sociable walkers on a budget this type of accommodation can be perfect; it is available in many towns and villages on the path, is relatively cheap and doesn't require you to carry a tent. The quality of the accommodation will vary widely though, so don't expect a room on your own or fluffy pillows and feather duvets; you will typically be sleeping in a dormitory/room with multiple bunk beds. In the height of the season these can be busy places and you need to be prepared for this; a busy bunkhouse kitchen can be a true test of patience and compromise and ear-plugs are an essential part of any hostelling kit list!

For many the appeal of this type of accommodation is the fact that you're bunking with fellow walkers, often following the same trail, and can take the time to sit down, talk and swap 'war stories', rather than just a passing greeting on the trail. Friendships that can span a lifetime are sometimes created in this way.

At the lowest end of the scale is the **camping barn** (£10-18 per person). This may be no more than a roof over your head, a raised wooden sleeping platform, a kitchen area, where you use your own stove, and a toilet with a shower if you're lucky. Assume that you'll need your full camping kit list (apart from the tent) for this type of accommodation.

Bunkhouses provide more facilities and you can expect to pay around £15-28pp per night. For this you will get a bunk bed, cooking facilities, hot showers and maybe even a drying room where you can hang wet gear. You will normally need a sleeping bag although some provide bedding for a small charge. Don't *expect* breakfast or an evening meal, though some bunkhouses do offer these. A hangover from Covid-19 is that many bunkhouses these days are only rented out to groups, though you might score a room to yourself mid-week.

There are two main types of **hostel** – privately run businesses and those that are part of the Youth Hostel Association (YHA). They both offer a similar level of service, but prices may vary depending on location and facilities.

If you are planning on using YHA hostels (☎ 0800-019 1700 or ☎ 01629-592700, 🖥 yha.org.uk) for the majority of your stops it is worth becoming a member, as you'll get 10% discount on all accommodation and food. You can join online, or at any hostel as you check in. YHA annual membership costs £20, with a £5 discount if you pay by direct debit and the discount applies to anyone in your booking. Those under 26 (and anyone in their party) can get an additional 5% discount. You can either book accommodation online through the YHA website or by phone. You'll need a photo ID to check in.

Hostels vary widely in size, age and user demographic. If you don't enjoy sharing an enclosed space with 50 intense children, high on fresh air and freedom from parental guidance, be sure to check in advance at places such as Edale and The Sill on Hadrian's Wall, as these are prime locations for school parties.

Rates for dorms and private rooms vary hugely according to the season and day of the week. Dorms start at around £15-20pp and double rooms £29-39 mid-week, but these can rise to £30pp for dorms and £79 for a double on a summer weekend (Fri & Sat). For this you'll get access to a shared hot shower (some rooms are en suite), free wi-fi and a self-catering kitchen, and maybe a

---

❏ SHOULD YOU BOOK YOUR ACCOMMODATION IN ADVANCE?

If you are walking the Pennine Way in summer, especially during school holidays (middle of July to the first week of September), and even more so on summer weekends or bank Holidays, and you aren't camping, then it's advisable to have your night's accommodation booked weeks in advance. Although it may compromise your spontaneity, booking enables you to enjoy the walk knowing you have a secure bed come nightfall. Several places along the route have only one or two places to stay and if these fill up then your whole itinerary suddenly becomes much trickier to piece together. There's nothing worse than getting to a place and finding all the accommodation booked up.

The situation is better outside of high summer, particularly in April/May or September, when as long as you're flexible and willing to take what's offered you should get away with booking just a few nights in advance. Be careful even when travelling out of high season as some YHA hostels and even B&Bs close between November and March. It can also be hard to get food in some places mid-week out of season.

Note that **bunkhouses** are often booked by groups on a sole-occupancy basis, particularly on weekends, so it is essential to book these in advance.

Campers can be much more flexible with their itinerary as most **campsites** have a policy of always finding space for a Pennine Way walker arriving on foot.

Obviously when booking in advance you want to be clear about the cancellation policy. You will generally be asked for a **deposit** when you book, which might be non refundable, or a refund may incur an administration charge. Some places are completely nonrefundable. If you have to cancel do try and telephone your hosts; it saves a lot of worry and allows them to provide a bed for someone else.

PLANNING YOUR WALK

drying room; most hostels provide an evening meal and breakfast for an additional fee and many are licensed to serve alcohol. Most don't open their doors until 5pm.

To find out if any hostels are closing for refurbishment or any other important changes visit the YHA website. Hostels should be booked well in advance in summer if you have fixed dates.

Camping pods and 'glamping'
Acting as a halfway house between camping and staying in a B&B, several sites now have **camping pods** – basic but comfortable 'sleeping sheds', usually simply furnished with a table and sleeping platform, though you'll often need your own bedding/sleeping bag. Prices vary widely but the better ones are around the £30pp mark.

Even a walk as remote as the Pennine Way hasn't entirely been immune to the current craze for **glamping** – where the campsite provides you with a luxury tent (often a bell tent or yurt) fitted out with rugs, furniture and a proper bed to sleep in. Indeed, even Edale, right at the start of the trek, now boasts its own (very upmarket) 'glampsite'. It's great fun of course, though not cheap, with prices more akin to an upmarket B&B (or, in Edale's case, an upmarket hotel!) than a campsite.

Bed and Breakfast (B&B)
The title says it all; in this type of accommodation you get a bed for the night and a breakfast in the morning. In most cases you will be staying in someone's home; they may run it as a business with a dozen rooms in a converted farmhouse or you may be sleeping in little Johnny's room now that he's left for university. The quality and facilities of Pennine Way B&Bs range from luxurious to spartan, but they are nearly always clean, tidy and efficient.

The real benefit of B&B accommodation is the fact that you get a room to yourself and you can travel light. A hot shower, or bath, at the end of the day, followed by a good night's sleep and a hearty cooked breakfast are enough to revive most walkers after a gruelling day on the fells. B&Bs in remote locations, where there is no pub nearby, may also offer an evening meal for an additional fee and if booked in advance. Many also offer a packed lunch option.

Any B&B on the Pennine Way will be accustomed to taking in walkers, often dripping wet on their doorstep, wind-blown and mud-spattered. The best ones have drying facilities, some will even do your washing (for a small charge). The psychological boost of putting on clean, dry clothing in the morning should not be underestimated!

Guesthouses, hotels, pubs and inns
Guesthouses are hotel-like B&Bs. They're generally slightly more expensive but can offer more space, an evening meal and a comfortable lounge or even bar for guests.

Pubs and inns often turn their hand to B&B accommodation in country areas and, although these businesses are less personal, you may find the anonymity preferable. They can be good fun if you plan to down a few pints at

---

❏ **B&B-STYLE ACCOMMODATION**

● **Rooms** Single rooms are likely to be small and their availability is limited. **Twin rooms** have two single beds while a **double** generally has one double bed though sometimes has two single beds that can be separated to make twin beds when required. **Triples** generally have a double and a single, or three single beds, and **quads** often have a double bed with bunk beds/two single beds, or four single beds; thus for a group of three/four people two may have to share a double bed; however, these rooms can also be used as a double or twin.

● **Facilities** An **en suite room** typically attracts a higher rate and often this is just a small shower cubicle with a toilet and basin squeezed into the room. So don't automatically turn your nose up at a **bathroom** across the corridor which could be much more spacious and there's nothing quite as relaxing as a proper bath at the end of a long day. Bathrooms may be shared with other rooms (**shared facilities**) or they may be for the sole use of the guests in a particular room (**private facilities**).

● **Rates** In this guide rates are quoted as the establishment quotes them, which is normally **per room**. Rates start at around £50/70 for a single/double (S/D) room with a shared bathroom up to £100-130 for a very comfortable room with an en suite bathroom and all mod cons. Hotel rates do not always include breakfast so check in advance. Some hotels (and some hostels including those owned by the YHA) change their tariffs at a moment's notice in response to the number of visitors, so use the prices in this book as a rough guide. In the low season (Sep-Mar) prices may come down to some extent. Most places offer the best rates to those booking directly with them and many have their own online booking systems. Bigger places can be booked on websites like 🖥 booking.com but you won't find any great discounts there.

Solo walkers can sometimes pay a single rate for a smaller, single bed room, but mostly you will have to pay a double room rate minus a modest £10 or so discount for eating one less breakfast. In the height of the season, in some places, you could even be expected to pay the full room rate and, unless you pay for two people, there are establishments that won't accept bookings from solo travellers at weekends, as they can usually be sure to fill them with two people and expect those two to eat there.

the bar, but not such fun if you're worn out and trying to sleep within earshot of that same rowdy bar. In this case it's best to ask to see the room first or specifically ask for a quiet room, preferably in a separate block, not above the bar. This is particularly important on a Friday and Saturday night. Pubs boasting both rooms and food allow you to avoid an extra walk to find an evening meal. After many days in boots, the relief of being able to pad down to the bar in just your socks cannot be understated. Sadly rural pubs are closing down at an alarming rate in England, a trend only accelerated by Covid-19, and several along the Way were closed at the time of research, hoping to reopen with new landlords or a new buyer.

Some **hotels** are fantastic places with great character and worth the treat – but more likely they are places you're forced to go to when all the cheaper alternatives are full.

Airbnb

The rise and rise of Airbnb (🖥 airbnb.co.uk) has seen private homes and apartments opened up to overnight travellers on an informal basis. While accommodation is primarily based in cities, the concept is spreading to tourist hotspots in more rural areas, but do check thoroughly what you are getting and the precise location. While the first couple of options listed may be in the area you're after, others may be far too far afield for walkers. At its best, this is a great way to meet local people in a relatively unstructured environment, but do be aware that these places are not registered B&Bs, so standards may vary, yet prices may not necessarily be any lower than the norm. Many require a minimum of two nights' booking, which is difficult for Pennine Way walkers.

FOOD AND DRINK

After 20 miles of wind and rain (though it's highly unlikely that every day will be like that!) there really is nothing like sitting down to a good meal and rehydrating with a refreshing drink. The Pennine Way is littered with fine establishments, with grand home-cooked meals and well-tended beer cellars, that fulfil this requirement perfectly. Unfortunately there are also one or two places that seem to thrive despite their obvious mediocrity and even open rudeness.

If you wish to sample the best of Britain's beer always choose a pint from a hand-pulled pump; ask the bar staff for a recommendation. Many places will even let you sample a small portion before you order. Yorkshire in particular is renowned for its brewing tradition and a rest day in Hawes will not be wasted in the many pubs.

A busy café, restaurant, pub or hotel is often a sign of a good kitchen, especially if the locals are eating there; your B&B owner will probably be able to make a recommendation, they will have heard the high praise or horror stories from other guests. If you've had your fill of sausages & mash, steak & ale pie and fish & chips, the box opposite may offer some inspiration for regional dishes along the Pennine Way.

Breakfast

Most B&Bs, pubs and guesthouses will offer you a **cooked breakfast** to begin your day on the fells. A walker can go a long way on a good 'Full English', certainly all the way to lunch time! Depending on where you are, the items on the plate will vary but normally include: sausages, bacon, fried egg, tomatoes, black pudding and mushrooms. This will usually be served with toast and marmalade, orange juice and tea or coffee. In the northern reaches of the Way and in Scotland the black pudding may be white pudding and potato cakes may make an occasional appearance.

Many places also offer a lighter **continental breakfast** option, including a vegan alternative. If you want to get an early start some places may be happy to provide a packed lunch instead of breakfast.

Lunch, cream tea and evening meals

For **lunch** you may like to take a packed lunch from wherever you stayed the night before or buy something in the many bakeries, cafés, and local shops en route. If you need sustenance in the afternoon look out for places serving coffee and cake and even **cream teas** (a scone served with jam and cream, possibly

❏ REGIONAL DISHES

● **Cumberland sausage** Common on pub menus, this is a long, coiled or curved sausage where the meat (pork) inside is chopped rather than minced and pepper, rather than herbs, is added. Served with chips or mashed potato.

● **Yorkshire pudding** This is a hollow, baked batter savoury pudding, typically served with roast beef and gravy on a Sunday, but many pubs serve it every day and you may sometimes find large versions filled with meat and gravy.

● **Lamb Henry** With all those sheep out on the hills it comes as no surprise that lamb is popular. Lamb Henry is lamb shank or shoulder cooked slowly, often with mint or rosemary, and served with gravy, chips and some vegetables. It's a cheap but filling meal though is mostly served in the winter months.

● **Parkin** A Yorkshire ginger cake, said to be the ideal accompaniment to a cup of strong Yorkshire tea.

● **Wensleydale cheese** It's been around a long time but had a

Lamb Henry with chips
© Chris Scott

surge of popularity thanks to its endorsement by global superstars Wallace and Gromit. You can visit the factory and shop in Hawes (see p166).

● **Bilberry pie** A sweet pastry pie filled with bilberries which are found growing wild across the northern moors in late summer. Usually served hot with custard.

● **Curd tarts** Pastry tarts of curd cheese often with currants, best served cold as an afternoon snack with a cup of tea.

● **Rag pudding** Invented in Oldham in the 19th century, when the town was the centre of Lancashire's cotton mill industry, this is a dish of minced meat and onions wrapped in suet pastry and steamed in a cheesecloth (or 'rag', hence the name).

PLANNING YOUR WALK

with a cake or two, and a pot of tea). In towns with a Co-op supermarket you can get a meal deal (sandwich, snack and drink) for a good value lunch on the go. Those on a budget should also bear in mind that many pubs offer a simpler and notably cheaper lunchtime menu, compared to their dinner options.

Pennine pubs are a great place to unwind in the **evening** and, apart from the few towns with restaurants, are often your only choice for a meal. With Britain's long overdue food revolution continuing apace, pubs have also been forced to become more than drinking dens. Places where your meal flips from freezer to microwave to plate are thankfully in decline. Indeed most pubs are more interested in serving meals than pouring pints, which is one reason why it's worth making a dinner reservation in the more popular pubs. Be careful if arriving late in the day as many pubs stop serving meals at 8pm, or early in the week as some smaller villages have nothing open on a Sunday, Monday or Tuesday. Despite the name, bar meals can be eaten at a regular table and at best have a home-cooked appeal which won't find you staring bleakly at an artfully carved radish

---

❏ REAL ALES

● **Black Sheep Brewery** (🖥 blacksheepbrewery.com) has been brewing since 1992 and produces a number of cask ales but its most popular is simply called Black Sheep. You'll see it in pubs up and down the Pennine Way.

● **Theakston** (🖥 theakstons.co.uk) brew in the heart of the Yorkshire Dales. Keep a particular eye out for the exceptional, multi-award-winning Old Peculier dark ale, as well as the more easily found Best Bitter.

● **Peak Ales** (🖥 peakales.co.uk) produces a number of award-winning beers from their base on the Chatsworth Estate, including Swift Nick, a traditional English bitter; the amber-coloured Bakewell Best; and Chatsworth Gold, a honey beer. They also brew seasonal (summer and winter) ales. You might find some of these in the pubs in the southern sections of the Way.

● **Timothy Taylor** (🖥 www.timothytaylor.co.uk) is a famous brewery that has been in the business for over 150 years. Their Landlord is a strong pale ale while the award-winning Boltmaker is named after one of their favourite local pubs.

---

entwined around a lone prawn. All menus include some vegetarian/vegan options and, if there is a traditional Pennine Way dish it must be Lamb Henry, found on menus from Edale to Dufton and beyond. How better to recharge your stomach than with a juicy shank of Pennine lamb and a pint of Black Sheep (see above). It makes the walk worth walking.

Buying camping supplies

With a bit of planning ahead there are enough shops to allow self-sufficient campers to buy supplies along the way. All the known shops are listed in the Town & Village Facilities table on pp34-5 and detailed in Part 4. The longest you should need to carry food for is two days, although hours can be irregular in village shops. Camp stoves, Bhutane/propane gas canisters or meths are usually available in outdoor stores. Coleman Fuel is not so widely found.

Drinking water

Very few of us drink enough water during a normal day, never mind when we're working hard climbing hills and walking several miles a day. **A walker should, on average, be drinking between three and four litres per day** in order to maintain optimum hydration and personal well-being.

One of the best ways to carry water is in a hydration pack (such as a Camelback or Platypus), which can be slipped into a purpose-built sleeve in the back of your pack. Access to the water is through a bite-valve at the end of a tube looped over your shoulder and enables you to sip water regularly without stopping to find a water bottle.

On longer days where you aren't likely to encounter a village or a pub, you may want to consider topping up the hydration pack from water sources you find along the path. A lightweight water filter such as the Sawyer Squeeze Filter or Lifestraw can be used to clean most water found in UK streams and rivers. The advantage of these sort of devices over a sterilising tablet is speed, simplicity and taste; you can drink straight from the filter or squeeze the water through into your hydration pack – selecting one that closes at the top does help in this regard. A steripen, which uses UV light to kill off any bugs in the water, is a quick and effective alternative though more expensive and susceptible to malfunction.

In general terms the higher up a hill you source your water and the faster that water is flowing, the more likely it is to be clean and pure. In many places along the Way the water will be discoloured from the peat it has flowed through to reach the river. This may be off-putting, but doesn't affect the quality of the water in any other way, especially if you filter it as well. Use your common sense; avoid standing pools, murky water or water with lots of insects or algae present. If in doubt, filter it.

As refreshing as a pint of beer may be at lunchtime, it is no substitute for water and should be avoided on hot summer days as the alcohol encourages blood flow to the surface of your skin and can result in overheating.

If you are wild camping near running water, please abide by the toilet guidelines provided on pp75-6.

MONEY

Cash and a couple of **credit/debit cards** are the best means of paying your way on the walk. Post-pandemic, many more businesses now accept card payments, even the smallest cafés or fish & chip shops. Nevertheless, it's a good idea to carry some cash as back up for those that don't. Don't expect an **ATM (cash machine)** in every village but remember that many supermarkets/convenience stores now have an ATM inside (which may charge), or offer 'cashback' when you buy something – though clearly these are only available during opening hours. **Cheques** are accepted in fewer places each year, although some B&Bs will still accept them from a British bank.

While there may not be banks or ATMs in every village, most **post offices** allow cash withdrawals at the counter. However, as the era of the country post office is in decline, check (🖥 postoffice.co.uk) to see branch opening hours, which banks offer withdrawal facilities through post offices and which branches have an ATM.

There will be occasions when you can't pay by card, notably at smaller campsites. It's also useful to carry a couple of 20p and 50p coins for campsite showers and for honesty boxes, where you often need to leave exact change.

OTHER SERVICES

Wi-fi is available and free almost everywhere, though at times only in public areas and sometimes it is unreliable. Places that didn't have wi-fi at the time of research are noted in the route guide.

Where they exist, special mention is made in Part 4 of other services such as outdoor gear shops, launderettes, pharmacies/chemists, medical centres and tourist information centres. Where we found phone boxes they were noted on the maps, mostly for navigation though, as these days most have been given over to defibrillators/book exchanges or have simply been vandalised beyond use.

WALKING COMPANIES

If you'd rather someone else made some or all of your holiday arrangements for you the companies on pp29-32 will be able to help. You can either choose just baggage transfer, or a self-guided/guided holiday in which case accommodation booking will also be included.

Baggage transfer

Baggage transfer means collecting your gear and delivering it to your next accommodation by late afternoon; all you need on the hill is a daypack with essentials. The cost is usually around £10 per bag per day, but varies between companies and you should check firstly that the company covers the whole walk (some do not) and secondly, whether there is a minimum number of bags that they require before they will accept a booking. You could also ask your B&Bs or local taxi firms if they provide an ad-hoc transfer service for specific sections though this will usually be more expensive.

● **Brigantes Walking Holidays** (☎ 01756-770402, ⌨ brigantesenglishwalks .com; Malham) run a family-operated baggage courier service which support trails across the north of England (single bag limit is 17kg). Contact them for a price.

● **Pennine Way Bag Transfer** (☎ 07891-584874, ⌨ penninewaybagtransfer .uk; Torside) They cover only the southern portion from Edale to Malham. with a minimum of two bags required per booking. Contact them for a quotation.

❑ **WALKING THE PENNINE WAY IN THE 1960s**

In August 1963, clad in cotton and wool that was spun, woven and stitched in the smoky industrial towns each side of the Pennine Way, we raced up Grindsbrook. Fuelled by adrenaline, over-confident, we failed to consult the compass and blundered too long amid the mist-shrouded peat hags of Kinder Scout. We didn't make that mistake twice. As far north as Blackstone Edge, and in places beyond, the Way was largely undefined on the ground. Guidebooks were things of the future. Ordnance Survey maps had yet to show the route. A Ramblers' Association leaflet described the line in sufficient detail for us to trace it onto borrowed maps.

We slogged across tussocks, heather, groughs, streams and bogs, occasionally encouraged by the sighting of a boot-print or a wooden stake but referring always to map and compass. Above Hebden Bridge we crossed fields dulled by soot from coal fires, and at the end of the third day our baptism of wet peat and trackless moors was over. We descended into the pastoral greenery of Craven and found our second wind on home ground in the Yorkshire Dales. On our seventh night we soaked in the bath at a B&B in Middleton in Teesdale. Previously we'd stayed in Youth Hostels without showers, making do with strip washes. Men didn't use deodorants then, and our single set of spare clothes was reserved for evenings. Enough said!

The famous crossing of the Pennines via High Cup was, and remains, a highlight of the Way. It was easier than expected, so fit had we become. Arriving in Dufton, we learned our hostel lay two miles away in the village of Knock. Next morning, without map, we negotiated the Cross Fell range in dubious visibility by dint of walking due

● **Sherpa Van Project** (☎ 01748-826917, 🖥 sherpavan.com) Sherpa operates a baggage-transfer service for the whole walk. Contact them for a quote.

Self-guided walking holidays

These packages usually include accommodation with breakfast and baggage transfer. Some also include personal transfer to and from the walk, and may include secure car parking and even optional lifts between accommodation if you don't feel like walking that day. Each company offers different services, so check the details carefully. The companies can also tailor-make holidays.

● **Absolute Escapes** (☎ 0131-610 1210, 🖥 absoluteescapes.com; Edinburgh) Offer the complete path as well as in sections.

● **Alpine Exploratory** (☎ 0131-214 1144, 🖥 alpineexploratory.com; Edinburgh) Offer the whole walk over 21-24 nights, or the southern, central or northern part of the route in about a week. In addition they welcome dogs.

● **Brigantes Walking Holidays** (see opposite) They offer the full route but are also happy to work on shorter or longer itineraries.

● **Contours Holidays** (☎ 01629-821900, 🖥 contours.co.uk; Derbyshire) Walks (Apr-Oct) along the whole Way (13-20 days), as well as the southern (6-8 days), central (6-11 nights) and northern (4-6 days) sections and 3-day 'taster' treks.

● **Discovery Travel** (☎ 01983-301133, 🖥 discoverytravel.co.uk; Isle of Wight) They have a 19-walking-day/20-night holiday covering the whole route available between March and October and also offer bespoke itineraries to suit.

● **Great British Walks** (☎ 01600-713008, 🖥 www.great-british-walks.com;

PLANNING YOUR WALK

north until reaching the Old Corpse Road. On a cold September night at Once Brewed hostel we slept snugly on mattresses in rope 'hammocks'. Next day we picked a way through miles of conifers, hoping the infrequent splashes of white paint on tree trunks indicated our route. On the penultimate day we realised our maps of Redesdale were ancient: they showed none of the huge Forestry Commission plantations, but we found our way by compass bearing. The Cheviot ridge gave us our first sight of Scotland as well as a fitting and final test of our stamina.

Our limited knowledge came from Kenneth Oldham's slim volume, *The Pennine Way*. The mass of information now available on websites lay decades ahead. We saw few signposts, and Tom Stephenson's 'long green trail' hadn't been formed, let alone turned into the spreading morass that necessitated the controversial paving. Few pubs served food, but shops were more plentiful than now. We had none of today's technical fabrics, phones, walking poles, GPS, plastic cards or plastic bags. We never dreamed such things might one day exist, and we felt we had the right kit for the job.

I'd never spent more than a week outside my home county, so the Pennine Way was an exceptional adventure. Since then the world has shrunk. The Way may no longer appear exotic, but still it challenges the walker to meet its mental and physical demands. Somewhere between Hadrian's Wall and Bellingham, the northbound Wayfarer will realise success is nigh. For the southbound traveller, an identical moment lightens the rucksack on the level track between Stoodley Pike and Blackstone Edge. Those feelings are worth your walk, and they will carry you with an inner smile all the way to the end. **Peter Stott**

Monmouth) Offer the complete trail in 21 nights, or any length and any part of the walk according to clients' wishes.

● **Macs Adventure** (☎ 0141-530886, 🖳 macsadventure.com; Glasgow) They offer the complete trek (15-22 days' walking), the northern section (5-7 days), the south (8-9 days) and central (8-10 days) between April and September.

● **Walkers' Britain** (☎ 020-8875 5070, 🖳 walkersbritain.co.uk; London) Itineraries for the whole path in 19/20 days' walking and also in half sections.

❏ INFORMATION FOR FOREIGN VISITORS

● **Currency** The British pound (£) comes in notes of £100, £50, £20, £10 and £5, and coins of £2 and £1. The pound is divided into 100 pence (usually referred to as 'p', pronounced 'pee') which come in silver coins of 50p, 20p, 10p and 5p, and copper coins of 2p and 1p.

● **Money** Up-to-date **rates of exchange** can be found on 🖳 xe.com/currencyconverter, at some post offices, or at any bank or travel agent. These days rarely used, **travellers' cheques** can be cashed only at banks, foreign exchanges and some of the large hotels; it makes much more sense to use a combination of **debit card and cash**.

● **Business hours** Most **grocery shops** are open Monday to Saturday 9am-5pm though some open as early as 7.30/8am; many also open on Sundays but not usually for the whole day. **Supermarkets** are open daily 8am-8pm (often longer) and on Sunday from about 9am to 5 or 6pm, though main branches of supermarkets generally open 10am-4pm or 11am-5pm.

Main **post offices** generally open Monday to Friday 9am-5pm and Saturday 9am-12.30pm; **banks** typically open at 9.30/10am Monday to Friday and close at 3.30/4pm, though in some places both post offices and banks may open only two or three days a week and/or in the morning, or limited hours, only.

ATMs (cash machines) located outside a bank, shop, post office or petrol station are open all the time, but any that are inside will be accessible only when that place is open. Most are free to use, but note that those with a charge, such as Link machines (🖳 link.co.uk/consumers/locator) may not accept foreign-issued cards.

Pub hours are less predictable as each pub may have different opening hours. However, most pubs on the Path open daily 11am-11pm (some close at 10.30pm on Sunday) but **some close in the afternoon**.

The last entry time to most **museums and galleries** is usually half an hour, or an hour, before the official closing time.

● **Public holidays** Most businesses in the South-West are shut on 1 January, Good Friday (March/April), Easter Monday (March/April), the first and last Monday in May, the last Monday in August, 25 December and 26 December.

● **School holidays** State-school holidays in England are generally as follows: a one-week break late October, two weeks over Christmas and the New Year, a week mid February, two weeks around Easter, one week at the end of May/early June (to coincide with the bank holiday at the end of May) and six weeks from late July to early September. Private-school holidays fall at the same time, but tend to be slightly longer.

● **Documents** If you are a member of a National Trust organisation in your country bring your membership card as you should be entitled to free entry to National Trust properties and sites in the UK. See also p62.

● **Travel/medical insurance** All visitors to Britain should be properly insured, including comprehensive health coverage. Before Brexit on 1st January 2021, the

● **Weather Goat Walks** (☎ 07483-870210; N Yorks) Help with planning and all aspects of walking support from the absolute beginner to the experienced walker; offer free parking.

Guided walking holidays

● **Footpath** (☎ 01985-840049, ▭ footpath-holidays.com) offers the walk for the southern section (based at Hebden Bridge), the central section (based at Hawes) and the northern section (based at Hexham). The holidays (6-7 days)

European Health Insurance Card (EHIC) entitled EU nationals (on production of the card) to necessary medical treatment under the National Health Service (NHS) while on a temporary visit here. Since Brexit this system is still valid for the time being but check the current situation (▭ nhs.uk/nhs-services, then click on Visiting or moving to England) before travelling. In any case, not all treatment will be covered and it is not a substitute for proper medical cover on your travel insurance for unforeseen bills and for getting you home should that be necessary. Also consider getting cover for loss and theft of personal belongings, especially if you are camping or staying in hostels, as there will be times when you'll have to leave your luggage unattended.

● **Weights and measures** Milk in Britain is still sometimes sold in pints (1 pint = 568ml), as is beer in pubs, though most other **liquids** including petrol (gasoline) and diesel are sold in litres.

Distances on road and path signs are given in miles (1 mile = 1.6km) rather than kilometres, and yards (1yd = 0.9m) rather than metres. The population remains divided between those who still use inches (1 inch = 2.5cm), feet (1ft = 0.3m) and yards and those who are happy with metric measurements; you'll often be told that 'it's only a hundred yards or so' to somewhere, rather than a hundred metres or so.

Most **food** is sold in metric weights (g and kg) but the imperial weights of pounds (lb: 1lb = 453g) and ounces (oz: 1oz = 28g) are frequently displayed too.

The **weather** – a frequent topic of conversation – is also an issue: while most forecasts predict temperatures in Celsius (C), some people continue to think in terms of Fahrenheit (F; see the temperature chart on p16 for conversions).

● **Smoking** Smoking in enclosed public spaces is banned. The ban relates not only to pubs and restaurants, but also to B&Bs, hostels and hotels. These latter have the right to designate one or more bedrooms where the occupants can smoke, but the ban is in force in all enclosed areas open to the public – even if they are in a private home such as a B&B. If you light up in a no-smoking area, which includes almost any indoor public place, you could be fined £50, but it will be the owners of the premises who suffer most if they fail to stop you, with a potential fine of £2500.

● **Time** During the winter, the whole of Britain is on Greenwich Mean Time (GMT). The clocks move one hour forward on the last Sunday in March, remaining on British Summer Time (BST) until the last Sunday in October.

● **Telephone** From outside Britain the international country access code for Britain is ☎ 44 followed by the area code minus the first 0, and then the number you require. Within Britain, to call a landline number with the same code as the landline phone you are calling from, the code can be omitted. If your mobile phone is registered overseas, consider buying a local SIM card to keep costs down.

● **Emergency services** For police, ambulance, fire or coastguard dial ☎ 999, or the EU standard number ☎ 112.

PLANNING YOUR WALK

are operated once a year in July-August and are arranged so that it would be possible to walk the whole route.
● **River Mountain Experience** (☎ 01677-426112, 🖳 rivermountainexperience .com; Northallerton) Offer guided walks along part of the Way.

WALKING WITH DOGS   [see pp282-4]

For many, walking without their dog would be as inconceivable as walking without boots, but the Pennine Way is tough, not just for us humans, but for dogs as well. Be sure that your dog is as prepared for the walk as you are. Dog-friendly accommodation is available in many places along the walk, and is specified in the route guide, but your selection will be restricted; all but one of the hostels along the trail do not allow dogs save for registered assistance dogs (take a bow, Greenhead Hostel, see p232, the only exception to this rule) and some campsites will also be closed to you if you're walking with your dog.

Although the Pennine Way is a public right of way along its whole length, there are restrictions for dogs in certain places and at certain times of year. Dogs must always be under close control, ideally on a lead, when near livestock and must always be on a lead when walking through areas of ground nesting birds in spring and early summer. There will be signs on stiles and gates to give you adequate warning. Even a well-trained dog will be hard pressed to resist the temptation to chase a fledgling grouse as it flees from cover.

Budgeting

When it comes to budgeting, there is a happy compromise somewhere between the hardened backpacker, who wild camps every night and forages for wild roots, berries and roadkill, and the five-star traveller, who insists on the best accommodation available, baggage transfer as well as fine wines and comestibles in the evening. Your budget depends on the level of comfort you're prepared to lavish upon yourself and, up to a point, how fast you can walk! Even if you're unlikely to come across any Michelin star restaurants along the Pennine Way, there is still a tendency for walkers to under-estimate their budget. Your walking holiday is likely to cost about the same as a fortnight in the sun.

ACCOMMODATION STYLES

Camping
Wild camping and river water is free and if you carried your own dehydrated meals you may conceivably complete the walk for nothing, and without contributing anything to the communities through which you pass. Campsites typically charge around £10pp per night, though the simpler ones are around £5. The additional luxuries of an occasional shower, a cooked breakfast and the odd pint and a meal in the evening will probably bring the cost up to £25pp per day.

Bunkhouses, camping barns and hostels

You can't always cook your own food in bunkhouses/camping barns (though all YHA hostels have a kitchen) so costs can rise: £35-40pp per day will allow you to have the occasional meal out and enjoy a few local brews. If staying in a YHA hostel expect to pay around £20-25pp per night though more in the high season; breakfast costs £5-8 as does a packed lunch; for an evening meal expect to pay £12. Many hostels are licensed so budget for more if you're a drinker.

B&B-style accommodation

B&B rates per person range from £35pp to £65pp or more a night, assuming you are sharing a double room, and of course you get a good breakfast to set you up for the day. On top of that add £20 to cover both a packed lunch and a pub meal in the evening. Solo walkers will spend a lot more, as single room rates (£50-90) are often not that much cheaper than a double. You'll soon find doing the walk at a relaxed three-week pace could put your budget into four figures.

OTHER EXPENSES

Think carefully about how you're going to get to Edale – fairly straightforward – and back from Kirk Yetholm – more convoluted. If using trains, buying an Advance ticket as soon as they are released (12-24 weeks ahead) will give you the best savings, though note that they are non-flexible and non-refundable. Incidental expenses can add up: soft drinks or beer, cream teas, taxis to take you to a distant pub or back onto the trail in the morning. This does not include finding out that some vital item of your equipment has been left at home or is not performing well. We estimate adding another £100-200 to your total budget for these 'incidentals'.

PLANNING YOUR WALK

❑ WALKING THE PENNINE WAY – A PERSONAL EXPERIENCE

I did the whole walk during the hot dry summer of 2013. It took me 20 days, averaging about 15 miles a day. For some of the first four days I was very aware of evidence of the nearby cities such as reservoirs, pylons, masts and drainage channels, which may come as a disappointment if you are looking for a 'wilderness walk'. However I am glad I was patient as this gradually changes when the walk enters the Yorkshire Dales National Park and becomes wilder and more unspoilt through the North Pennines Area of Outstanding Natural Beauty (AONB) until you reach The Cheviots in the Borders which are really remote. It has some spectacular landmarks including High Force, High Cup Nick and Hadrian's Wall. The enormous job of laying flagstones along the boggy areas of the route has helped tame the bogs, so I didn't have any problems.

Overall it is a tough but really exhilarating walk which needs preparation and stamina to complete, having a total of 11,350m of ascent. The Pennine Way stretched my boundaries, involving as it does good map-reading skills, some short scrambles and a lot of hill climbing. The route, which has had a lot of restoration work done to it, is the perfect antidote to crowded routes such as Hadrian's Wall, and really deserves a renaissance. **Rucksack Rose (Twitter: @RucksackRose)**

VILLAGE & TOWN FACILITIES & DISTANCES
Edale to Kirk Yetholm – Walking North

PLACE* & DISTANCE* APPROX MILES / *KM*	ATM (BANK)	POST OFFICE	INFO	EATING PLACE	FOOD SHOP	CAMP-SITE	HOSTEL BARN	B&B HOTEL
Edale/Nether Booth			VC	✔✔✔	✔	✔	Y/B†/G	✔✔✔
Upper Booth 1½ / *2.5*						✔	B†	
Torside 13½ / *21.5*								
(Padfield + 2 / *3.3*)				✔				✔✔
Crowden 1 / *1.6*						✔P		
Standedge 11 / *17.5*								
(Diggle +1½ / *2.5*)				✔				✔✔
(Marsden + 2 / *3.3*)	✔			✔✔✔	✔			✔✔
Blackstone Edge 5½ / *9*				✔				
Mankinholes 6 / *9.5*				✔			Y†	✔
Calder Valley 3 / *5*								
(Hebden Bridge +1¼ / *2*)	✔	✔		✔✔✔	✔		H	✔✔✔
Blackshaw Head 1½ / *2.5*								
Colden ½ / *1*				✔	✔	✔		
Widdop 2½ / *4*				✔				
Ponden & Stanbury 6 / *9.5*				✔		✔	G	✔✔
(Haworth +3.5/*5.5*)	✔	✔		✔✔✔	✔		Y	✔✔✔
Ickornshaw (& Cowling) 5 / *8*				✔✔✔	✔	✔P		✔
Lothersdale 2½ / *4*				✔				
(Earby+1¼ / *2*)	✔	✔		✔✔✔	✔		H	
East Marton 6 / *9.5*				✔		✔		
Gargrave 2½ / *4*	✔			✔✔✔	✔	✔		✔✔
Airton 4 / *6.5*				✔	✔		B	✔
Kirkby Malham 1½ / *2.5*				✔				
Malham 1 / *1.6*			NPC	✔✔✔		✔	Y/B†/G	✔✔✔
Horton-in-Ribblesdale 14½ / *23.5*				✔✔✔	✔	✔	B	✔✔✔
Hawes 13½ / *21.5*	✔	✔	NPC/TIC	✔✔✔	✔	✔	Y	✔✔✔
Hardraw 1½ / *2.5*				✔✔		✔		✔✔
Thwaite 8 / *13*				✔		✔		✔
(Muker+1¼ / *2*)				✔✔	✔			✔✔
Keld 3 / *5*				✔	✔	✔	B/G	✔✔✔
Tan Hill 4 / *6.5*				✔		✔	B	✔
Baldersdale 10 / *16*								
(Cotherstone + 5 / *8*)		(✔)		✔				✔
Lunedale 3 / *5*						✔P		
Middletn-in-Tsdale 3½ / *5.5*	✔	✔	TIC	✔✔✔	✔	✔		✔✔✔
Holwick 2½ / *4*				✔			B	
High Force 2½ / *4*				✔				✔
(Langdon Beck + ¾ / *1.2*)				✔			Y	✔
Dufton 14½ / *23.5*				✔✔	✔	✔P	Y	✔

cont'd on p36

NOTES *PLACE & DISTANCE Places in **bold** are on the Pennine Way; places in brackets and not in bold – eg (Earby+1¼) – are nearby. The backeted distance shows the additional distance off the route – eg Earby is 1¼ miles from the Way. Distance is given from the place above that is on the path.

ATM ✔ = ATM in bank, post office or outside shop

POST OFFICE (✔) = limited opening hours or pop-up

VILLAGE & TOWN FACILITIES & DISTANCES
Kirk Yetholm to Edale – Walking South

PLACE* & DISTANCE* APPROX MILES / *KM*	ATM (BANK)	POST OFFICE	INFO	EATING PLACE	FOOD SHOP	CAMP-SITE	HOSTEL BARN	B&B HOTEL
Kirk/Town Yetholm		✔		✔✔	✔	✔	H	✔✔✔
Byrness 25½ / *41*				✔		✔P		✔
Bellingham 15 / *24*	✔	✔	TIC	✔✔✔	✔	✔P		✔✔✔
Once Brewed 15 / *24*			NPC/TIC	✔✔		✔	Y/B/G	✔✔✔
(Stonehaugh +1 / *1.6*)						✔		
Burnhead 2½ / *4*				✔				✔
Greenhead 4 / *6.5*				✔✔		✔	H/B†	✔✔✔
Slaggyford &Knarsdale 9½ / *15.5*				✔		✔		✔
Alston 7 / *11.5*	✔	✔	TIC	✔✔✔	✔	✔	Y/B	✔✔✔
Garrigill 4/*6.5*		✔		✔	✔	✔	B	✔✔
Dufton 15½ / *25*				✔✔	✔	✔P	Y	✔
High Force 14½ / *23.5*				✔				✔
(Langdon Beck + ¾ / *1.2*)				✔			Y	✔
Holwick 2½ / *4*				✔			B	
Middletn-in-Tsdale 2½ / *4*	✔	✔	TIC	✔✔✔	✔	✔		✔✔✔
Lunedale 3½ / *5.5*						✔P		
Baldersdale 3 / *5*								
(Cotherstone + 5 / *8*)		(✔)		✔				✔
Tan Hill 10 / *16*				✔		✔	B	✔
Keld 4 / *6.5*				✔	✔	✔	B/G	✔✔✔
Thwaite 3 / *5*				✔		✔		✔
(Muker+1¼ / *2*)				✔✔	✔			✔✔
Hardraw 8 / *13*				✔✔		✔		✔✔
Hawes 1½ / *2.5*	✔	✔	NPC/TIC	✔✔✔	✔	✔	Y	✔✔✔
Horton-in-Ribblesdale 13½ / *21.5*				✔✔✔	✔	✔	B	✔✔✔
Malham 14½ / *23.5*			NPC	✔✔✔		✔	Y/B†/G	✔✔✔
Kirkby Malham 1 / *1.6*				✔				
Airton 1½ / *2.5*				✔	✔		B	✔
Gargrave 4 / *6.5*	✔			✔✔✔	✔	✔		✔✔
East Marton 2½ / *4*				✔		✔		
Lothersdale 6 / *9.5*				✔				
(Earby+1¼ / *2*)	✔	✔		✔✔✔	✔		H	
Ickornshaw (& Cowling) 2½ / *4*				✔✔✔	✔	✔P		✔
Ponden & Stanbury 5 / *8*				✔		✔	G	✔✔
(Haworth +3.5/*5.5*)	✔	✔		✔✔✔	✔		Y	✔✔✔
Widdop 6 / *9.5*				✔				
Colden 2½ / *4*				✔	✔	✔		
Blackshaw Head ½ / *1*								
Calder Valley 1½ / *2.5*								
(Hebden Bridge +1¼ / *2*)	✔	✔		✔✔✔	✔		H	✔✔✔

cont'd on p37

B&B/HOTEL ✔ = one place ✔✔ = two ✔✔✔ = three or more
INFO TIC = Tourist Info Centre NPC = National Park Centre VC = Visitor Centre
EATING PLACE (✔) = seasonal or open daytime only or only limited days
CAMPSITE (✔) = basic campsite ✔P = with camping pods
HOSTEL/BARN Y = YHA hostel H = independent hostel B = Bunkhouse or camping barn
† groups only at time of research G = Glamping

VILLAGE & TOWN FACILITIES & DISTANCES
Edale to Kirk Yetholm – Walking North

PLACE* & DISTANCE* APPROX MILES / KM	ATM (BANK)	POST OFFICE	INFO	EATING PLACE	FOOD SHOP	CAMP-SITE	HOSTEL BARN	B&B HOTEL
Garrigill 15½ /25		✔		✔	✔	✔	B	✔
Alston 4/6.5	✔	✔	TIC	✔✔	✔	✔	Y/B	✔✔
Slaggyford &Knarsdale 7/11.5				✔		✔		
Greenhead 9½ /15.5				✔✔		✔	H/B†	✔✔
Burnhead 4/6.5				✔				✔
Once Brewed 2½ /4			NPC/TIC	✔✔		✔	Y/B/G	✔✔
(Stonehaugh +1/1.6)						✔		
Bellingham 15/24	✔	✔	TIC	✔✔	✔	✔P		✔✔
Byrness 15/24				✔		✔P		✔
Kirk/Town Yetholm 25½ /41	✔			✔✔	✔	✔	H	✔✔

NOTES ***PLACE & DISTANCE** Places in **bold** are on the Pennine Way; places in brackets and not in bold – eg (Earby+1¼) – are nearby. The backeted distance shows the additional distance off the route – eg Earby is 1¼ miles from the Way. Distance is given from the place above that is on the path.
ATM ✔ = ATM in bank, post office or outside shop
POST OFFICE (✔) = limited opening hours or pop-up

❏ WALKING THE PENNINE WAY – A PERSONAL EXPERIENCE

I remember exactly when I decided I needed to walk the Pennine Way, it was April 2005 and I was driving home from a meeting in Slough; Radio 4 were doing a feature on the 40th birthday of the path. I'd only just started walking, in an effort to lose some weight and the Pennine Way seemed like a worthy goal to aim for. My love of desolate moorland and mist-shrouded hills was still a long way into the future, but it seemed like a challenge, something I could aspire to.

Over the next few years my walking became prolific; I started with small day walks, built up to longer mountain walks in the Lake District and finally, in May 2010, I set out from Edale.

Over the next 17 days I met only the occasional PW walker; if you're walking the Pennine Way alone, you need to be happy with your own company. I loved the quiet, the solitude on the hills and the emptying of the mind that resulted in having no other responsibility than getting up each morning and putting one foot in front of the other. No other path has offered me that sense of calm and inner peace. It was a joy and a pleasure, as well as a physical and mental challenge at times; it is, after all a long path!

My arrival in Kirk Yetholm, dripping in sweat on a blistering hot day, after walking about 26 miles from Byrness in 10 hours, was welcomed by no-one. A witty local at the bar in the Border Hotel asked me if it was raining outside and the barmaid made no remark when I asked for the Pennine Way book to sign. The path is a personal challenge, don't do it for anyone but yourself.

Stuart Greig (Twitter: @LoneWalkerUK)

VILLAGE & TOWN FACILITIES & DISTANCES
Kirk Yetholm to Edale – Walking South

PLACE* & DISTANCE* APPROX MILES / KM	ATM (BANK)	POST OFFICE	INFO	EATING PLACE	FOOD SHOP	CAMP-SITE	HOSTEL BARN	B&B HOTEL
Mankinholes 3 / 5				✔			Y†	✔
Blackstone Edge 6 / 9.5				✔				
Standedge 5½ / 9								
(Diggle +1½ / 2.5)				✔				W
(Marsden + 2 / 3.3)	✔			WW	✔			W
Crowden 11 / 17.5						✔P		
Torside 1 / 1.6								
(Padfield + 2 / 3.3)				✔				W
Upper Booth 13½ / 21.5						✔	B†	
Edale/Nether Booth 1½ / 2.5			VC	WW	✔	✔	Y /B† /G	WW

INFO TIC = Tourist Info Centre   NPC = National Park Centre   VC = Visitor Centre
B&B/HOTEL ✔ = one place W = two WW = three or more
EATING PLACE (✔) = seasonal or open daytime only or only limited days
CAMPSITE (✔) = basic campsite ✔P = with camping pods
HOSTEL/BARN Y = YHA hostel H = independent hostel B = Bunkhouse or camping barn
          † groups only at time of research   G = Glamping

PLANNING YOUR WALK

❏ WALKING THE PENNINE WAY – A PERSONAL EXPERIENCE

It started for me as a trip with a friend who later dropped out leaving me with the daunting prospect of doing the Pennine Way as my first trail, and alone!

I expected a few problems along the way and ended up packing way too much equipment into my rucksack to cover as much as possible. Even though I had made a couple of trial weekend treks, the weight was a complete killer.

The first half was difficult and engulfed by setbacks. On day one my train was late into Manchester, resulting in me missing the connection to Edale! A cancellation later found me taking another route and walking directly to Crowden for my first night's sleep. I actually went back after to complete the first day's walking.

By the time I got to Thornton-in-Craven my ill-fitting boots meant I had to come away to buy new boots and restart a few days later. The second part was much more enjoyable, my rucksack repacked with less in it, the new boots, and better weather, at least until High Cup Nick, where the weather was so terrible I only knew I was there because the ground vanished! Dufton Hostel was wonderful and I made some lifelong friends there in the pub that night, who completed the walk with me and we still walk together every year. For all of us who walked the rest of the Way, the icing on the cake was spending our last night at Davidson's Linn, a beautiful spot, enhanced only slightly by curry and malt whisky.

I plan to do it again one day, in one go, with no break in the middle. I think there are two secrets to enjoying the Pennine Way; travel as light as possible and take enough time to enjoy the scenery. The walk really is possible for anyone and provided memories that will stay with me forever; from fording swollen streams at Black Hill to the biggest plate of food I have ever seen in Bellingham.

Mark Smith (Twitter: @markj_smith)

Itineraries

All walkers are individuals. Some like to cover large distances as quickly as possible, others like to stroll along and stop frequently – indeed this natural variation in pace is what causes most friction in groups. You may want to walk the Pennine Way all in one go, tackle it over a series of weekends, or use the trail for linear day walks; the choice is yours. This book has been divided into stages, and many will use it that way, but these are not rigid. Instead, the book has been designed to make it easy for you to plan your own optimal itinerary.

The **planning map** (see inside back cover) and **table of village/town facilities** (see pp34-7) summarise the essential information. Alternatively, have a look at the **suggested itineraries** (pp39-41) and choose your preferred type of accommodation and pace. There are also suggestions for those who want to experience the best of the trail over a day or a weekend (see opposite). The **public transport maps and service table** (pp54-9) will also be useful.

Having made a rough plan, turn to Part 4, where you will find summaries of the route, full descriptions of the accommodation options, suggestions for where to eat and information about other services in each village and town; as well as the detailed trail maps.

Which direction?

Most people walk the Pennine Way **south to north**. There are practical reasons for this; the prevailing south-westerly wind and rain are behind you, as is the

---

❑ **WALKING THE PENNINE WAY – A PERSONAL EXPERIENCE**

I used to love walking around Edale as a teenager and made my first attempt at the Pennine Way when I was 16. Woefully ill-prepared we aborted after 3 days when my companion got sick. Now 62, newly retired, and a lot wiser, I made it on my second attempt, end-to-end in 19 days.

A lot has changed in the meantime. Underfoot has improved a lot, and signage is much better, no more wandering between walls of peat trying to hold a compass bearing while your boots disappear at each step. There is even an app which tells you where you are! This is all good and helps you appreciate what has not changed and why I love the Pennine Way. The wildness and rough beauty of the moors, the bucolic, green dales, the welcoming villages and pubs and the no-nonsense locals that you meet along the way.

The other thing that remains is the wind. It is rare that you know the exact wind speed when you are out on the hills but my friend and I happened to be blown off our feet on Great Dun Fell at the exact time that the weather station there was officially recording gusts up to 175km/hr. With the wisdom of age, and because we could not physically stand, we slid and crawled down off the ridge, skirted round the summit of Cross Fell and eventually made it to Garrigill. The Pennine Way certainly retains its teeth. So I still haven't completely cracked Cross Fell, but I will be back.

Steve Oxley (2018)

sun. Head north–south if you want a better face tan! The maps in Part 4 give timings for both directions and, as route-finding instructions are on the maps rather than in blocks of text, it ought to be straightforward using this guide back to front.

THE BEST DAY AND WEEKEND (TWO-DAY) WALKS

Not everyone is able to devote the best part of three weeks to walking the Pennine Way in one continuous journey. That doesn't mean, however, that you can't sample the delights of the path and this section may help your decision-making process by describing some of the one- and two-day walk options that

	WILD CAMPING* AND CAMPSITES (▲)				
	Relaxed pace		**Medium pace**		**Fast pace**
		Approx distance		Approx distance		Approx distance
Night	**Place**	miles (km)	**Place**	miles (km)	**Place**	miles(km)
0	Edale		Edale		Edale	
1	Crowden ▲	16 (26)	Crowden ▲	16 (26)	Black Hill	20½ (33)
2	Standedge ▲	11 (18)	Blackst Edge	16½ (26.5)	Blackshaw Hd	22½ (36)
3	Withins Moor	11 (18)	Walshaw	15½ (25)	Pinhaw Beacon	18½ (30)
4	Withins Height	12 (19.5)	Pinhaw Beacon	13½ (22)	Fountains Fell	20½ (33)
5	East Marton ▲	15½ (25)	Fountains Fell	20½ (33)	Hawes ▲	20½ (33)
6	Fountains Fell	16½ (26.5)	Dodd Fell	16 (26)	Sleightholme	18½ (30)
7	Old Ing Moor	11 (18)	Keld ▲	17 (27)	Middleton	14½ (23.5)
8	Gt Shunner Fell	15½ (25)	(Rest day)	0 (0)	Rail wagon	6 (9.5)
9	Tan Hill ▲	10½ (17)	Deepdale Beck	12 (19.5)	Greg's Hut	23 (37)
10	Deepdale Beck	8 (13)	Rail wagon	14½ (23.5)	Glendue Burn	18½ (30)
11	Middleton ▲	8½ (13.5)	High Cup	10 (16)	Wark Forest	20½ (33)
12	(Rest day)	0 (0)	Greg's Hut	13 (21)	Byrness Hill	25 (40)
13	High Cup	16 (26)	Alston ▲	10 (16)	Kirk Yetholm#	24½ (39.5)
14	Greg's Hut	13 (21)	Glendue Burn	8½ (13.5)		
15	Alston ▲	10 (16)	Wark Forest	20½ (33)		
16	Glendue Burn	8½ (13.5)	Deer Play	14½ (23.5)		
17	Wark Forest	20½ (33)	Coquet Head	13½ (22)		
18	Deer Play	14½ (23.5)	Kirk Yetholm#	21½ (34.5)		
19	Byrness Hill	10½ (17)				
20	Windy Gyle	12 (19.5)				
21	Kirk Yetholm#	12½ (20)				

* See p19-20 for important information about wild camping. Wild camping obviously allows overnighting where you please. Where possible the approximate locations of wild camps have been proposed on the fells, ie where discreet and unobtrusive stays are most easily made. Most places have also been chosen for their scenic appeal, the vicinity of Glendue Burn being a notable but unavoidable exception. On other days the ideal distance – be it 'relaxed' or 'fast' – puts you so near a town it's simpler to stay on a campsite or even at a B&B. The flexibility of wild camping enables greater daily distances to be covered so the three proposed itineraries above may not take as many days.

　　　▲ Campsite　　# The campsite is in Town Yetholm, not Kirk Yetholm.

PLANNING YOUR WALK

are available. This is by no means a definitive list, it simply selects some of the highlights of the Way.

The day walks are mostly circular so you can return to the start point without relying on public transport, or you could simply backtrack from the point at which the walks leave the Way. Some of these walks use paths not covered in the maps in this book, so you will need the appropriate Ordnance Survey maps to complete them. The correct map is identified in the text for each walk.

However, in order to maximise your time on the Pennine Way and to try and simulate the experience those end-to-enders will get, the two-/three-day walks described here are linear and will typically require the use of public transport (or two vehicles) to get back home, or back to your car at the start. With the inclusion of a couple of long stages, it is possible to complete the whole route using this method, even if the dwindling supply of regular bus services north of the Wall conspires against you.

PLANNING YOUR WALK

STAYING IN HOSTELS, BUNKHOUSES & CAMPING BARNS

	Relaxed pace		Medium pace		Fast pace	
Night	Place	Approx distance miles (km)	Place	Approx distance miles (km)	Place	Approx distance miles(km)
0	Edale		Edale		Edale	
1	Torside*	16 (26)	Torside*	16 (26)	Torside*	16 (26)
2	Standedge*	11 (18)	Standedge*	11 (18)	Mankinholes◊	22½ (36)
3	Mankinholes◊	11½ (18.5)	Mankinholes◊	11½ (18.5)	Ickornshaw*	18½ (30)
4	Haworth§	11½ (18.5)	Ickornshaw*	18½ (30)	Malham	17½ (28)
5	Earby•	14 (22.5)	Malham	17½ (28)	Horton-in-Rib	14½ (23.5)
6	Malham	10½ (17)	Horton-in-Rib	14½ (23.5)	Keld	26 (42)
7	Horton-in-Rib	14½ (23.5)	Hawes	13½ (22)	Middleton-in-T*	20½(33)
8	Hawes	13½ (22)	(Rest day)	0 (0)	Dufton	19½ (31.5)
9	(Rest day)	0 (0)	Keld	12½ (20)	Alston	19½ (31.5)
10	Keld	12½ (20)	Baldersdale†	14 (22.5)	Greenhead	16½ (26.5)
11	Baldersdale†	14 (22.5)	Langdon Beck	14 (22.5)	Bellingham*	21½ (34.5)
12	Middleton-in-T*	6½ (10.5)	Dufton	12 (19.5)	Byrness*	15 (24)
13	Langdon Beck	7½ (12)	Alston	19½ (31.5)	Kirk Yetholm	25½ (41)
14	Dufton	12 (19.5)	Greenhead	16½ (26.5)		
15	Garrigill	15½ (25)	Once Brewed	6½ (10.5)		
16	Slaggy/Knars*	11 (18)	Bellingham*	15 (24)		
17	Greenhead	9½ (15)	Byrness*	15 (24)		
18	Once Brewed	6½ (10.5)	Kirk Yetholm	25½ (41)		
19	Bellingham*	15 (24)				
20	Byrness*	15 (24)				
21	Byrness*#	13 (21)				
22	Kirk Yetholm	12½ (20)				

* No hostel/bunkhouse/barn; stay in B&B
◊ If YHA Mankinholes is still not taking individual bookings continue to Hebden Bridge 3 miles (5km) further on   § 3½ miles (6km) to/from town each way
• 1½ miles (2km) to/from town each way   † The nearest B&B is at Cotherstone
 # Use Forest View Inn's transport scheme (see p258), or sleep in Auchope refuge hut

One-day circular walks

● **Edale to Kinder Downfall** (see p87) **returning by the old route over Kinder Scout and Grindsbrook Clough** At around **10 miles (16km)** this route will let you experience the start of the Pennine Way as it is today and as it was originally. The crossing of the Kinder plateau should be done with care, good navigation skills and ideally in fine weather. (Explorer OL01: Peak District Dark Peak Area).

● **Rochdale Canal to Top Withins** (see p119) **returning via Dean Gate and Hebden Dale** Follow the Pennine Way from the Rochdale Canal at Charlestown across Heptonstall Moor to Top Withins, where you will need to dodge the Brontë tourists before returning along Dean Gate and any one of a dozen footpaths through Hebden Dale back to the canal, a round trip of around **11 miles (17.7km)** in all. (Explorer OL21: South Pennines).

● **Airton to Malham Tarn** (see p143) **returning along the same path**

STAYING IN B&B-STYLE ACCOMMODATION

	Relaxed pace		Medium pace		Fast pace	
		Approx distance		Approx distance		Approx distance
Night	Place	miles (km)	Place	miles (km)	Place	miles(km)
0	Edale		Edale		Edale	
1	Torside §	15 (24)	Torside §	15 (24)	Torside §	15 (24)
2	Standedge ●	12 (19.5)	Standedge ●	12 (19.5)	Mankinholes	23½ (38)*
3	Hebden Br*	14½ (23.5)	Hebden Br*	14½ (23.5)	Ponden	13½ (21.5)
4	Ponden	10½ (17)	Ickornshaw & Cowling	15½ (25)	Malham	22½ (36)
5	Earby	12 (19.5)	Malham	17½ (28)	Horton-in-Rib	14½ (23.5)
6	Malham	10½ (17)	Horton-in-Rib	14½ (23.5)	Keld	26 (42)
7	Horton-in-Rib	14½ (23.5)	Hawes	13½ (21.5)	Middleton-in-T	20½ (33)
8	Hawes	13½ (21.5)	(Rest day)	0 (0)	Dufton	19½ (31.5)
9	(Rest day)	0 (0)	Keld	12½ (20)	Alston	19½ (31.5)
10	Keld	12½ (20)	Cotherstone*	14 (22.5)	Greenhead	16½ (26.5)
11	Cotherstone*	14 (22.5)	Langdon Beck	14 (22.5)	Bellingham	21½ (34.5)
12	Langdon Beck	14 (22.5)	Dufton	12 (19.5)	Byrness	15 (24)
13	Dufton	12 (19.5)	Alston	19½ (31.5)	Kirk Yetholm	25½ (41)
14	Garrigill	15½ (25)	Greenhead	16½ (26.5)		
15	Knarsdale	11 (17.5)	Once Brewed	6½ (10.5)		
16	Greenhead	9½ (15.5)	Bellingham	15 (24)		
17	Once Brewed	6½ (10.5)	Byrness	15 (24)		
18	Bellingham	15 (24)	Kirk Yetholm	25½ (41)		
19	Byrness	15 (24)				
20	Byrness #	13 (21)				
21	Kirk Yetholm	12½ (20)				

* *Additional distance to B&B accommodation from Pennine Way*

§ *then 2½ miles (4km) to Padfield*
● *then 1½ miles (2km) to Diggle or 2 miles (3km to Marsden*
Use Forest View Inn's transport scheme (see p258)

PLANNING YOUR WALK

❏ **WALKING THE PENNINE WAY – A PERSONAL EXPERIENCE**
There were a few raised eyebrows when I announced that I was going to walk the Pennine Way on my own. Non-walking friends worried about my safety. Walking friends wondered if I would finish. Happily, they were all wrong. I encountered nothing but kindness and respect and I finished in 18 days wishing it would go on forever. Never once did I think about quitting and to anyone considering it I'd say walk your own walk. Your mind is by far your greatest asset or your greatest liability. The first and last hour of every day are the hardest – no matter how long or short the day is.

Highlight: sharing the last day with my husband and getting my certificate at the Border Hotel. Lowlight: sharing a YHA room with a girl who snored louder than an express train. Top tip: ignore anyone who says that you can't get lost – trust me, you can. If you think you need to stop and consult the map – you do!

I loved every single soggy exhausting moment of it and I'd do it again in a heartbeat except that I worry that it won't be as good second time and I'd rather keep those wonderful memories.   **Janet Donnelly (Twitter: @celebrantjanet)**

Sometimes an 'out and back' path is rewarding, allowing you to see the landscape from different perspectives. This is one such walk; starting at Airton and taking in Malham Cove and Malham Tarn as well as the wonderful Watlowes valley. Around **12 miles (19.3km)**. (Explorer OL02: Yorkshire Dales Southern & Western Area).

● **Horton-in-Ribblesdale to Cam End** (see p157) **returning via the Ribble Way** Climb out of Horton on the Pennine Way along a lovely lane as far as the logging road at Cam End, where you turn left and drop down to pick up the Ribble Way back into Horton. There are some splendid views of the Yorkshire Three Peaks along this **13-mile (21km)** route. (Explorer OL02: Yorkshire Dales Southern & Western Area).

● **Thwaite to Tan Hill** (see p176) **returning via West Stones Dale road** This walk takes you round the foot of Kisdon Hill, a rustic track with great views into the head of Swaledale, before striking out across East Stonesdale Moor to the enigmatic Tan Hill Inn. Return by the same path, or the quiet West Stonesdale road for a walk of around **14 miles (22.5km)**. (Explorer OL30: Yorkshire Dales Northern & Central Area).

● **Middleton-in-Teesdale to High Force** (see p196) **returning via Holwick Scars** The best waterfall walk in the country – unless you decide to walk on to Cauldron Snout (an extra 11 miles/18km) – along the Pennine Way to High Force and using the high-level route up Holwick Scars and over Crossthwaite Common to return to Middleton, around **13 miles (21km)** in all. (Explorer OL31: North Pennines & OL19: Howgill Fells & Upper Eden Valley).

● **Dufton to High Cup** (see p210) **returning via Harbour Flatt** Follow the Pennine Way in reverse from Dufton, up to the incredible glacial bowl of High Cup then take the lofty path along its eastern lip, down Middle Tongue and around the nose of Middletongue Crag, passing the farm of Harbour Flatt and back along the lane to Dufton, for an exhilarating **10-mile (16km)** walk. (Explorer OL19: Howgill Fells & Upper Eden Valley).

● **Greenhead to Once Brewed** (see p231) Another 'out and back' day walk, but justified on the basis that the path is accompanied by the Roman Wall and what you miss on the way out you may spot on the way back. You walk a total of about **14 miles (22.5km)** beside some of the finest sections of the Wall; ramparts, mile-castles and turrets are all visited. (Explorer OL43: Hadrian's Wall).

Two- and three-day linear walks

● **Edale to Standedge** (see p87) This **30-mile (50km)** walk takes in the Kinder Scout, Bleaklow and Black Hill massifs and offers a chance to experience some of the best 'Dark Peak' walking there is. Where there's gritstone there's also peat, but thankfully the worst of the mire is now slabbed, so although you may not keep your boots dry, you are unlikely to be swallowed whole! The railway stations at Edale and Marsden will facilitate your travel and a Padfield B&B or camp at Crowden will break the journey into two days.

● **Gargrave to Horton-in-Ribblesdale** (see p141) This **22-mile (35km)** section may be within the reach of some as a day walk, using the stations at Gargrave and Horton, both on the Leeds–Settle–Carlisle line to facilitate transfer. However, it is best experienced as a weekend walk, with a break in Malham before tackling the tough stretch over Fountains Fell and Pen-y-ghent down into Horton.

● **Horton-in-Ribblesdale to Bowes** (see p157) This is best undertaken as a three-day walk, totalling, as it does, **around 42 miles (68km)**. The route includes the waterfall in Hardraw, an ascent of Great Shunner Fell, a pint at the highest pub in Britain at Tan Hill Inn and the crossing of the desolate Sleightholme Moor. The railway station in Horton is a great starting point but a second car, or a bus or taxi to Kirkby Stephen station, will be needed for the return leg.

● **Dufton to Greenhead** (see p210) The high point of the Pennine Way on Cross Fell is also the highlight of this section, unless you decide to extend it slightly to take in the Roman Wall, which could be done by using Bardon Mill station (Newcastle–Carlisle Line) instead of Haltwhistle; both require a diversion of a couple of miles from the Wall. Indeed the start point of Dufton is three miles (5km) from Appleby station, but a taxi can whisk you over this short distance easily enough. Expect to cover **about 40 miles (64km)** on this walk.

❏ **WALKING THE PENNINE WAY – A PERSONAL EXPERIENCE**
The first time I walked the Pennine Way, south to north, was magic. I enjoyed it so much I decided to do it again, north to south. The countryside is a given – fantastic – but the weather can be totally unpredictable, which adds to the experience; however, the outstanding memory, each time, was of the people I met and how friendly they were.

  Each time I camped most of the way. There was one time I asked a farmer for permission to pitch on his land and ended up helping him with a new born calf. Unforgettable! I didn't plan ahead and relied on picking up supplies locally, or, more often than not, eating in pubs. Camping outside Tan Hill Inn was wonderful, waking up with the ducks in the morning. The Pennine Way is one of walking's great 'must do's' and it will more than repay the effort. **Gordon Green (Twitter: @aktovate1)**

● **Bellingham to Kirk Yetholm** (see p248) Both ends of this **40-mile (64km)** section of the Way require some logistical jiggery-pokery, as neither has a railway station within easy reach. The 25-mile (40km) stretch over the Cheviot range can be broken down using the accommodation options described on p258 & p262, or make use of one of the mountain shelters; both have sleeping space for three or four people in comfort. Better still, yomp the whole ridge in one go and feel what it must be like to have walked all the way from Edale.

What to take

It's easy enough to find online tales of Pennine Wayfarers broken and beaten by their huge loads. Taking too much is an easy mistake to make when you don't know what to expect and many over-compensate by packing everything they think may be needed. This isn't a problem if you plan on using a baggage-transfer service, but will be if you intend carrying it all yourself.

The ability to pack light comes with experience and requires a degree of discipline. Every ounce you remove from your load will enable you to walk that little bit further, make the day that little bit easier and reduce the strain on feet that need to carry you over 250 miles. Be careful in your selection of equipment and ruthless in your decision to take something at all.

If you've done any hill-walking you will probably have most of the equipment you need, but if you are starting fresh look out for online deals and special offers in the outdoor supermarkets; shopping around can save you a small fortune. However, beware of cheap, low-quality products; 'buy cheap, buy twice' is often very true and you need equipment to last the full length of the trail.

TRAVELLING LIGHT

Baggage-transfer services (see pp28-9) enable you to walk every day with nothing more than a daypack, water, lunch, waterproofs and the other bare essentials. This lightweight approach and the fact that you can have clean clothes every day appeals to many walkers. Consider, though, the feeling of setting out from Edale with everything you need to walk over 250 miles to Kirk Yetholm and the sense of satisfaction that may engender upon arrival.

HOW TO CARRY YOUR LUGGAGE

Today's **rucksacks** are hi-tech affairs that make load-carrying as tolerable as can be expected. Don't get hung up on anti-sweat features; unless you use a wheelbarrow your back will always sweat. It's better to ensure a good fit, especially in the back-length if you are above average height. In addition to padded hip belts, an unelasticated cross-chest strap will keep the pack snug; it can make a real difference. Envy-inducing backpack features include hip belt pockets, a water bottle holster that you can access without removing your pack, top flap pockets and an inner compartment for a water bladder. If you're camping you'll need a pack of no less than 60-litres' capacity. Staying in hostels, 40 litres should be ample, and for those eating out and staying in B&B-style accommodation a 30- to 40-litre pack should suffice; anything less than this and you will almost certainly be using a baggage transfer service. It is worth noting that baggage carriers will impose a weight limit on your bag of around 17-20kg.

Although many rucksacks claim to be waterproof, this isn't always the case so it is worth using a waterproof **pack cover** or at least a strong plastic **bin liner**. It's also handy to compartmentalise the contents into coloured or distinguishable bags so you know what is where. Take **dry bags** for your wet clothes and towel, **plastic bags** for rubbish etc and plenty of Ziploc bags; they're always useful. Finally, pack the most frequently used things so they are readily accessible.

FOOTWEAR

Boots

If you have to get one item of equipment right, it's your boots. Although modern boots don't need 'breaking in' the way boots used to, you would still be a brave (or possibly foolish) person to turn up at Edale with a pair of boots you'd never tried before. **Always test equipment** before a long walk and this is all the more true for boots; a weekend walk with the pack weight you intend to use on the Pennine Way should be enough to tell you what you need to know.

Boot selection is best done with the advice of a professional, so an online purchase or an outdoor supermarket may not be the best place, unless you are repeat buying boots. **Fit and comfort are paramount** – there's nothing worse than descending a long stony track, such as the Corpse Road off Cross Fell, and finding your boots are smashing your toes or don't protect your feet from the surface beneath. You have about half a million steps to do along the Way, so choose wisely. Most reputable outdoor stores will let you try boots at home, around the house, for a few days and allow you to return them if you find they don't fit. Expect to pay £100-150 for a good pair, or £150-200 for Gore-Tex boots. All boots can be transformed with **shock-absorbing insoles**, as long as you leave a little extra space when choosing them (wear extra thick socks). Some are thermally moulded to your foot in the shop but the less-expensive examples are also well worth the investment.

A significant proportion of walkers don't bother with boots at all, relying on lightweight running shoes or walking shoes. These don't offer the ankle support of boots but they do dry quicker and can help you walk lighter and faster. Strong Vibram soles are important to protect your feet from rocks. The key thing is that your footwear is comfortable enough to wear for 10 hours a day.

See p79 for blister-avoidance strategies.

Although not essential, it's a treat to have **alternative footwear** when not on the trail to give your feet a break or let boots dry. Sport sandals, Crocs or flip-flops are all suitable as long as they're light. They can also be useful when crossing particularly wet boggy areas.

PLANNING YOUR WALK

Socks

A **two-layer** approach to socks helps to prevent blisters; the idea being that the inner sock stays with your foot and the outer sock moves with your boot, which reduces friction on the skin and thereby blisters. A thin liner sock works best for this, with a thicker, cushioning sock used for the outer layer. Foot care is one of those places where you don't want to cut corners, so consider Merino wool for liner socks, they are light, tough and seem, miraculously, to fail to hold smells!

Waterproof socks made by reputable brands such as Sealskinz or DexShell are becoming increasingly popular and are useful when dealing with boggy moors, if your boots aren't completely waterproof. The waterproof membrane might make your feet sweat a bit more but a built-in, merino-blend lining will keep this to a minimum.

CLOTHES

Tops

Multiple layers of clothing provide the most effective and flexible approach to upper body protection. Three layers typically provides enough flexibility for an English spring or summer walk.

A quick-drying synthetic **base layer**, or better still a Merino wool or Icebreaker layer that stays fresh for weeks, may be enough on its own for warm days, or for when you're working hard up the face of Pen-y-ghent. A warm **mid layer**, typically a fleece or wind shirt will add some protection when you reach the summit and begin to cool down, or for those days when the sun just refuses to shine. A lightweight down jacket will give you maximum warmth for its weight. Finally, a waterproof, windproof **outer layer**, or 'shell' is your final defence against strong winds, rain and really cold days. A good-quality jacket will have armpit vents that you can open to allow some air to flow around your upper body, while still repelling the worst of the rain. It would also be useful to help prevent hypothermia. The layers can be mixed and matched depending on how bad the weather is. Summer rain showers are often warm enough to leave the fleece in your pack and quickly throw the outer shell over your base layer.

Avoid cotton; as well as being slow to dry, when it's wet cotton saps away body heat and will cause chafing if worn next to the skin. Take a change of base layers (including underwear); if you hand wash underwear in the evening, it may not be dry by the time you leave in the morning.

A **spare set of 'evening' clothes** will guarantee you always have something clean and dry to change into at the end of the day, which makes life more comfortable for your companions as well as yourself. Having a spare set of clothes also provides an emergency layer in case you or someone you're with goes down with hypothermia (see p79).

Leg wear

Your legs will probably feel the cold less than any other part of your body so, unless you're walking at the extreme ends of the season, a lightweight, quick-drying pair of **synthetic trousers** will almost certainly suffice. Denim jeans are cotton so are not recommended – they tend to chafe once wet and stay wet for much longer than synthetic materials.

Waterproof overtrousers can be awkward and time-consuming to put on unless they have full length side zips and can generate as much internal moisture through sweat as they repel in a light shower; consider a pair of quick-drying trousers instead.

On a warm day you may also want to consider **shorts** – some trousers have the option to zip off the bottom half of the legs to turn them into shorts. Check that you can do this without having to take your boots off though, or convert them first thing, before you set out.

Gaiters are not as essential as they once were. The slabs have tamed the worst of the bogs, but you may be surprised how well they serve to protect your boots and lower legs when walking through tall wet vegetation.

Headwear and other clothing

A peaked cap or a full-brimmed **hat** such as a Tilley will help with UV protection on sunny days. At the beginning or end of the summer you should pack a woolly hat and maybe **gloves** to combat wind chill on an exposed summit.

TOILETRIES

Besides **toothpaste** and a brush, **liquid soap** can also be used for shaving and washing clothes, although a ziplock bag of detergent is better if you're laundering regularly. Carry **toilet paper** and a lightweight **trowel** to bury the results out on the fells (see pp75-6). Less obvious items include **ear plugs** (for hostel dormitories and campsites), **lip balm**, **moisturiser** and, particularly if camping, **Smidge midge repellent** (though we never encountered any, some people claim to have been bitten half to death by midges, particularly when camping by water) and a **water filter bottle or purification system**. Optimists should bring SPF50 **sun protection**.

FIRST-AID KIT

Apart from aching limbs your most likely ailments will be blisters so a first-aid kit can be minimal. Include **painkillers** such as paracetamol or ibuprofen (provided you are not asthmatic) which is more effective against pain with inflammation although rest, of course, is the best cure. **Blister treatments** include brands such as 'Moleskin', 'Compeed', or 'Second Skin'. An **elastic knee support** is a good precaution for a weak knee. A few sachets of **rehydration powders** will quickly remedy mineral loss through sweating. Also consider taking a small selection of different-sized **sterile dressings** for wounds.

GENERAL ITEMS

Essential

Carry a **compass** and know how to use it with a map; also take a **whistle** (the **international distress (emergency) signal** is six blasts on a whistle, or six flashes with a torch, repeated regularly) and a **mobile phone** for emergencies, but don't rely on getting a signal in remote places; a **hydration pack** (at least two litres); a **headtorch** with spare **batteries**; **emergency snacks** which your body can quickly convert into energy; a **penknife**, **watch**, **plastic bags**, **safety pins** and **scissors**.

Useful

If you're not carrying a proper bivi bag or tent a compact **foil space blanket** is a good idea in the cooler seasons. A compact **camera** is a great way to capture and record memorable moments – though most people will have this facility on their smartphone. A **notebook** or journal and a **paperback** for the evenings can now be combined in a mobile device such as a Kindle or small electronic tablet (but remember to wrap it safely against water). A **flask** for tea, coffee or hot soup will pay its own way if you're walking in the cooler parts of the year. Also consider **sunglasses**, a small pair of **binoculars** and a **battery pack** and cables to recharge your phone en route.

    Walking poles are a personal choice and not something you should take unless you usually walk with them; the Pennine Way is not a place to test new equipment of any sort. However, significant benefits can be gained from using one, or a pair of poles.

SLEEPING BAG

If you're camping or planning to stay in camping barns you'll need a sleeping bag. Some bunkhouses offer bedding but you'll keep your costs down if you don't have to hire it. Most hostels provide bedding.

    A **two-season bag** will do for indoor use, but if you can afford it or anticipate outdoor use, go warmer; it's better to be too warm than too cold. A bag rated with a comfort level of around 0°C should be fine. Sleeping bags come in two main types: **synthetic and down**. Synthetic bags are cheaper (around £100 compared to £200 or more) but are bulkier and weigh more than a down bag rated for a similar temperature range. A synthetic bag deals with damp better than a down bag,

---

❏ **WALKING THE PENNINE WAY – A PERSONAL EXPERIENCE**

When I accompanied a friend in fulfilling his lifelong ambition to walk the PW, I thought I was an experienced walker (Dales Way, Camino de Santiago, Machu Pichu etc). Let's just say I finished a lot more experienced than I started, especially crawling to the stone shelter of Little Dun Fell in the mist and pelting needle-rain accompanying Hurricane Ali, with overtrousers billowing around my knees. The conditions, even at the end of one of the driest summers on record and despite the huge bonus of many solid footings over the interminable marshes, were nearly always challenging with rain, wind and penetrating drizzle sometimes obscuring the views or slowing the pace, especially raising the heart rate for the occasional scrambling up rocky paths or over riverside boulders. The views are quite stunning and remind you how beautiful Britain is. The best ones can be accessed in a few weekends but Edale to Kirk Yetholm in 3 weeks, as Wainwright once implied, is only for an elite order of headbangers! **Steve Davies** (2018)

retaining some thermal properties, but down water-repellent treatments are becoming more common and this difference is now less significant. An 800-fill down bag will be warmer, lighter and more expensive than a 650-fill bag.

CAMPING GEAR

If you have no desire to camp on the hills (wild camping) you may well get away with a cheap festival **tent** for summer campsites, as long as the weather is good. You will need something a little more technical for the hills though, something able to stand up to buffeting from the wind and properly waterproof. Expect to pay around £100 for a good one-man tent and anything up to £300 for a lightweight, two-man example. Aim to select a tent weighing no more than 2kg and remember that you need to be very good friends with anyone you intend to share a two-man tent with! Long-distance ultralight backpackers often make do with a groundsheet and tarp held up with a trekking pole, though you get much less protection from rain and bugs this way.

The technology associated with inflatable **sleeping mats** has developed rapidly over the last few years and you will sleep much better with one beneath your sleeping bag. They are lightweight, incredibly comfortable and pack away small. Self-inflating mattresses are usually more robust, slightly cheaper but also a little less comfortable than the modern 'air-bed' mattresses produced by brands such as Thermarest.

Give serious consideration to **cooking gear**. The variety of stoves and fuels is bewildering, each with their own merits and pitfalls. Some campers swear by white or methylated spirits as fuel, others prefer the convenience of gas cannisters. Consider using pubs and cafés as an alternative to carrying any cooking gear at all. That said, there is nothing quite like a hot drink in the morning or on a cold, rainy day. You'll need a pot, cup, and bowl, preferably a set that nests inside each other. Always bring a spork.

MAPS

The hand-drawn maps in this book cover the trail at a scale of just under 1:20,000 but are in a strip, the scale equivalent to two miles wide. In some places, particularly on high moors where navigation points are scant, a proper **topographical map** and a compass could be of great use. But, as mentioned on pp17-18, when the mist comes down and all landmarks disappear, a **GPS** or smartphone used with a map comes into its own.

In Britain the **Ordnance Survey** (🖳 ordnancesurvey.co.uk) maps are peerless. Their orange 1:25,000-scale 'Explorer' series features pin-sharp cartography and detail that makes navigation a doddle. From south to north nine sheets cover the Pennine Way: **OL01** The Peak District – Dark Peak area; **OL21** South Pennines; **OL02** Yorkshire Dales – Southern & Western areas; **OL30** Yorkshire Dales – Northern & Central Areas; **OL31** North Pennines – Teesdale & Weardale; **OL19** Howgill Fells & Upper Eden Valley; **OL43** Hadrian's Wall; **OL42** Kielder Water and Forest; **OL16** The Cheviot Hills. Packing such a stack of maps, especially the bulky laminated weatherproof versions, isn't really fea-

PLANNING YOUR WALK

❑ DIGITAL MAPPING   see also pp17-18

There are numerous software packages now available that provide Ordnance Survey (OS) maps for a smartphone, tablet, PC, or GPS unit. Maps are downloaded into an app from where you can view, print and create routes on them.

For a subscription of £4.99 for one month or £28.99 for a year (on their current offer) **Ordnance Survey** (🖥 ordnance survey.co.uk) allows you to download and use their UK maps (1:25,000 scale) on a mobile or tablet without a data connection for a specific period. Their app works well.

Memory Map (🖥 memory-map.co.uk) currently sell OS Explorer 1:25,000 and Landranger 1:50,000 mapping covering the whole of Britain with prices from £19.99 for a one year subscription. **Anquet** (🖥 anquet.com) has the full range of OS 1:25,000 maps covering all of the UK from £28 per year annual subscription.

Maps.me is free and you can download any of its digital mapping to use offline. You can install the Trailblazer waypoints for this walk on its mapping but you'll need to convert the .gpx format file to .kml format before loading it into maps.me. Use an online website such as 🖥 gpx2kml.com to do this then email the kml file to your phone and open it in maps.me.

Harvey (🖥 store.avenza.com/collections/harvey-maps) currently use the US Avenza maps app for their two *Pennine Way* maps (1:40,000 scale, $15.99 each).

It is important to ensure any digital mapping software on your smartphone uses pre-downloaded maps, stored on your device, and doesn't need to download them on-the-fly, as this may be expensive and will be impossible without a signal. Remember that battery life will be significantly reduced, compared to normal usage, when you are using the built-in GPS and running the screen for long periods.

---

sible. Old-school walkers either post them ahead or mark the Way and trim off the flab, but remember that you can access OS maps on your smartphone via the OS app (see above).

OS Explorers are the ultimate Pennine maps but there is a series of handy maps which give the big picture during planning and work fine on the trail as a back up to this book's maps: Harvey Maps (🖥 harveymaps.co.uk) produce two waterproof maps covering Pennine Way South: Edale to Middleton, and Pennine Way North: Middleton to Kirk Yetholm (2019: £16.50 each or £30 for the set) in a series of north-oriented strip panels at a scale of 1:40,000. The panels cover a broader area each side of the path and, crucially, they include the OS grid to work with GPS. Alternatively consider the two AZ Adventure Series maps (🖥 collins.co.uk/pages/a-z) for the Way: South (Edale to Bowes) and North (Bowes to Kirk Yetholm). They are lightweight, cheap (£8.95), use OS's mapping on the same 1:25,000 scale as their Explorer series and have an index.

RECOMMENDED READING

● *Pennine Way Companion*, Alfred Wainwright. Originally published in 1968 in Wainwright's Lakeland Pictorial Guides series, second-hand copies of later editions are available online at 🖥 alfredwainwright.co.uk.
● *Pennine Walkies*, Mark Wallington (Arrow, 1997) describes in wry humour, the highs and lows of walking the Way with a crazy dog.

● *Walking Home: Travels with a Troubadour on the Pennine Way*, Simon Armitage (Faber & Faber, 2012) Another personal account, this time from Britain's poet laureate (and Marsden's favourite son), walking from Scotland back home, describing the highs and lows of walking the Pennine Way while giving poetry readings en route.

● *End to End – An Adventure on the Pennine Way*, Dean Carter (2018) A wonderfully honest account of a personal journey along the Way; not a guidebook, but it will certainly help to prepare you for what's to come.

● *The Pennine Way: The Path, the People, the Journey*, Andrew McCloy (Cicerone, 2016) A personal portrait of the Way through its history, people and an account of walking the trail today.

   Although the following are currently out of print you may find second-hand copies online:

● *The Pennine Way*, Roly Smith (2011) A beautifully illustrated celebration of the Pennine Way, including its history and geography.

● *Wainwright on the Pennine Way*, Alfred Wainwright & Derry Brabbs (2014)

❏ SOURCES OF FURTHER INFORMATION

Trail information
● **Pennine Way National Trail** (🖳 nationaltrail.co.uk/pennine-way) The website provides an interactive map with accommodation guide, events and information as well as FAQs and even GPS waypoints.
● **Pennine Way Walkers Facebook Group** (🖳 facebook.com/groups/penninewaywalkers) Helpful and supportive group of Pennine Way walkers, past and present, who can collectively answer almost any question you throw at them.

Tourist information centres, Visitor centres and National Park centres
Most **tourist information centres** (TICs) are open daily from Easter to September/October, and thereafter more limited days/hours. Unless you have a specific query, they're usually of little use to an organised walker once underway. There are **visitor centres** with some tourist information at Edale (p83), Hebden Bridge (p116), Once Brewed (p241) and Bellingham (p248).
   The Pennine Way goes through the Peak District, Yorkshire Dales and Northumberland national parks; see box p62 for contact details; both Malham (p148) and Hawes (p168) are **national park centres** and have some tourist information.

Organisations for walkers
● **Backpackers Club** (🖳 backpackersclub.co.uk) For people interested in lightweight camping. Members receive a quarterly magazine, access to a comprehensive information service (including an online forum) and a farm-pitch directory. Membership costs £20 per year, or £30 for a family.
● **The Long Distance Walkers' Association** (🖳 ldwa.org.uk) An association of people with the common interest of long-distance walking. Membership includes a journal, *Strider*, three times per year giving details of challenge events and local group walks as well as articles on the subject. Individual membership costs £18 a year whilst family membership for two adults and all children under 18 is £25.50 a year.
● **Ramblers** (🖳 ramblers.org.uk) Looks after the interests of walkers throughout Britain. They publish a large amount of useful information including their quarterly *Walk* magazine. Annual membership costs £36.60/49 individual/joint.

Legendary fell walker Alfred Wainwright teams up with photographer Derry Brabbs to provide a large-format overview of the path.

The BBC produced a couple of well-made programmes in 2015 to celebrate the 50th anniversary of the Pennine Way. You may still be able to find the three-part TV series *The Pennine Way* with Paul Rose on BBC iPlayer, while the three-part radio documentary *The Folk of the Pennines* with Mark Radcliffe is available on BBC Sounds.

Getting to and from the Pennine Way

Travelling to the start of the Pennine Way by public transport makes sense in so many ways. There's no need to trouble anyone for a lift or worry about your vehicle while walking, there are no logistical headaches about how to return to your car when you've finished the walk and it's a big step towards minimising your ecological footprint. If you book in advance, even the train fares aren't that

---

❑ **GETTING TO BRITAIN**

● **By air** There are plenty of cheap flights from around the world to London's airports: Heathrow, Gatwick, Luton, London City and Stansted. However, Manchester (🖥 manchesterairport.co.uk) and Edinburgh (🖥 edinburghairport.com) airports are the closest to the start and finish points of the Pennine Way and both have plenty of international flights, including with budget airlines. There are also airports at Newcastle (🖥 newcastleairport.com) and Leeds (🖥 leedsbradfordairport.co.uk). Visit the airport websites to see which airlines fly there and from where.

● **From Europe by train** Eurostar (🖥 eurostar.com) operates a high-speed passenger service via the Channel Tunnel between a number of cities in Europe (particularly Paris, Brussels and Amsterdam) and London (St Pancras International). See opposite for details of how to get to and from the start/end of the walk by train from London; all the railway stations in London have connections to the London underground. For more information about rail services from Europe contact your national rail company or Railteam (🖥 railteam.eu).

● **From Europe by coach** Eurolines (🖥 eurolines.eu) have a huge network of long-distance coach services connecting over 500 cities in 25 European countries to London. Flix Bus (🖥 global.flixbus.com) also operates low-cost coach services to London. Check carefully, however: often, once such expenses as food for the journey are taken into consideration, it does not work out that much cheaper than taking a flight, particularly when compared to the fares on some of the budget airlines.

● **From Europe by car** P&O Ferries (🖥 poferries.com) and DFDS Seaways (🖥 dfdsseaways.com) are just two of the many ferry operators that operate services between Britain and continental Europe; the main routes are between all the major North Sea and Channel ports. Direct Ferries (🖥 directferries.co.uk) lists all the main operators/routes and sells discounted tickets.

Eurotunnel (🖥 eurotunnel.com) operates 'Le Shuttle', a shuttle train service for vehicles via the Channel Tunnel between Calais and Folkestone taking one hour between the motorway in France and the motorway in Britain.

❏ **NATIONAL EXPRESS COACH SERVICES**

426 London to Newcastle via Sheffield, Leeds & Middlesborough, daily 3-4/day
540 London to Manchester, daily 1/hr
560 London to Sheffield daily 2/day
561 London to Bradford via Sheffield & Leeds, daily 7-9/day
564 London to Halifax via Sheffield, daily 2/day
565 London to Hull via Sheffield, daily 1/day
590 London to Glasgow via Birmingham, Penrith & Carlisle, daily 1/day
591 London to Glasgow via Sheffield, Leeds, Newcastle, Berwick-upon-Tweed
    & Edinburgh, daily 1/day

eye-watering. Quite apart from that, you'll simply feel your holiday has begun the moment you step out of your front door, rather than when you've slammed the car door behind you.

NATIONAL TRANSPORT

By rail

Frequent and direct rail connections to Edale from both Manchester and Sheffield make these two cities the most obvious gateways to the start of the Pennine Way. The 30- or 45-minute train journey makes them very convenient as well. At the northern terminus of the walk you need to aim for Berwick-upon-Tweed, which is reached via two bus journeys from Kirk Yetholm, via Kelso, and will take at least 2¼ hours.

East Midlands Railway (🖳 eastmidlandsrailway.co.uk) have direct services from St Pancras mainline station to Sheffield; change there to Northern Rail services to Edale (see box p59). Alternatively, Avanti West Coast (🖳 avantiwestcoast.co.uk) operate from Euston station to Manchester (from where you can also change to a Northern train to Edale). Cross Country Trains (🖳 crosscountrytrains.co.uk) also provide services to both Sheffield and Manchester.

At the end of the walk, or if you are walking north to south, you will need LNER's (London North Eastern Railway; 🖳 lner.co.uk) King's Cross to Edinburgh service as it calls at Berwick-upon-Tweed.

There are stations on the Pennine Way at Edale, Hebden Bridge, Gargrave and Horton-in-Ribblesdale. Other useful stations with good bus services linking them to various parts of the Way include Huddersfield, Marsden, Skipton, Darlington, Appleby, Bardon Mill, Haltwhistle and Hexham. Services are provided by Northern Rail and Trans-Pennine Express (see box p59).

National Rail (☎ 03457-484950, 24hrs, 🖳 nationalrail.co.uk) has timetable and fare information for rail travel in the whole of Britain. You can buy tickets through the relevant rail operator, in person at a railway station, or online at 🖳 thetrainline.com. It's worth planning and booking ahead, at least two weeks, as it's the only way to get a reasonably discounted advance train fare. It helps to

[cont'd on p56]

PLANNING YOUR WALK

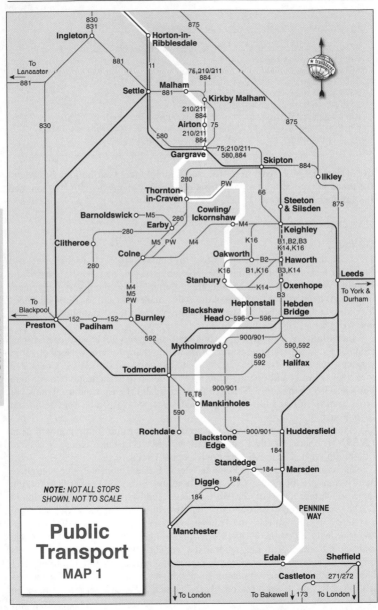

NOTE: NOT ALL STOPS
SHOWN. NOT TO SCALE

Public Transport
MAP 1

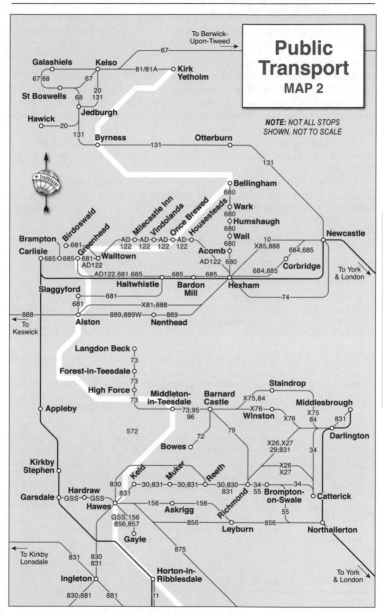

Public Transport MAP 2

NOTE: NOT ALL STOPS SHOWN. NOT TO SCALE

To Berwick-Upon-Tweed

Galashiels — Kelso — 67
67;68
St Boswells
67
68
20
131
Hawick — 20 — Jedburgh
131
Byrness — 131 — Otterburn
131

Kelso — 81/81A — Kirk Yetholm

Bellingham
680
Wark
680
Humshaugh
680
Wall
680
Acomb
AD122 680

Brampton
685 — 685
Carlisle
Birdoswald
681
Greenhead
681
Walltown
AD122
Milecastle Inn Vindolanda Once Brewed Housesteads
AD — AD — AD — AD
122   122   122   122

X85,888
10
Newcastle
684,685
Corbridge
684,685
To York & London

AD122,681,685
Slaggyford
681
Haltwhistle — 685 — Bardon Mill — 685 — Hexham
74
Alston
681
X81;888
889;889W — 889 — Nenthead
888
To Keswick

Langdon Beck
73
Forest-in-Teesdale
73
High Force
73
Middleton-in-Teesdale
73;95 96

Appleby
572
Bowes
72

Barnard Castle
Staindrop
X75,84
Winston
X76
X76
79
Middlesbrough
X75 84
831
Darlington
34
X26,X27 29;831
X26 X27
34
Brompton-on-Swale
Catterick
55
55

Kirkby Stephen
Garsdale
GSS — GSS
Hardraw
830
831
Hawes
Keld — 830;831 — Muker — 830;831 — Reeth — 30;830 831 — 34
156 — Askrigg — 156 — Richmond
GSS;156 856,857
Gayle
856 — Leyburn — 856 — Northallerton

875
To Kirkby Lonsdale
831
830 831
Ingleton
830;881
881
Horton-in-Ribblesdale
11
To York & London

PLANNING YOUR WALK

be as flexible as possible and don't forget that most discounted tickets generally limit you to a specific date and time of train; check the restrictions before you buy your ticket.

By coach (long-distance bus)

National Express (🖳 nationalexpress.com) is the principal coach operator in Britain. There are services from most towns in England and Wales to a number of towns and cities near the route (see box p53). The most useful route is No 591 between London and Glasgow via Berwick-upon-Tweed (8 hours), which also stops in Newcastle and Leeds.

Megabus (🖳 uk.megabus.com) operates low-cost services from all over Britain to Manchester, Sheffield, and Newcastle. Fares start from just £1 plus a 50p booking fee.

Travel by coach is usually much cheaper than by train but takes a lot longer. Advance bookings carry discounts so be sure to book at least a week ahead. If you don't mind an uncomfortable night there are overnight services on some routes.

By car

Both Edale and Kirk Yetholm are easily reached using the motorway and A-road

---

❑ PUBLIC TRANSPORT – BUS SERVICES – see pp54-5 for Maps 1 & 2

Notes: ● Not all stops are listed
● Many bus services in rural areas operate on a hail-and-ride basis ie the driver will stop to set passengers down or pick them up as long as it's safe to do so.
● The services listed were operating at the time of research but it is essential to check, especially in rural areas and for less frequent services.

Arriva in the North-East (🖳 arrivabus.co.uk/North-East)   (MAP 2)
X26/X27 Darlington to Catterick via Richmond, Mon-Sat 2/hr, Sun 1/hr
X75 Darlington to Barnard Castle via Staindrop, Mon-Sat 1/hr, Sun 5/day
685 Newcastle to Carlisle via Corbridge, Hexham, Bardon Mill, Haltwhistle,
       Greenhead & Brampton, Mon-Sat 1/hr, plus Sun 1/hr Newcastle to Hexham,
       5/day Hexham to Carlisle

Blackburn Bus Company (🖳 transdevbus.co.uk/blackburn)   (MAP 1)
152 Burnley to Preston via Padiham & Blackburn, Mon-Sat 2/hr, Sun 1/hr

Borders Buses (☎ 01289-308719, 🖳 bordersbuses.co.uk)   (MAP 2)
67 Galashiels to Berwick via St Boswells & Kelso, Mon-Sat 1/hr
68 Galashiels to Jedburgh via St Boswells, Mon-Sat 1/hr

Burnley Bus (🖳 transdevbus.co.uk/burnley   (MAP 1)
M4 Burnley to Keighley via Colne & **Cowling**, Mon-Sat 2/hr, Sun 1/hr
M5 Burnley to Barnoldswick via Colne & **Earby**, Mon-Sat 2/hr, Sun 1/hr
PW **Pendle Wizz:** Burnley to Skipton via Colne & **Thornton-in-Craven**,
       Mon-Fri 2/hr, Sat & Sun 1/hr

Cumbria Classic Coaches (🖳 cumbriaclassiccoaches.co.uk)   (MAP 2)
572 Ravenstonedale to Barnard Castle via Kirkby Stephen, Wed 1/day

network from the rest of Britain. Unless you're just out for a day walk however, you'd be better leaving the car at home as there is nowhere safe to leave a vehicle unattended for a long period.

LOCAL TRANSPORT

Getting to and from most parts of the Pennine Way is relatively simple due to the public transport network including trains, coaches and local bus services.

The public transport map on pp54-5 gives an overview of routes which are of particular use to walkers and the table below lists the operators (and their contact details), the route details and the approximate frequency of services in both directions. Note that services may be less frequent in the winter months or stop completely. It is also essential to check services before travelling as details may change. If the operator details prove unsatisfactory contact traveline (☎ 0871-200 2233, daily 8am-8pm, 🖥 traveline.info), which has timetable information for the whole of the UK; details about services in Scotland are also available on 🖥 travelinescotland.com. Local timetables can also be picked up from tourist information centres along the Way.

P L A N N I N G   Y O U R   W A L K

Dales & District (🖥 dalesbus.org)   (MAPS 1 & 2)
830   Preston to Richmond via Ingleton, **Hawes**, Muker, Gunnerside & Reeth,
          May-mid Oct Sun & Bank Hols 1/day
831   Middlesborough to Kirkby Lonsdale via Darlington, Richmond, Keld, **Hawes**
          & Ingleton, Apr-mid Oct Sun 1/day
856   **Wensleydale Flyer**: Northallerton to Gayle via Leyburn & **Hawes**,
          Sun only 3/day
875   Leeds to **Hawes** via Ilkley, Apr-mid Oct Sun 1/day (DalesBus)
881   Lancaster to **Malham** via Ingleton & Settle, Apr-mid Oct Sun 1/day
          (Malham DalesBus)
884   Ilkley to **Malham** via Skipton, **Gargrave**, **Airton** & **Kirkby Malham**,
          Sun & Bank Hols 4/day (Craven Link)

First (🖥 firstgroup.com/ukbus)   (MAP 1)
184   Huddersfield to Oldham via **Marsden**, Brun Clough **(Standedge)** & **Diggle**,
          Mon-Sat 1/hr, Sun 6/day (First Greater Manchester)
271/272 Sheffield to Castleton, daily approx 1/hr (also operated by
          Hulleys of Baslow)
590   Halifax to Rochdale via **Hebden Bridge** & Todmorden, Mon-Fri 2/hr
592   Halifax to Burnley via **Hebden Bridge** & Todmorden, daily 1/hr

Hodgsons Buses (☎ 01833-630730, 🖥 hodgsonsbuses.com)   (MAP 2)
29   Darlington to Richmond, Mon-Sat 6/day
34   Darlington to Richmond via Catterick & Brompton-on-Swale, Mon-Sat 4/day
55   Northallerton to Richmond via Brompton-on-Swale, Mon-Sat 3/day
73   Langdon Beck to Barnard Castle via **High Force**, Newbiggin & **Middleton-in-Teesdale**, Wed only 2/day plus 1/day Langdon Beck to **Middleton-in-Teesdale**
79   Richmond to Barnard Castle, Mon-Sat 4/day   *[cont'd overleaf]*

PLANNING YOUR WALK

❏ PUBLIC TRANSPORT – BUS SERVICES [cont'd]

Go North East (🖥 gonortheast.co.uk)   (MAP 2)
AD122 Hexham to Haltwhistle circular route via Chesters Fort, Housesteads, **Once
          Brewed** (The Sill Visitor Centre), Vindolanda, **Milecastle Inn**, Walltown &
          Greenhead, mid Apr to end Sep daily 5/day, winter Sat & Sun only 4/day
10   Newcastle to Hexham, Mon-Sat 2/hr, Sun 1/hr
74   Newcastle to Hexham, Mon-Fri 4/day, Sat 5/day
680   Hexham to **Bellingham** via Acomb, Wall, Humshaugh & Wark, Mon-
          Sat 7-8/day
681   **Alston** to Birdoswald via **Slaggyford**, Haltwhistle, **Greenhead**,
          Gilsland & Walltown, Mon-Fri 2/day, Sat 3/day
684   Newcastle to Hexham via Corbridge, Mon-Sat 1/hr

Peter Hogg of Jedburgh (☎ 01835-863755, 🖥 roadhoggs.net)   (MAP 2)
20   Kelso to Hawick via Jedburgh, Mon-Sat 3-5/day, Sun 4/day
81/81A Morebattle to **Kirk Yetholm** circular route via Kelso & **Town Yetholm**,
          Mon-Sat 6/day
131   Jedburgh to Newcastle via **Byrness** & Otterburn, Mon-Sat 1/day
          plus Kelso to Newcastle Mon-Fri 1/day

Hulleys of Baslow (☎ 01246-582246, 🖥 hulleys-of-baslow.co.uk)   (MAP 1)
173   Bakewell to Castleton, Mon-Sat 5/day
271/272 Sheffield to Castleton, daily approx 1/hr (also First)

Keighley Bus Company (🖥 transdevbus.co.uk/keighley)   (MAP 1)
B1   Keighley to **Stanbury** via **Haworth**, Mon-Sat 1/hr
B2   Keighley to Oakworth via **Haworth**, daily 1/hr
B3   Keighley to **Hebden Bridge** via **Haworth** & Oxenhope, daily 1/hr
K14   Keighley circular route via Oxenhope, **Haworth** & **Stanbury**, daily 5-6/day
K16   Keighley circular route via Oakworth & **Stanbury,** Mon-Fri 2/day of which
          1/day via **Haworth**
66   Keighley to Skipton, Mon-Sat 2/hr, Sun 1/hr

Kirkby Lonsdale Coach Hire (🖥 klch.co.uk)   (MAP 1)
75   Skipton to **Malham** via **Gargrave** & **Kirkby Malham**, Sat only 2/day
          of which 1/day in summer continues to Settle
580   Skipton to Settle via **Gargrave**, Mon-Sat 1/hr

Little White Bus (aka Upper Wensleydale Community Partnership;
          office ☎ 01969-667400, 🖥 littlewhitebus.co.uk)   (MAP 2)
GSS   **Garsdale Station Shuttle**: Gayle to Garsdale via **Hawes** & **Hardraw**,
          Mon-Sat 4/day, Sun & bank hols 2-3/day.
          *Additional journeys can be provided if prebooked; the office is open
          Mon-Fri 9am-5.30pm, Sat 9am-12.30pm, or out of hours call the driver
          on ☎ 07816-986448.*
30   **Swaledale Shuttle**: **Keld** circular route via **Thwaite**, Muker, Gunnerside,
          Reeth, Grinton, Reeth & Richmond, Mon-Sat 2-3/day
          Community minibus service – must be prebooked 24 hrs in advance
156   **Wensleydale Voyager**: Gayle to Leyburn via **Hawes**, Askrigg & Aysgarth,
          Mon-Sat 6-9/day

See pp54-5 for Maps 1 & 2

NYCC (North Yorkshire County Council; 🖳 northyorks.gov.uk/bus-timetables)
(MAPS 1 & 2)
11   Settle to **Horton-in-Ribblesdale**, Mon-Sat 3/day plus Tosside to Settle 2/day
210/211 Skipton to **Malham** via **Gargrave**, **Airton** & **Kirkby Malham**,
Mon-Fri 2/day

Stagecoach (🖳 stagecoachbus.com)   (MAP 1)
280   Preston to Skipton via Clitheroe, **Earby** & **Thornton-in-Craven**, Mon-Sat
1/hr, Sun 4/day

Scarlet Band Bus & Coach (☎ 01740-654247, 🖳 scarletbandbuses.co.uk) (MAP 2)
72   **Bowes** to Barnard Castle, Mon-Fri 2/day
84   Darlington to Barnard Castle via Staindrop, Mon-Sat 3/day
95/96 Middleton-in-Teesdale to Barnard Castle via **Cotherstone,** Mon-Sat 1/hr

TLC Travel (☎ 01274-727811, 🖳 www.tlctravelltd.co.uk)   (MAP 1)
T6/T8 Todmorden circular via **Mankinholes**, daily 1/hr
596   **Hebden Bridge** to Blackshaw Head via **Heptonstall**, daily 1/hr
900/901 Huddersfield to **Hebden Bridge** via **Blackstone Edge** & Mytholmroyd,
Mon-Sat1/hr, Sun 3/day

Wright Brothers' Coaches (☎ 01434-381200, 🖳 wrightscoaches.co.uk)   (MAP 2)
888   Newcastle to Keswick via Hexham & **Alston**, July-end Sep Fri, Sat, Sun &
Mon 1/day
889   **Alston** to Hexham via Nenthead, Tue only 1/day
889W Alston to Nenthead, Mon, Wed & Fri 1-2/day

RAIL SERVICES Note: not all stops are listed   (MAPS 1 & 2)

Northern Rail (☎ 0800 200 6060, 🖳 northernrailway.co.uk)
● Manchester Piccadilly to Sheffield via **Edale**, daily 1/hr
● Manchester Piccadilly to Hadfield, daily 2/hr
● Leeds to Manchester (V) via **Hebden Bridge** & Todmorden, Mon-Sat 2/hr, Sun 1/hr
● Leeds to Preston via **Hebden Bridge** & Todmorden, daily 1/hr
● Leeds to Blackpool North via **Hebden Bridge** & Todmorden, daily 1/hr
● Leeds to Carlisle via Keighley, Skipton, **Gargrave**, Settle, **Horton-in-Ribblesdale**,
Garsdale, Kirkby Stephen & Appleby, Mon-Sat 8/day, Sun 5-6/day
(note: not all services stop at Gargrave)
● Newcastle to Carlisle via Hexham & Haltwhistle, daily 1/hr; some services also call
at Bardon Mill which is two miles off the Pennine Way and is a stop on
Arriva's No 685 bus service.

Trans Pennine Express (🖳 tpexpress.co.uk)
● Manchester to Newcastle via Leeds, York & Durham, Mon-Sat 1/hr, Sun 8/day
● Manchester to Middlesbrough via Leeds, York, Northallerton, Darlington, daily 1/hr
● Manchester Victoria (V) to Huddersfield via **Marsden**, daily 2/hr

See p128 for information about **Keighley & Worth Valley Railway** and p168
for details about **DalesRail**'s seasonal Sunday Blackpool to Carlisle service

PLANNING YOUR WALK

2   THE ENVIRONMENT & NATURE

Conserving the Pennines

GOVERNMENT AGENCIES AND SCHEMES

Government responsibility for the countryside is handled in England by **Natural England** (🖳 gov.uk/government/organisations/natural-england). Natural England is responsible for 'enhancing biodiversity and landscape and wildlife in rural, urban, coastal and marine areas; promoting access, recreation and public well-being, and contributing to the way natural resources are managed, so they can be enjoyed now and by future generations'. Amongst other things it designates the level of protection for areas of land, as outlined below, and manages England's national trails (see box opposite).

The highest level of landscape protection is the designation of land as a **national park** which recognises the national importance of an area in terms of landscape, biodiversity and as a recreational resource. The Pennine Way passes through three National Parks: the Peak District (🖳 peakdistrict.gov.uk), the Yorkshire Dales (🖳 yorkshiredales.org.uk) and Northumberland (🖳 northumberlandnationalpark.org.uk). Although they wield a considerable amount of power and can easily quash planning applications from the local council, their management is always a balance between conservation, the needs of visitors, and protecting the livelihoods of those who live within the park.

Land which falls outside the remit of a National Park but which is nonetheless deemed special enough for protection may be designated an **Area of Outstanding Natural Beauty** (**AONB**; 🖳 landscapesforlife.org.uk), the second level of protection after National Park status. The North Pennines is one such AONB (🖳 www.northpennines.org.uk). Designated in 1988, it is valued for its upland habitats and wildlife, containing a third of England's upland heathland and a third of its blanket bog. These fragile habitats make the North Pennines one of England's most important regions for upland wildlife – it is home to the majority of England's black grouse and is upland England's hotspot for breeding wading birds.

Of course, it wouldn't get AONB status unless it was a beautiful area; the moors, hills and wooded valleys certainly make it so. And it

The Pennine Way was the first of the National Trails in England and Wales; the officially designated long-distance paths, now supported and funded by Natural England and Natural Resources Wales. There are now 16 National Trails in England and Wales, totalling approximately 2500 miles (4000km) of path, each one looked after by a National Trail Officer who co-ordinates the management, maintenance and marketing of the trail, with the assistance of volunteers and other agencies.

A similar system of trails exists in Scotland, where they are called **Long Distance Routes**.

is the underlying geology that gives the region its character which led to the area being designated a UNESCO European Geopark (🖳 europeangeoparks.org) in 2003, the first in Britain. A year later it became a founding member of the Global Geoparks Network (🖳 www.globalgeopark.org).

National Nature Reserves (NNRs) are places where wildlife comes first. They were established to protect the most important areas of wildlife habitat and geological formations in Britain, and as places for scientific research. This does not mean they are 'no-go areas' for people. It means that visitors must be careful not to damage the wildlife of these fragile places. Kinder Scout (see box p86) is a NNR.

Local Nature Reserves (LNRs) are for both people and wildlife. They are living green spaces in towns, cities, villages and countryside which are important to people, and support a rich and vibrant variety of wildlife. They are places which have wildlife or geology of special local interest. These can be created by local authorities or councils.

Sites of Special Scientific Interest (SSSIs) purport to afford extra protection to unique areas against anything that threatens the habitat or environment. They range in size from a small site where orchids grow, or birds nest, to vast swathes of upland, moorland and wetland.

The country through which the Pennine Way passes has its share of SSSIs but they are not given a high profile for the very reason that this would draw unwanted attention. They are managed in partnership with the owners and occupiers of the land but it seems this management is not always effective.

Special Areas of Conservation (SACs) are areas which have been given special protection under the European Union's Habitats Directive. They provide increased protection to a variety of wild animals, plants and habitats and are a vital part of global efforts to conserve the world's biodiversity.

CAMPAIGNING AND CONSERVATION ORGANISATIONS

The idea of conservation started back in the mid 1800s with the founding of the Royal Society for the Protection of Birds (see box p62). The rise of its membership figures accurately reflects public awareness and interest in environmental issues as a whole: it took until the 1960s to reach 10,000, but rocketed to

THE ENVIRONMENT & NATURE

200,000 in the 1970s and had mushroomed to around 1.2 million by 2022. There are now many campaigning and conservation groups – see box below for the details of some. Independent of government but reliant on public support, they can concentrate their resources either on acquiring land which can then be managed purely for conservation purposes, or on influencing political decision-makers by lobbying and campaigning.

The huge increase in public interest and support during the last 20 years indicates that people are more conscious of environmental issues and believe that it cannot be left to our political representatives to take care of them for us without our voice. We are becoming the most powerful lobbying group of all; an informed electorate.

❑ CAMPAIGNING/CONSERVATION ORGANISATIONS AND CHARITIES

● **National Trust** (NT; 🖳 nationaltrust.org.uk) A charity with over 5 million members which aims to protect, through ownership, threatened coastline, countryside, historic houses, castles and gardens, and archaeological remains for everybody to enjoy.

NT land/properties on the Pennine Way include Kinder Scout (see box p86), Housesteads Fort (see box p240; though it is managed by English Heritage, see below), Malham Tarn and Moor (see p150) in Yorkshire Dales National Park, Marsden Moor and Hardcastle Crags near Hebden Bridge.

● **Royal Society for the Protection of Birds** (RSPB; 🖳 rspb.org.uk) The largest voluntary conservation body in Europe now has over 200 nature reserves in the UK. The closest reserves to the Pennine Way are Geltsdale, off the A689 west of Knarsdale (off MAP 99), and Dove Stone, west of Wessenden Head (off MAP 12).

● **The Wildlife Trusts** (🖳 wildlifetrusts.org) The umbrella organisation for the 47 wildlife trusts in the UK; the trust is concerned with all aspects of nature conservation and manages around 2300 nature reserves. Wildlife trusts along the Pennine Way include Broadhead Clough (near Hebden Bridge), Globe Flower Wood (near Malham), Brae Pasture (near Horton), Hannah's Meadow (right on the Pennine Way), Greenlee Lough (just north of Hadrian's Wall) and Yetholm Loch (near Kirk Yetholm).

● **English Heritage** (🖳 www.english-heritage.org.uk) English Heritage looks after, champions and advises the government on historic buildings and places in England. In April 2015 it was divided into a new charitable trust that retains the name English Heritage and a non-departmental public body, **Historic England** (🖳 historiceng land.org.uk). English Heritage cares for over 400 historic buildings, monuments and sites and manages parts of Hadrian's Wall (see National Trust above) and also Bowes Castle.

● **Forestry Commission** (🖳 gov.uk/government/organisations/forestry-commission) Government department for establishing and managing forests for a variety of uses.

● **Woodland Trust** (🖳 woodlandtrust.org.uk) The trust aims to conserve, restore and re-establish native woodlands throughout the UK.

● **Butterfly Conservation** (🖳 butterfly-conservation.org) was formed in 1968 by some naturalists who were alarmed at the decline in the number of butterflies and moths, and who aimed to reverse the situation. They now have 31 branches throughout the British Isles and operate 33 nature reserves and also sites where butterflies are likely to be found.

Flora and fauna

WILD FLOWERS, GRASSES AND OTHER PLANTS

Many grasses, wild flowers, heather, mosses and liverworts (lichen-type plants with liver-shaped leaves) owe their continued existence to man's land management; global warming notwithstanding, if left to its own devices much of the land would return to the natural state of temperate regions: the woodland of 10,000 years ago. Rare breeds of livestock are often excellent grazers for rough grassland because they are hardier so do not need to be given extra food that will then over-fertilise the ground. They also seem to be more selective in what they eat (and taste better too).

Intensive agriculture took its toll on the wild flower population in the same way that it did on the birds and mammals. The flowers are making a comeback but it is illegal to pick many types of flowers now and the picking of most others is discouraged; it is always illegal without the landowners' permission, no matter what the type. Cut flowers only die, after all. It is much better to leave them to reseed and spread and hopefully magnify your or someone else's enjoyment another year. Spring and early summer is the best time to see wild flowers.

Bogs and wet areas

Look out for **cotton grass** (not actually a grass but a type of sedge), **deer-grass, cloudberry** (a dwarf blackberry with a light orange berry when ripe that can be used as a substitute for any fruit used in puddings and jams) and the **insect-eating sundew**. Drier areas of peat may be home to **crowberry** (a source of vitamin C) and **bilberry** (see below).

Peat itself is the ages-old remains of vegetation, including **sphagnum mosses** (see box p87). This type of moss is now rare, but may be found in 'flushes' where water seeps out between gritstone and shale. Also look out for **bog asphodel, marsh thistle** and **marsh pennywort**.

Woodlands

Not much grows in coniferous plantations because the dense canopy prevents light getting in. But in oak woodlands the floor is often covered with interesting plants such as **bilberries**, whose small, round black fruit is ripe for picking from July to September and is much tastier than the more widely commercially sold

---

❏ **WHY ARE FLOWERS THE COLOUR THEY ARE?**
The vast majority of British wild flowers range in colour from yellow to magenta and do not have red in them; the poppy is the most notable exception. This is because most flowers are insect-pollinated as opposed to being pollinated by birds. Birds see reds best, insects see yellow to magenta best.

THE ENVIRONMENT & NATURE

American variety. It's recommended in jams, jellies, stews and cheesecake. Bilberry pie is known in Yorkshire as 'mucky-mouth pie', for reasons you can work out, and is eaten at funerals. **Moorland cowberry** (also used in jams), **wavy hair grass** and **woodrush** are other species you may see. Other shrubs to look out for include **guelder rose** and **bird cherry**.

Higher areas

Much of the high land is peaty and many types of grass turn brown in winter. Those present include **matgrass, heath rush, bent, fescues** and **wavy hair grass**. Flowers include **tormentil** and **harebell**.

Heather is the main plant of higher areas and is carefully farmed for grouse. It is burnt in strips over the winter to ensure new growth as a food supply for the birds. It has many uses, including as a tea and flavouring beer, and makes a very comfortable mattress on a warm, sunny afternoon. When it flowers around August time, the moors can turn purple. **Bracken**, **gorse** and **tufted hair grass** are all signs that the land is not being intensively managed.

Lower areas

These places are where you'll see the most flowers, whose fresh and bright colours give the area an inspiring glow, particularly if you have just descended from the browns and greens of the higher, peaty areas.

On valley sides used for grazing you may see **self heal, cowslips** (used to make wine and vinegar), **bloody cranesbill** and **mountain pansy**. **Hawthorn** seeds dropped by birds sprout up energetically and determinedly but are cropped back by sheep and fires. This is a good thing; these shrubs can grow to 8 metres (26ft) and would try to take over the hillsides to the detriment of the rich grasslands. They do, however, have a variety of uses: the young leaves are known as 'bread and cheese' because they used to be such a staple part of a diet; the flowers make a delicious drink and when combined with the fruit make a cure for insomnia. **Rushes** indicate poor drainage.

❏ **ORCHIDS**

These highly prized plants, the occasional object of professional thefts, are often mistakenly thought to grow only in tropical places. They come from one of the largest families in the world and their range is in fact widespread, right up to the Arctic Circle in some places. In Britain over 40 types grow wild and you'd be unlucky not to see any on the Pennine Way, especially in quarries and on hillsides. The **lady's slipper**, first discovered in Ingleborough in 1640, the **narrow-lipped helleborine**, which grows in Northumberland, and the **frog orchid** are just some you may come across. The **early purple orchid** (see photo opposite) is made into a drink called Saloop, which was popular before coffee became the staple.

Although they have a tendency to grow on other plants, orchids are not parasites, as many believe; they simply use them for support. They are distinctive as having one petal longer than the other two and many growers say they're no more difficult to grow at home than many other houseplants. With their flowers being generally spectacular and the wonderful strong scent they're well worth the effort.

Common Vetch
Vicia sativa

Meadow Cranesbill
Geranium pratense

Heartsease (Wild Pansy)
Viola tricolor

Lousewort
Pedicularis sylvatica

Germander Speedwell
Veronica chamaedrys

Common Dog Violet
Viola riviniana

Self-heal
Prunella vulgaris

Heather (Ling)
Calluna vulgaris

Harebell
Campanula rotundifolia

Early Purple Orchid
Orchis mascula

Bell Heather
Erica cinerea

Common Butterwort
Pinguicula vulgaris

Gorse
Ulex europaeus

Meadow Buttercup
Ranunculus acris

Marsh Marigold (Kingcup)
Caltha palustris

Bird's-foot trefoil
Lotus corniculatus

Water Avens
Geum rivale

Tormentil
Potentilla erecta

Primrose
Primula vulgaris

St John's Wort
Hypericum perforatum

Yellow Rattle
Rhinanthus minor

Common Ragwort
Senecio jacobaea

Hemp-nettle
Galeopsis speciosa

Cowslip
Primula veris

ICRO-ORGANISMS AND INVERTEBRATES

neath your feet and under the yellow leaves of autumn are millions,
ons, of organisms beavering away at recycling anything that has had its
n to decay. One gram of woodland soil contains an estimated 4000-
of bacteria. Almost all of them are unknown to science and the vitally
le they play in maintaining the natural balance of our ecosystems is only
g to be appreciated. Many scientists now believe these organisms actu-
earth. Research into them is at an early stage but as one American aca-
, 'As we walk across leaf litter we are like Godzilla walking over New

ued apace into the 1970s and '80s with big grants and tax breaks
owners and wealthy investors.
the result of this 'blanket planting' in the northern Pennines;
trees with such a dense canopy that nothing grows beneath.
tive is that these forests are virtually the only habitat where
e is used. Many probably think moorland is the same but
ome of the most noxious chemicals in use today and then
nto which the insecticide gradually washes off.
ts under way to replant felled coniferous timber with a
d the number of conifer plantations has fallen by 7%
e new woodlands are not only planted for timber, but
urism and are good for wildlife. Kielder Forest now
bic metres of timber a year, the majority going into
aller wood from the tops of the trees going to the
by Hexham.

ur walk and the best way of identifying them
ification apps are available to help with this).
nd not just for your pleasure. It is their way
tory is still occupied and not up for grabs,
horus is such a cacophony because most
when they wake and are still alive they
ow it. They also have a call, or alarm,

rform incredible annual migrations,
same nest they occupied the previ-
rds ingest their own organs to keep
elieved to fly non-stop for up to
period to lay eggs. They can also
r.
tphones and tablets, including
g as well as by their appear-
g.

Honeysuckle
Lonicera periclymemum

Dog Rose
Rosa canina

Forget-me-not
Myosotis arvensis

Scarlet Pimpernel
Anagallis arvensis

Common Fumitory
Fumaria officinalis

Wood Sorrel
Oxalis acetosella

Ramsons (Wild Garlic)
Allium ursinum

Common Hawthorn
Crataegus monogyna

Ox-eye Daisy
Leucanthemum vulgare

Silverweed
Potentilla anserina

Yarrow
Achillea millefolium

Hogweed
Heracleum sphondylium

Cotton Grass
Eriophorum angustifolium

Spear Thistle
Cirsium vulgare

Common Knapweed
Centaurea nigra

Rowan (tree)
Sorbus aucuparia

Herb-Robert
Geranium robertianum

Red Campion
Silene dioica

Bluebell
Hyacinthoides non-scripta

Rosebay Willowherb
Epilobium angustifolium

Foxglove
Digitalis purpurea

The **adder** (see pp72-3) is the only common snake in the north of England, and the only venomous one of the three species in Britain.

© Henry Stedman

Also look out for **bird's eye primrose, white clover** and as **crested dog's tail** and **bent**.

TREES, WOODS AND FORESTS

Woods are part of Britain's natural heritage as reflected in the Red Riding Hood and Robin Hood for example, and also in it hunting grounds of Henry VIII and his subsequent felling of construct the fleets that led to Britannia 'ruling the waves'. T at the start of the walk, is the small town of Chapel-en-l name means 'chapel in the forest' because it used to be enormous forest that stretched to Edale and beyond.

Ten thousand years ago as Europe emerged fro man started to exert his influence on the landscap wooded. In 1086 when William the Conqueror or to 15% and it then shrank to 4% by the 1870s. V was established woodland cover in Britain wa to 6.5%. A survey in 2022 estimated that th woodland across the UK, representing 13% figures disguise is that a huge proportion c 900 years ago or even 100 years ago, i Although the Forestry Commission w the vast numbers of acres of conifer behind diversification of tree speci cism of 'blanket conifers' the Fo turing of Kielder Forest in the l late to break up the even-age a with the vast landscape ener broadleaves were planted Bro

Oak and broadleaf w
Oak trees are one of t
species: the **commo**
of the woodland o
are made up o
poplar and **s**
However, th
National P
rowan, s
ronmen

Con
Th
hen
strategic
plant fast-g.
spruce across

Streams, rivers and lakes

Both the **great-crested grebe** and the **little grebe** live on natural lakes and reservoirs. In spring you can see the great-crested grebe's 'penguin dance', where they raise themselves from the water breast to breast by furiously paddling their feet, and then swing their heads from side to side. They also have their full plumage, including an elaborate collar that could well have served as inspiration for the Elizabethans. They nearly became extinct in Britain in the 19th century, but have now recovered despite plenty of enemies including pike, rooks, mink and even the wake from boats, which can flood their nests. The little grebe is small and dumpy but very well designed for hunting sticklebacks under water.

Yellow wagtails are summer visitors that are as likely to be seen on lakesides as in water meadows, pasture and even moors. How do you recognise them? They have a yellow underneath, unlike the **grey wagtail** which has a black chin and then a yellow belly. If the bird is by a fast-flowing stream it will almost certainly be a grey wagtail.

Reservoir water tends to be relatively acidic so supports little wildlife except wildfowl including **goosanders**, especially in winter, and the similar-looking **red-breasted mergansers**. They are both members of the sawbill family which use serrated bill edges to seize and hold small fish. The trout in the reservoirs will have been introduced for anglers.

In streams and rivers you may see **common sandpipers**. Most of them head for Africa in the winter, but about 50 are thought to brave it out in ever-milder Britain. You might see them stalking insects, their head held fixed and horizontal before a sudden snap brings the hunt to an end.

Dippers are the only songbirds that can 'fly' underwater or walk along streambeds. You may see them 'curt-seying' on rocks in the middle of swift-flowing streams before they dive under the surface. They fly extremely quickly, because their tiny wings are designed for maximum efficiency in the water and are far too small to keep the comparatively huge bodies airborne without enormous amounts of flapping and momentum.

Woodland

Although rare in the Pennines, broad-leaved woodland harbours a variety of birdlife. You may see, or more likely hear, a **green woodpecker**, the largest woodpecker in Britain. They are very shy and often hide behind branches. They trap insects by probing holes and cavities with their tongue, which has a sticky tip like a flycatcher.

The further north you go the more likely you are to see **pied flycatchers**, summer visitors from Africa. The male can have multiple mates and is known to keep territories well over a mile apart, perhaps to keep a quiet life.

GREEN
WOODPECKER
L: 330MM/13"

Nuthatches are sparrow-sized with blue backs, orange breasts and a black eye-stripe, and have the rare ability to clamber up and down trunks and branches. Here all year, in summer they eat insects and in the autumn crack open acorns and hazelnuts with hard whacks of their bill.

Treecreepers also cling to trees. They have a thin, downward-curved bill that is ideal for picking insects out of holes and crevices. They are brown above and silvery-white underneath, which should help you distinguish them from the similar sized and behaviourally similar **lesser-spotted woodpecker**, which is black and white and not seen on the more northern sections of the Way. The male woodpecker also has a red crown.

Coniferous woodland is not home to much wildlife, because the tree canopy is too dense. You may, however, see nesting **sparrowhawks**. They suffered a big decline in the 1950s due to the use of pesticides in farming. In all the British raptor (bird of prey) species the female is larger than the male, but the male sparrowhawk is one of the smallest raptors in Britain. It feeds entirely on fellow birds and has long legs and a long central toe for catching and holding them. It has a square-ended tail and reasonably short wings for chasing birds into trees.

You may also see **short-eared owls** in young plantations because of the preponderance of short-tailed vole, their principal prey. They also hunt over open moors, heaths and rough grasslands. This owl is probably the one that is most often seen in daylight. It has two ear-tufts on the top of its head which are, you've guessed it, shorter than the **long-eared owl**'s. You may also see a **black grouse** (see box p161), also known as **black game**. Conifer plantations provide temporary havens for them while they try to regain some of their numbers. The black male birds perform in a mock fight known as a *lek* in front of the grey females. This happens year-round and if you see a male fluffing up the white of its tail and cooing like a dove don't necessarily expect to see a female present; they are quite happy to perform for anyone.

BLACK GROUSE
L: 580mm/23"

Coniferous woods are also home to the greeny-yellow **goldcrest**, Britain's smallest bird. It weighs less than 10 grams but along with the **coal tit** is possibly the dominant species in coniferous woods. Because it is one of the few species that can exploit conifers it is growing in number.

Moor, bog and grazing

Many birds have developed to live in the wettest, windiest, most barren places in England; the places along which the best of the Pennine Way passes. On heather moors you will almost certainly see **red grouse** (see also box, p161), for whom the heather is intensively managed to ensure a good supply of young shoots for food. They are reddish-brown, slightly smaller than a pheasant and likely to get up at your feet and fly off making a lot of noise.

Moorland is also home to Britain's smallest falcon, the **merlin**. The male is slate-grey, the female a reddish-brown. They eat small birds, catching them with low dashing flights. Their main threat comes from the expense of maintaining moorland for grouse shooting; as costs grow, fewer and fewer farmers are doing this and with the disappearance of the moor we will see the disappearance of the merlin. Another moorland raptor is the **short-eared owl** (see opposite).

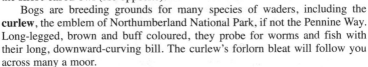

CURLEW
L: 600MM/24"

Bogs are breeding grounds for many species of waders, including the **curlew**, the emblem of Northumberland National Park, if not the Pennine Way. Long-legged, brown and buff coloured, they probe for worms and fish with their long, downward-curving bill. The curlew's forlorn bleat will follow you across many a moor.

Snipe live in wet areas. They are smaller than grouse, but they share very similar plumages. They have particularly long bills for feeding in water and rely on being camouflaged rather than escaping predators by flight, and hence often get up right at your feet. Once airborne their trajectory is fast and zig-zags.

In summer **golden plover** live in upland peaty terrain, are seen in pairs and will be visible to walkers (as well as audible because of their plaintive call); in winter they are seen in flocks and in lowland grassland. They are a little larger than a snipe, have golden-spotted upper parts and can be recognised by their feeding action of running, pausing to look and listen for food (seeds and insects) and bobbing down to eat it. **Dunlins** also live in peaty terrain and are half the size of a golden plover but not dissimilar in colouring to the inexperienced eye. They are a very common wader.

SKYLARK
L: 185MM/7.25"

You may also see but are more likely to hear the continuous and rapid song of the **skylark**. They tend to move from moorland to lower agricultural land in the winter. Just bigger than a house sparrow, they have brown upper parts and a chin with dark flakes and a white belly.

Patches of gorse and juniper scrub are often chosen as a nesting site for **linnets**, which flock together during the winter but operate in small colonies at other times. They are small birds that will also be seen on open farmland, as will the slightly larger **yellowhammer**, recognisable by its

THE ENVIRONMENT & NATURE

LAPWING/PEEWIT
L: 320MM/12.5"

yellow head and chest. It too nests in gorse and juniper bushes.

The **lapwing** is relatively common, quite large and can be recognised by its wispy black plume on the back of its head and, in summer, the aerial acrobatics of the male. They fly high to dive steeply down, twisting and turning as if out of control before pulling out at the last minute.

The **meadow pipit** is a small, classic LBJ (little brown job). They make plenty of noise and on a still day climb to about 15 metres (50ft) and then open their wings to parachute gently down. They can sometimes be recognised by their white outer tail feathers as they fly away from you. The **wheatear** is a small grey bird with white tail feathers and its call is a hard 'tack'. It is seen in western and northern Britain in summer but winters in central Africa.

The **peregrine falcon** (see p148) had a hard time in the 20th century, being shot during WW2 to protect carrier pigeons and then finding it hard to rear their young after eating insects that had fed on pesticide-soaked plants. Their comeback is therefore a sign that things are picking up again in the British countryside.

Buildings and cliffs

Swallows, **house martins** and **swifts** nest in barns and other buildings. They are hard to tell apart, but as a simple guide: swallows are the largest, are blue-black above and have a white belly and a long-forked tail; swifts are the next down in size, are essentially all black with a shallow forked tail that is usually closed and probably fly the fastest; house martins are the smallest, have a relatively short tail and a completely white underneath and, most usefully for identification purposes, a white rump (on top, near the tail). As a walker, you may be able to relate to why a non-breeding swift will fly 100 miles to avoid rain. If insects are bugging you, thank nature for swifts. A single one will eat 10,000 of the pesky buzzers a day, so think how many more bites you would suffer if it were not for them.

BARN OWL
L: 355MM/14"

Peregrine falcons, **kestrels** and **jackdaws** (similar to a crow but with a whitish back of the head) nest on cliffs. At Malham Cove the RSPB have set up a peregrine-viewing site (see box p148) allowing visitors to see the resident pair on the limestone cliffs. The kestrel, Britain's most common and most familiar bird of prey, also nests in man-made structures and is sometimes seen in city centres. It can be distinguished from the sparrowhawk, the second most common raptor, by its pointed wings and hovering when hunting. The male has a blue-grey head and a rich chestnut-coloured back, while the female is a duller chestnut both above and on her head. Jackdaws are very common in villages and towns; if you see a crow-like bird sitting on a chimney top, reckon on it being a jackdaw.

Owls may also nest in cliffs and barns. You are most likely to see a little owl, which is a non-native resident that will often occupy the same perch day after day. Local knowledge can be useful for finding one of these.

Barn owls have been affected by intensive agriculture and are on the decline but are also one of the most widely distributed birds in the world.

MAMMALS

Roe deer are the smallest of Britain's native deer, and are hard to see. They normally inhabit woodland areas but you may see one in grassland or, if you're very lucky, swimming in a lake. The males (bucks) claim a territory in spring and will chase a female (doe) round and round a tree before she gives in to his pursuit. This leaves circles of rings round the base of the tree, which are known as 'roe rings'.

Badgers like to live in deciduous woodland. Their black-and-white striped heads make them highly recognisable, but you're most likely to see them at night. They are true omnivores eating almost anything including berries, slugs and dead rabbits. The female (sow) gathers dry grasses and bracken in February for her nest. She then tucks them between her chin and forequarters and shuffles backwards, dragging them into her home (sett). The young are born blind in February and March and stay underground until spring.

Foxes are common wherever there are animals or birds to be preyed on, or dustbins to scavenge from, which is just about everywhere. Britain is estimated to have 40 times the fox population of northern France. They are believed to have been here since before the last Ice Age when the sabre-toothed tiger would have prevented them from enjoying their current supremacy in the food chain. Although now banned, fox hunting is an emotive countryside issue. A lot of conservationists believe that the fox itself is the best control of its numbers. If an environment is unsuitable they tend not to try and inhabit it and, like some marsupials, a pregnant vixen will reabsorb her embryos if conditions are unfavourable for raising cubs. Foxes do a useful job eating carrion, which sometimes includes dead lambs and rabbits. If they could learn to lay off the capercaillie and other protected birds they'd even get the RSPB on their side.

The **otter** is a sensitive indicator of the state of our rivers. They nearly died out in the last century due to a number of attacks on them, their habitat and their environment, but law has protected them since 1981. Due to the work of conservationists they're now making a comeback, but even small amounts of pollution can set back the efforts to give them a strong foothold in the wild. They are reclusive so you'll be incredibly lucky if you see one. They not only eat fish, but water voles and small aquatic birds. Their most successful hunting tactic is to launch a surprise attack from below as an otter's eyes are set on the top of its head and they have unique muscles that compensate for the visual distortion caused by water.

THE ENVIRONMENT & NATURE

Mink were introduced from North America and only exist in the wild because they escaped or were set free from mink farms. They are one of the most serious pests in the countryside; as they are an alien species, nature has yet to work out how to balance their presence. They spend a lot of time in rivers feeding on aquatic birds and fish and can be distinguished from otters by their considerably smaller size and white chin patch.

The **stoat** is a small but fierce predator. They are native and fairly wide-spread and can be recognised by their elongated and elegant form, reddish-brown coats and white bellies. They are very adaptable, moving in wherever they can find a den, including old rabbit burrows, and may live for up to 10 years. Minks, stoats, polecats, otters, badgers, weasels (the world's smallest carnivores) and pine martens are all from the same family.

The **red squirrel** is native, unlike the grey squirrel, but it is now rare to see one. They are smaller than their reviled grey cousins and feature a vibrant red coat and fabulously bushy tail (although their coat turns a little browner in winter). Note, too, the tufts that grow at the tips of their ears. Despite their rarity, people often see them on the Pennine Way, either near the YHA hostels in Dufton and Alston, or near Hadrian's Wall. The alien **grey squirrel** has played a big part in the demise of the red squirrel, partly because it is able to eat the red squirrel's food before it ripens. Efforts to reintroduce the red squirrel have not had a great deal of success, partly because they're reluctant to move from tree to tree along the ground and therefore need a dense tree canopy.

The **common shrew** is a tiny animal that lives in woodland and hedgerows. It needs to eat every four hours, and in a 24-hour period will eat twice its body weight in insects, using its long sensitive nose to sniff them out. It spends a lot of time underground eating earthworms. The mother and babies are sometimes seen traversing open ground in a train-like procession, with each shrew holding the tail of the one in front. It is the second most common British mammal.

The **mole** is armed with powerful forearms that it uses to burrow a network of underground tunnels that act as traps for unsuspecting earthworms. They patrol these every four hours, either eating all the visitors on the spot or gathering them up to save for later after immobilising them through decapitation.

In woodland or anywhere near buildings you may see the smallest of Britain's resident species of **bat**, the **pipistrelle**. Bats have been here consistently since the Ice Age and are now a protected species. Even though the pipistrelle weighs a tiny 3-8 grams (about the same as a single clove of garlic, or two sheets of kitchen roll), in one night it may eat as many as 3500 insects. Bats, hedgehogs and dormice are the only British mammals that truly hibernate throughout the whole winter from October to April. They will wake, however, if the temperature increases to unseasonal levels.

REPTILES

The **adder**, or viper, is Britain's only venomous snake but is harmless if left alone. It can be recognised by a black zig-zag down its back and is found in woodland and moorland. Adders hibernate in winter and when possible laze around in the morning and evening sun in spring and summer, eating everything from slugs to small birds. The males fight for females by rearing up and twisting themselves round each other as if trying to climb a tree; victory is often down to length. While this strenuous activity is going on the females are still asleep. They wake to find the victorious male rubbing his body against her and sticking his tongue out. It may sound all too familiar to many.

Although the **slow worm** looks like a snake it is, in fact, a legless lizard, sharing its notched tongue (rather than a snake's forked tongue), moveable eyelids (snakes have no eyelids) and fixed jaw (snakes have a free jaw for swallowing large prey); they eat slugs and insects and inhabit thick vegetation and rotting wood. The **common lizard** inhabits grass, in woods, moorland or grassland; they feed on insects and spiders.

BUTTERFLIES AND MOTHS

Butterfies you may see include the **red admiral**, **peacock** and the **painted lady** which can, on first flutter, be mistaken for a **small tortoiseshell** but look up close and you'll spot several differences to the markings including, most noticeably, the absence of a blue border at the bottom edge of its wings which is present on the tortoiseshell; the painted lady's story is significantly more interesting too as it will have migrated thousands of miles from North Africa to feed on the wildflowers here in late summer. Another eye-catching butterfly is the **green hairstreak**, though to fully appreciate its metallic green wings you need to see it at rest with its wings folded up; in flight it actually looks a fairly dull brown colour.

In mid summer you may see the **emperor moth**, a spectacular moor-dwelling moth that feeds on the heather. Both the brown hindwings and grey forewings have striking 'eye' markings on them, fooling the predators by making them think they are up against a much larger creature.

❏ WALKING THE PENNINE WAY – A PERSONAL EXPERIENCE

I never intended to walk the Pennine Way. I spent a day and a half walking from Gargrave to Horton-in-Ribblesdale, just for something to do over a long weekend away. Yet at the end I found myself staring at Ingleborough and Whernside, thinking that I could do with a bit more of this. Six months later I was back staring at those same hills, ready to set off to do some more. Having never done any long-distance walking before, I was suddenly hooked.

Walking in stages, fitted in when my annual leave allowed, it took three years to complete the whole thing, mostly completed in spring and autumn, when the weather was often at its worst. More than once I arrived at a B&B or hostel soaking wet, wondering why I was doing this, but the magic of those wild moorlands and hills kept me going. Well, that and the thought of a reviving pint in one of the many pubs along the way. It was an amazing experience – and a great pub crawl – and I have every intention of doing it again one day, preferably all in one go, and maybe even going north to south for a change. One thing is for sure, I'll do it in the summer when it might (hopefully) be just a bit drier!

Andrew Bowden (Twitter: @RamblingManUK)

THE ENVIRONMENT & NATURE

MINIMUM IMPACT & OUTDOOR SAFETY

Minimum impact walking

Britain has little wilderness, at least by the dictionary definition of land that is 'uncultivated and uninhabited'. But parts of the Pennine Way include the closest we have and it's a fragile environment. Trapped between massive conurbations, the Peak District and South Pennines in particular are among the most crowded recreational areas in England and inevitably this has brought its problems. As more and more people enjoy the freedom of the hills so the land comes under increasing pressure and the potential for conflict with other land-users is heightened. Everyone has a right to this natural heritage but with it comes a responsibility to care for it too.

ENVIRONMENTAL IMPACT

A walking holiday in itself is an environmentally friendly approach to tourism. The following are some ideas on how you can go a few steps further in helping to minimise your impact on the environment while walking the Pennine Way. Some of the latter practices become particularly relevant if you are wild camping.

Use public transport

As more and more cars are added to Britain's road network, traffic congestion is becoming a much more common occurrence, particularly on the motorway network, but increasingly also in rural areas as people head to the countryside. The roads in the Peak District and Yorkshire Dales can become very busy, especially in the summer and on Bank Holiday weekends. Despite popular myth, public transport is regular and frequent in many places, although some rural outposts only see a bus once a week. If public transport services aren't used they will decline even faster than they have in recent years.

Never leave litter

'Pack it in, pack it out'. Leaving litter is antisocial so carry a degradable plastic bag for all your rubbish, organic or otherwise and even other people's too, and pop it in a bin in the next village. Or better still, reduce the amount of litter you take with you by getting rid of packaging in advance.

Don't leave litter even if it is biodegradable. Apple cores and especially banana skins and orange peel are unsightly, encourage flies, ants and wasps and so ruin a picnic spot for others. A piece of orange peel left on the ground takes six months to decompose; silver foil 18 months; a plastic bag 10 years; clothes 15 years; and a can 85 years. In high-use areas such as the Pennine Way take all your litter with you.

Buy local
Look and ask for local produce to buy and eat. Not only does this cut down on the amount of pollution and congestion that the transportation of food creates, so-called 'food miles', it also ensures that you are supporting local farmers and producers.

Erosion
Stay on the main trail The effect of your footsteps may seem minuscule but when they are multiplied by thousands of walkers each year they become rather more significant. Although it can be a bit much to ask when the actual pathway is waterlogged, avoid taking shortcuts, widening the trail or creating more than one path; your footprints will be followed by many others. When slabs have been laid, please use them, even if the surrounding landscape is dry. The stones protect the delicate peat from erosion and allow the regrowth of grasses which stabilise the peat bog.

Consider walking out of season The maximum disturbance caused by walkers coincides with the time of year when nature wants to do most of its growth and recovery. In high-use areas, like that along much of the Pennine Way, the trail often never recovers. Walking at less busy times eases this pressure while also generating year-round income for the local economy. Not only that, but it may make the walk more enjoyable as there are fewer people on the path and (where it's open) there's less competition for accommodation.

Respect all flora and fauna
Care for all wildlife you come across. Tempting as it may be to pick wild flowers leave them so the next people who pass can enjoy them too. Don't break branches off or damage trees in any way. If you come across wildlife keep your distance and don't watch for too long. Your presence can cause considerable stress particularly if the adults are with their young or in winter when the weather is harsh and food scarce. Young animals are rarely abandoned. If you come across deer calves or young birds keep away so that their mother can return.

Outdoor toiletry
As more and more people discover the joys of the outdoors, answering the call of nature is becoming an increasing issue. In some national parks in North America visitors are provided with waste alleviation gelling (WAG) bags and are required to pack out their excrement. Ideally this should be the case in the UK; similar bags are available online and in some outdoors stores. Human excrement is not only offensive to our senses but, more importantly, can infect water sources.

Where to go Wherever possible **use a toilet**. Public toilets are marked in this guide and you'll also find facilities in pubs and cafés.

If you do have to go outdoors choose a site **at least 30 metres away from running water**. Carry a small towel and **dig a hole** about 15cm (6") deep to bury your excrement. It will decompose quicker when in contact with the top soil or leaf mould. Do not squash it under rocks as this slows down the composting process. However, do not attempt to dig any holes on land that is of historical or archaeological interest, such as around Hadrian's Wall.

Toilet paper and tampons Toilet paper decomposes slowly and is easily dug up by animals. It can then blow into water sources or onto the trail. The best method for dealing with it is to **pack it out**, along with tampons and sanitary towels; don't be tempted to burn the paper as this could lead to fire spreading, especially in a dry moorland environment.

ACCESS AND THE RIGHT TO ROAM

Right to roam
Following a concerted effort by groups such as the Ramblers (see box p51) and the British Mountaineering Council, the principle of access to open countryside and registered common land was finally allowed under the Countryside and Rights of Way Act 2000, affectionately known as CroW. In England, the act came into effect in full in 2005, creating a new right of access to the English countryside for recreation on foot.

© Chris Scott

This confusing sign does not mean 'no access for walkers' but advises that you're leaving a Right to Roam area and thereafter must stick to footpaths.

There are restrictions, of course: some land (such as gardens, parks and cultivated land) is excluded, and high-impact activities such as driving a vehicle, cycling, and horse-riding may not be permitted. The act also: gives greater protection to SSSIs (see p61) and AONBs (see p60); lists habitats and species important to biological diversity in England; and covers the conduct of those walking with dogs (see p32 and pp282-4).

❏ LAMBING AND GROUSE SHOOTING
Lambing takes place between mid March and mid May; during this period dogs should not be taken along the path. Even a dog secured on a lead can disturb a pregnant ewe. If you see a lamb or ewe that appears to be in distress contact the nearest farmer.

Grouse shooting is an important part of the rural economy and management of the countryside. Britain is home to 20% of the world's moorland, and is under a duty to look after it. The season runs from 12 August to 10 December but shooting is unlikely to affect your walk.

❑ THE COUNTRYSIDE CODE

The Countryside Code, originally described in the 1950s as the Country Code, was revised and relaunched in 2004, in part because of the changes brought about by the CRoW Act (see opposite); it has been updated several times since then, most recently in 2022. The Code seems like common sense but sadly some people still appear to have no understanding of how to treat the countryside they walk in.

An adapted version of the 2022 Code (🖳 gov.uk/government/publications/the-countryside-code), headed 'Respect. Protect. Enjoy.', is given below:

Respect other people

● **Consider the local community and other people enjoying the outdoors** Be sensitive to the needs and wishes of those who live and work there. If, for example, farm animals are being moved or gathered keep out of the way and follow the farmer's directions. Being courteous and friendly to those you meet will ensure a healthy future for all based on partnership and co-operation.

● **Leave gates and property as you find them and follow paths unless wider access is available** A farmer normally closes gates to keep farm animals in, but may sometimes leave them open so the animals can reach food and water. Leave gates as you find them or follow instructions on signs. When in a group, make sure the last person knows how to leave the gates. Follow paths unless wider access is available, such as on open country or registered common land (known as 'open access land'). Leave machinery and farm animals alone – if you think an animal is in distress try to alert the farmer instead. Use gates, stiles or gaps in field boundaries if you can – climbing over walls, hedges and fences can damage them and increase the risk of farm animals escaping. The path is well supplied with stiles where it crosses field boundaries. If you have to climb over a gate because you can't open it always do so at the hinged end. Also be careful not to disturb ruins and historic sites. Minimise erosion by not cutting corners or widening the path.

Protect the natural environment

● **Leave no trace of your visit and take your litter home** Take special care not to damage, destroy or remove features such as rocks, plants and trees. Take your litter with you; litter and leftover food doesn't just spoil the beauty of the countryside, it can be dangerous to wildlife and farm animals.

Fires can be as devastating to wildlife and habitats as they are to people and property – so be careful with naked flames and cigarettes at any time of the year.

● **Keep dogs under effective control** This means you should keep your dog on a lead or in sight at all times, be aware of what it's doing and be confident it will return to you promptly on command. Across farmland dogs should always be kept on a short lead; during lambing time they should not be taken at all. Always clean up after your dog and get rid of the mess responsibly – 'bag it and bin it' – in any public waste bin if no dedicated bin is available.

Enjoy the outdoors

● **Plan ahead, check what facilities are open and be prepared** You're responsible for your own safety: be prepared for natural hazards, changes in the weather and other events. Wild animals, farm animals and horses can behave unpredictably if you get too close, especially if they're with their young – so give them plenty of space. Check the weather forecasts.

● **Follow advice and local signs** In some areas temporary diversions may be in place; take notice of these and other local trail advice.

Outdoor safety

AVOIDANCE OF HAZARDS

In walking, as in life, most hazards can be avoided through the application of common sense and with some forethought and planning. The Pennine Way is not an expedition into the unknown, you will probably meet people every day, but some sections are remote and you need to be prepared for problems and adverse conditions. Abiding by the following rules should minimise the risks.

Safety on the Pennine Way

Your safety is your responsibility! Organisations are there to help you if an emergency arises, but you should make every effort to ensure you stay safe in the first place. Here are some tips that may help:

● Avoid walking alone if possible.

● Make sure that someone knows your plans for every day you are on the trail. This could be a friend or relative that you have promised to call every night, or the establishment you plan to stay in at the end of each day's walk. That way, if you fail to turn up or call, they can raise the alarm.

● If visibility is suddenly reduced and you become uncertain of the correct trail, wait. You'll find that mist often clears, at least for long enough to allow you to get your bearings. If you are still uncertain – and the weather does not look like improving – return the way you came to the nearest point of civilisation and try again another time when conditions have improved.

● Always fill your water bottle at every opportunity (but don't empty it until you are certain you can refill it) and pack some food such as high-energy snacks.

● Always carry a torch, compass, map, whistle and wet-weather gear with you.

● Be extra vigilant if walking with children, dogs or the unfit.

● Be cautious of herds of cows with calves, especially if you have a dog (see p283).

Dealing with an accident

● Use basic first aid to treat the injury to the best of your ability.

● Try to attract the attention of anybody else who may be in the area. The **international distress (emergency) signal** is six blasts on a whistle, or six flashes with a torch, repeated regularly.

● If possible leave someone with the casualty while others go to get help. If there are only two people, you have a dilemma. If you decide to get help, leave all spare clothing and food with the casualty.

● In an emergency dial ☎ 999 (or the EU standard number ☎ 112). Don't assume your mobile won't work up on the fells. However, before you call work out exactly where you are; on the app What3words (🖥 what3words.com) the world is divided into three-metre squares and each has its own three-word geocode so it makes it easy to tell people where you are. **See pp273-4 for the what3words refs for the waypoints in this book**.

WEATHER FORECASTS

The UK has notoriously unpredictable weather and the Pennine range, like any mountainous area, generates its own weather patterns as well. A check of the weather forecast before you leave in the morning could help you avoid a dangerous situation later in the day. Hostels, TICs and some good B&Bs will have that morning's summary pinned up by the door. Alternatively check the forecast online or on an app, ideally using a mountain weather service such as MWIS (see below) as the weather on the high tops can be much more extreme than in the valleys and lowlands.

If the forecast is really bad, consider either an alternative low-level route if there is one, or a rest day if plans allow, or a taxi to your next accommodation if they don't. Some baggage-transfer services allow you to ride with the bags, but check with them first if this is part of their service. Even on what should be a fine day, ensure you have waterproofs in your pack, just in case.

Access to forecasts

The **UK Met Office** (⌨ metoffice.gov.uk) has a comprehensive range of services, including weather apps, and dedicated forecasts for mountain areas (⌨ www.metoffice.gov.uk/weather/specialist-forecasts/mountain).

The **Mountain Weather Information Service** (MWIS; ⌨ mwis.org.uk) has a very detailed service for the high hills of the Peak District and the Yorkshire Dales.

BLISTERS

The Pennine Way is no place for experimenting with new equipment and this applies particularly for new boots. Even though most new boots do not require 'breaking in' these days, they do need to be tested for comfort before you set out. Blisters are often caused by wet feet, so waterproof boots may help; try to avoid getting them wet inside, perhaps by using gaiters, although these aren't to everyone's taste. Airing your feet at rest stops is a great policy and always address hotspots as soon as they develop. Zinc oxide will help reduce a hotspot, but if you leave it too long and it develops into a blister you will need a 'moleskin' patch or a blister plaster such as Compeed. Avoid popping blisters if at all possible as this can lead to infection. If the skin breaks, clean it with an antiseptic wipe or cream and cover it with a non-adhesive dressing, taped into place.

HYPOTHERMIA

Also known as **exposure**, hypothermia occurs when the body can't generate enough heat to maintain its normal temperature, usually as a result of being wet, cold, unprotected from the wind, tired and hungry. It's usually more of a problem in upland areas on the moors or, of course, outside summer. Hypothermia is easily avoided by wearing suitable clothing, carrying and eating enough food and drink, being aware of the weather conditions and keeping an eye on the condition of your companions. Feeling cold and tired is par for the course on the Pennine Way, but along with shivering, these are the early symptoms of hypothermia; so find (or fashion) shelter as soon as possible and get into whatever dry clothes you have.

If symptoms worsen just adding layers will not help, you will need to add warmth, either in the form of a hot drink, food or fire or through the sharing of body warmth with a companion; this is best achieved through skin-to-skin contact in a sleeping bag or bivi bag. If symptoms aren't addressed behaviour may become erratic, speech slurred and co-ordination poor, leading eventually to unconsciousness, followed by coma and even death. Do not delay in seeking medical assistance, including mountain rescue.

HYPERTHERMIA

Although uncommon, it is possible to suffer from **heat exhaustion**, even in the north of England. Brought on by a long, strenuous walk in hot temperatures, the symptoms are a result of the loss of body fluids and salts and a sufferer may feel faint, nauseous and sweat heavily. Additional symptoms include: skin that feels hot to the touch, a rapid heart rate, feeling confused and urinating less often.

A person with heat exhaustion should be moved quickly to somewhere cool and given fluids, preferably water, to drink. Follow this, if possible, with a weak salt solution of one teaspoon of salt per litre of water and assist the casualty to drink it. If spotted and addressed quickly, they should start to feel better within half an hour. Certain groups of people – including diabetics using insulin, people with kidney, heart or circulation problems and the young and elderly – are more at risk of getting heatstroke and should seek medical attention as soon as possible.

Heatstroke (hyperthermia) is a much more serious problem altogether. It occurs when the body's temperature becomes dangerously high due to excessive heat exposure. The body is no longer able to cool itself and starts to overheat. Early symptoms will include a high body temperature and an absence of sweating, followed by erratic behaviour, slurred speech and poor co-ordination, leading eventually to convulsions, coma and possibly death. Rehydration is not enough; shade the victim and sponge them down, wrap them in wet towels or soak their lower layers, fan them, and get help immediately; this is an emergency situation, dial ☎ 999.

SUNBURN

Sunburn can happen, even in northern England and even on overcast days. The best way to avoid it – and the extra risk of developing skin cancers that sunburn brings – is to keep your skin covered at all times in light, loose-fitting clothing, and to cover any exposed areas of skin in sunscreen (with a minimum factor of 30). Sunscreen should be applied regularly throughout the day. Don't forget your lips, nose, ears and the back of your neck, and even under your chin to protect you against rays reflected from the ground. Most importantly of all, always wear a hat! A broad-brimmed hat will provide much better protection than a baseball cap, which just shades your eyes.

Using this guide

The trail guide has been divided into 15 stages (walking from south to north, the direction taken by 80% of walkers on the Pennine Way), though these are not to be taken as rigid daily itineraries since people walk at different speeds and have different interests.

The **route overviews** introduce the trail for each of these stages. They're followed by **navigation notes** that will help you identify and overcome potential route-finding trouble spots. To enable you to plan your itinerary, practical information is presented on the trail maps; this includes walking times for both directions, all places to stay and eat, as well as useful shops and other services. Further details are given in the text under the entry for each place. For an overview of all this information see the town and village facilities table, pp34-7. For cumulative **distance chart** see p290 and for **map profiles** and **overview maps** see the colour pages at the end of the book.

TRAIL MAPS [key map inside back cover; symbols key p284]
Scale and walking times

The trail maps are to a **scale** of just under 1:20,000 (1cm = 200m; 3¹⁄₈ inches = one mile). Each full-size map covers about two miles but that's a very rough estimate owing to variety of terrain.

Walking times are given along the side of each map; the arrow shows the direction to which the time refers. The black triangles indicate the points between which the times have been taken. **See note on walking times in the box below**. These time-bars are a rough guide and are not there to judge your walking ability; actual walking times will be different for each individual. There are so many variables that affect walking speed from the weather conditions to how many beers you drank the previous evening as well as how much you are carrying. After the first hour or two of walking you'll be able to see how your speed relates to the timings on the maps.

> ❏ **IMPORTANT NOTE – WALKING TIMES**
> Unless otherwise specified, **all times in this book refer only to the time spent walking**. You should add 20-30% to allow for rests, photos, checking the map, drinking water etc, not to mention time simply to stop and stare. When planning the day's hike count on 5-7 hours' actual walking.

Up or down?

The trail is shown as a dashed line. An arrow across the trail indicates the slope; two arrows show that it is steep. The arrows always point uphill. If, for example, you are walking from A (at 80m) to B (at 200m) and the trail between the two is short and steep, it would be shown thus: A – – – >> – – – – B. Reversed arrow heads indicate a downward gradient.

Other map features

The numbered GPS waypoints refer to the list on pp275-82 Features are marked on the map when they are pertinent to navigation. In order to avoid cluttering the maps and making them unusable not all features have been marked each time they occur.

ACCOMMODATION

Apart from in large towns where some selection has been necessary, all accommodation on or close to the trail is marked on (or indicated off) the maps with details in the accompanying text.

Details of each place are given in the accompanying text. The number of **rooms** of each type is given at the beginning of each entry, ie: **S** = Single, **D** = Double room, **T** = Twin room with two beds, **Tr** = Triple room and **Qd** = Quad. Note that many of the triple/quad rooms have a double bed and one/two single beds (or bunk beds) thus for a group of three or four, two people would have to share the double bed but it also means the room can be used as a double or twin.

Rates quoted for B&B-style accommodation are generally **per room** at a single/double (S/D) rate; sometimes the single rate is in a smaller room with a single bed, sometimes it's single occupancy (sgl occ) of a double room. At other places there are no single rates. A few older fashioned B&B quote rates **per person (pp)** based on two people sharing a room for a one-night stay; single travellers will almost always pay more than that per person rate. The rates quoted were accurate at the time of research but may well change. See box on p23 for more information on rates.

The text also mentions whether the rooms are **en suite**, or if facilities are **private** or **shared** (in either case this may be a bathroom or shower room just outside the room – if private then you will be the only person using that bathroom). For those who prefer a relaxed soak at the end of the day ☛ signifies that a **bath** is available in, or for, at least one room.

Also noted is whether the premises allow **dogs to stay** (🐾 – see also pp282-4), subject to prior arrangement, and any associated charges; and if **packed lunches** (Ⓛ) are available (usually these must be requested at least 24 hours in advance). These generally cost around £7-8. **Wi-fi** is available almost everywhere, except in some campsites, so the text only notes where, at the time of research, it was not available.

Several B&B proprietors based a mile or two off the trail will, subject to prior arrangement, be happy to collect walkers from the nearest point on the trail and take them back the next morning; a small charge may be payable though.

The route guide

EDALE [Map 1, p85]

Surrounded by hills and providing access to hundreds of miles of footpaths, it's no surprise that Edale is a mecca for walkers from all over the UK. This ancient and beautiful village comprises a scattering of stone cottages, an impressive village church and an old pub; at weekends it has hundreds of visitors. Some of these will be embarking on the Pennine Way and this walk and the village have become synonymous. Upon arrival, visitors are drawn towards the focal point of the village, the Old Nag's Head (see p86), and for Pennine Wayfarers this is an absolute must, as it's the official start point for the walk.

See p14 for details about Edale Country Day in June.

Transport

All great adventures should start with a train journey and the Pennine Way is no different, so the best way to arrive in Edale is by **train**. (Indeed, given that there are no bus services to Edale, train is pretty much the only way to arrive, at least if you're relying on public transport.) There are frequent connections – services are operated by Northern Rail (see box on p59) – from both Sheffield (30 mins away) and Manchester (45 mins away) and you are unlikely to step onto Edale platform alone.

Undoubtedly a very scenic way to approach Edale is by **car**, using the minor road from the south, over Mam Tor, to see the Vale of Edale spread out below and the village nestled amongst the heather moors around it. If you plan on parking your car here for a few days, give Andrew Critchlow of Shaw Wood Farm a call (☎ 07792-446753); he has a field behind the farmhouse, just five minutes from the station. He usually charges around £3 per day, with all money going to charity. The village's official car park (see Map 1) charges £6 a day, or £7 overnight.

For a **taxi** try SOS Taxis Grindleford (☎ 07541-101076, 🖳 rajsostaxis.com).

Services

Pop into **The Moorland Centre** (Peak District National Park Centre; ☎ 01433-670207, 🖳 visitpeakdistrict.com; May-Sep daily 9.30am-5pm, Oct-Nov & Feb-Apr 10am-4.30pm, Dec, Jan closed). **Edale Visitor Centre** here has maps, guidebooks, snacks, souvenirs, and a limited selection of outdoor clothing. The village website (🖳 edale.org.uk) is also useful. See also box p87.

At the top end of the village there's **Edale General Store** (☎ 01433-670599, 🖳 edalegeneralstore.com; Apr-Oct Mon-Thur 9am-12.30pm, Fri & Sat until 6pm, Sun 10am-4pm) which caters for walkers' needs. They sell groceries, such as bread, eggs and ham, as well as camping equipment and locally brewed beer; they accept card payment but don't offer cashback. There are limited **post office** services here on Wednesday morning (9.30am-noon). This is the last shop you will see, unless you divert from the route, until Hebden Bridge (which itself is off the trail).

There is basically no mobile phone coverage but you may get a weak signal on the road just above the railway station. However, there are two public **phones** in the village.

Where to stay

The first day out from Edale requires a full day's walking and is one of the toughest first days of any long-distance walk in the UK. Unless you can arrive early it makes sense, therefore, to stay the night in the village, or very close by. The popularity of Edale makes it important to secure your accommodation prior to arrival, especially if, like most walkers, you plan to begin the Pennine Way at the weekend.

Note that some B&Bs may not be keen to take solo travellers at weekends unless they pay the full room rate and may not accept single-night bookings.

In Edale There are two **campsites** in the centre of the village both of which are open most of the year (just closing at times in winter). *Fieldhead* (☎ 01433-670386, 🖳 fieldheadcampsite.co.uk; no wi-fi; 🐕) by the Moorland Centre, charges from £10pp. There are toilets, showers (20p for two minutes) and basic drying facilities. Backpackers tend to head for the lower riverside pitches but all three manicured fields are nicely away from vehicle parking (there are wheelbarrows for luggage). Booking is recommended; the online booking system works well.

Newfold Farm (☎ 01433-670401, 🖳 newfoldfarmedale.com; space for 120 tents; wi-fi; 🐕 but on a lead at all times), up the hill by the post office, charges £15/22 for 1/2 people and tent. Shower, toilet facilities and picnic tables are available and there's plenty of space. Of the two campsites it's better suited to car or van campers (electric hookups are available). They also offer ten large bell **glamping tents** (sleep 2-4; £80-100; min 2 nights at weekends, min 3 nights in school holidays) with mattresses, chairs and fire pit. Booking is essential for Bank Holiday weekends when there is a minimum of three nights; at other times it is first come first served.

There are two farms offering **bunkhouse** accommodation for groups only. *Edale Camping Barn* (☎ 01433-651901, 07739 878383, 🖳 www.cotefield tarmcottages.co.uk, Mar-Nov; sleeps 8) is a simple barn with outside (chemical) toilet, water tap and cooking area (no electricity or hot water). It's 10 minutes' walk to the east of Edale village at Cotefield Farm. There is also *Ollerbrook Farm Bunkhouse* (☎ 01433-670235, 🖳 ollerbrookfarm.co .uk; min group size 6), actually two bunkhouses with a total of 32 beds (£20-25pp) in seven rooms. They have kitchens and cooking facilities.

At the top of Edale's group-accommodation tree is *Edale Gathering* (off Map 1; ☎ 01433-670612, 🖳 edalegathering.com; ☛; 🐕; lodge apartments open all year, tents Apr-Dec). **Glamping** doesn't get any more fabulous than this, with four tented safari lodges each sleeping six (1D/2T rooms per tent; min 4 nights; from £700) all kitted out with wood-burning stoves, roll-top baths with showers and fully equipped open-plan kitchen/dining areas. They have also restored an old 19th-century shooting lodge for larger parties (4 rooms sleep 2-4; min 2 nights; from £1300. It's all rather luxurious and lovely but with no single-night bookings and eye-watering prices, it's better for groups walking in the region than Pennine Way walkers. The site lies about a quarter of a mile above the start of the trail at the very top of the village.

Walkers requiring **B&B** have a limited

❏ TALKING THE TALK

Although we all speak English after a fashion, the finely honed ear will perceive at least five distinct accents along the Pennine Way, each with its own dialect, with greetings being most evident to the walker. These will be most noticeable in deeply rural areas, particularly among agricultural workers who may sound unintelligible to an unacclimatised foreigner.

From the High Peak of northern Derbyshire ('*ahyallrait*?') you'll flit between the cultural frontier of erstwhile county rivals, Yorkshire and Lancashire, who both share a curt 'ow do?' Then, as you leave the Dales another invisible boundary is crossed and the accent takes on the distinctive 'Geordie' tones of County Durham and Northumberland ('allreet?') before your final linguistic watershed over The Cheviots into Scotland where a barely discernible nod means you've a new friend for life.

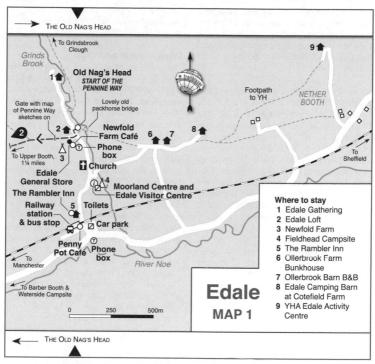

choice. ***Ollerbrook Barn*** (☎ 01433-670200, 🖳 ollerbrookbarn.co.uk; 2D en suite, 1D private bathroom; ➽; Ⓛ; 🐾) is a beautiful ivy-clad converted barn in a quiet spot away from the village. B&B costs S £40-55 or D £80-90. If arranged in advance they are happy to pick people up from Edale station free of charge.

Another cosy spot is ***Edale Loft*** (☎ 01433-670014, 🖳 airbnb.co.uk,western. house @btinternet.com; 1D/T or Tr en suite; ➽; 🐾; min 2 nights), sometimes known as Western House, just past the Old Nag's Head pub, which charges £125-130 B&B for its one attic suite.

Originally built as the Railway Hotel, ***The Rambler Inn*** (☎ 01433-670268, 🖳 theramblerinn.co.uk; 3D/2T/2Tr/2Qd, all en suite; ➽; Ⓛ; 🐾 bar only) is a friendly pub that charges D/Tr £130/150 for a room.

In Upper Booth Located 1¼ miles (2km) into the Pennine Way, Upper Booth (Map 2) can make a nice warm up the night before you start your walk proper. The nearest food is in Edale.

Upper Booth Farm Campsite (Map 2; ☎ 07811-043836, 🖳 nationaltrust.org.uk/holidays/upper-booth-farm-campsite; 🐾; Apr-Oct) is a National Trust-owned site with a lovely location and online **camping** rates starting at £20/27 S/D per pitch. Walk-in Pennine Way campers pay £13 but you can't book this online; if you book and pay online for the higher rate you'll get a refund when you check in. The site also has modern toilet and shower facilities but there is no wi-fi and almost no mobile phone signal. Ask about the secret backpacker pitches by the river. Booking is essential for summer weekends, when there is a two-night minimum stay. A basic **camping barn** (🐾) with room for up to 12 people but with no water, heating or electricity was only open to groups at the time of research, though check with them for the latest information.

In Nether Booth Most nights *YHA Edale* (Map 1; also known as YHA Edale Activity Centre; bookings ☎ 0345-371 9514, 🖳 yha.org.uk/hostel/yha-edale-activity-centre; sleeps 157 in total, 7 en suite rooms sleep 3-6, dorm beds in rooms of various sizes sleeping 1-12; ◐; open all year) may seem more of a 'hyperactivity centre' over-run with school kids than the old ramblers' hostel it once was. It's therefore essential to book in advance to see if beds are available to non-groups, especially as the hostel is 1½-miles east of Edale village. Dorm beds cost from £22pp, private rooms from S/D £25/39. Meals are available and there is a bar as well as laundry and drying facilities. You can reach the hostel via a network of footpaths from the village or along the road.

In Barber Booth This small hamlet is about half a mile south-west of Edale (off Map 1) or just under one mile south-east of Upper Booth (off Map 2) and if you're really stuck for accommodation *Waterside Campsite* (☎ 01433-670215; 40 pitches; no wi-fi; 🐾 on lead; Easter-Sep) offers **camping** from £10pp. Showers, toilets and

hot/cold water are available. Booking is essential for bank holiday weekends when a minimum stay of three nights is required.

Where to eat and drink
Being the traditional start of the Pennine Way, a meal at *The Old Nag's Head* (☎ 01433-670291, 🖳 dorbiere.co.uk/the-old-nags-head, **fb**; food Mon-Sat noon-9pm, Sun noon-8pm; 🐾) at the top of the village is a rite of passage. Start the trail as you mean to go on with a Pick 'n' Mix Sausage (£10.95), choosing from four types of sausage, three types of mash and three sauces, and then add on a giant Yorkshire pudding (£1.50) for luck.

The only alternative for a weekday evening meal is in Edale. Although less iconic, *The Rambler Inn* (see Where to stay; Mon-Sat noon-9pm, Sun to 8pm) down the road is actually more appealing, with a large beer garden and a full pub menu (meals £11-15), including a tempting lemon and gin cheesecake for dessert.

For a daytime flapjack and cup of tea as you get off the train try *Penny Pot Café* (🖳 pennypotcafe.com, daily 8am-5pm) near the station; cards only.

Newfold Farm (see Where to stay in Edale) has a licensed **café** (9am-5pm; 🐾) offering sandwiches, soups and sharing platters with nice outdoor seating, and they also serve **pizzas** on Friday and Saturday nights in summer.

❏ **KINDER SCOUT – A BIT OF HISTORY**
Kinder Scout, a hugely popular recreational area, with Manchester and Sheffield just a curlew's whistle away, became synonymous with the so-called 'right to roam' when in 1932 it was the scene of a mass 'trespass' in which thousands of people demonstrated their belief that wild land should be accessible to all by marching across the plateau. It took a while but the event eventually led to the National Parks and Access to the Countryside Act of 1949. Today rights of access to the countryside have improved further with the Countryside & Rights of Way Act 2000 (see p62).

In October 2009 Kinder Scout plateau became a National Nature Reserve (NNR; see p61), originally covering 800 hectares and extended in 2022 to 1082 hectares, affording blanket bog and sub-alpine dwarf shrub heath the protection that NNR status brings. The National Trust, who own the land, are continuing to restore much of the damaged habitat; repairing eroded patches and aiding the recovery of sphagnum moss – see box opposite.

EDALE TO CROWDEN

MAPS 1-9

Route overview

As can be seen from the table (right), the Pennine Way throws you straight in at the deep end. If the weather is poor, it may also test your navigation and equipment as you

Distance	**16 miles (25.5km)**
Ascent	**2600ft (793m)**
Time	**5¾-7¼ hours***

skirt around the notorious Kinder Scout (see box opposite) and ascend the remote summit of Bleaklow. The days of wading knee deep through peat bog are long gone however, thanks to the use of stone slabs, reclaimed from demolished cotton mills and laid over the worst of the bogs to prevent erosion and provide, almost incidentally, a dry path and perfect navigation aid for walkers.

Having left Edale you pass through sheep pastures, the hamlet of **Upper Booth** (Map 2) and along a lane, all the time the hills encroaching closer and closer. The path soon arrives at the picturesque bridge at the foot of **Jacob's Ladder** (Map 3) and the first stiff climb of the walk up to the towering **Edale Rocks**. A five-minute detour from here can take you to the medieval wayside boundary marker known as the **Edale Cross** (Map 3).

Back at Edale Rocks, you begin the classic edge walk around **Kinder Scout** passing impressive gritstone outcrops to reach **Kinder Downfall** (Map 4). If you're lucky you may see water cascading down over the edge and if you're even luckier you may see it being blown upwards by the wind as it whistles up the valley and onto the plateau.

❏ MOORS FOR THE FUTURE

Based at The Moorland Centre in Edale, the Moors for the Future Partnership was established with a Heritage Lottery Fund grant in 2003. It was given a remit to: restore and conserve our important moorland resources; raise awareness of the value of this environment; and to develop expertise on how to protect and manage the moors in a sustainable way in the Peak District and South Pennines.

Peat bogs, such as those on the summit of Bleaklow and Kinder Scout, play an important environmental role as carbon dioxide (CO_2) banks, storing large amounts of the greenhouse gas. As these delicate landscapes are eroded, through pollution, overgrazing, summer wildfires and the weather, the CO_2 is slowly leaked back into the atmosphere. It is estimated that the UK's peat bogs store the equivalent of ten times the country's total CO_2 emissions. Erosion of the southern Pennine hills is causing the release of something like the CO_2 emission of a large town every year.

The work carried out by Moors for the Future Partnership on Kinder and Bleaklow includes projects such as spreading geotextiles to stabilise the bare peat, building footpaths and applying lime, seed and fertiliser and re-introducing **sphagnum** (see p63), a key peat-building moss. The best example of their work for the Pennine Wayfarer is the transformation of Black Hill (Map 12), from a peaty wasteland just a few years ago, to a more healthy revegetated moorland – better for wildlife, water quality and retaining carbon in the soil. More information on the work carried out can be found on their website (⌨ moorsforthefuture.org.uk).

---

* Your walking day will be longer than this! See **important note on walking times** on p81.

Keeping to the edge, you'll soon arrive at the steep, stepped descent to a crossroads of paths. Be sure to keep straight ahead, turning right here (too soon) will leave you with a long road walk to recover the path. Cross William Clough (a *clough* is a stream) and a short distance ahead you reach **Mill Hill** (Map 4); turn right across the bare peat expanse of featherbed moss, now thankfully slabbed, to meet the A57 at **Snake Pass** (Map 6). The pass gets its name from the serpent adorning the coat of arms of local landowners the Cavendish family.

Devil's Dike (Map 6) awaits and a long, steady ascent of Bleaklow (a *low* is a small hill or burial ground). The path follows a sunken course between walls of peat, meandering all the way, crossing small streams and the occasional open expanse of cotton-grass if the season is right. In good weather this is a joy to walk, the section up and beside **Hern Clough** (Map 7) being the highlight. In bad weather and poor visibility in particular this can be a nervous test of navigation. The path is mostly obvious though and knee-high stone blocks are interspersed along the length carrying the acorn symbol of the National Trail. Several sites off the trail near here offer an opportunity for **wild camping**, notably at the rocky areas of Wain Stones (near Bleaklow Head) and Hern Stones.

Where the Way crosses Hern Clough by two tall milestones, an unmarked trail detours west off the trail for about half a mile to Higher Shelf Stones and the scattered remains of a **B29 Superfortress** plane, which crashed here in 1948. A memorial marks the site which is scattered with wreckage of fuselage and engines. Don't attempt to find the site in bad weather.

Bleaklow Head is soon reached, an impressive cairn with a stake marking the nominal summit – a huge expanse of peat, rocks and grassy hummocks can't

---

❏ PEAT

The Way has not become synonymous with miles of spirit-sapping bogs for nothing. Paving slabs have alleviated much of the misery, but why is it so darn soggy?

Peat and the underlying geology are to blame. The British Isles (and indeed much of the landmass of planet earth) was once covered in trees. Everywhere except the highest mountains and sandy beaches was wooded. Sabre-toothed tigers prowled

in the forests alongside elephants and rhinos. Today these ancient woodlands and rampaging carnivores are no longer around. The reason for the disappearance of this habitat is not a natural phenomenon but the activities of early man.

When early Britons felled primeval forests for building and farming, groundwater was no longer absorbed and evaporated by the trees. Add the impermeability of the underlying gritstone and the saturated vegetation rotted where it lay, forming the peat, which you squelch through today. So, next time your boots fill with black peaty soup, don't curse nature, curse your axe-wielding forebears instead.

Wet feet? Blame the cavemen!

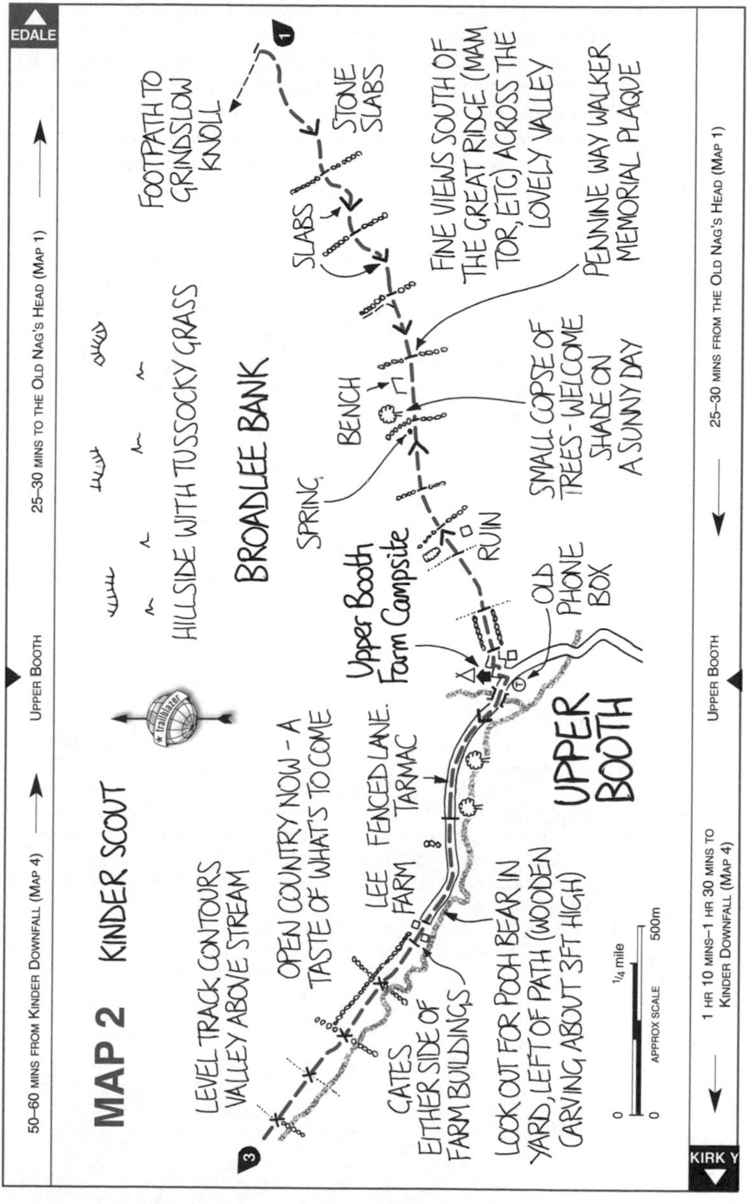
EDALE
MAP 2 KINDER SCOUT
50–60 MINS FROM KINDER DOWNFALL (MAP 4)
UPPER BOOTH
25–30 MINS TO THE OLD NAG'S HEAD (MAP 1)
LEVEL TRACK CONTOURS VALLEY ABOVE STREAM
OPEN COUNTRY NOW - A TASTE OF WHAT'S TO COME
HILLSIDE WITH TUSSOCKY GRASS
BROADLEE BANK
FOOTPATH TO GRINDSLOW KNOLL
STONE SLABS
SLABS
SPRING
BENCH
LEE FARM
FENCED LANE. TARMAC
Upper Booth Farm Campsite
RUIN
GATES EITHER SIDE OF FARM BUILDINGS
LOOK OUT FOR POOH BEAR IN YARD, LEFT OF PATH (WOODEN CARVING ABOUT 3FT HIGH)
UPPER BOOTH
OLD PHONE BOX
SMALL COPSE OF TREES - WELCOME SHADE ON A SUNNY DAY
FINE VIEWS SOUTH OF THE GREAT RIDGE (MAM TOR, ETC) ACROSS THE LOVELY VALLEY
PENNINE WAY WALKER MEMORIAL PLAQUE
APPROX SCALE
0
1/4 mile
0
500m
1 HR 10 MINS–1 HR 30 MINS TO KINDER DOWNFALL (MAP 4)
UPPER BOOTH
25–30 MINS FROM THE OLD NAG'S HEAD (MAP 1)
KIRK Y

really be called a summit. The exit from Bleaklow isn't obvious, but a stone block guide post points the way and it's mostly downhill now to Torside, still four miles (6.5km) and two hours away. On the way you'll follow **Clough Edge** (Map 8), a lofty path with great views down to your destination. The steep descent brings you to the B6105 road (Map 9) at **Torside**, where you'll have to either camp in **Crowden** (see p94) or stay in a B&B in **Padfield** (see p93); for the latter you can either arrange to be picked up by your accommodation or walk the two miles along the Longdendale Trail. Sixteen miles down, 240 to go!

Navigation notes

The path is obvious and clear as far as Kinder Low (Map 3), at which point it becomes somewhat faint and intermittent across the sandy rock-strewn area beside the trig point, but keep an eye out for the cairns beside the path, or better still use a GPS if you lose the faint track. If you find the Kinder Low trig point on your left at any point you've gone wrong. But if, having passed the trig point, you then make for the escarpment to the north of it and keep to the edge you'll be on the right track.

The trickiest part of the day is the summit of Bleaklow Head (Map 7), but providing you seek out the two knee-high, stone block guide markers that are located beside the huge summit cairn, you should end up going in the right direction. GPS waypoints are provided and the summit cairn is an excellent reference for a compass bearing. The final troublespot is encountered at the end of the descent down Wildboar Grain (Map 8). Before you turn right (north-west) down

---

❏ PENNINE WAY GEOGRAPHICAL GLOSSARY

Maps of northern England can require a bit of decoding if you aren't used to them. The following definitions should help you extract a bit more information.

When it comes to water features, a *beck* is a stream, a *burn* is a larger stream or river and a *clough* is a steep river or stream valley. A *lough* is a lake and, as you'd imagine, it shares the same root as the Scottish word loch. A *knowe* is a hill (as in a knoll), a *rigg* is a bigger hill and a *pike* is a large hill with a peaked summit. A *tor* is a rocky outcrop; you'll pass Torside at the end of your first day's walking. A *grough* is a deep channel in peat bog. Several features along the Pennine Way get their names from old Scandinavian, including a *ghyll* (or gill), which is a ravine, a *foss* (or force), meaning waterfall, and any town that features the name *kirkby*, which is Norse for a village with a church.

Town places names can also give you a clue to the past. Anything ending in *-dale* is, of course, a valley. A place name ending in *-ton* started as a farm or hamlet (think Middleton, Alston or Horton), while a *-ham*, such as Malham or Bellingham, denotes a former village or estate. The *-bury* in Standbury indicates that it was once a fort. Celtic names are also thrown into the linguistic mix, one notable example being *pen* (hill), as in Pen-y-ghent.

As noted, many place names along the Pennine Way date from the Viking invasions; a Thwaite is a clearing in a forest, and a Keld is a spring, while Ickornshaw gets its name from the Norse words for squirrel (*icorni*) and woods (*shaw*) – thus 'Squirrel Woods'. Lumbutts is somewhat disappointingly just a *butt* (small piece of land) next to a *lum* (pool).

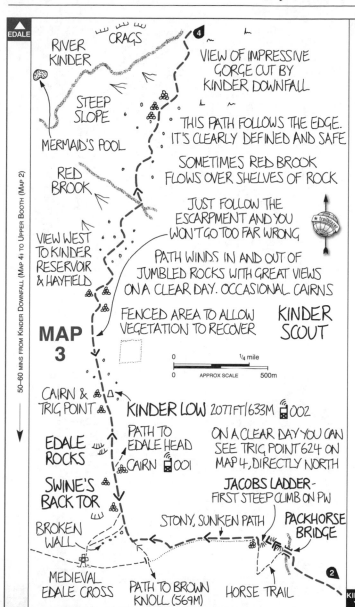

▲ EDALE

RIVER KINDER

CRAGS

4

VIEW OF IMPRESSIVE GORGE CUT BY KINDER DOWNFALL

STEEP SLOPE

MERMAID'S POOL

THIS PATH FOLLOWS THE EDGE. IT'S CLEARLY DEFINED AND SAFE

RED BROOK

SOMETIMES RED BROOK FLOWS OVER SHELVES OF ROCK

JUST FOLLOW THE ESCARPMENT AND YOU WON'T GO TOO FAR WRONG

VIEW WEST TO KINDER RESERVOIR & HAYFIELD

trailblazer

PATH WINDS IN AND OUT OF JUMBLED ROCKS WITH GREAT VIEWS ON A CLEAR DAY. OCCASIONAL CAIRNS

FENCED AREA TO ALLOW VEGETATION TO RECOVER

MAP 3

KINDER SCOUT

0   ¼ mile
0   APPROX SCALE   500m

CAIRN & TRIG POINT

KINDER LOW 2077 FT/633M 📱 002

EDALE ROCKS

PATH TO EDALE HEAD

CAIRN 📱 001

ON A CLEAR DAY YOU CAN SEE TRIG POINT 624 ON MAP 4, DIRECTLY NORTH

SWINE'S BACK TOR

JACOBS LADDER - FIRST STEEP CLIMB ON PW

BROKEN WALL

STONY, SUNKEN PATH

PACKHORSE BRIDGE

MEDIEVAL EDALE CROSS

PATH TO BROWN KNOLL (569M)

HORSE TRAIL

2

KIRK Y ▼

50-60 MINS FROM KINDER DOWNFALL (MAP 4) TO UPPER BOOTH (MAP 2)

1 HR 10 MINS-1 HR 30 MINS FROM UPPER BOOTH (MAP 2) TO KINDER DOWNFALL (MAP 4)

ROUTE GUIDE AND MAPS

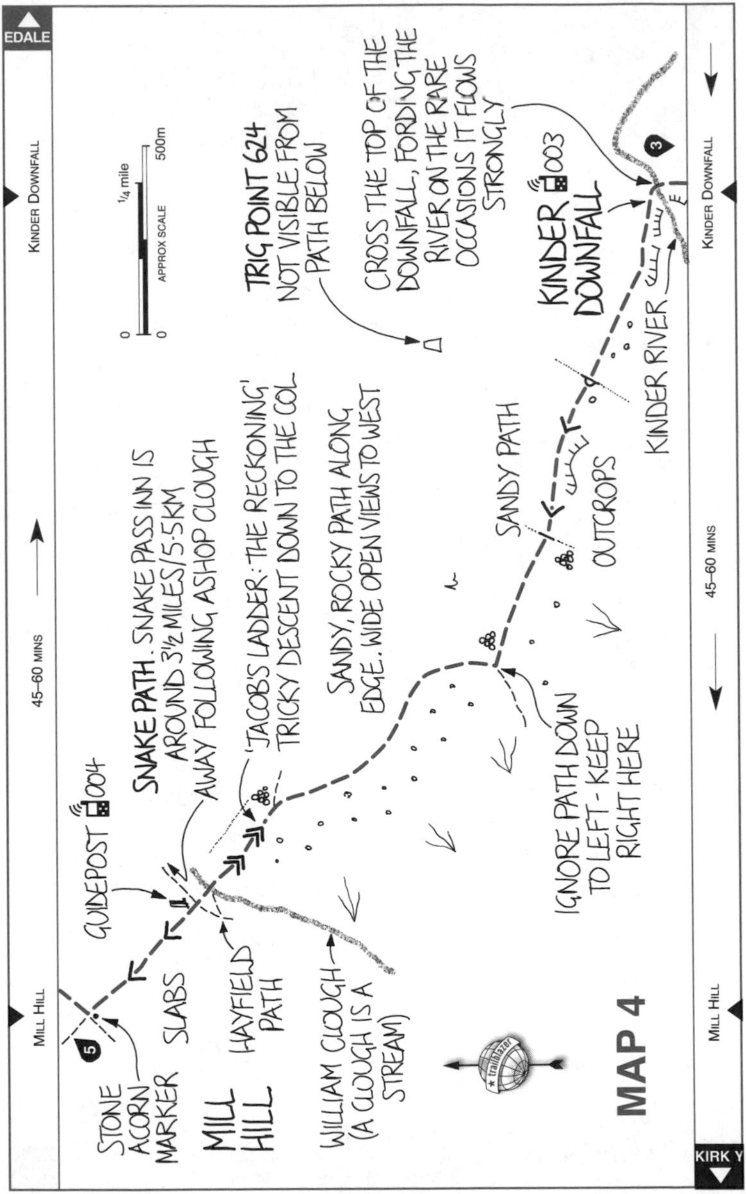

ROUTE GUIDE AND MAPS

EDALE ▲

◀ Kinder Downfall

¼ mile

500m

APPROX SCALE

0

0

TRIG POINT 624
NOT VISIBLE FROM
PATH BELOW

△

CROSS THE TOP OF THE
DOWNFALL, FORDING THE
RIVER ON THE RARE
OCCASIONS IT FLOWS
STRONGLY

KINDER 📷 003
DOWNFALL

KINDER RIVER

◀ Kinder Downfall

❸

45–60 MINS

SNAKE PATH. SNAKE PASS INN IS
AROUND 3½ MILES/5·5KM
AWAY FOLLOWING ASHOP CLOUGH

'JACOB'S LADDER: THE RECKONING'
TRICKY DESCENT DOWN TO THE COL

SANDY, ROCKY PATH ALONG
EDGE. WIDE OPEN VIEWS TO WEST

SANDY PATH

OUTCROPS

GUIDEPOST 📷 004

45–60 MINS

IGNORE PATH DOWN
TO LEFT - KEEP
RIGHT HERE

◀ Mill Hill

STONE
ACORN
MARKER

MILL
HILL

HAYFIELD
PATH

WILLIAM CLOUGH
(A CLOUGH IS A
STREAM)

SLABS

❺

MAP 4

KIRK Y ▼

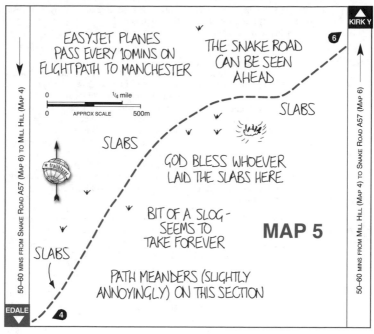

EASYJET PLANES PASS EVERY 10MINS ON FLIGHTPATH TO MANCHESTER

THE SNAKE ROAD CAN BE SEEN AHEAD

6

KIRK Y

0   ¼ mile

0   APPROX SCALE   500m

SLABS

SLABS

GOD BLESS WHOEVER LAID THE SLABS HERE

BIT OF A SLOG - SEEMS TO TAKE FOREVER

MAP 5

SLABS

PATH MEANDERS (SLIGHTLY ANNOYINGLY) ON THIS SECTION

50-60 MINS FROM SNAKE ROAD A57 (MAP 6) TO MILL HILL (MAP 4)

50-60 MINS FROM MILL HILL (MAP 4) TO SNAKE ROAD A57 (MAP 6)

EDALE

4

ROUTE GUIDE AND MAPS

Torside Clough, you need to scramble up the steep slope on the other side of the junction of rivers. There is a path, but it's not obvious until you look for it. At the top of the scramble there's an acorn post to prove you're still on the path.

PADFIELD [off Map 9, p97]

Padfield is about 2½ miles west of the Way at Torside, adjacent to Hadfield, better known to many as the fictional 'Royston Vasey' from the 1990s TV series *League of Gentlemen*; not a distinction most 'local people' would cherish in reality. The nicest way to get here from the Pennine Way is along the Longdendale Trail from Torside Reservoir. Neighbouring Hadfield has a **railway station** with a frequent service to Manchester Piccadilly operated by Northern Rail (see box p59).

Windy Harbour (☎ 01457-853107, 🖥 windyharbour.co.uk; 5D/1T, all en suite; Ⓛ ; 🐾) is two miles along the B6105 en route to Padfield, but if you call or book ahead they'll come and pick you up where the

Way meets the B6105. For **B&B** they charge £85 for a double (no single rates) but note that it's a popular wedding venue so is often busy on weekends. **Food** is offered (Tue-Sat noon-8pm, Sun noon-4pm), with main courses between £13 and £20, or take a 10-minute walk to the Peels Arms.

A little further west is *White House Farm* (☎ 01457-854695, 🖥 thepennineway .co.uk/whitehousefarm; 2T en suite/1D private bathroom; 🛶; Ⓛ; 🐾) with B&B for S/D £50/80. Owner Sheila offers a free lift to/from Torside.

Just across the road, the *Peels Arms* (☎ 01457-852719, **fb**; 🐾 back bar only), Temple St, is the best place for a meal (**food**

Mon-Fri noon-2.30pm & 5-9pm, Sat noon-9pm, Sun noon-8pm). There are good homemade pies (main courses £14-16), mid-week food specials, Wainwright beer and a garden.

CROWDEN   [Map 9, p97]

For some years Crowden was synonymous with the YHA hostel but the site is now an Outdoor Education Centre

The only option for a night here is **camping** at *Crowden Camping and Caravanning Club Site* (☎ 01457-866057, 🖥 campingandcaravanningclub.co.uk; 45 pitches; 🐾; late Mar/early Apr to early Nov), on Woodhead Rd, with good facilities including a **shop** (9am-11am, 1-6pm), showers, laundry facilities and a drying room. Online rates start at £19.20 for non-members but walk-in Pennine Way hikers are charged £10-12.50 (cash only); if you book online at the higher rate they will refund you when you arrive. Those arriving on foot will always be accommodated; find a spot between the pods or along the side wall. They also have three carpeted camping **pods** (£35-50, min 2 nights), with electricity but no beds; PW walkers can often get these for £30 (no minimum stay) on arrival, if they are available.

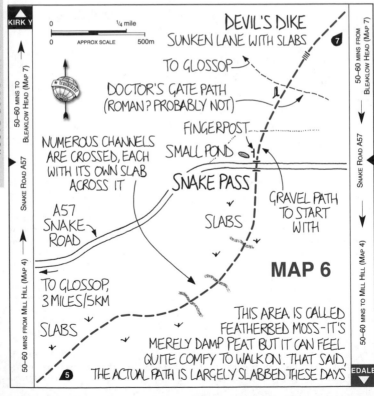

KIRK Y

50-60 MINS TO BLEAKLOW HEAD (MAP 7)

SNAKE ROAD A57

50-60 MINS FROM MILL HILL (MAP 4)

50-60 MINS FROM BLEAKLOW HEAD (MAP 7)

SNAKE ROAD A57

50-60 MINS TO MILL HILL (MAP 4)

EDALE

0   ¼ mile
0   APPROX SCALE   500m

★ trailblazer

DEVIL'S DIKE
SUNKEN LANE WITH SLABS   7

TO GLOSSOP

DOCTOR'S GATE PATH
(ROMAN? PROBABLY NOT)

FINGERPOST

NUMEROUS CHANNELS
ARE CROSSED, EACH
WITH ITS OWN SLAB
ACROSS IT

SMALL POND

SNAKE PASS

A57
SNAKE
ROAD

SLABS

GRAVEL PATH
TO START
WITH

TO GLOSSOP,
3 MILES/5KM

MAP 6

SLABS

THIS AREA IS CALLED
FEATHERBED MOSS - IT'S
MERELY DAMP PEAT BUT IT CAN FEEL
QUITE COMFY TO WALK ON. THAT SAID,
THE ACTUAL PATH IS LARGELY SLABBED THESE DAYS

5

ROUTE GUIDE AND MAPS

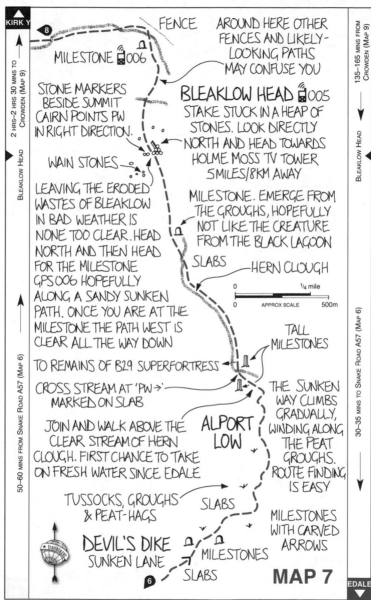

KIRK Y

8

FENCE

AROUND HERE OTHER FENCES AND LIKELY-LOOKING PATHS MAY CONFUSE YOU

MILESTONE 📱006

STONE MARKERS BESIDE SUMMIT CAIRN POINTS PW IN RIGHT DIRECTION.

BLEAKLOW HEAD 📱005
STAKE STUCK IN A HEAP OF STONES. LOOK DIRECTLY NORTH AND HEAD TOWARDS HOLME MOSS TV TOWER 5 MILES/8KM AWAY

WAIN STONES

LEAVING THE ERODED WASTES OF BLEAKLOW IN BAD WEATHER IS NONE TOO CLEAR. HEAD NORTH AND THEN HEAD FOR THE MILESTONE GPS 006 HOPEFULLY ALONG A SANDY SUNKEN PATH. ONCE YOU ARE AT THE MILESTONE THE PATH WEST IS CLEAR ALL THE WAY DOWN TO REMAINS OF B29 SUPERFORTRESS

MILESTONE. EMERGE FROM THE GROUGHS, HOPEFULLY NOT LIKE THE CREATURE FROM THE BLACK LAGOON

SLABS

HERN CLOUGH

0 .... ¼ mile
0 .... 500m
APPROX SCALE

TALL MILESTONES

CROSS STREAM AT 'PW→' MARKED ON SLAB

JOIN AND WALK ABOVE THE CLEAR STREAM OF HERN CLOUGH. FIRST CHANCE TO TAKE ON FRESH WATER SINCE EDALE

ALPORT LOW

THE SUNKEN WAY CLIMBS GRADUALLY, WINDING ALONG THE PEAT GROUGHS. ROUTE FINDING IS EASY

TUSSOCKS, GROUGHS & PEAT-HAGS

SLABS

DEVIL'S DIKE
SUNKEN LANE

MILESTONES

6

SLABS

MILESTONES WITH CARVED ARROWS

MAP 7

trailblazer

2 HRS–2 HRS 30 MINS TO CROWDEN (MAP 9)

BLEAKLOW HEAD

50–60 MINS FROM SNAKE ROAD A57 (MAP 6)

135–165 MINS FROM CROWDEN (MAP 9)

BLEAKLOW HEAD

30–35 MINS TO SNAKE ROAD A57 (MAP 6)

ROUTE GUIDE AND MAPS

EDALE

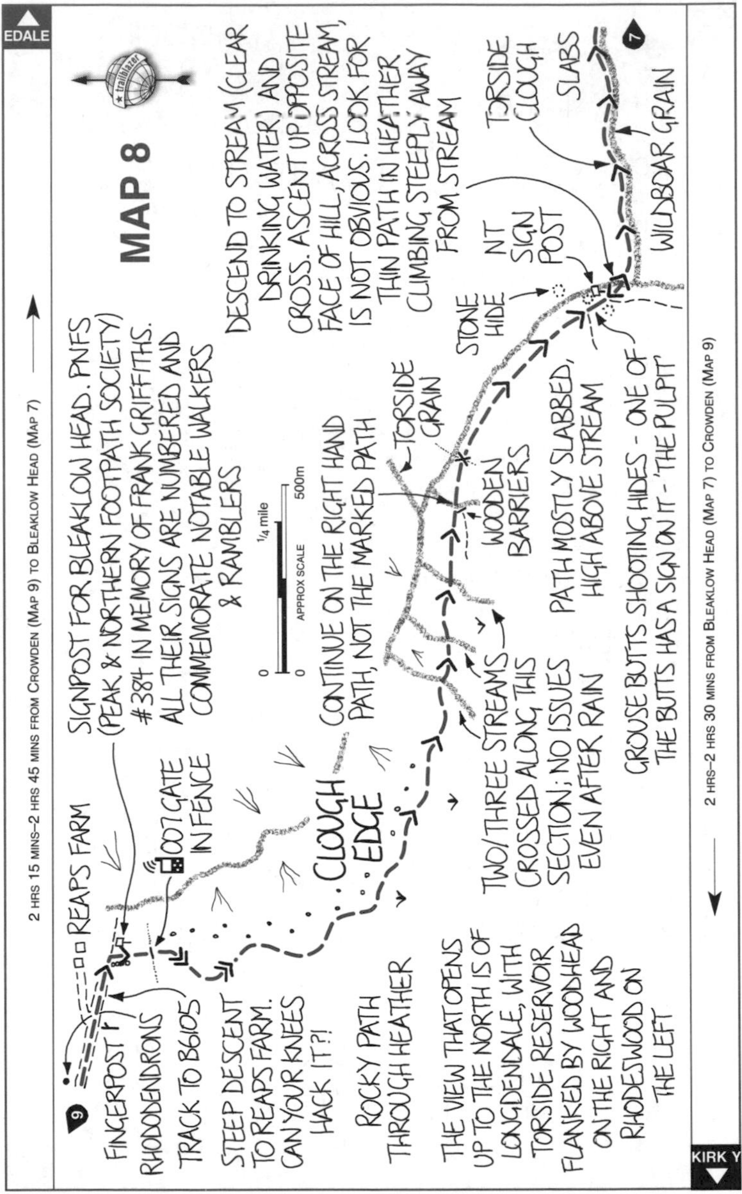

EDALE

MAP 8

2 HRS 15 MINS–2 HRS 45 MINS FROM CROWDEN (MAP 9) TO BLEAKLOW HEAD (MAP 7)

SIGNPOST FOR BLEAKLOW HEAD. PNFS (PEAK & NORTHERN FOOTPATH SOCIETY) #384 IN MEMORY OF FRANK GRIFFITHS. ALL THEIR SIGNS ARE NUMBERED AND COMMEMORATE NOTABLE WALKERS & RAMBLERS

DESCEND TO STREAM (CLEAR DRINKING WATER) AND CROSS. ASCENT UP OPPOSITE FACE OF HILL, ACROSS STREAM, IS NOT OBVIOUS. LOOK FOR THIN PATH IN HEATHER CLIMBING STEEPLY AWAY FROM STREAM

REAPS FARM

DON'T GATE IN FENCE

CONTINUE ON THE RIGHT HAND PATH, NOT THE MARKED PATH

TORSIDE GRAIN

STONE HIDE

NT SIGN POST

TORSIDE CLOUGH

SLABS

WILDBOAR GRAIN

7

0   ¼ mile

0   APPROX SCALE   500m

CLOUGH EDGE

TWO/THREE STREAMS CROSSED ALONG THIS SECTION; NO ISSUES EVEN AFTER RAIN

WOODEN BARRIERS

PATH MOSTLY SLABBED, HIGH ABOVE STREAM

GROUSE BUTTS SHOOTING HIDES - ONE OF THE BUTTS HAS A SIGN ON IT - 'THE PULPIT'

FINGERPOST & RHODODENDRONS TRACK TO B6105

STEEP DESCENT TO REAPS FARM. CAN YOUR KNEES HACK IT?!

ROCKY PATH THROUGH HEATHER

THE VIEW THAT OPENS UP TO THE NORTH IS OF LONGDENDALE, WITH TORSIDE RESERVOIR FLANKED BY WOODHEAD ON THE RIGHT AND RHODESWOOD ON THE LEFT

9

2 HRS–2 HRS 30 MINS FROM BLEAKLOW HEAD (MAP 7) TO CROWDEN (MAP 9)

KIRK Y

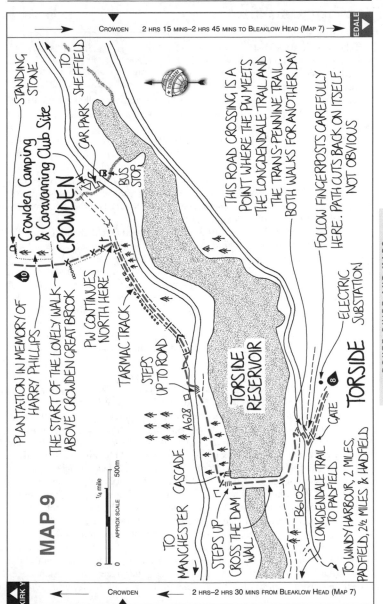

CROWDEN   2 HRS 15 MINS–2 HRS 45 MINS TO BLEAKLOW HEAD (MAP 7) →

EDALE ▶

STANDING STONE

TO SHEFFIELD

CAR PARK

Crowden Camping & Caravanning Club Site

THIS ROAD CROSSING IS A POINT WHERE THE PW MEETS THE LONGDENDALE TRAIL AND THE TRANS-PENNINE TRAIL. BOTH WALKS FOR ANOTHER DAY

BUS STOP

CROWDEN

FOLLOW FINGERPOSTS CAREFULLY HERE. PATH CUTS BACK ON ITSELF. NOT OBVIOUS

PLANTATION IN MEMORY OF HARRY PHILLIPS

THE START OF THE LONELY WALK ABOVE CROWDEN GREAT BROOK

PW CONTINUES NORTH HERE

TARMAC TRACK

STEPS UP TO ROAD

ELECTRIC SUBSTATION

TORSIDE RESERVOIR

TORSIDE

MAP 9

¼ mile

500m

APPROX SCALE

0

0

CASCADE

A628

TO MANCHESTER

STEPS UP

CROSS THE DAM WALL

GATE

B6105

LONGDENDALE TRAIL TO PADFIELD

TO WINDY HARBOUR, 2 MILES, PADFIELD, 2½ MILES & HADFIELD

ROUTE GUIDE AND MAPS

KIRK Y

CROWDEN TO STANDEDGE

MAPS 9-15

Route overview

Another classic Peak District walk awaits, with a mixture of remote moorland and reservoir access roads, wide views and plenty of hills. There is a similar amount

Distance	11 miles (17.5km)
Ascent	2300ft (701m)
Time	5-6¼ hours

of height gain as yesterday, so this stage is no pushover. You'll also have to factor in how you'll get to your accommodation at Marsden or Diggle, which could add on another 1½ miles by foot.

The day starts with a series of short climbs taking you away from Torside and up to the gritstone outcrops of **Laddow Rocks** (Map 10). Almost half the day's total ascent is in these first three miles or so, but the height gain pays dividends, weather permitting, with outstanding views all around. This is the most scenic section of today's walk so be sure to soak up the views. Keep one eye on the path though, for it is one of the only exposed stretches on the Pennine Way, with a sharp drop off down to your right.

This high-level path soon drops to meet **Crowden Great Brook** (Maps 10-11), where wild campers will find an excellent wide flat pitch, before a long, gentle climb (on slabs now), up to the recently transformed **Black Hill** (Map 12). No longer a barren, black wasteland of peat bog, it is now green and lush thanks to much replanting and sheep control. Dropping down from Black Hill you may see the spire of Emley Moor Mast on the far horizon (see box on p100) and the much closer Holme Moss Mast across the moor, before meeting the A635; if you've arrived on a weekend morning there may even be a van doing a roaring trade in bacon butties and tea. Sit with your back to the road and admire the hills behind, because ahead the Way follows a series of access roads, linking together a string of reservoirs.

Although not completely devoid of scenic value this man-made landscape feels harsh in comparison to the natural, remote beauty of Kinder and Bleaklow. Once you pass beyond **Wessenden Head**, and the **Wessenden reservoirs** (Map 13) you at least return to moorland. The walking is not too strenuous, though the midges can be relentless near the reservoirs in high summer. The reservoirs were built in 1877 and 1836, respectively, to supply water for the mills and then the towns downstream. A lovely track takes you between **Swellands** and **Black Moss reservoirs** (Map 14) and down to **Redbrook reservoir** (Map 15) and the goal for the day, the **Standedge Cutting** at Brun Clough Reservoir car park on the A62.

About 150m directly beneath you at this point are the four **Standedge Tunnels**, three rail tunnels and a canal tunnel (built 1811) that is simultaneously the highest, deepest and longest canal tunnel in Britain. The tunnel reopened in 2001 and visitors can join a weekend sightseeing boat tour (Fri & Sat, tickets £8) into the tunnel, or even navigate their own narrowboat through the three-mile long tunnel (3 hours) between Marsden and Diggle. Contact the **Standedge Visitor Centre** (🖳 canalrivertrust.org.uk/places-to-visit/standedge-tunnel-and-visitor-centre) outside Marsden for details. [cont'd on p103]

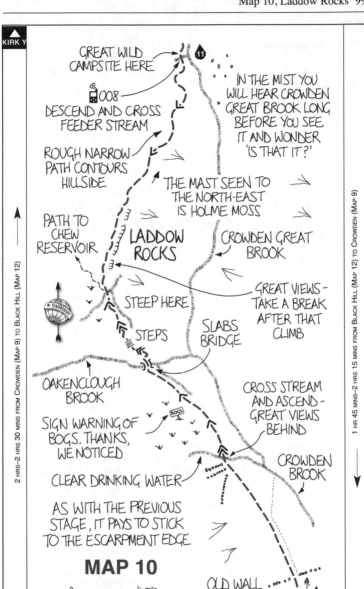

GREAT WILD CAMPSITE HERE

📱008
DESCEND AND CROSS FEEDER STREAM

ROUGH NARROW PATH CONTOURS HILLSIDE

IN THE MIST YOU WILL HEAR CROWDEN GREAT BROOK LONG BEFORE YOU SEE IT AND WONDER 'IS THAT IT?'

THE MAST SEEN TO THE NORTH-EAST IS HOLME MOSS

PATH TO CHEW RESERVOIR

LADDOW ROCKS

CROWDEN GREAT BROOK

GREAT VIEWS - TAKE A BREAK AFTER THAT CLIMB

STEEP HERE

STEPS

SLABS BRIDGE

OAKENCLOUGH BROOK

CROSS STREAM AND ASCEND - GREAT VIEWS BEHIND

SIGN WARNING OF BOGS. THANKS, WE NOTICED

BOGS

CLEAR DRINKING WATER

CROWDEN BROOK

AS WITH THE PREVIOUS STAGE, IT PAYS TO STICK TO THE ESCARPMENT EDGE

MAP 10

0   ¼ mile
0   APPROX SCALE   500m

OLD WALL

9

KIRK Y

EDALE

ROUTE GUIDE AND MAPS

KIRK Y

0 ¼ mile

0 APPROX SCALE 500m

CROSS STREAM AND THEN STILE IN FENCE

009

12

SLABS START HERE. SHORT BREAK AT ONE POINT BUT THEY CONTINUE TO CAIRN AT TOP RIGHT OF THIS MAP

SLABS ON ASCENT OF BLACK HILL MAKE FOR EASY NAVIGATION

trailblazer

MEADOWGRAIN CLOUGH

HEREABOUTS CROWDEN LOSES THE DRAMA OF THE PRECEDING VALLEY

STEEP SHALE ASCENT

CROWDEN GREAT BROOK

IN DRY CONDITIONS THE PATH CUTS ACROSS THE SMALL MEANDER. IF IT'S IN FLOOD SCRAMBLE UP THE SHALEY ASCENT ON THE WEST SIDE, CROSS THE HILL OVERLOOKING THE MEANDER AND DROP BACK DOWN INTO THE BOG

CROSS STREAMS

PATH FOLLOWS STREAM HERE

10 BROAD WITH POOLS AT INTERVALS

MAP 11

2 HRS–2 HRS 30 MINS FROM CROWDEN (MAP 9) TO BLACK HILL (MAP 12)

1 HRS 45 MINS–2 HRS 15 MINS FROM BLACK HILL (MAP 12) TO CROWDEN (MAP 9)

EDALE

❏ EMLEY MOOR TRANSMITTER MAST [off Map 12]

At 1084ft (330m), Emley Moor Mast is the tallest free-standing structure in the UK and can be seen clearly for much of the second day along the Pennine Way, assuming the mist isn't down! As you stand on the summit of Black Hill the beautifully tapered concrete structure is over 10 miles distant; because of its 'significant architectural or historic interest' it was granted Grade II Listed status in 2003. The mast transmits radio and TV signals to millions of people across the north of England.

On the bitterly cold and windy evening of 19th March 1969 there was a build-up of ice and snow on top of the cylindrical steel tower that stood there at the time. This caused the guide wires to fail and the structure buckled and collapsed, partially destroying the nearby Emley Moor Methodist Chapel and missing the local school bus by just a few minutes. Miraculously no-one was seriously injured. A temporary mast was quickly raised and the tower seen today was built over the next couple of years, this time from concrete instead of steel. At the time of research a new but temporary 317m tall mast was under construction next to the Emley mast, to be used to transmit signals while modifications are made to the original mast.

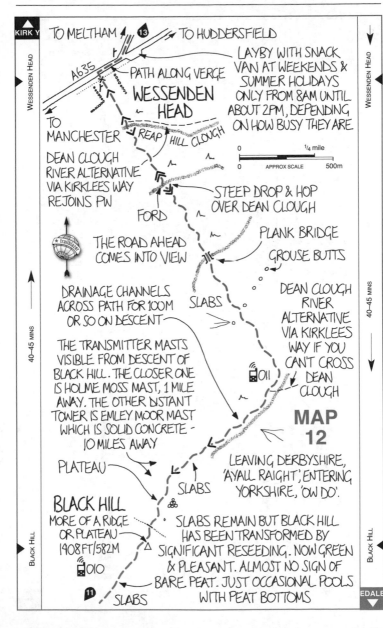

KIRK Y

WESSENDEN HEAD

TO MELTHAM **13** TO HUDDERSFIELD

A635

PATH ALONG VERGE

WESSENDEN HEAD

LAYBY WITH SNACK VAN AT WEEKENDS & SUMMER HOLIDAYS ONLY FROM 8AM UNTIL ABOUT 2PM, DEPENDING ON HOW BUSY THEY ARE

TO MANCHESTER

REAP HILL CLOUGH

DEAN CLOUGH RIVER ALTERNATIVE VIA KIRKLEES WAY REJOINS PW

0   ¼ mile
0   APPROX SCALE   500m

STEEP DROP & HOP OVER DEAN CLOUGH

FORD

THE ROAD AHEAD COMES INTO VIEW

PLANK BRIDGE

GROUSE BUTTS

★ trailblazer

DRAINAGE CHANNELS ACROSS PATH FOR 100M OR SO ON DESCENT

SLABS

DEAN CLOUGH RIVER ALTERNATIVE VIA KIRKLEES WAY IF YOU CAN'T CROSS DEAN CLOUGH

THE TRANSMITTER MASTS VISIBLE FROM DESCENT OF BLACK HILL. THE CLOSER ONE IS HOLME MOSS MAST, 1 MILE AWAY. THE OTHER DISTANT TOWER IS EMLEY MOOR MAST WHICH IS SOLID CONCRETE – 10 MILES AWAY

011

MAP 12

PLATEAU

SLABS

LEAVING DERBYSHIRE, 'AYALL RAIGHT', ENTERING YORKSHIRE, 'OW DO'.

BLACK HILL
MORE OF A RIDGE OR PLATEAU
1908FT/582M
010

SLABS REMAIN BUT BLACK HILL HAS BEEN TRANSFORMED BY SIGNIFICANT RESEEDING. NOW GREEN & PLEASANT. ALMOST NO SIGN OF BARE PEAT. JUST OCCASIONAL POOLS WITH PEAT BOTTOMS

11 SLABS

WESSENDEN HEAD

40-45 MINS

40-45 MINS

BLACK HILL

EDALE

ROUTE GUIDE AND MAPS

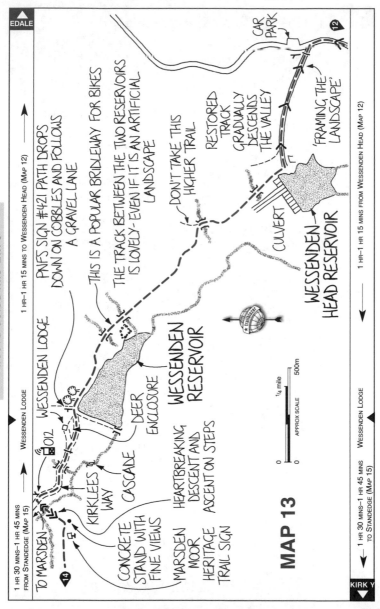

1 HR 30 MINS–1 HR 45 MINS FROM STANDEDGE (MAP 15)

WESSENDEN LODGE

1 HR–1 HR 15 MINS TO WESSENDEN HEAD (MAP 12)

EDALE

PNFS SIGN #421 PATH DROPS DOWN ON COBBLES AND FOLLOWS A GRAVEL LANE

THIS IS A POPULAR BRIDLEWAY FOR BIKES

THE TRACK BETWEEN THE TWO RESERVOIRS IS LOVELY - EVEN IF IT IS AN ARTIFICIAL LANDSCAPE

DON'T TAKE THIS HIGHER TRAIL

RESTORED TRACK GRADUALLY DESCENDS THE VALLEY

CAR PARK

12

'FRAMING THE LANDSCAPE'

WESSENDEN HEAD RESERVOIR

CULVERT

WESSENDEN LODGE

1012

DEER ENCLOSURE

WESSENDEN RESERVOIR

KIRKLEES WAY

CASCADE

HEARTBREAKING DESCENT AND ASCENT ON STEPS

TO MARSDEN

CONCRETE STAND WITH FINE VIEWS

MARSDEN MOOR HERITAGE TRAIL SIGN

14

★ trailblazer

MAP 13

0

0

¼ mile

APPROX SCALE

500m

1 HR 30 MINS–1 HR 45 MINS TO STANDEDGE (MAP 15)

WESSENDEN LODGE

1 HR–1 HR 15 MINS FROM WESSENDEN HEAD (MAP 12)

KIRK Y

[*cont'd from p98*]   Unless you have arranged for a lift from Standedge Cutting you are likely to have to wait for a bus or continue walking until you reach your accommodation for the night. If you get a phone signal at Brun Clough then check ⌨ www.tfgm.com for live information on the next bus departure to either Diggle or Marsden. Alternatively a footpath leads to Diggle from Brun Clough via Boat Lane; for Marsden you should branch off the Pennine Way before you hit the A62, at the marker stone by Redbrook Reservoir.

Navigation notes

Thanks to the good path out of Crowden and the judicious use of slabs across the worst sections of bogs, this stage has surprisingly few navigational challenges. The only possible area of confusion may arise if you are forced, by particularly heavy rain, to navigate around the flooded meander of Crowden Great Brook (Map 11). In which case the river should be easy to see and follow until you reach the slabs at GPS 009.

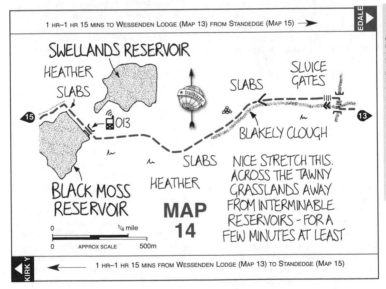

DIGGLE   [Map 15]

On the outskirts of Diggle about 1½ miles south-west of the Pennine Way (all steeply downhill) is *Diggle Hotel* (☎ 01457-872741, **fb**; 2T/1D/1Tr/1Qd, all en suite; Ⓛ), a family-run free house (Mon bar only from 5pm; **food** Tue-Thur noon-8pm, Fri & Sat to 9pm, Sun to 7pm) with several real ales. Look out on the menu for rag pudding

(a local speciality of mince and onions wrapped in suet pastry) with chips, mushy peas & gravy (£10.95). Rooms cost from £75 for a double (no single rates), with full breakfast an extra £10.

Sunfield Accommodation (☎ 01457-874030, ⌨ sunfieldaccom.co.uk; 5D/1T, all en suite; Ⓛ), to the east of Diggle hotel, charges S/D from £55/80 for simple farm-house B&B. They offer a lift back to the trail the next morning and packed lunches if requested at the time of booking.

First's No 184 **bus** (see p56) runs to Diggle from Brun Clough. Take the bus back to the Way (or on to Marsden) the next morning.

MARSDEN   [off Map 15]

If you prefer to go to Marsden where there are more services, short of waiting for First's hourly No 184 bus service (see p56) at Brun Clough Reservoir, the quickest way (2 miles) is to take the Standedge Trail east-wards from the southern end of Redbrook Reservoir (Map 15). It's also possible to walk to Marsden from Wessenden Reservoir (Map 13), via Blakely and Butterfly reservoirs (also 2 miles).

Marsden has a Co-op **supermarket** (daily 7am-11pm) with an **ATM**, the Village Green (🖵 tvgmarsden.co.uk, Mon-Sat 9am-5.30pm) community-owned **gro-cery**, a Boots **pharmacy** (Mon-Fri 9am-6pm, Sat 9am-1pm), some B&B accommo-dation, some cafés and a couple of pubs and restaurants. All the services are within five minutes of the **railway station** and First's **bus** service No 184; see p56.

At the end of Manchester Rd, the main street leading away from the station, but close to the town's facilities, is *The New Inn* (☎ 01484-841917, 🖵 newinnmarsden .co.uk, **fb**; 3D/1Tr, all en suite; 🛁; ⓛ; 🐕), a former coaching inn; rooms cost £75-89 for a double (sgl occ £55-69), plus £5pp for a full breakfast. Pub **food** is served Mon-Thur 5-8pm, Fri & Sat noon-8pm, Sun noon-7pm. Rooms are above the pub, so karaoke nights every other Saturday might make things noisy until closing.

Olive Branch Inn (☎ 01484-844487, 🖵 olivebranch.uk.com, **fb**), on the main Manchester Rd, one mile northeast of town, has a mouthwatering menu (**food** served

Tue-Thur 6.30-9pm, Fri 6.30-9.30pm, Sat 1-9.30pm, Sun 1-8pm) of top-notch French-inspired seafood, game and poultry; ask if they are offering their fixed price menu. **B&B** (3D, all en suite; 🛁) costs S/D £90/130; they also do a dinner, bed & breakfast deal (£210 for two) with good Sunday and Thursday discounts – see the website for details.

Crumbals on the Corner (**fb**; Wed-Sat 8.30am-4pm, Sun 9am-4pm) is a warm and cosy café that serves great coffee, cakes, all-day breakfasts, and paninis (£6).

Marsden Fisheries (☎ 01484-520483, Wed-Fri 11.30am-2pm & 4.30-8pm, Sat 11.30am-7pm) offers excellent fish and chips (£6.50) to take away.

Riverhead Brewery Tap (☎ 01484-844324, 🖵 theriverheadmarsden.co.uk, **fb**) is the best place for a pint, pouring ten real ales, some brewed in house (and named after the region's reservoirs), and offering delightful riverside seating. **Food** (Wed-Thur 4-9pm, Fri & Sat noon-9pm, Sun noon-4pm) here is limited to Chinese *baozi* dumplings, loaded fries and desserts.

Arcade (☎ 01484-442409, **fb**; open Tue-Sun 10am-late, except Wed from noon) is Marsden's hippest drinking venue, a blend of craft beer taproom and café, decked out in black industrial beams and with a bright interior riverside seating area. They offer a daily brunch menu until 3pm, as well as weekend burgers (Thur-Sat 5-8.30pm), otherwise it's good for beer or coffee.

SYMBOLS USED IN TEXT

🛁 Bathtub in, or for, at least one room; WI-FI is available at most places but see p82
ⓛ packed lunch available if requested in advance
🐕 Dogs allowed subject to prior arrangement (see p32)
fb signifies places that have a Facebook page (for latest opening hours)

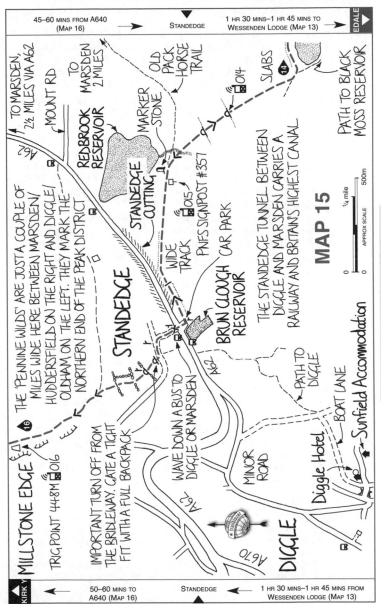

TO MARSDEN, 2½ MILES VIA A62

MOUNT RD

TO MARSDEN 2 MILES

OLD PACK HORSE TRAIL

REDBROOK RESERVOIR

MARKER STONE

SLABS

14

014

PATH TO BLACK MOSS RESERVOIR

A62

STANDEDGE CUTTING

PNFS SIGNPOST #357

015

MAP 15

THE STANDEDGE TUNNEL BETWEEN DIGGLE AND MARSDEN CARRIES A RAILWAY AND BRITAIN'S HIGHEST CANAL

0   ¼ mile
0   APPROX SCALE   500m

WIDE TRACK

BRUN CLOUGH RESERVOIR

CAR PARK

A62

THE 'PENNINE WILDS' ARE JUST A COUPLE OF MILES WIDE HERE BETWEEN MARSDEN/ HUDDERSFIELD ON THE RIGHT AND DIGGLE/ OLDHAM ON THE LEFT. THEY MARK THE NORTHERN END OF THE PEAK DISTRICT

STANDEDGE

PATH TO DIGGLE

WAVE DOWN A BUS TO DIGGLE OR MARSDEN

IMPORTANT TURN OFF FROM THE BRIDLEWAY. GATE A TIGHT FIT WITH A FULL BACKPACK

16

MILLSTONE EDGE

TRIG POINT 448M   016

MINOR ROAD

Diggle Hotel

A62

A670

BOAT LANE

Sunfield Accommodation

DIGGLE

ROUTE GUIDE AND MAPS

STANDEDGE TO CALDER VALLEY   MAPS 15-22
Route overview

This section is punctuated by road cross-
ings and trig points – four of the former
and three of the latter – with a huge monolith of a monument at Stoodley Pike to

Distance	14½ miles (23.5km)
Ascent	1400ft (426m)
Time	5¾-7½ hours

round off the day. The path almost completely loses the sense of remoteness
you'll have been experiencing so far and the conurbations of Lancashire and
Yorkshire squeeze the Pennine Way into a narrow corridor, almost smothering
it in the process. The walk planners have done all they can to avoid urban walking, however, so this day still retains some scenic highpoints.

   Millstone Edge (Map 15) is the first of several gritstone edges you'll need
to traverse. The Pennine Way is joined for a while by the Oldham Way (Map
16) before they part company and you reach the **A640 road** (Map 16) between
Huddersfield and Oldham/Manchester.

   The high, airy path across **White Hill** (Map 17) with its trig point is soon
interrupted by the A672, where you can restore yourself with a cup of tea and a
bacon roll (£3.50), full breakfast (£3.50-7.50) or a lunch sandwich at the white
shipping container of *Nicky's Foodbar* (see Map 17; **fb**; Tue-Fri 9am-4pm, Sat
& Sun 10am-4pm). You can also fill up your water bottle here, use the bathroom
and invest in a muffin the size of your fist for the walk ahead.

   The nearby **Windy Hill radio tower** has an interesting history, built in the
1950s as part of a secret microwave relay link to maintain communications in
case of nuclear war with the USSR. Almost immediately beyond the tower is
the soaring arch of the bridge across the **M62 Trans-Pennine Motorway**. The
65ft (20m) high bridge is perhaps the most impressive motorway crossing of
any footpath in the country. Thank the foresight of Ernest Marples, the
Transport Minister at the time and a keen walker, for its existence.

   The crossing of the peaty expanse of **Redmires** (Map 18) has been tamed
by the slabs and the climb up to the gritstone splendour of **Blackstone Edge** and
its trig point is now much easier. The modern concrete guide marker stands in
stark contrast to the ancient **Aiggin Stone** just beyond, which has been guiding
travellers for over 600 years. The road you join for a few short yards is thought
to be even older, possibly even as old as the Romans.

   The White House (Map 19) marks the end of the moorland scenery. It's rare
that a pub pops up so opportunely so make the most of this former packhorse

---

❏ PEAK & NORTHERN FOOTPATH SOCIETY (PNFS)
The PNFS (🖥 peakandnorthern.org.uk) has been providing informative, durable and,
many people would say, beautiful signposts for walkers for over a hundred years. In
addition, the charitable organisation has installed a number of toposcopes and erected several bridges to help walkers across rivers and streams. Their distinctive square,
green, metal-plate signs can be found at various points along the Pennine Way. There
are seven PNFS signs on the Pennine Way path – see how many you can spot!

inn. **Wild campers** will find a doable pitch in the disused quarry just before the pub and another better location, about a mile beyond it, in Cow's Mouth quarry on Light Hazzles Edge (Map 19). Carved on the cliffs here is the Simon Armitage poem 'Rain' (see box p108).

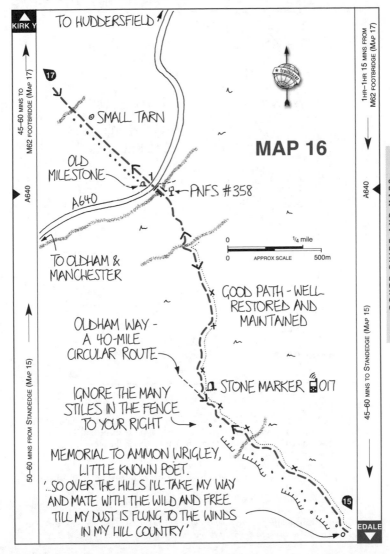

KIRK Y

TO HUDDERSFIELD

45–60 MINS TO M62 FOOTBRIDGE (MAP 17)

A640

17

SMALL TARN

OLD MILESTONE

A640

PNFS #358

TO OLDHAM & MANCHESTER

MAP 16

1HR–1HR 15 MINS FROM M62 FOOTBRIDGE (MAP 17)

A640

0   ¼ mile

0   APPROX SCALE   500m

GOOD PATH - WELL RESTORED AND MAINTAINED

OLDHAM WAY - A 40-MILE CIRCULAR ROUTE

STONE MARKER 017

45–60 MINS TO STANDEDGE (MAP 15)

IGNORE THE MANY STILES IN THE FENCE TO YOUR RIGHT

50–60 MINS FROM STANDEDGE (MAP 15)

MEMORIAL TO AMMON WRIGLEY, LITTLE KNOWN POET.
'..SO OVER THE HILLS I'LL TAKE MY WAY
AND MATE WITH THE WILD AND FREE
TILL MY DUST IS FLUNG TO THE WINDS
IN MY HILL COUNTRY'

15

EDALE

ROUTE GUIDE AND MAPS

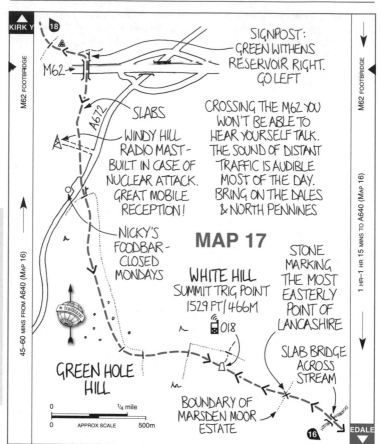

KIRK Y
18
M62 →
A672
SLABS

SIGNPOST:
GREEN WITHENS
RESERVOIR RIGHT.
GO LEFT

CROSSING THE M62 YOU
WON'T BE ABLE TO
HEAR YOURSELF TALK.
THE SOUND OF DISTANT
TRAFFIC IS AUDIBLE
MOST OF THE DAY.
BRING ON THE DALES
& NORTH PENNINES

WINDY HILL
RADIO MAST-
BUILT IN CASE OF
NUCLEAR ATTACK.
GREAT MOBILE
RECEPTION!

NICKY'S
FOODBAR-
CLOSED
MONDAYS

MAP 17

WHITE HILL
SUMMIT TRIG POINT
1529 FT / 466M
018

STONE
MARKING
THE MOST
EASTERLY
POINT OF
LANCASHIRE

SLAB BRIDGE
ACROSS
STREAM

GREEN HOLE
HILL

BOUNDARY OF
MARSDEN MOOR
ESTATE

0   ¼ mile
0   APPROX SCALE   500m

trailblazer

16
EDALE

M62 FOOTBRIDGE

M62 FOOTBRIDGE

45-60 MINS FROM A640 (MAP 16)

1 HR-1 HR 15 MINS TO A640 (MAP 16)

ROUTE GUIDE AND MAPS

❑ THE RAIN STONE   [Map 19]

Carved on the cliffs at Light Hazzles Edge is *Rain*, one of **Simon Armitage**'s six Stanza Stones poems, 'celebrating the element which gave shape and form to this region, namely water'. See 🖥 stanzastones.co.uk for more on the project.

Be glad of these freshwater tears,
Each pearled droplet some salty old sea-bullet
Air-lifted out of the waves, then laundered and sieved, recast as a soft bead and
returned.
And no matter how much it strafes or sheets, it is no mean feat to catch one rain-
drop clean in the mouth,
To take one drop on the tongue, tasting cloud pollen, grain of the heavens, raw sky.
Let it teem, up here where the front of the mind distils the brunt of the world.

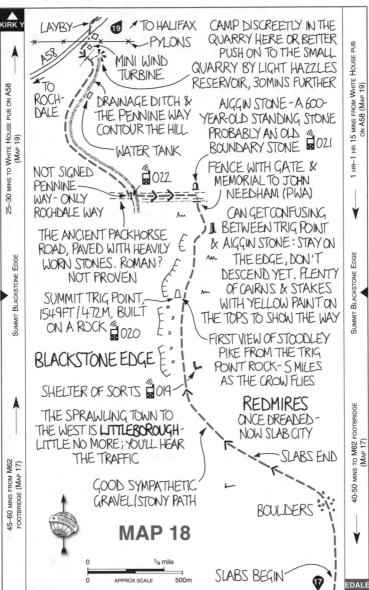

KIRK Y

LAYBY TO HALIFAX
PYLONS
A58
MINI WIND
TURBINE
TO ROCH-DALE
DRAINAGE DITCH &
THE PENNINE WAY
CONTOUR THE HILL
WATER TANK

CAMP DISCREETLY IN THE QUARRY HERE OR BETTER PUSH ON TO THE SMALL QUARRY BY LIGHT HAZZLES RESERVOIR, 30 MINS FURTHER

AIGGIN STONE - A 600-YEAR-OLD STANDING STONE PROBABLY AN OLD BOUNDARY STONE 📱021

FENCE WITH GATE & MEMORIAL TO JOHN NEEDHAM (PWA)

NOT SIGNED PENNINE WAY - ONLY ROCHDALE WAY

📱022

THE ANCIENT PACKHORSE ROAD, PAVED WITH HEAVILY WORN STONES. ROMAN? NOT PROVEN

CAN GET CONFUSING BETWEEN TRIG POINT & AIGGIN STONE: STAY ON THE EDGE, DON'T DESCEND YET. PLENTY OF CAIRNS & STAKES WITH YELLOW PAINT ON THE TOPS TO SHOW THE WAY

SUMMIT TRIG POINT, 1549FT / 472M, BUILT ON A ROCK 📱020

BLACKSTONE EDGE

FIRST VIEW OF STOODLEY PIKE FROM THE TRIG POINT ROCK - 5 MILES AS THE CROW FLIES

SHELTER OF SORTS 📱019

REDMIRES ONCE DREADED - NOW SLAB CITY

THE SPRAWLING TOWN TO THE WEST IS LITTLEBOROUGH - LITTLE NO MORE; YOU'LL HEAR THE TRAFFIC

SLABS END

GOOD SYMPATHETIC GRAVEL/STONY PATH

BOULDERS

MAP 18

0 ————— 1/4 mile
0 ————— 500m
APPROX SCALE

SLABS BEGIN 17

25-30 MINS TO WHITE HOUSE PUB ON A58 (MAP 19)

SUMMIT BLACKSTONE EDGE

45-60 MINS FROM M62 FOOTBRIDGE (MAP 17)

1 HR-1 HR 15 MINS FROM WHITE HOUSE PUB ON A58 (MAP 19)

SUMMIT BLACKSTONE EDGE

40-50 MINS TO M62 FOOTBRIDGE (MAP 17)

ROUTE GUIDE AND MAPS

EDALE

The pretence of remoteness that you may have shrouded yourself in all day is gone, as you walk along a wide gravel track beside three reservoirs. As you round the corner at the end of the last of these, Stoodley Pike comes into view, still some two miles (3km) distant along a fine path over the charming **Coldwell Hill** (Map 20). Before reaching the monument you'll pass **Withen's Gate**, which is the point at which anyone destined for **Mankinholes** (see below) should turn left, or continue on to **Stoodley Pike** (Map 21, see box p114), an impressive stone monolith. The path now drops steadily and steeply in places, from the open moor, through fields to meet a wide farm track. This in turn winds downhill though **Callis Wood** into the **Calder Valley** and towards **Rochdale Canal**.

If your accommodation lies in Hebden Bridge you have another couple of miles as the path turns right along the canal into the town. You can break this canal walk at the *Stubbing Wharf* (see p120) before arriving in the slightly eccentric and wonderfully lively town of **Hebden Bridge** (Map 22a).

Navigation notes

There is little chance of going astray; even in winter-white-out conditions the path is obvious and mostly well signed. Blackstone Edge may be the only exception, but provided you stay high, the cairns and stakes should see you through to Aiggin Stone.

If you are headed into Hebden Bridge or plan to camp at Old Chamber Farm you'll find it easier to branch off the main Pennine Way and follow the **Hebden Bridge Loop** (see p114) into the town.

BLACKSTONE EDGE   [Map 19]

The White House (☎ 01706-378456, 🖳 thewhitehousepub.co.uk; **food** served Mon-Thur noon-2pm & 5.30-8pm, Fri & Sat noon-2pm & 5.30-8.30pm, Sun & bank hols noon-8pm) dates from 1671 and is a serviceable place for a pint or a meal (£12.50-16) – however, note that it is closed most afternoons.

TLC Travel's No 901 **bus** service (see pp54-9) calls by the pub en route between Huddersfield and Hebden Bridge.

MANKINHOLES & LUMBUTTS   [Map 20, p112]

Unless you're content to curl up in a curlew's nest, the only accommodation between Standedge and the Calder Valley is in Mankinholes. It means a diversion down off the route and unless you retrace your steps steeply uphill back to Withen's Gate to rejoin the trail proper, you'll have missed out part of the Pennine Way and the resultant guilt could torment you for eternity.

At the time of research, *YHA Mankinholes* (☎ 0345-371 9751, 🖳 yha .org.uk/hostel/mankinholes; sleeps 32 in 8 rooms; no wi-fi; Mar-early Nov) was only available to groups on an exclusive hire basis so check with them to see if anything has changed. It's in an old manor house.

For food head to *The Top Brink Inn* (☎ 01706-812696, 🖳 topbrink.co.uk, **fb**; 🐾; **food** served Apr-Sep daily noon-9pm, rest of year Mon-Fri noon-2.30pm & 5-9.30pm, Sat, Sun & Bank Holidays noon-9.30pm) in next-door **Lumbutts**. The menu includes mixed grill (£22.95), cumberland sausage & mash (£13.50) and a range of vegetarian dishes.

For **B&B**, try *Two Hoots Cottage Guest House* (off Map 21; ☎ 07792-447356, 🖳 twohootsguesthouse.co.uk; 1D or T private bathroom; 🛏; Ⓛ) on Lee Bottom Rd, about a mile away from (and 200 vertical metres below) Stoodley Pike.

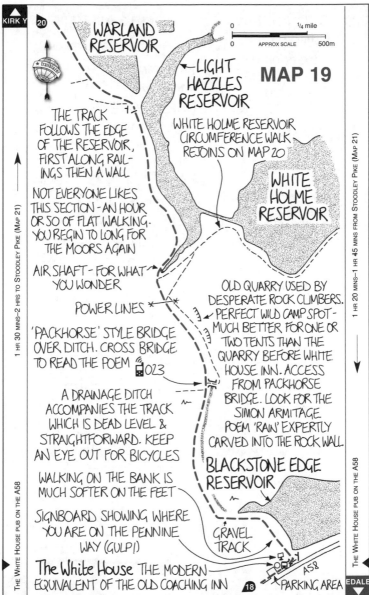

KIRK Y

20

WARLAND RESERVOIR

0   1/4 mile

0   APPROX SCALE   500m

←LIGHT HAZZLES RESERVOIR

MAP 19

WHITE HOLME RESERVOIR CIRCUMFERENCE WALK REJOINS ON MAP 20

WHITE HOLME RESERVOIR

THE TRACK FOLLOWS THE EDGE OF THE RESERVOIR, FIRST ALONG RAIL-INGS THEN A WALL

NOT EVERYONE LIKES THIS SECTION - AN HOUR OR SO OF FLAT WALKING. YOU BEGIN TO LONG FOR THE MOORS AGAIN

AIR SHAFT - FOR WHAT YOU WONDER

POWER LINES

'PACKHORSE' STYLE BRIDGE OVER DITCH. CROSS BRIDGE TO READ THE POEM 📱023

A DRAINAGE DITCH ACCOMPANIES THE TRACK WHICH IS DEAD LEVEL & STRAIGHTFORWARD. KEEP AN EYE OUT FOR BICYCLES

OLD QUARRY USED BY DESPERATE ROCK CLIMBERS. PERFECT WILD CAMP SPOT - MUCH BETTER FOR ONE OR TWO TENTS THAN THE QUARRY BEFORE WHITE HOUSE INN. ACCESS FROM PACKHORSE BRIDGE. LOOK FOR THE SIMON ARMITAGE POEM 'RAIN' EXPERTLY CARVED INTO THE ROCK WALL.

BLACKSTONE EDGE RESERVOIR

WALKING ON THE BANK IS MUCH SOFTER ON THE FEET

SIGNBOARD SHOWING WHERE YOU ARE ON THE PENNINE WAY (GULP!)

The White House THE MODERN EQUIVALENT OF THE OLD COACHING INN

GRAVEL TRACK

A58

18

PARKING AREA

1 HR 30 MINS-2 HRS TO STOODLEY PIKE (MAP 21)

THE WHITE HOUSE pub on the A58

1 HR 20 MINS-1 HR 45 MINS FROM STOODLEY PIKE (MAP 21)

THE WHITE HOUSE pub on the A58

ROUTE GUIDE AND MAPS

EDALE ▼

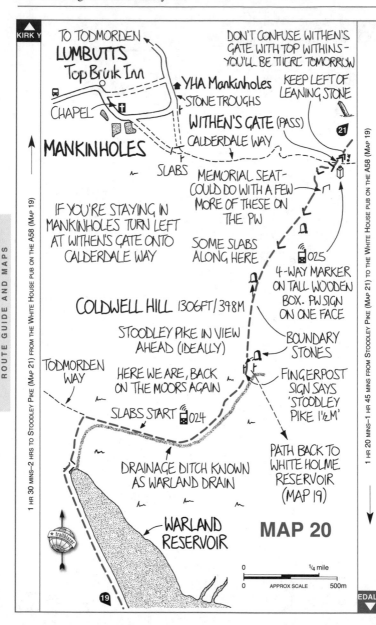

TO TODMORDEN

LUMBUTTS
Top Brink Inn

DON'T CONFUSE WITHEN'S
GATE WITH TOP WITHINS –
YOU'LL BE THERE TOMORROW

CHAPEL

YHA Mankinholes

STONE TROUGHS

KEEP LEFT OF
LEANING STONE

WITHEN'S GATE (PASS)

CALDERDALE WAY

MANKINHOLES

SLABS

MEMORIAL SEAT –
COULD DO WITH A FEW
MORE OF THESE ON
THE PW

IF YOU'RE STAYING IN
MANKINHOLES TURN LEFT
AT WITHEN'S GATE ONTO
CALDERDALE WAY

SOME SLABS
ALONG HERE

025

4-WAY MARKER
ON TALL WOODEN
BOX. PW SIGN
ON ONE FACE

COLDWELL HILL 1306FT / 398M

STOODLEY PIKE IN VIEW
AHEAD (IDEALLY)

BOUNDARY
STONES

TODMORDEN
WAY

HERE WE ARE, BACK
ON THE MOORS AGAIN

FINGERPOST
SIGN SAYS
'STOODLEY
PIKE 1½M'

SLABS START 024

DRAINAGE DITCH KNOWN
AS WARLAND DRAIN

PATH BACK TO
WHITE HOLME
RESERVOIR
(MAP 19)

WARLAND
RESERVOIR

MAP 20

★ trailblazer

0   ¼ mile
0   APPROX SCALE   500m

19

21

1 HR 30 MINS–2 HRS TO STOODLEY PIKE (MAP 21) FROM THE WHITE HOUSE PUB ON THE A58 (MAP 19)

1 HR 20 MINS–1 HR 45 MINS FROM STOODLEY PIKE (MAP 21) TO THE WHITE HOUSE PUB ON THE A58 (MAP 19)

ROUTE GUIDE AND MAPS

KIRK Y

EDALE

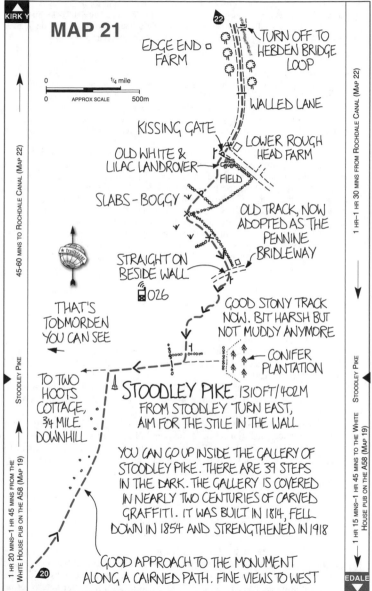

MAP 21

EDGE END FARM

22

TURN OFF TO HEBDEN BRIDGE LOOP

WALLED LANE

0 ... ¼ mile
0 ... 500m
APPROX SCALE

KISSING GATE

OLD WHITE & LILAC LANDROVER

LOWER ROUGH HEAD FARM

FIELD

SLABS - BOGGY

OLD TRACK, NOW ADOPTED AS THE PENNINE BRIDLEWAY

STRAIGHT ON BESIDE WALL
026

GOOD STONY TRACK NOW. BIT HARSH BUT NOT MUDDY ANYMORE

THAT'S TODMORDEN YOU CAN SEE

CONIFER PLANTATION

TO TWO HOOTS COTTAGE, ¾ MILE DOWNHILL

STOODLEY PIKE 1310FT/402M
FROM STOODLEY TURN EAST, AIM FOR THE STILE IN THE WALL

YOU CAN GO UP INSIDE THE GALLERY OF STOODLEY PIKE. THERE ARE 39 STEPS IN THE DARK. THE GALLERY IS COVERED IN NEARLY TWO CENTURIES OF CARVED GRAFFITI. IT WAS BUILT IN 1814, FELL DOWN IN 1854 AND STRENGTHENED IN 1918

GOOD APPROACH TO THE MONUMENT ALONG A CAIRNED PATH. FINE VIEWS TO WEST

20

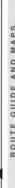

45-60 MINS TO ROCHDALE CANAL (MAP 22)

STOODLEY PIKE

1 HR 20 MINS-1 HR 45 MINS FROM THE WHITE HOUSE PUB ON THE A58 (MAP 19)

1 HR-1 HR 30 MINS FROM ROCHDALE CANAL (MAP 22)

ROUTE GUIDE AND MAPS

STOODLEY PIKE

1 HR 15 MINS-1 HR 45 MINS TO THE WHITE HOUSE PUB ON THE A58 (MAP 19)

EDALE

The smart room costs from £60/95 for S/D occupancy. If requested in advance excellent evening meals are available for around £15 for two courses. Booking is essential, as is tasting one of Patricia's cakes.

TLC Travel's circular T6/T8 **bus** operates every hour or so between Mankinholes and Todmorden; see p59.

❏ **STOODLEY PIKE**   [Map 21, p113]

This needle-shaped monument above the Calder Valley (Calderdale) was erected on a site where there had been an ancient burial cairn, assumed to be that of a chieftain. It seems plausible, the height being a commanding one and the ideal spot to erect a memorial. It was also an ideal site for a beacon since the chain that warned of the approach of the Spanish Armada included Halifax's Beacon Hill and Pendle Hill above Clitheroe, Stoodley being the link between the two.

Be that as it may, in 1814 it was decided to celebrate the defeat of Napoleon by erecting a monument by public subscription. Local bigwigs were quick to put their name down; then as now a chance to appear influential was not to be missed. Unfortunately Napoleon escaped from Elba, raised his armies and overthrew the restored monarchy, cutting short the erection of the monument. After Wellington finally put paid to Napoleon at Waterloo, work began again and it was completed before the end of 1815. Disaster struck in 1854 when the tower collapsed as the country was going to war again, this time in the Crimea, an evil omen indeed. Rebuilt, it has survived to this day although it is said it wobbled a bit on the eve of the Falklands War (1982).

For walkers along the Pennine Way the 120ft (37-metre) high spire is a landmark that beckons from afar. Inside the graffiti-decked gallery you can climb the 39 steps in the dark. Roughly at the 40-mile (60km) mark from Edale, Stoodley Pike marks a change in the countryside. The peat moors are largely behind you and ahead lie more pastoral scenes as the gritstone gives way to limestone.

THE HEBDEN BRIDGE LOOP

If you're visiting Hebden Bridge for any reason (and we strongly advise that you do), you can take a short-cut from the Pennine Way shortly after Edge End Farm (Map 21). This is part of the Hebden Bridge Loop, a walk that was established by the Hebden Bridge Walkers Action to coincide with the 50th anniversary of the Pennine Way. The full loop is 3¾ miles (6km) long and adds an extra 1¼ miles (2km) to the direct route.

To return to the Pennine Way after visiting Hebden Bridge purists will want to retrace their steps back to the point where they left it; but those who are more relaxed about such things can walk along the Rochdale Canal to rejoin the main way at Callis Bridge, or may instead prefer to follow the Loop north from Hebden Bridge and return to the main trail at Hebble Hole, via the rather lovely village of **Heptonstall** (see box p117).

The places where the Loop meets the Pennine Way are marked on maps 21 and 23. You can read more about the Loop (including directions and a map) by visiting 💻 hbwalkersaction.org.uk/pennine-way-loop. There are also several maps posted on the loop at strategic locations.

The Loop Route into Hebden Bridge

From the turnoff to the Hebden Bridge Loop near Edge End Farm (Map 21) the trail descends through woods to cross a stream and then climbs to join the first cobblestoned and then tarmac road at Horsehold. Just after here is a fine

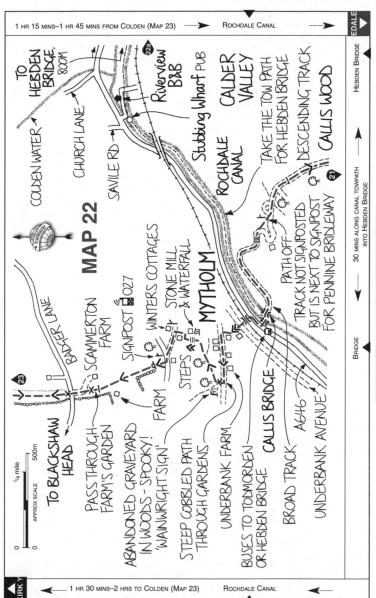

1 HR 15 MINS–1 HR 45 MINS FROM COLDEN (MAP 23) ⟶

ROCHDALE CANAL ⟶

EDALE ▶

HEBDEN BRIDGE

30 MINS ALONG CANAL TOWPATH INTO HEBDEN BRIDGE ⟶

BRIDGE

◀ KIRK Y...

1 HR 30 MINS–2 HRS TO COLDEN (MAP 23) ⟵

ROCHDALE CANAL ⟵

MAP 22

TO HEBDEN BRIDGE, 800M

COLDEN WATER

CHURCH LANE

SAVILE RD

Riverview B&B

22a

Stubbing Wharf PUB

ROCHDALE CANAL

CALDER VALLEY

TAKE THE TOW PATH FOR HEBDEN BRIDGE

DESCENDING TRACK

CALLIS WOOD

21

PATH OFF

TRACK NOT SIGNPOSTED BUT IS NEXT TO SIGNPOST FOR PENNINE BRIDLEWAY

BADGER LANE

TO BLACKSHAW HEAD

23

PASS THROUGH FARM'S GARDEN

SCAMMERTON FARM

SIGNPOST 0027

WINTERS COTTAGES

STONE MILL & WATERFALL

MYTHOLM

FARM

STEPS

ABANDONED GRAVEYARD IN WOODS - SPOOKY! 'WAINWRIGHT SIGN'

STEEP COBBLED PATH THROUGH GARDENS

UNDERBANK FARM

CALLIS BRIDGE

BUSES TO TODMORDEN OR HEBDEN BRIDGE

BROAD TRACK

A646

UNDERBANK AVENUE

¼ mile

0   500m

APPROX SCALE

0

Trailblazer

resting spot beneath a large cross, with views of Mytholm below. From here follow New Road down into Hebden Bridge, or branch off right to follow footpaths to camping at Old Chamber Farm (see opposite).

Hebden Bridge Loop to the Pennine Way

To rejoin the Loop in Hebden Bridge, find the steep steps (aka the 'Cuckoo Steps') of Stoney Lane, 300ft west of the Hebden Bridge Co-op. Climb uphill and then take a right onto Heptonstall Rd for 80m until you see a public footpath on the left leading up through the woods. You'll continue straight past cliffs and then up steep steps to arrive at Hell Hole Rocks, a popular local climbing spot. From here continue through suburban housing, across Beckett's Close, to swing left at Acres Lane by a Hebden Bridge Loop sign and map. Take a few minutes at St Thomas' Church to visit Sylvia Plath's grave (see box opposite) and the nearby ruins of the original church.

To continue on the Hebden Bridge Loop turn left up Heptonstall's cobbled main street until the village peters out and look for a Hebden Bridge Loop sign on the left pointing across a field. (Alternatively continue a little further to take a break on two convenient benches; from here you can rejoin the Loop down Green Lane after 50m.) The loop branches off Green Lane at Lumb Bank to trace stone paths and tracks above Golden Water to finally rejoin the Pennine Way at Hebble Hole (Map 23).

HEBDEN BRIDGE   [Map 22a, p119]

Hebden Bridge, a half-hour stroll east of the Pennine Way, is our vote for the most interesting town along the route and is well worth the short detour. It was along the Calder Valley that the Industrial Revolution was born, fuelled by the Rochdale Canal which passes through town. Since the mills closed the town has attracted a large 'alternative' population (a 2018 *Guardian* article described it as 'a little rain-soaked paradise'); as a result the town is stuffed with craft breweries, ethnic restaurants (Tibetan, Thai, Turkish, Persian), organic grocers, vintage clothing shops, art galleries and at least one bespoke milliner. It's that kind of town. This is *the* place to take a half or full day break from the trail.

The town has a vibrant arts scene. **Picture House cinema** (🖳 hebdenbridge picturehouse.co.uk) shows afternoon matinées and the main programme is at 7.45pm daily. There are regular drama performances at the **Little Theatre** (🖳 hblt.co.uk) and excellent live music (and Indonesian food) at the famous next-door **Trades Club** (🖳 thetradesclub.com).

St **George's Square** is worth a visit for its market stalls (until 4pm), selling second hand goods (Fri), arts and crafts (Sat) and locally produced food (Sun).

See also 🖳 hebdenbridge.co.uk/events.

Transport

[See also pp52-9] There are frequent **trains** (operated by Northern Rail) from Leeds, Bradford, Manchester and Preston.

Hebden Bridge is also a stop on several **bus** services including: First's Nos 590 & 592; TLC Travel's Nos 596 & 901; and Keighley Bus's B3.

For a taxi call **Hebden Cars** (☎ 01422-845555).

Services

The Co-op **supermarket** (Mon-Sat 7am-10pm, Sun 11am-5pm) on the main road has an **ATM**. There's also a **post office** (Mon, Tue, Thur, Fri 9am-5.30pm, Wed 10am-3pm, Sat 9am-1pm) on Holme St and a Boots **chemist** (Mon-Fri 8.30am-6.30pm, Sat 9am-5.30pm). If you need some **outdoor gear** (already?) try Mountain Wild (🖳 mountain-wild.com, Mon-Sat 9.30am-4.30pm, Sun 11.30am-4.30pm) on Crown St or Rohan (Tue-Sat 9.30am-5pm, Sun 11am-4pm) on St George's Square.

Where to stay

The town only has one **campsite**, at *Old Chamber Farm* (off Map 22a; ☎ 07814 321606, 🖳 oldchambercamping.com), but luckily it's a gem. The terraced sites cost £10pp and give you access to a barn-sized sitting area with tables and chairs, electrical plugs, showers, a toilet, kettle, fridge and washing machine. Sunday morning breakfasts (bacon sandwiches £3) are available and the sunset views are wonderful. The site is a 15-minute walk direct from the Hebden Bridge Loop (no need to walk into Hebden Bridge). The walk into town is an easy 15 minutes downhill and a sweaty, heart-pumping 20 minutes back up; the owners have helpfully painted light blue markers to guide you through the woods into town.

If you'd rather use a **hostel**, the non-profit *IOU Hebden Bridge Hostel* (☎ 01422 843183, 🖳 hebdenbridgehostel.org; 1D/2Tr/7Qd, all en suite 2x6-/2x4-bed dorms; Easter to early Nov) is on the eastern side of town. A dorm bed costs £25pp; the four-bed rooms are £50-85 and triples are £60-90 depending on how many are sharing. There are two accessible rooms for £60/80 S/D. There's a self-catering kitchen but the hostel is vegetarian so no meat or fish can be brought onto the premises.

The Smithery B&B (☎ 07957 256154, 🖳 smithery.co.uk, 1D/1T shared bathroom) is squeezed between busy New Road and the Rochdale Canal and offers two rooms, one with charming canal views, the other smaller with bunk bed accommodation. B&B costs S/D £60/75.

Thorncliffe B&B (☎ 01422-842163, 07949 729433, 🖳 thorncliffe.uk.net; 1D en suite/1D private bathroom; ▬) is on Alexandra Rd, off Birchcliffe Rd; it is a steep walk (about 5 mins) up from Market St. Expect a nice spacious room and good continental breakfasts as well as a selection of cereal bars and fruit in the room on arrival. They charge from S/D £75/85.

Riverview B&B (Map 22; ☎ 01422-844943, ☎ 07715-582378, 🖳 riverviewbnb .co.uk; 1D/1T, en suite; ▬; ◐; 🐾) is on Stubbing Drive; it is less than a mile from the Pennine Way, along the towpath on the route into Hebden Bridge. B&B here costs from S/D £75/95.

The White Lion Hotel (☎ 01422-842197, 🖳 whitelionhotel.net, **fb**; 2D or T/8D, all en suite; ▬; ◐; 🐾), Bridge Gate, charges £120-150 for B&B and is popular for both its accommodation and restaurant.

Croft Mill (☎ 01422-846836, 🖳 www. croftmill.com; 18 self-contained apart-

---

❏ HEPTONSTALL DETOUR

The charming village of Heptonstall is worth a visit if you are walking the Hebden Bridge Loop or if you have a day off in Hebden Bridge; see opposite on how to get here on the Hebden Bridge Loop trail. Literary pilgrims will want to visit the grave of American poet and novelist **Sylvia Plath** at St Thomas' Church in Heptonstall. Plath was married to British poet Ted Hughes, who was born in nearby Mythoimroyd. Her grave is in the Commonwealth graveyard, not the main cemetery, and is surprisingly hard to find; keep heading straight from the entrance and then look three-quarters of the way along the graves, about four or five tiers in. Rival groups of Plath and Hughes fans keep rubbing off (and then repainting) the 'Hughes' after Sylvia Plath's name. The inscription on the gravestone ('Even amidst fierce flames, the golden lotus can be planted') comes from the Bhagavad Gita.

From the graveyard follow Church Lane past the atmospheric ruins of the **St Thomas Becket Church**, parts of which date back to the 12th century, until you reach the 16th-century **Heptonstall Cloth Hall** and the choice of two pubs serving food; the *Cross Inn* (☎ 01422-846607, **fb**; Mon-Thur 3pm-late, Fri-Sun noon-late) to the right and the *White Lion* (🖳 whitelionheptonstall.com; food Wed 3-11pm, Thur-Sat noon-11pm, Sun noon-7pm) to the left. From here it's downhill back to Hebden Bridge, or uphill on the Hebden Bridge Loop to the Pennine Way.

ments sleeping 2-4; ☕), just off Albert St, comes recommended: 'Quiet, top of the range, with helpful, interested owners'. An apartment costs from £120, with a minimum of two nights. This rate includes a generous continental 'breakfast pack', and the full cooking facilities (with a couple of supermarkets close by) mean that you could save money on dinner by cooking your own; also it would be easy to make your own packed lunch for the next day.

Where to eat and drink

If sandwiches and full English breakfasts are getting a bit repetitive, make the most of the variety and choice in Hebden. For example, where else on the Pennine Way can you tuck into some delicious Himalayan fare such as that provided by the ***Tibetan Kitchen*** (☎ 01422-292306, 🖳 tibetankitchen.co.uk; Fri-Sun 1-7pm) on Market St? Choose three dishes and rice for £7-8 (the *shasha* chicken stir fry with peppers is particularly good), or try six *momos* (filled dumplings) for £5.

Market St also contains some excellent cafés, our favourite being ***Mooch*** (☎ 01422-846954, 🖳 moochcafebar.wordpress.com; 🐕; food Mon-Fri 9am-8pm, Sat & Sun 10am-8pm; may close later Fri & Sat) which becomes a bar in the evenings. Dog-friendly and pleasant to humans too, they serve food that is both ethically sourced and eclectic, with breakfasts ranging from the full English (£6.50) to a vegan soya yogurt pot with maple syrup, dates & goji berries (£4).

In the heart of town in the pedestrianised section is the licensed ***Watergate Tea Rooms*** (☎ 01422-842978; daily 9am-4.30pm, last hot food 3pm) which does great lunches such as Welsh rarebit (£4.50) as well as a giant Yorkshire pudding with sausages & gravy (£6.20) and full breakfasts. Try a 'Buck Royale' – black pudding and poached eggs on a crumpet.

A little further on is ***Coffee Cali*** (Mon-Fri 8.30am-5pm, Sat & Sun 9am-5pm), where you can get a coffee and a grilled ciabatta. Still further on, ***Innovation Café Bar*** (☎ 01422-844094, 🖳 innovationhebdenbridge.co.uk, **fb**; Mon-Sat 9.45am-5pm, Sun 11am-5pm), in **Hebden Bridge Mill**, does a range of hot and cold sandwiches.

For evening dining, next door is ***Il Mulino*** (☎ 01422-845986, 🖳 ilmulino.co.uk; Tue-Thur 5-9pm, Fri & Sat 5-10pm, Sun 4-9pm) which does a good range of Italian food, including a wide choice of pasta dishes (£10-12) and pizzas (from £9.50). From Italy we move east along the Mediterranean coast to ***Aya Sophia*** (☎ 01422-845337, 🖳 ayasophia.co.uk, **fb**; food daily 11am-11pm) with Greek and Turkish specialities from £13 including a lovely vegetable moussaka (£13.95).

The Olive Branch (☎ 01422-842299, 🖳 theolivebranchrestaurants.com, **fb**; food daily noon-10pm) offers ciabatta sandwiches and salads for lunch and Turkish grills (£13-17), meze and pizza (from £9.50) in the evening.

For Thai food you can't do better than the riverside ***Rim Nam Thai*** (☎ 01422-846888, 🖳 rimnamthairestaurant.co.uk, **fb**; Tue Fri 5-11pm, Sat 3-11pm, Sun 3-10pm). Curries cost around £10, plus £2.50 for rice, and there are some wonderfully spicy salads.

We are pretty sure that ***Leila's Kitchen*** (☎ 01422-843587, 🖳 leilaskitchen.co.uk, **fb**; Mon & Wed-Sat 9am-4pm, Sun 10am-4pm; 🐕) is the only vegetarian Persian-inspired café-bar you'll find on the Pennine Way. For a crash course on Persian cuisine try the *ash reshtash* (noodle stew) followed by *yatimcheh* (aubergine and courgette in a garlic tomato sauce) with rice. It occupies the wonderful old Oxford House building and also has outside seating.

On Bridge Gate, off the square, ***Shoulder of Mutton*** (🖳 shoulderofmuttonhebden.com, **fb**; Mon-Sat noon-8.30pm, Sun noon-8pm; 🐕) serves tapas-style platters (3 items for £15) as well as pies, sausages and sandwiches, though it can get truly hectic on a hot weekend afternoon in summer. ***The White Swan*** (🖳 thewhiteswanhebdenbridge.co.uk, **fb**; Mon-Sat from 11am, Sun from noon) is more traditional and cheaper, serving classic pub grub for under £6.

At the northern end of the town, ***The White Lion*** (see Where to stay) does classy,

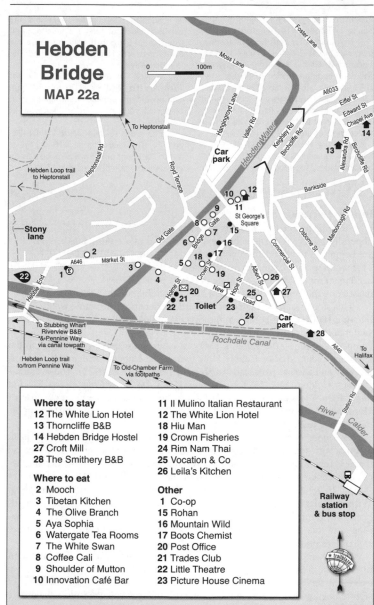

Hebden Bridge
MAP 22a

0   100m

To Heptonstall

Hebden Loop trail
to Heptonstall

Stony
lane

Heptonstall Rd

Royd Terrace

Moss Lane

Hangingroyd Lane

Valley Rd

Car
park

Hebden Water

Keighley Rd

Birchcliffe Rd

Foster Lane

A6033

Eiffel St

Edward St

Chapel Ave

14

13

Alexandra Rd

Birchcliffe Rd

Bankside

Osborne St

Marlborough Rd

10 12
11

9

8 Gate

7

6 Bridge

5

18

19

17

16

15

St George's
Square

Commercial St

Old Gate

A646   Market St

2

1 £

3

4

Crown St

Albert St

26

27

25

New

Hope St

20

21

22

23

Toilet

24

28

Hope St

Road

Car
park

A646

To
Halifax

To Stubbing Wharf
Riverview B&B
& Pennine Way
via canal towpath

Hebble End

22

Hebden Loop trail
to/from Pennine Way

To Old Chamber Farm
via footpaths

Rochdale Canal

River Calder

Station Rd

Railway
station
& bus stop

trailblazer

Where to stay
12 The White Lion Hotel
13 Thorncliffe B&B
14 Hebden Bridge Hostel
27 Croft Mill
28 The Smithery B&B

Where to eat
 2 Mooch
 3 Tibetan Kitchen
 4 The Olive Branch
 5 Aya Sophia
 6 Watergate Tea Rooms
 7 The White Swan
 8 Coffee Cali
 9 Shoulder of Mutton
10 Innovation Café Bar

11 Il Mulino Italian Restaurant
12 The White Lion Hotel
18 Hiu Man
19 Crown Fisheries
24 Rim Nam Thai
25 Vocation & Co
26 Leila's Kitchen

Other
 1 Co-op
15 Rohan
16 Mountain Wild
17 Boots Chemist
20 Post Office
21 Trades Club
22 Little Theatre
23 Picture House Cinema

ROUTE GUIDE AND MAPS

imaginative fare (Mon-Sat noon-8.45pm, Sun to 7.45pm) for £14-19 a main course.

If you are after craft beer rather than real ales, local Hebden Bridge brewers *Vocation & Co* (🖳 vocationbrewery.com, **fb**; daily noon-late) offer 20 of their own IPAs and pale ales on tap, alongside some European and guest beers and serve up epic burgers and loaded fries (daily noon-9pm). They sell third pints, allowing you to try a wider range of brews.

Stubbing Wharf (Map 22; ☎ 01422-844107, 🖳 greatpubs.co.uk/stubbing-wharf-hebden-bridge, **fb**; food daily 11am-9pm;

🍴), situated between the river and the canal, provides pub food in a great location. You'll pass the pub if walking along the canal between Hebden Bridge and the Pennine Way.

If you prefer fast food, *Crown Fisheries* (**fb**; Wed-Sat 11.30am-6.30/7pm, Sun noon-5pm) provides traditional fish & chips and you can eat in or take away as you please.

The Chinese *Hiu Man* (☎ 01422-844724, Tue-Thur & Sun 5-10pm, Fri & Sat to 10.30pm) on Crown St is take-away only, with a main dish and rice £7-8.

CALDER VALLEY TO ICKORNSHAW   MAPS 22-31

Route overview

It hasn't exactly been easy to this point, but hopefully by day four the aches and pains are beginning to subside and you've found your walking legs, because you're going to need them for today. Only a couple of other

Distance 15½ miles (25km)
Ascent 3100ft (945m)
Time 5½-7½ hours

days along the Pennine Way have a greater height gain than this section.

This stretch starts with one of the hardest ascents of the whole walk, a lung-bursting 1000ft (304m) climb in the first two miles (3.2km) as the Way ascends switchbacking tracks and pathways west of **Mytholm** (Map 22). The effort is compensated for by the varied scenery of lanes, steps, passages, fields and the charming picnic spot of Hebble Hole, where the Hebden Bridge Loop rejoins the Way and another path leads to *Hebden Camping* (see p122). You eventually reach **Colden** (Map 23) for a stop at *May's Aladdin's Cave* (see p122) and then Mount Pleasant Farm, one of the last houses before the open expanse of **Heptonstall Moor** (Map 24), where you will find the first wild camping opportunity since leaving Hebden Bridge.

The moor is crossed on a good path which then drops down to the lush, green beauty spot at **Graining Water** (Map 25). Make the most of it, because the next few miles are either along reservoir access roads or on the harsh gravel paths beside them. You'll pass two of the three **Walshaw Dean reservoirs** (Maps 25 & 26) before turning away and climbing the moorland path up **Withins Height** (Map 27) to the old farmhouse of Top Withins that many associate with Emily Brontë's *Wuthering Heights*. In the summer this place is bristling with tourists but at quieter times it's a potential **wild camp**, with a water source five minutes' walk further along the trail

From here many choose to divert from the Pennine Way to visit **Haworth** (3½ miles, 5.5km, 1½hrs), for the full immersive Brontë experience. An overnight stay here will break up this long section and allow an afternoon of sightseeing and indulgence in this wonderful village. You can follow the scenic **Brontë Way** (Maps 27 & 28), from Top Withins down to your accommodation.

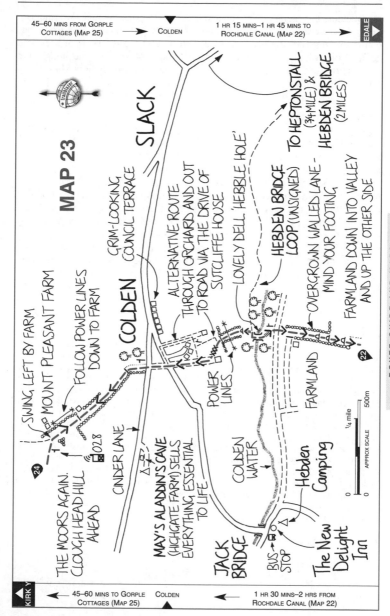

MAP 23

SLACK

GRIM-LOOKING COUNCIL TERRACE

TO HEPTONSTALL (¾ MILE) & HEBDEN BRIDGE (2 MILES)

ALTERNATIVE ROUTE THROUGH ORCHARD AND OUT TO ROAD VIA THE DRIVE OF SUTCLIFFE HOUSE

HEBDEN BRIDGE LOOP (UNSIGNED)

LOVELY DELL 'HEBBLE HOLE'

OVERGROWN WALLED LANE – MIND YOUR FOOTING

FARMLAND DOWN INTO VALLEY AND UP THE OTHER SIDE

SWING LEFT BY FARM

MOUNT PLEASANT FARM

FOLLOW POWER LINES DOWN TO FARM

COLDEN

POWER LINES

FARMLAND

THE MOORS AGAIN. CLOUGH HEAD HILL AHEAD

CINDER LANE

MAY'S ALADDIN'S CAVE (HIGHGATE FARM) SELLS EVERYTHING ESSENTIAL TO LIFE

COLDEN WATER

HEBDEN CAMPING

JACK BRIDGE

BUS STOP

The New Delight Inn

¼ mile

500m

APPROX SCALE

If you ignore this literary diversion and proceed along the Pennine Way, the path drops down across moorland to **Ponden** (Map 28) with a couple of accommodation options and a rather contrived path around the reservoir of the same name. Another long ascent lies beyond, only 800ft (244m) this time though, and you are rewarded with the crossing of the heather-clad **Ickornshaw Moor** (Map 30), past the wooden huts (called *cowlings*) and down, across fields into the tiny village of **Ickornshaw** (Map 31) and food options in nearby Cowling.

Navigation notes

Trying to find the Pennine Way path among the myriad other green footpaths leaving Hebden Bridge is a bit like trying to find a needle in a haystack! The route through the maze is well signed though and you'll be walking slowly up the steep slope so will have little trouble spotting them.

The crossing of Heptonstall Moor (Map 24) is aided by slabs and a well-trodden path and provided you don't miss the sharp right turn at GPS 030 that takes you down to Gorple Cottages, this potentially tricky section should be a breeze. Similarly, the path from Walshaw Dean Middle Reservoir across the moor may look desolate on the map, but the slabs are here too and the signposts which prevent the day-trippers from straying from the path serve just as well.

Leaving Ickornshaw Moor is more likely to cause confusion than the crossing of it, so keep an eye out for the left turn at GPS 045, down through the fields to the waterfall at Lumb Head (Map 31). There is a path around Lower Summerhouse Farm, but it is well signed and exits into the field beyond at almost the same point.

COLDEN & JACK BRIDGE
[Map 23, p121]

Within a mile of leaving the valley, you will see signs pointing the way to **Aladdin's Cave**, promising untold excesses such as sweets, cakes, groceries and hot drinks. This is *Highgate Farm* (☎ 01422-842897) run by the redoubtable May Stocks who has a natural instinct for what wayfarers want and has provided for them accordingly for several decades now. Besides the **shop** (daily 7am-9pm), May allows basic **camping** (🐾 on lead) for free for walkers staying one night; there are toilet facilities and spring water for your water bottle. A fine selection of hot pies and cakes can be bought here, along with cold beer, saving you the toil of carrying them up the hill from Hebden Bridge, plus some pharmacy items.

With a friendly atmosphere and a well-tended cellar, *The New Delight Inn* (☎ 01422-844628, 🖳 newdelightinn.co.uk; 🐾; bar Thur & Fri 5-9pm, Sat noon-11pm, Sun noon-9pm; **food** Thur & Fri 5-8pm, Sat noon-8pm, Sun to 6pm; closed Mon-Wed), at **Jack Bridge**, provides a haven for thirsty or just plain miserable Pennine Way walkers. Attached to the pub is *Hebden Camping* (☎ 07763 574060, 🖳 hebden bridge-camping.co.uk; 🐾; closed Nov) which charges Pennine Way walkers £5 for a tent (usually £10-20 per pitch) plus £3 per person. Shower and toilet facilities are available just outside the pub. OK for a night, it's a very hands-off place so don't expect much.

❏ **IMPORTANT NOTE – WALKING TIMES**
All times in this book refer only to the time spent walking. You will need to add 20-30% to allow for rests, photography, checking the map, drinking water etc.

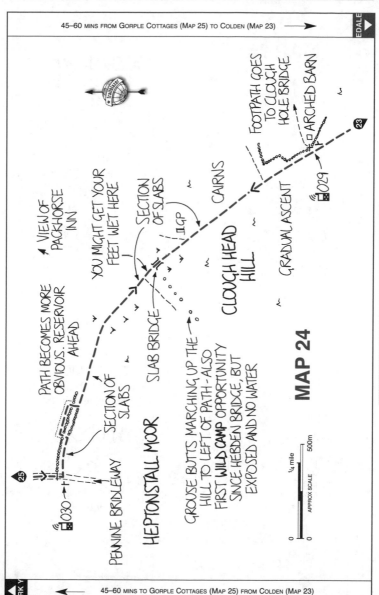

EDALE ►

KIRK Y ◄

ROUTE GUIDE AND MAPS

VIEW OF PACKHORSE INN →

PATH BECOMES MORE OBVIOUS. RESERVOIR AHEAD

YOU MIGHT GET YOUR FEET WET HERE

SECTION OF SLABS

FOOTPATH GOES TO CLOUGH HOLE BRIDGE

☐ ARCHED BARN

23

📷 029

CAIRNS

IIGP

SECTION OF SLABS

SLAB BRIDGE

CLOUGH HEAD HILL

GRADUAL ASCENT

PENNINE BRIDLEWAY

📷 030

25

HEPTONSTALL MOOR

SECTION OF SLABS

GROUSE BUTTS MARCHING UP THE HILL TO LEFT OF PATH - ALSO FIRST WILD CAMP OPPORTUNITY SINCE HEBDEN BRIDGE, BUT EXPOSED AND NO WATER

MAP 24

¼ mile

500m

APPROX SCALE

0

0

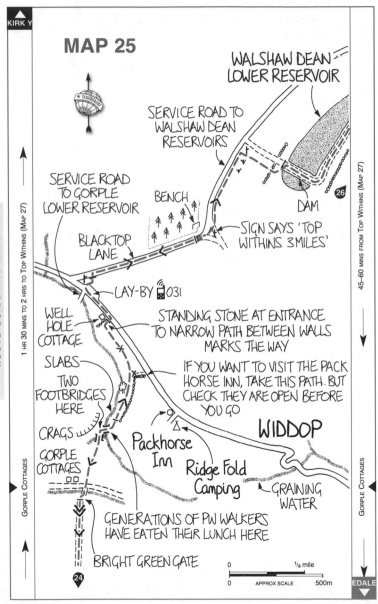

KIRK Y

MAP 25

WALSHAW DEAN LOWER RESERVOIR

SERVICE ROAD TO WALSHAW DEAN RESERVOIRS

SERVICE ROAD TO GORPLE LOWER RESERVOIR

BENCH

BLACKTOP LANE

DAM

26

SIGN SAYS 'TOP WITHINS 3 MILES'

LAY-BY 📱031

WELL HOLE COTTAGE

STANDING STONE AT ENTRANCE TO NARROW PATH BETWEEN WALLS MARKS THE WAY

SLABS

IF YOU WANT TO VISIT THE PACK HORSE INN, TAKE THIS PATH. BUT CHECK THEY ARE OPEN BEFORE YOU GO

TWO FOOTBRIDGES HERE

CRAGS

WIDDOP

GORPLE COTTAGES

Packhorse Inn

Ridge Fold Camping

GRAINING WATER

GENERATIONS OF PW WALKERS HAVE EATEN THEIR LUNCH HERE

BRIGHT GREEN GATE

24

1 HR 30 MINS TO 2 HRS TO TOP WITHINS (MAP 27)

45–60 MINS FROM TOP WITHINS (MAP 27)

GORPLE COTTAGES

GORPLE COTTAGES

ROUTE GUIDE AND MAPS

0   ¼ mile

0   APPROX SCALE   500m

EDALE

WIDDOP [Map 25]

The next pub north from Colden is the **Packhorse Inn** (☎ 01422-842803, 🖥 the packhorseinn.co.uk, **fb**; 🐾; **food** summer Wed-Sat noon-8pm, Sun noon-6pm), a few hundred metres off route and beckoning with a cosy fire and outside seating. If you spent the night in Hebden, lunchtime could be about now but note that they're closed Monday and Tuesday and don't always do food on Wednesday. Mains (£12-18) include venison, fish pie and liver with bacon .

Ridge Fold Camping (☎ 07989 322617, 🖥 ridgefoldcamping@gmail.com, **fb**; Jul-Sept) is a new farm-run campsite located right next to the Packhorse Inn. Prices are £20 per pitch, though solo Pennine Way backpackers pay £10. There is a toilet block with hot water (no showers), drinking water and a drying room/canteen where campers can shelter from the rain. Plus you are crawling distance from the pub.

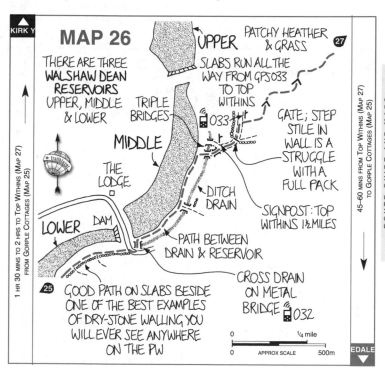

PONDEN & STANBURY
[Map 28, p127]

Ponden is now much smaller than it was when weaving was dominant in the area. The only option here these days is *Ponden Mill* (☎ 01535-643923, 🖥 themillatponden

.com; 2D en suite, £75), where pleasant riverside **camping** costs £10/15 for one/two people, with access to toilets and a shower. Two **B&B** rooms are available in the Mill, or for the ultimate **glamping** experience there's the very romantic and secluded Falling Water Cabin (£145, min 2 nights, outdoor toilet, no shower), which featured in *George Clark's Amazing Spaces* TV programme. Note that the Georgian millhouse is a popular weekend wedding venue, so you might get some noise (and feel rather underdressed) on a Saturday night; the rest of the week is much more bucolic.

Your other alternative, if you don't want to stay in Haworth 2 miles away, is in **Stanbury**. The well-run *Old Silent Inn* (☎ 01535-647437, 🖥 theoldsilent.co.uk, **fb**; 6D/1T/1Tr, all en suite; ①; 🐾) gained its name after Bonnie Prince Charlie hid out

here in 1688 with a nod and a wink from the locals. Today room only costs S/D/Tr £70/90/100. The menu (**food** summer Mon-Fri noon-2.30pm & 5-8.30pm, Sat noon-8.30pm, Sun noon-7.45pm) includes steak & Old Peculier pie (£12). To reach it you've either got a slightly hairy walk down Ponden Lane (watch out for traffic), or you could leave the Way at WPT 036 to take a track to Hob Lane.

Keighley Bus Company's K14/K16 **bus** services (see pp54-9) call in at the eastern end of Ponden Lane every hour or two on the way to Stanbury and Haworth.

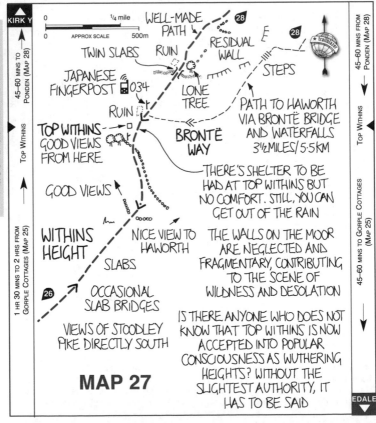

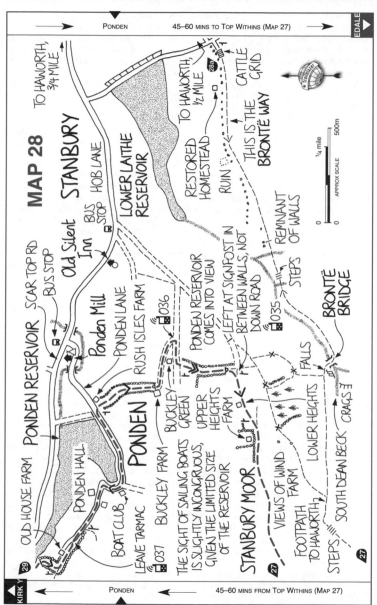

MAP 28

STANBURY

PONDEN

EDALE ►

PONDEN   45–60 MINS TO TOP WITHINS (MAP 27) ►

TO HAWORTH, ¾ MILE

TO HAWORTH, ½ MILE

THIS IS THE BRONTË WAY

CATTLE GRID

RESTORED HOMESTEAD

RUIN

28a

Old Silent Inn

SCAR TOP RD

BUS STOP

BUS STOP

HOB LANE

LOWER LAITHE RESERVOIR

PONDEN RESERVOIR

Ponden Mill

PONDEN LANE

RUSH ISLES FARM

036

PONDEN RESERVOIR COMES INTO VIEW

LEFT AT SIGNPOST IN BETWEEN WALLS, NOT DOWN ROAD

REMNANT OF WALLS

STEPS

BRONTË BRIDGE

035

FALLS

OLD HOUSE FARM

PONDEN HALL

BOAT CLUB

LEAVE TARMAC

037

PONDEN

BUCKLEY FARM

BUCKLEY GREEN

UPPER HEIGHTS FARM

THE SIGHT OF SAILING BOATS IS SLIGHTLY INCONGRUOUS, GIVEN THE LIMITED SIZE OF THE RESERVOIR

STANBURY MOOR

VIEWS OF WIND FARM

LOWER HEIGHTS FARM

SOUTH DEAN BECK

CRAGS

FOOTPATH TO HAWORTH

STEPS

27

27

¼ mile

500m

APPROX SCALE

0   0

KIRK Y ◄

PONDEN ◄

45–60 MINS FROM TOP WITHINS (MAP 27)

HAWORTH [Map 28a]

The Pennine Way does not go through Haworth, but there are good reasons for taking the 90-minute detour off the path, via the **Brontë Way**, to seek whatever solace may be required: refreshment, accommodation (which is in short supply on the Way itself), literary inspiration; all are there in abundance but the extra 3½ miles (6km) down also involves 3½ miles back up!

This gritstone town's appeal is firmly based on its association with the Brontë sisters. Year-round the streets throng with visitors, most of whom have probably never read the works of Emily, Charlotte or Anne. However, such is the romantic appeal of the family, whose home can still be visited, that crowds continue to be drawn here from all over the world.

Haworth is a major destination on the UK tour circuit for Japanese visitors; you'll have spotted PW signs in Japanese near Top Withins.

Walk into town on a weekend in late May and you'll likely see the main street full of flannel suits, patrolling GIs and antique cars, thanks to the town's **1940s Weekend**; it's like walking onto the set of *Dad's Army*. It's great fun but Haworth's accommodation and car parks will be full to bursting.

Brontë Parsonage Museum (☎ 01535-642323, 🖳 bronte.org.uk; Wed-Sun 10am-5pm, last admission 4pm; £11) is at the top of the town. It tells the fascinating story of the family (see box p130) and their tragic life. The dining room is where *Jane Eyre* and *Wuthering Heights* were written.

The **railway station** here is a stop on the **Keighley & Worth Valley Railway Line** (☎ 01535-645214, 🖳 kwvr.co.uk; 4-9 services/day most days, see website for times; return ticket £13.50, day rover £20), a preserved line which runs steam trips between Keighley (where it links up with the main Leeds–Settle–Carlisle line) and Oxenhope. Oakworth, one of the other stops on the line, is where part of *The Railway Children* was filmed. Its 2022 sequel *The Railway Children Return* was again filmed in Oakworth, and also in Haworth itself.

Transport

[See also pp54-9] Frequent **bus** services here include Keighley Bus Company's B1, B2, B3, K14 and K16. Only scenic steam excursions depart from the train station; for passenger services head to Keighley.

For a **taxi** call Brontë Taxis (☎ 01535-644442, 🖳 brontetaxis.com).

Services

Haworth has services aplenty including a **post office** (Mon-Fri 9am-5pm, Sat 9am-12.30pm), a Spar **supermarket** (daily 7am-10.30pm) near the station and a Co-op (daily 7am-10pm) 150m south. Both the Spar and the Co-op have **ATMs**. There's also a Day Lewis **pharmacy** (Mon-Fri 9am-12.45pm & 2-6.30pm, Sat 10am-12.30pm), and Peggy Tubs **Laundrette** (Mon & Tue 8am-2pm, Wed-Sun 8am-5pm).

Where to stay

YHA Haworth (off Map 28a; ☎ 0345-371 9520, 🖳 yha.org.uk/hostel/haworth; ⓛ; Feb-Sep) is on Longlands Drive out on the eastern side of town, 1½ miles up a long hill. This grand Victorian mansion has 89 beds (1 x 6-bed en suite, mix of rooms sleep 1-8 shared facilities) but the popularity of the town means that it gets very busy at peak times. A dorm bed costs £15-30pp, private rooms from S/D £25/29 (higher on weekends and in August). The hostel is licensed and meals are available; there is also a laundry room and drying facilities.

Weavers Guesthouse (☎ 01535-643209, 🖳 weaversguesthouse.co.uk; 1S/2T/3D, all en suite; 🛏; ⓛ; min 2 nights at weekends), at 15 West Lane, sits in the heart of the cobbled old town and charges £59 for a single and £83-89 a double B&B.

Halfway down the hill on Main St is *The Fleece Inn* (☎ 01535-642172, 🖳 fleeceinnhaworth.com, **fb**; 2S/1T/5D/2D or T, all en suite; 🛏; ⓛ; 🐾); it is one of the best pubs in town and has small singles for £55 and larger doubles for £90-105 – the rates include 10% off any meals taken at the bar and even a voucher for a complimentary 'tasting tray' of Timothy Taylor ales. Weekends can be noisy so ask for a room at the back.

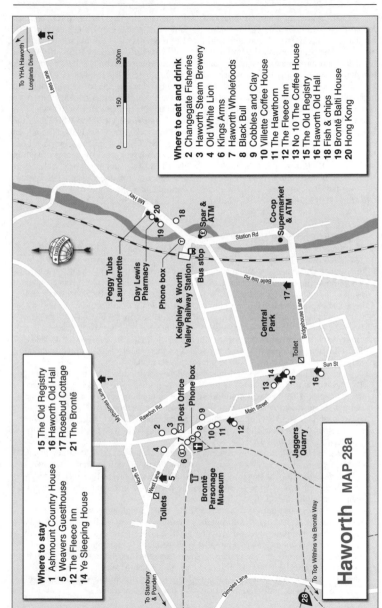

Where to stay

1 Ashmount Country House
5 Weavers Guesthouse
12 The Fleece Inn
14 Ye Sleeping House

15 The Old Registry
16 Haworth Old Hall
17 Rosebud Cottage
21 The Brontë

Where to eat and drink

2 Changegate Fisheries
3 Haworth Steam Brewery
4 Old White Lion
6 Kings Arms
7 Haworth Wholefoods
8 Black Bull
9 Cobbles and Clay
10 Villette Coffee House
11 The Hawthorn
12 The Fleece Inn
13 No 10 The Coffee House
15 The Old Registry
16 Haworth Old Hall
18 Fish & chips
19 Brontë Balti House
20 Hong Kong

Haworth **MAP 28a**

ROUTE GUIDE AND MAPS

At the bottom of Main St *The Old Registry* (☎ 01535-646503, 🖥 theoldreg istryhaworth.co.uk, **fb**; 8D, all en suite; 🍺), 2-4 Main St, is furnished with an eye for detail and an emphasis on luxury and pampering; some rooms have a whirlpool bath. B&B costs £80-115 per room; a two-night minimum stay applies most weekends (Fri & Sat) when rates are £10-20 higher.

Ye Sleeping House (☎ 01535-645992, 🖥 yesleepinghouse.co.uk; 1S/1Tr share bathroom, 1Qd en suite; 🍺; ⓛ; 🐾), at 8 Main St, is the perfect place to do what the name says. B&B here costs S/D £63/70 with shared bathroom or £75/84 en suite.

Not far away, on Sun St, is *Haworth Old Hall* (☎ 01535-642709, 🖥 haworthold hallpub.co.uk, **fb**; 1D or T/1D, both en suite; ⓛ; 🐾 bar only) which charges £90-120 room only (sgl occ full room rate).

Rosebud Cottage (☎ 01535-640321, 🖥 rosebudcottage.co.uk; 1S/3D/1T en suite; 🍺; ⓛ), 1 Belle Isle Rd, is a well-run establishment charging £55 for a small single and S/D £80/100 in a larger double room. It's a short uphill walk from here into town.

The Brontë (☎ 01535-644112, 🖥 the bronte.co.uk, **fb**; 2S/1T/3D/3Tr, all en suite, 1S/2T shared facilities; 🍺; ⓛ), Lees Lane, is a larger establishment not far from the YHA hostel and might be just the ticket for a group of walkers wanting accommodation under the same roof. Refurbished and rebranded in 2022, it's geared for over-

❑ THE BRONTËS & HAWORTH

The three Brontë sisters, Emily (*Wuthering Heights*, 1847), Charlotte (*Jane Eyre*, 1847) and Anne (*The Tenant of Wildfell Hall*, 1848), were brought up in Haworth by their father and an aunt – after their mother died of cancer in 1821 – in the Parsonage where Reverend Brontë had taken a living in 1820. The Parsonage still stands and is open to the public as a museum. As the only boy in the family Branwell had every hope and expectation lavished on him, taking precedence over his more talented sisters, but squandered his life in drink and drugs, dying in 1848. Emily, Charlotte, Branwell and their father Patrick are buried with other members of the family in a family vault in **St Michael's church**, where Patrick served as reverend for 41 years. The **Old School Room** next to the Parsonage was where all the Brontë children taught and where Charlotte's wedding reception was held.

The surrounding villages and moorland are tightly tied to the Brontës writings. The farmhouse of Top Withins has the air of a pilgrimage site thanks to its connections, in spirit if not physical description, to the eponymous residence of Wuthering Heights. Ponden Hall, also right on the Pennine Way, is thought to be the real-life location of Thrushcross Grange, home to the pampered Linton family in the same novel. Nearby Wycoller Hall, west of the Pennine Way, was the inspiration for Ferndean Manor in *Jane Eyre*.

Modern Haworth is not shy in promoting other, somewhat less authentic, Brontë connections. Visitors can lunch in the 'Wuthering Heights' pub in Stanbury, down a 'Charlotte Brontë IPA' at Haworth's 17th-century Kings Arms and then pick up a souvenir Branwell Brontë wine stopper from the Parsonage gift shop. The Brontës, it seems, are big business.

The lonely, unassuming sisters wrote under male pseudonyms but still their talents went largely unrecognised during their lifetimes and they all died comparatively young (Charlotte during pregnancy, aged 38; Emily aged 30; Anne aged 29) from tuberculosis (known then as 'consumption') exacerbated by the unhealthy conditions that plagued their village. Today their reputation as novelists endures, and *Wuthering Heights* in particular – set so obviously in the Haworth locality – continues to entrance readers with its vivid portrait of thwarted passion and unfulfilled lives shaped by the bleak, unforgiving landscape of the Yorkshire moors.

nighters and has good clean rooms with ample scope for eating and drinking downstairs. You can expect to pay from £50 for a single or from £90 for a double B&B. It's a bit out of town.

Ashmount Country House (☎ 01535-645726, ☐ ashmounthaworth.co.uk; 11D/1T, all en suite; ☞; ⓛ), on Mytholmes Lane, charges £150-250 for a room; several rooms have a hot tub.

Where to eat and drink

Haworth Old Hall (see Where to stay; food Mon-Sat noon-8.30pm, Sun noon-7.30pm) stands apart from the other pubs here and is recommended for its real ales and plentiful outdoor seating. A range of bar meals (from £12.50) in generous portions is available.

The cobbled Main St has a plethora of eating places. *The Fleece Inn* (see Where to stay; food Mon-Sat noon-8.30pm, Sun to 7.30pm) has a real fire (in winter) and real ales (Timothy Taylor) too. It's a good place to try some local flavours like pork tenderloin with black pudding (£13.50); main courses start at £12; they have a pie night on Wednesday (pie and a drink £10.95).

The Old Registry (See Where to stay, food Tue-Sat 6.30-8.30pm) is probably the best restaurant in town, with meaty main dishes (lamb neck, beef brisket) but also hard-to-find treats such as Mediterranean fish soup as a starter and roasted rhubarb with meringue for dessert; mains £16-19.

For lunches and afternoon teas you can't do better than *Villette Coffee House* (☎ 01535-644967, fb; Mon-Sat 9am-5pm, Sun 8am-6pm; ☞), named after the Charlotte Brontë novel. They serve such delights as Yorkshire curd tarts, large flat parkins and delicious sticky ginger buns; their Brontë brunch is a feast (£7.25).

No 10 The Coffee House (fb; Wed & Thur 11.30am-6pm, Fri from 10am, Sat & Sun from 9am) serves a variety of teas and freshly ground coffees, as well as homemade cakes and scones baked daily on the premises, in a relaxing environment. A substantial afternoon tea is available but must be booked in advance.

Haworth Steam Brewery (☎ 01535-646059, ☐ haworthsteambrewery.co.uk,

fb; bar Sun-Wed 11am-6pm, Thur-Sat 11am-11pm; food Tue-Sun 11am-3.30pm, Thur-Sat 6-8.30pm; no wi-fi; ☞ daytime only) is a micro-brewery and restaurant at the top of the cobbled Main St. There is an extensive food menu (mains £12-16) plus a range of their own beers and local gins.

Nearby are three decent pubs within a stone's throw of each other: the historic *Kings Arms* (fb) serving local Bridgehouse beers; the 18th century *Black Bull* (☐ blackbullhaworth.co.uk, fb); and the *Old White Lion* (☐ oldwhitelionhotel.com, fb), all offering pub grub.

Changegate Fisheries (Betty Sampson's; ☎ 01535-642336, fb; Wed-Fri 11.30am-2pm & 4-7pm, Sat & Sun 11.30am-5pm; small ☞) is a traditional chippy with pub tables outside. Haddock and chips costs £7.

Nearby is *Haworth Wholefoods* (☎ 01535 649217, ☐ haworthwholefoods.co .uk, fb; Mon-Sat 9am-5pm), home of the delicious Pennine Way pasty (£2.20), a wonderfully filling vegetarian concoction.

Cobbles and Clay (☐ cobblesandclay.co.uk, fb; daily 8.45am-5pm) is more than just a café; you can paint a plate whilst enjoying American-style pancakes or imaginative lunch dishes such as shakshuka or a Reuben sandwich (salt beef & sauerkraut; £8-9).

Shuffle further down the hill and you'll come across a couple of more formal dining options. *The Hawthorn* (☎ 01535-644477, ☐ thehawthornhaworth.co.uk, fb; food Wed-Fri 5-11pm, Sat 11am-midnight, Sun noon-5pm; ☞ downstairs only) is a 'gastropub' in a lovely old Georgian building with a roaring log fire, wood panelled walls and a frequently changing menu that specialises in dishes from the Josper charcoal grill (mains £12-18, grills £23-30).

In the eastern, non-touristy (and less charming) part of town is a collection of takeaways and restaurants. *Brontë Balti House* (fb; daily 4.30-11pm), a takeaway which offers chicken Balti and rice for £7.50. There is also *Hong Kong*, (Tue-Sun 5.30-9pm, dishes incl rice £6.50), a Chinese takeaway; and another *fish & chip* shop (Mill Hey Fisheries).

ICKORNSHAW [Map 31, p134]

The Pennine Way crosses the busy A6068 between Colne and Keighley at Ickornshaw. To blend in say 'Ick-<u>corn</u>-sher', with the emphasis on the 'corn' and no one need ever know your dark secret.

Ickornshaw is an off-shoot of Cowling which is a quarter of a mile off route to the east.

Winterhouse Barn (☎ 01535-632234, Ⓛ; 🐎) is very close to the trail and offers

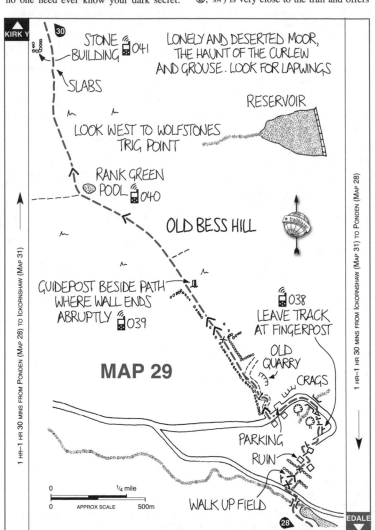

ROUTE GUIDE AND MAPS

KIRK Y

30

STONE BUILDING 📱041

LONELY AND DESERTED MOOR, THE HAUNT OF THE CURLEW AND GROUSE. LOOK FOR LAPWINGS

SLABS

RESERVOIR

LOOK WEST TO WOLFSTONES TRIG POINT

RANK GREEN POOL 📱040

OLD BESS HILL

trailblazer

GUIDEPOST BESIDE PATH WHERE WALL ENDS ABRUPTLY 📱039

📱038

LEAVE TRACK AT FINGERPOST

OLD QUARRY

MAP 29

CRAGS

PARKING

RUIN

WALK UP FIELD

28

EDALE ▼

1 HR–1 HR 30 MINS FROM PONDEN (MAP 28) TO ICKORNSHAW (MAP 31)

1 HR–1 HR 30 MINS FROM ICKORNSHAW (MAP 31) TO PONDEN (MAP 28)

0 ¼ mile
0 APPROX SCALE 500m

camping for £10pp in an enclosed area with a pub table, near a toilet and shower block. For £2 more it's worth upgrading to the **summerhouse** (sleeps 2), a potting shed that comes with electricity, light, a kettle with coffee, tea and milk, camp beds (you'll need a sleeping bag) and a lovely garden sitting area. Order your breakfast bacon or sausage sandwich the night before from the very helpful owners. Cash only. For an evening meal walk 15 minutes to Cowling (see below).

White House Farm (☎ 01535-637880, 🖳 smout.co.uk; 1D or T en suite; (L)), just off the trail north of Ickornshaw, is the only B&B in town and has only one large room, so book in advance. Dinner (£18) and packed lunches are available if reserved 48 hours in advance. Rates are S/D £55/80 and payment is by cash, cheque or bank transfer only. It's one mile by road down Lane House Road, or a third of a mile through fields further north along the Pennine Way.

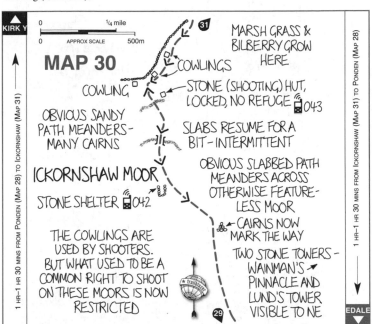

MAP 30

KIRK Y

0   1/4 mile
0   APPROX SCALE   500m

31

MARSH GRASS & BILBERRY GROW HERE

COWLINGS

COWLING

STONE (SHOOTING) HUT, LOCKED, NO REFUGE 📱043

OBVIOUS SANDY PATH MEANDERS- MANY CAIRNS

SLABS RESUME FOR A BIT-INTERMITTENT

ICKORNSHAW MOOR

OBVIOUS SLABBED PATH MEANDERS ACROSS OTHERWISE FEATURE- LESS MOOR

STONE SHELTER 📱042

CAIRNS NOW MARK THE WAY

THE COWLINGS ARE USED BY SHOOTERS. BUT WHAT USED TO BE A COMMON RIGHT TO SHOOT ON THESE MOORS IS NOW RESTRICTED

TWO STONE TOWERS - WAINMAN'S PINNACLE AND LUND'S TOWER VISIBLE TO NE

★ trailblazer

29

1 HR-1 HR 30 MINS FROM PONDEN (MAP 28) TO ICKORNSHAW (MAP 31)

1 HR-1 HR 30 MINS FROM ICKORNSHAW (MAP 31) TO PONDEN (MAP 28)

ROUTE GUIDE AND MAPS

EDALE

COWLING   [Map 31, p134]

Cowling has a useful **shop** (Village Local; Mon-Fri 8.30am-8pm, Sat 9am-8pm, Sun 10am-4pm) and several options for food and drink.

The friendly *Bay Horse Inn* (☎ 01535-633953, 🖳 bayhorsecowling.com; 🐾; food Mon 10am-2pm, Tue-Sat 10am-8pm, Sun noon-8pm) serves excellent-value pub fare (£8-10), including Minted Lamb Henry, and on Wednesday you can score a

double burger and a pint for £10. They also do takeaway.

There is a friendly chip shop (*Cowling Chippy*, **fb**; Tue-Fri 11.30am-2pm, 4.30-7pm, Sat 11.30-2pm) which has some indoor seating as well as the usual take-away service.

Further up the street is *Sam's Pizza* (☎ 01535-448466, 🖳 samspizzas.weebly.com, **fb**; Thur-Sat 4.30-9pm, Sun 5-8pm), sell-

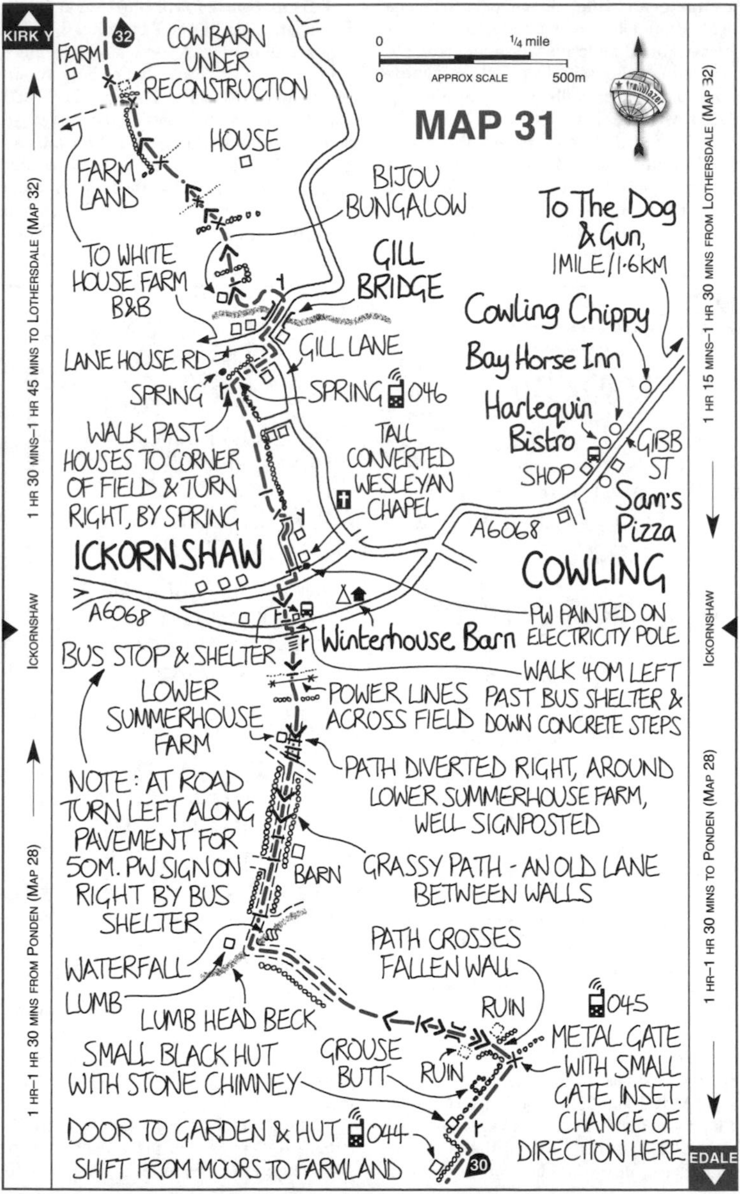

KIRK Y

FARM | 32

COW BARN UNDER RECONSTRUCTION

HOUSE

FARM LAND

TO WHITE HOUSE FARM B&B

LANE HOUSE RD

SPRING

WALK PAST HOUSES TO CORNER OF FIELD & TURN RIGHT, BY SPRING

ICKORNSHAW

A6068

BUS STOP & SHELTER

LOWER SUMMERHOUSE FARM

NOTE: AT ROAD TURN LEFT ALONG PAVEMENT FOR 50M. PW SIGN ON RIGHT BY BUS SHELTER

WATERFALL LUMB

LUMB HEAD BECK

SMALL BLACK HUT WITH STONE CHIMNEY

DOOR TO GARDEN & HUT 📱044

SHIFT FROM MOORS TO FARMLAND

0 ¼ mile

0 APPROX SCALE 500m

MAP 31

BIJOU BUNGALOW

GILL BRIDGE

GILL LANE

SPRING 📱046

TALL CONVERTED WESLEYAN CHAPEL

To The Dog & Gun, 1 MILE/1·6KM

Cowling Chippy

Bay Horse Inn

Harlequin Bistro

SHOP

GIBB ST

Sam's Pizza

A6068

COWLING

PW PAINTED ON ELECTRICITY POLE

Winterhouse Barn

WALK 40M LEFT PAST BUS SHELTER & DOWN CONCRETE STEPS

POWER LINES ACROSS FIELD

PATH DIVERTED RIGHT, AROUND LOWER SUMMERHOUSE FARM, WELL SIGNPOSTED

GRASSY PATH - AN OLD LANE BETWEEN WALLS

BARN

PATH CROSSES FALLEN WALL

RUIN

📱045

METAL GATE WITH SMALL GATE INSET. CHANGE OF DIRECTION HERE.

GROUSE BUTT

RUIN

30

ICKORNSHAW ← 1 HR 30 MINS–1 HR 45 MINS TO LOTHERSDALE (MAP 32)

1 HR 15 MINS–1 HR 30 MINS FROM LOTHERSDALE (MAP 32)

ICKORNSHAW

1 HR–1 HR 30 MINS FROM PONDEN (MAP 28)

1 HR–1 HR 30 MINS TO PONDEN (MAP 28)

ROUTE GUIDE AND MAPS

EDALE

ing kebabs and burgers plus 12-14" pizzas.

Between the two is *Harlequin Bistro* (☎ 01535-633223, 🖥 harlequinbistro.co .uk, **fb**; Fri & Sat 5.30-9pm, Sun noon-2pm & 4-7pm), the smartest place in town with mains like slow-roasted pork belly with cider gravy costing £13-18.

On a Monday evening when everything is closed, the next nearest place to eat

is *Dog & Gun* (☎ 01535-633855, 🖥 dog-and-gun-inn.co.uk, **fb**; **food** daily noon-9pm; no wi-fi; 🐾 bar area only), beyond Cowling 2 miles from the Winterhouse Barn (see p132). The menu is extensive (£11-14) and includes fish dishes, sizzlers and vegetarian options.

The only **bus** service is Burnley Bus's M4; see p56 for details.

ICKORNSHAW TO MALHAM   MAPS 31-41

Route overview

Nearly all the day's ascent is achieved in the first four miles (6.4km) and the latter half of the day sees a distinct change in scenery; from the dark gritstone and black

Distance	17 miles (27.5km)
Ascent	2500ft (762m)
Time	6¾-9¾ hours

peat of the Peak District to the light grey limestone and green grass of the Yorkshire Dales. You can lighten the load a little by forgoing a packed lunch as there are opportunities along the way to stop and take on refreshments.

Leaving Ickornshaw via **Gill Bridge** the path makes a short, sharp climb up **Cowling Hill**, then there's another up and over and down into **Lothersdale** (Map 32), with its incongruous chimney. It's probably too early for the Hare & Hounds (see p136) to be open, so it's out of the village and up into the fields for the climb up to **Elslack Moor** (Map 33) and the highpoint of the day at the trig point at **Pinhaw Beacon**. A new **Covid-19 memorial** here remembers those who died during the pandemic and offers thanks to the NHS workers who cared for them, while pointing out the surrounding geographical features. Take a moment to admire the views; on a clear day you may be able to identify Pen-y-ghent, 17 miles away. The rest of the day is mostly low level, through fields and pastures as you transition from one geography to the next.

The Way then drops down to **Thornton-in-Craven** (Map 34); a village with few amenities for the walker other than a shady seat beneath the trees just before you reach the road and some **bus** services (Stagecoach's No 280 & Burnley Bus's Pendle Wizz; see p56). If it's food and accommodation you are after, it's better to drop down to **Earby** (see p136), where you'll find a good hostel and lots of food options. However, most press on, over **Langber Hill** (Map 35) to the **Leeds–Liverpool canal**, with its famous double bridge carrying the very busy A59 past **East Marton**. As you leave the canal keep an eye out for *Abbots Harbour* (see p141), a lovely café and almost perfectly situated for lunch, but only on the weekends.

The path then goes through lush green fields, over **Scaleber Hill** (Map 36) – this will cause no problems to the hardened walker you now are – and down into the wonderful oasis of **Gargrave** (Map 37). For Pennine Wayfarers, this is the gateway to the Dales and offers all the refreshment options a walker could need. Stopping is mandatory, even if it's just for a bag of sweets from *Dalesman Café* (see p142).

Beyond Gargrave the Way climbs steadily through the fields of **Eshton Moor** (Map 38) and then down to meet the River Aire which you cross again, the first time having been in Gargrave, and then walk beside for the remainder of this section, through **Airton** (Map 39), where a diversion to the tea room of **Town End Farm Shop** (see p146) is possible, past **Hanlith Hall** and finally into **Malham**, a tourist hot-spot at the edge of limestone country.

If you arrive in Malham early enough it's well worth dumping your bag at your accommodation and then making the 3½ mile return detour to **Janet's Foss waterfall** and **Goredale Scar** (off Map 40), two of the most impressive natural features you'll see on the Pennine Way. Have a good night's rest in this friendly village, for tomorrow hills await.

Navigation notes

The number of fields, stiles and gates on today's route will inevitably lead to confusion and although the path on the ground is often not obvious, especially on the way into Gargrave, the signage is mostly excellent. Keeping one eye (and a finger) on the map and the other on the lookout for Pennine Way markers should be enough to see you through.

LOTHERSDALE   [Map 32]

The *Hare & Hounds* (☎ 01535-631200, 🖳 hareandhoundslothersdale.com; 🐾) serves food every day (Mon-Sat noon-9pm, Sun to 8pm). There's a great range of lunchtime sandwiches (£8-10), including steak, or brie and bacon, as well as heftier dinners (£12-16), from fish pie to Korean barbecue beef salad.

EARBY   [Map 34, p139]

Earby is quite a large community but it doesn't have much accommodation. It does have a **general store** cum **post office** (Mon-Thur 9am-9pm, Fri & Sat 9am-10pm, Sun noon-8pm), a **chemist** (Mon-Fri 8.30am-6.30pm, Sat 9am-2pm) and a Co-op **supermarket** (daily 7am-10pm) with **ATM**.

The main reason to detour to Earby is to stay in the historic *Earby Holiday Hostel* (☎ 07791 903454, 01282-842349, 🖳 earby hostel.co.uk; 1x2-, 2x6-, 1x7-bed rooms; shared facilities; Mar/Easter to early Nov; Ⓛ), a fine place with a kitchen, dining room, lounge and drying room. A bed costs £25pp, including bed linen and towel, and if it's not busy you'll likely score your own room. Breakfast (£5), dinner and packed lunches are possible if arranged 48 hours in advance. They also have a cottage (£70-75; min 2 nights) that is perfect for couples or families.

In Earby itself *Aspendos* (Sun-Thur 3-10pm, Fri 3-11pm, Sat noon-11pm) has pizzas and kebabs to take away and there's a Kashmiri Indian restaurant, *Musafir* (☎ 01282-843943, 🖳 musafirtakeaway.com, **fb**; daily 4-11pm) with chef's specials from £8.25. *Orient Pearl* (🖳 orientpearlearby.co .uk; Wed-Mon 4.30-10pm) is a Chinese takeaway; *Quality Fish Bar* (☎ 01282-842546; Tue-Sat 11.30am-6.30/7pm) for fish & chips, and there's a **bakery**. *Humble Pie* (**fb**; Wed-Sun 9am-3pm), near the Co-op, is a good place for coffee and breakfast.

Earby has two pubs, the *Red Lion* (🖳 redlionearby.co.uk), closest to Earby hostel and serving local real ales but no food, and the *Punch Bowl* (🖳 thepunchbowlearby.co .uk), further away on Skipton Rd but serving pub grub daily from noon.

There is even a craft brewery, *BB 18 Brewery* (**fb**; Mon, Wed & Thur 4-9pm, Fri & Sat 2-10pm, Sun 2-9pm), where you can get a taster flight of three of the beers they brew on site.

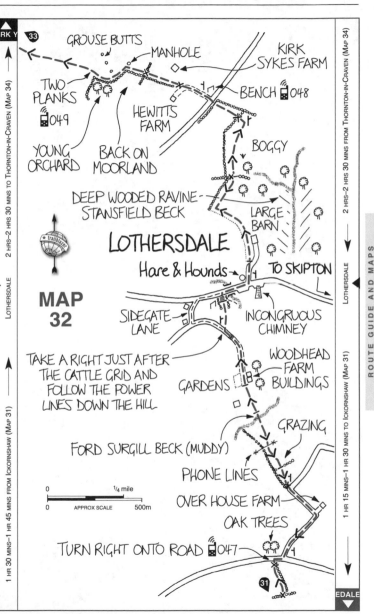

KIRK Y

33

GROUSE BUTTS

MANHOLE

KIRK SYKES FARM

TWO PLANKS 📱049

HEWITTS FARM

BENCH 📱048

YOUNG ORCHARD

BACK ON MOORLAND

BOGGY

DEEP WOODED RAVINE - STANSFIELD BECK

LARGE BARN

LOTHERSDALE

Hare & Hounds

TO SKIPTON

MAP 32

SIDEGATE LANE

INCONGRUOUS CHIMNEY

TAKE A RIGHT JUST AFTER THE CATTLE GRID AND FOLLOW THE POWER LINES DOWN THE HILL

WOODHEAD FARM BUILDINGS

GARDENS

FORD SURGILL BECK (MUDDY)

GRAZING

PHONE LINES

OVER HOUSE FARM

OAK TREES

TURN RIGHT ONTO ROAD 📱047

31

0   ¼ mile

APPROX SCALE   500m

2 HRS–2 HRS 30 MINS TO THORNTON-IN-CRAVEN (MAP 34)

LOTHERSDALE

1 HR 30 MINS–1 HR 45 MINS FROM ICKORNSHAW (MAP 31)

2 HRS–2 HRS 30 MINS FROM THORNTON-IN-CRAVEN (MAP 34)

LOTHERSDALE

1 HR 15 MINS–1 HR 30 MINS TO ICKORNSHAW (MAP 31)

EDALE

ROUTE GUIDE AND MAPS

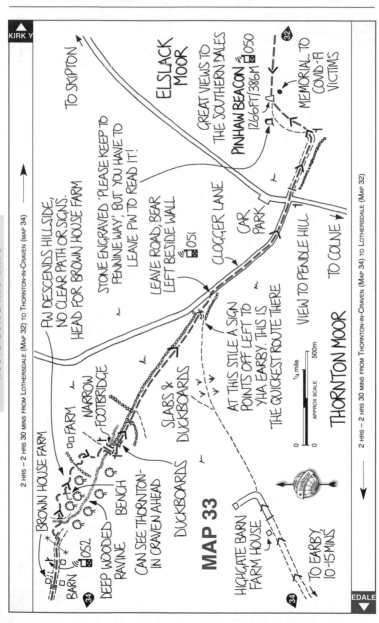

KIRK Y

2 HRS – 2 HRS 30 MINS FROM LOTHERSDALE (MAP 32) TO THORNTON-IN-CRAVEN (MAP 34) ——→

TO SKIPTON

ELSLACK
MOOR

GREAT VIEWS TO
THE SOUTHERN DALES

32

PINHAW BEACON 🏔 📷 050
1266FT/386M

MEMORIAL TO
COVID-19
VICTIMS

PW DESCENDS HILLSIDE,
NO CLEAR PATH OR SIGNS.
HEAD FOR BROWN HOUSE FARM

STONE ENGRAVED 'PLEASE KEEP TO
PENNINE WAY', BUT YOU HAVE TO
LEAVE PW TO READ IT!

LEAVE ROAD, BEAR
LEFT BESIDE WALL

📷 051

CLOGGER LANE

CAR
PARK

VIEW TO PENDLE HILL

TO COLNE ↓

THORNTON MOOR

BROWN HOUSE FARM

🏠 FARM

NARROW
FOOTBRIDGE

SLABS &
DUCKBOARDS

AT THIS STILE A SIGN
POINTS OFF LEFT TO
YHA EARBY. THIS IS
THE QUICKEST ROUTE THERE

¼ mile
APPROX SCALE
0   500m
0

BARN 📷 052

34

DEEP WOODED RAVINE

BENCH

DUCKBOARDS

CAN SEE THORNTON-
IN-CRAVEN AHEAD

MAP 33

HIGHGATE BARN
FARM HOUSE

TO EARBY
10-15 MINS

34

EDALE

2 HRS – 2 HRS 30 MINS FROM THORNTON-IN-CRAVEN (MAP 34) TO LOTHERSDALE (MAP 32) ——→

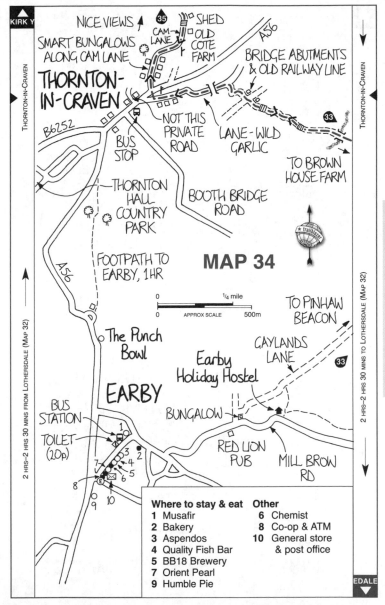

KIRK Y

THORNTON-IN-CRAVEN

NICE VIEWS

SMART BUNGALOWS ALONG CAM LANE

THORNTON-IN-CRAVEN

B6252

35 CAM LANE

SHED OLD COTE FARM

BRIDGE ABUTMENTS & OLD RAILWAY LINE

A56

THORNTON-IN-CRAVEN

NOT THIS PRIVATE ROAD

LANE - WILD GARLIC

33

BUS STOP

TO BROWN HOUSE FARM

THORNTON HALL COUNTRY PARK

BOOTH BRIDGE ROAD

A56

FOOTPATH TO EARBY, 1HR

MAP 34

trailblazer

0 ¼ mile
0 APPROX SCALE 500m

The Punch Bowl

EARBY

Earby Holiday Hostel

TO PINHAW BEACON

GAYLANDS LANE

33

BUS STATION

TOILET (20p)

BUNGALOW

RED LION PUB

MILL BROW RD

2 HRS–2 HRS 30 MINS FROM LOTHERSDALE (MAP 32)

2 HRS–2 HRS 30 MINS TO LOTHERSDALE (MAP 32)

ROUTE GUIDE AND MAPS

Where to stay & eat	Other
1 Musafir	**6** Chemist
2 Bakery	**8** Co-op & ATM
3 Aspendos	**10** General store
4 Quality Fish Bar	& post office
5 BB18 Brewery	
7 Orient Pearl	
9 Humble Pie	

EDALE

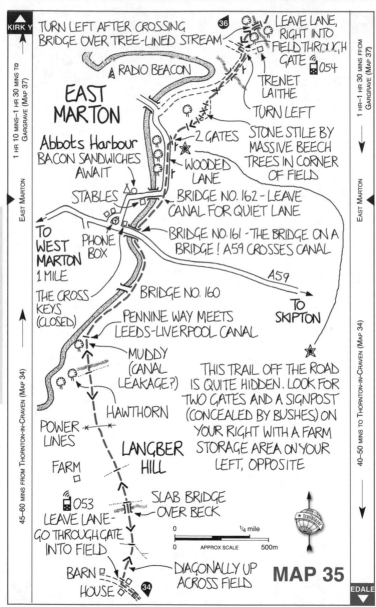

KIRK Y

TURN LEFT AFTER CROSSING
BRIDGE OVER TREE-LINED STREAM

36

LEAVE LANE,
RIGHT INTO
FIELD THROUGH
GATE 📱054

RADIO BEACON

TRENET
LAITHE

EAST
MARTON

TURN LEFT

1 HR 10 MINS–1 HR 30 MINS TO GARGRAVE (MAP 37)

1 HR–1 HR 30 MINS FROM GARGRAVE (MAP 37)

Abbots Harbour
BACON SANDWICHES
AWAIT

2 GATES

STONE STILE BY
MASSIVE BEECH
TREES IN CORNER
OF FIELD

WOODED
LANE

STABLES

EAST MARTON

EAST MARTON

BRIDGE NO. 162 – LEAVE
CANAL FOR QUIET LANE

TO
WEST
MARTON
1 MILE

PHONE
BOX

BRIDGE NO. 161 – THE BRIDGE ON A
BRIDGE! A59 CROSSES CANAL

A59

THE CROSS
KEYS
(CLOSED)

BRIDGE NO. 160

TO
SKIPTON

ROUTE GUIDE AND MAPS

PENNINE WAY MEETS
LEEDS-LIVERPOOL CANAL

MUDDY
(CANAL
LEAKAGE?)

THIS TRAIL OFF THE ROAD
IS QUITE HIDDEN. LOOK FOR
TWO GATES AND A SIGNPOST
(CONCEALED BY BUSHES) ON
YOUR RIGHT WITH A FARM
STORAGE AREA ON YOUR
LEFT, OPPOSITE

HAWTHORN

POWER
LINES

LANGBER
HILL

FARM

45–60 MINS FROM THORNTON-IN-CRAVEN (MAP 34)

40–50 MINS TO THORNTON-IN-CRAVEN (MAP 34)

📱053
LEAVE LANE–
GO THROUGH GATE
INTO FIELD

SLAB BRIDGE
OVER BECK

0   ¼ mile
0   APPROX SCALE   500m

trailblazer

BARN
HOUSE

34

DIAGONALLY UP
ACROSS FIELD

MAP 35

EDALE

EAST MARTON [Map 35]

East Marton is a hidden treasure known only to canal users and walkers looking for a mooring or way station alongside the PW.

Although it has limited opening hours, *Abbots Harbour* (☎ 01282-843207, **fb**; 🐾; Fri & Sat 10am-4pm, Sun 10am-5pm) still deserves an accolade for its atmosphere and **food**. A bacon sandwich costs £3.10, all-day breakfast with tea or coffee £7.25. You can also **camp** here; £5pp will see you

securely ensconced, with toilet and shower facilities at your disposal.

Up the lane facing the main road, the **Cross Keys** pub (☎ 01282-844326, 🖳 the crosskeys.uk.com;) was closed and seeking new management at the time of writing. Check online whether it has reopened.

Should you need to get out of town fast ring **Gill's Taxis** (☎ 01282-841301) for a **taxi**.

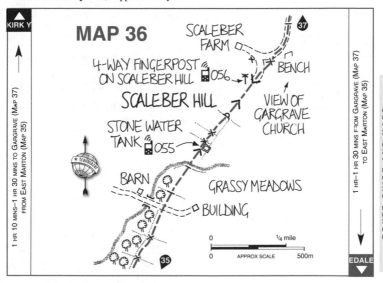

GARGRAVE [Map 37a, p143]

This small attractive town has most things you will want. Say 'hello' to the River Aire which you'll be following later in the day.

All the shops here are on the main road and close together. There is a **pharmacy** (Mon-Fri 9am-1pm, 2-5.30pm, Sat 9am-12.30pm) and a well-stocked Co-op **supermarket** (daily 7am-10pm) with an **ATM**.

See p14 for details of the agricultural show here in August.

Transport

Gargrave is a stop on Northern Rail's Leeds to Carlisle **railway** line (see p59), with seven trains a day to Settle, Horton,

Carlisle, Leeds and Lancaster.

Bus services calling here include: Kirkby Lonsdale Coaches' Nos 580 & 75 (Saturdays only); North Yorkshire County Council (NYCC)'s No 210/211; and the DalesBus No 884 (Sundays only). For more details see pp54-9.

Where to stay

Since the accommodation options here are limited plan ahead or take a bus (see p54) to Skipton (see 🖳 welcometoskipton.com for details of the many accommodation options there as well as other information).

Coming off the Pennine Way, just

before the bridge, you'll pass the *Masons Arms* (☎ 01756-749304, 🖳 masonsarms-gargrave.co.uk; 3D/2T/1Tr, all en suite; 🍴; Ⓛ; 🐾), on the corner close to the church. It has rooms for £80-90 (sgl occ £55-60, weekends & school hols full room rate); breakfast costs £5.50 extra for the continental version, £10 for the full English.

The Old Swan Inn (☎ 01756-749232, 🖳 classicinns.co.uk/old-swan-gargrave; 4D/1T, all en suite; 🍴; clean 🐾) charges from S/D £89/99 for room only, about £20 more on weekends.

Head east out of town on the A65 and you'll get to *Eshton Road Caravan Site* (☎ 01756-749229; 🐾) with an enclosed **camping** area for £10pp; toilet and shower facilities are available. It is advisable to book ahead for summer weekends.

Where to eat and drink
As you cross the bridge over the River Aire you will face *Dalesman Café* (☎ 01756-749250; Tue-Sun 9am-4pm; 🐾), a nostalgic place stuffed with 1950s memorabilia. It offers a good range of food: a 'Dalesman

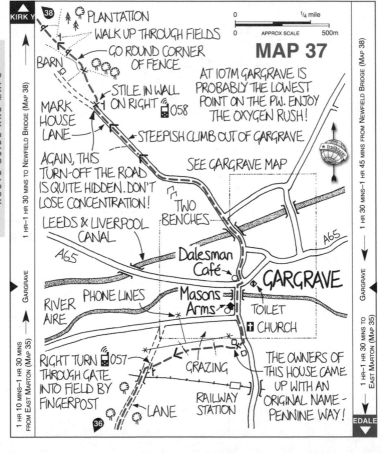

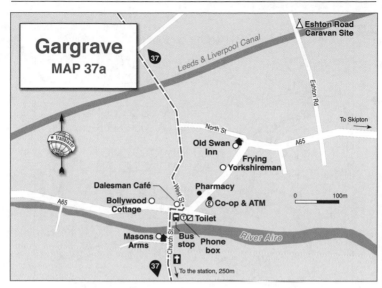

Gargrave
MAP 37a

Eshton Road
Caravan Site

Leeds & Liverpool Canal

37

To Skipton

North St

A65

Old Swan
Inn

Frying
Yorkshireman

Eshton Rd

Dalesman Café

Pharmacy

Bollywood
Cottage

£ Co-op & ATM

0   100m

Toilet

A65

River Aire

Masons
Arms

Bus
stop

Phone
box

37

To the station, 250m

Lunch' with ham, Wensleydale cheese &
chutney is £8.50; home-made cakes are £3;
soup (always vegetarian) is £5.50 as well as
indulgences such as quality ice-cream,
scones, and around 200 varieties of old-
fashioned sweets in jars. They always have
something gluten-free on the menu.

Nearby is a very good Indian restaurant, *Bollywood Cottage* (☎ 01756-749252,
🖳 bollywoodcottage.co.uk; Tue-Sat 5-
11pm, Sun 5-10.30pm) with biryani dishes
from £9.50 and curries £8.50-12.

Masons Arms (see Where to stay; food
Mon-Sat noon-8.30pm, Sun noon-7pm) is a
friendly local with interesting pub food
(£13-15), including a red lentil, sweet potato and spinach dahl. Ask about the
'Yorkshire tapas'. The lunchtime (noon-

4pm) snack menu has sandwiches, salads
and jacket potatoes for £8.

The Old Swan Inn (see Where to stay;
bar daily noon to 11pm; food Mon-Fri
noon-8pm, Sat & Sun 11am-8pm) has a
variety of traditionally themed rooms such
as a flagstone floor 'Snug' with an open fire
in winter, and a 'Parlour' with a darts board.
The menu largely consists of the usual pub
favourites (steaks, burgers and a pie of the
day), costing £11-14.

For fish & chips, steak pie or, God for-
bid, a spam butty, try the excellently-named
Frying Yorkshireman (fb; Mon-Fri
11.30am-2.30pm, 4-8.30pm, Sat 11.30am-
8.30pm). The lunchtime menu is particularly good value, with a small fish and chips
just £5.25. You can take away or eat in.

AIRTON   [Map 39, p145]

Right by the left bank of the river, tiny
Airton has two places to stay: *Airton Barn*
(☎ 01729-830263, 07379 508195, 🖳 air-
tonbarn.org.uk; 1 x 6 bunk beds; shared
facilities; booking essential) located at the
Quaker Meeting House, has a dormitory
which is open to anyone. A bunk bed costs

from £20pp but they also have fold out mattresses and airbeds, making a total capacity
of 18 people, and there are a couple of
camping spaces out back. There are shower facilities and access to two kitchens.
Sheet, duvet cover and pillow slips (£5 per
stay) can be rented or bring a sleeping bag.

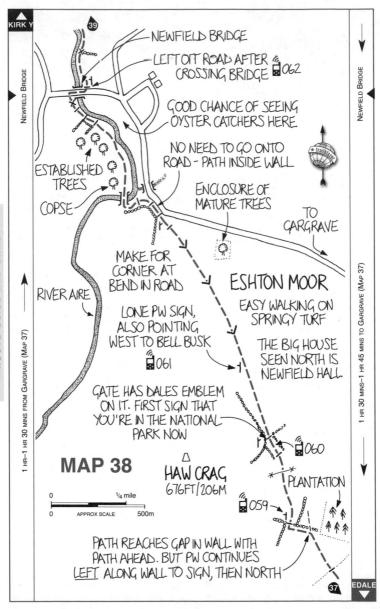

KIRK Y
39

NEWFIELD BRIDGE
LEFT OFF ROAD AFTER CROSSING BRIDGE 062

GOOD CHANCE OF SEEING OYSTER CATCHERS HERE

NO NEED TO GO ONTO ROAD - PATH INSIDE WALL

ESTABLISHED TREES
COPSE

ENCLOSURE OF MATURE TREES

TO GARGRAVE

NEWFIELD BRIDGE

MAKE FOR CORNER AT BEND IN ROAD

ESHTON MOOR

EASY WALKING ON SPRINGY TURF

RIVER AIRE

LONE PW SIGN, ALSO POINTING WEST TO BELL BUSK 061

THE BIG HOUSE SEEN NORTH IS NEWFIELD HALL

GATE HAS DALES EMBLEM ON IT. FIRST SIGN THAT YOU'RE IN THE NATIONAL PARK NOW

060

MAP 38

△
HAW CRAG
676FT/206M

PLANTATION

059

0   ¼ mile
0   APPROX SCALE   500m

PATH REACHES GAP IN WALL WITH PATH AHEAD. BUT PW CONTINUES <u>LEFT</u> ALONG WALL TO SIGN, THEN NORTH

1 HR 30 MINS—1 HR 30 MINS FROM GARGRAVE (MAP 37)

1 HR 30 MINS—1 HR 45 MINS TO GARGRAVE (MAP 37)

EDALE
37

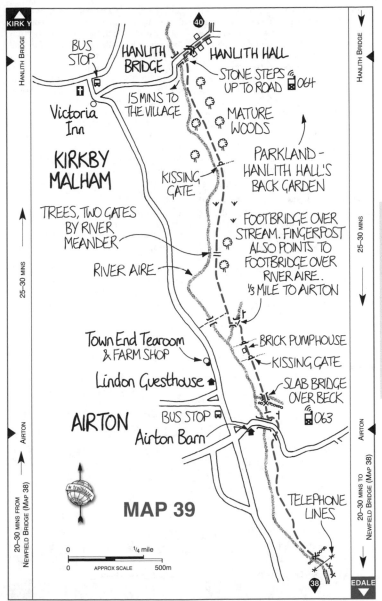

MAP 39

Evening meals are not available here but if you expect to arrive after 5pm the staff there are happy to collect any food order from Town End Farm Shop (see below).

Towards the other end of the scale is the characterful *Lindon Guesthouse* (☎ 01729-830418, 💻 lindonguesthouse.co.uk; 1T/4D, all en suite; ⓛ; 🦮), a little way out of the village along the Malham road. B&B costs S/D from £70/85; evening meals (£17.95) are available subject to prior arrangement, but not usually on Thursdays and Sundays or during lambing time.

Town End Farm Shop & Post Office (☎ 01729-830902, 💻 townendfarmshop.co

.uk; Tue-Sat 9.30am-5pm, Sun & Bank Hol Mons 10am-5pm) also has a *tea room* (hot food served to 3pm, tea room closes at 4pm; 🦮) which is a little further along the road, towards Kirkby Malham. Sandwiches, soups and desserts are available (£9-12) and most of the food is made in-house, even the chorizo. A handy footpath and footbridge over the Aire, just to the north of the farm, leads back to the Pennine Way.

NYCC's Nos 210/211 **bus services** call here twice a day en route between Skipton and Malham, as does the DalesBus No 884 (Sundays only). see pp54-9 for details.

KIRKBY MALHAM   [Map 39]

Standing back from the river, this village is another gem, carefully preserved by its inhabitants and unspoilt by anything as common as a shop. The church has a set of stocks into which anyone putting up a satellite dish would probably be clapped and pelted with rotting fruit.

Victoria Inn (☎ 01729-830499; 💻 victoriakirkbymalham.co.uk, **fb**; 1D/2D or T/1Tr, all en suite) offers four **rooms** for £110-145. The pub (Tue 3-10pm, Wed-Sat

11am-10/11pm, Sun & bank hols noon-9pm) serves standard pub fare (**food** Tue 5-8pm, Wed-Fri noon-2pm & 5-8pm, Sat noon-8pm, Sun noon-4pm), with main dishes £12-19.

NYCC's No 210/211 **bus** service calls here as do Kirkby Lonsdale Coaches' No 75 (Saturdays only) and DalesBus No 884 (Sundays only) services; see pp54-9 for details.

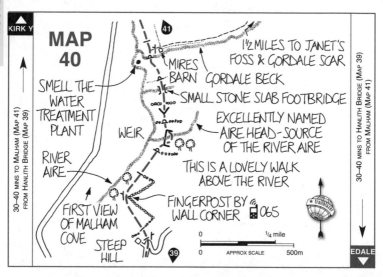

ROUTE GUIDE AND MAPS

KIRKBY

MAP 40

41

SMELL THE WATER TREATMENT PLANT

MIRES BARN

CORDALE BECK

1½ MILES TO JANET'S FOSS & GORDALE SCAR

SMALL STONE SLAB FOOTBRIDGE

WEIR

EXCELLENTLY NAMED AIRE HEAD-SOURCE OF THE RIVER AIRE

RIVER AIRE

THIS IS A LOVELY WALK ABOVE THE RIVER

FIRST VIEW OF MALHAM COVE

FINGERPOST BY WALL CORNER 065

STEEP HILL

39

30-40 MINS TO MALHAM (MAP 41) FROM HANLITH BRIDGE (MAP 39)

30-40 MINS TO HANLITH BRIDGE (MAP 41) FROM MALHAM (MAP 39)

★ trailblazer

0   ¼ mile
0   APPROX SCALE   500m

EDALE

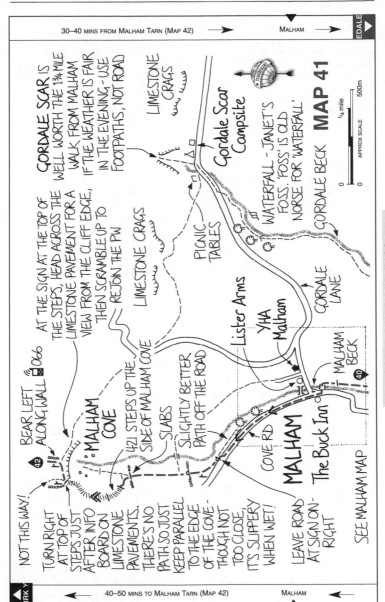

CORDALE SCAR IS WELL WORTH THE 1¾ MILE WALK FROM MALHAM IF THE WEATHER IS FAIR IN THE EVENING – USE FOOTPATHS, NOT ROAD

LIMESTONE CRAGS

Cordale Scar Campsite

MAP 41

¼ mile

APPROX SCALE

0   500m

WATERFALL – JANET'S FOSS. 'FOSS' IS OLD NORSE FOR 'WATERFALL'

CORDALE BECK

AT THE SIGN AT THE TOP OF THE STEPS, HEAD ACROSS THE LIMESTONE PAVEMENT FOR A VIEW FROM THE CLIFF EDGE, THEN SCRAMBLE UP TO REJOIN THE PW

LIMESTONE CRAGS

PICNIC TABLES

CORDALE LANE

BEAR LEFT ALONG WALL 066

Lister Arms
YHA Malham

421 STEPS UP THE SIDE OF MALHAM COVE

MALHAM COVE

SLABS

SLIGHTLY BETTER PATH OFF THE ROAD

MALHAM BECK

40

NOT THIS WAY!

TURN RIGHT AT TOP OF STEPS JUST AFTER INFO BOARD ON LIMESTONE PAVEMENTS. THERE'S NO PATH SO JUST KEEP PARALLEL TO THE EDGE OF THE COVE – THOUGH NOT TOO CLOSE, IT'S SLIPPERY WHEN WET!

42

COVE RD

MALHAM
The Buck Inn

LEAVE ROAD AT SIGN ON RIGHT

SEE MALHAM MAP

MALHAM   [Map 41a]

Probably the busiest village between Haworth and the Roman wall, Malham is world-renowned for its incredible limestone amphitheatre and more recently its peregrine falcons (see box below). A wise walker will aim to arrive in Malham during the week, or certainly outside the school holiday period, as accommodation is often booked up well in advance. This was once a mining village known for calamine, the ore which produces zinc.

Services

Malham National Park Centre (NPC; ☎ 01729-833200, 🖳 yorkshiredales.org.uk; Easter-Oct daily 10am-5pm, Nov-Dec & Feb-Mar Sat & Sun 10am-4pm) is just to the south of the village and has some modest displays about the geology and history of the area, as well as general information about the region and Yorkshire Dales National Park while the **Town Head Barn** to the north has a few small displays on rural life.

The town's **website** (🖳 malhamdale .com) is also useful for information about the area in general, including yet more accommodation (what follows below is a selection).

A small **general store** (Malham Shop; ☎ 01729-830319) is located right on the bridge in the heart of the village, but its rather unconventional opening times, 'weekends and most afternoons' make it hard to rely on for walkers. If it's open it's worth popping in just to see what can be achieved in such a small space – Dr Who's TARDIS has nothing on this place. The stock is very limited but it's the last chance to buy anything until Hawes.

See p14 for details of events held here in the summer.

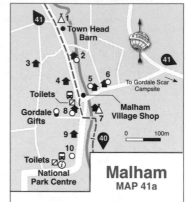

Malham
MAP 41a

Where to stay and eat
1 Riverside Campsite at
   Town Head Farm
2 Beck Hall B&B
3 Hill Top Farm Bunkhouse
4 Lister Barn
5 Lister Arms
6 YHA Malham
7 Miresfield Farm (B&B & camping)
8 The Buck Inn
9 River House B&B
10 Old Barn Tea Room

Transport

[See pp54-9] NYCC's 210/211 **bus** calls here as do Kirkby Lonsdale Coaches' No 75 (Saturdays only) and DalesBus Nos 881 (seasonal) and 884 (both Sundays only).

For a 24-hour **taxi** service call Skipton & Craven Taxis (☎ 01756-701122, 🖳 skip tontaxis.com).

Where to stay

Even though there is a good supply of accommodation here visitor numbers are high so it's worth booking in advance. If it's

---

❏ PEREGRINE FALCON VIEWING

Every year the RSPB run a peregrine-viewing site at **Malham Cove** (Map 41) where a resident pair of these raptors nest on the limestone cliffs. The site is right in the bowl of the cove and RSPB wardens are on hand with telescopes during the nesting season; this is generally March/April-July (Thur-Mon 10.30am-4.30pm) but the staff at the National Park Centre (see Services) will know the days/hours nearer the time.

B&B you're after, note that during peak times some places will accept bookings only for a **two-day stay at weekends** and, as in some other places, solo travellers need expect no favours on pricing. As far as room quantities and ambience goes, most of the B&Bs in Malham can be classified in the 'small hotel' category. It's a busy place.

To **camp** in an awesome setting walk one mile east to the slightly eccentric *Gordale Scar Campsite* (Map 41; ☎ 01729-830333; ☐ gordalescarcampsite.co.uk; 🐾), Gordale House Farm, where they charge £8-10 per person. There's a very basic toilet and shower block.

North of the village there's spacious camping at *Riverside Campsite* at **Town Head Farm** (☎ 01729-830287, ☐ malhamdale.com/camping.htm; no wi-fi; 🐾 on a lead; Easter to Oct); they charge £8pp for walkers, and for £2 more walkers can get out of the rain and sleep in Bessie the caravan (no electricity or water). Shower (£1 per 7 mins, buy a token) and toilet facilities are available.

Simple camping (£10pp) is also possible at *Miresfield Farm* (☎ 01729-830414, ☐ miresfieldfarm.co.uk; 🐾); toilets are available. At the time of research the five B&B rooms were being renovated so check with them for availability.

There's **bunkhouse** accommodation at *Hill Top Farm* (☎ 01729-830320, ☐ hilltopmalham.co.uk; 5 rooms sleep 2-6, 1 x 15-bed room; 🐾) costing £35pp. There are showers, a drying room and a fully equipped kitchen. However, it is important to note that individuals can only book a bed outside of school holidays and weekends and only if there are no group bookings, so they don't take individual bookings until near the requested date.

Near the centre of the village is the very popular *YHA Malham* (☎ 0345-371 9529, ☐ yha.org.uk/hostel/malham; wi-fi in communal areas; ©). The 81-bed (1 x 3-, 2 x 2-, 1 x 6-bed rooms en suite, 8 x 4-, 4 x 6-, 1 x 8-bed rooms shared facilities) purpose-built hostel now boasts two **camping pods** too (sleep 2; £59-79 per pod) as well as a licensed *café/restaurant* which is also open to non-residents, though as always

there is a self-catering kitchen. There is also a drying room and laundry facilities as well as a **shop** selling basic food supplies. Private rooms swing wildly in price, with a two-bed room with shared facilities costing anywhere between £29 and £79. Check with them about the availability of dorm beds. The whole hostel is sometimes booked out with school groups.

B&B at *River House B&B* (☎ 01729-830315, ☐ riverhousemalham.co.uk; 2D or T/6D, all en suite; 🛏; ©; 🐾; summer min 2 nights) costs £70-110 for a double, or £60-99 for single occupancy. The hotel has a drying room, bar, lounge and laundry service.

The Buck Inn (☎ 01729-830317, ☐ vixen-pubs.co.uk/buck-inn-pub-malham; 9D/1T, all en suite; 🛏; ©; 🐾) has decent rooms above the pub; B&B costs £90-100.

Over the road *Lister Arms* (☎ 01729-830444, ☐ listerarms.co.uk; 2D or T/16D/5Qd, all en suite; 🛏; ©; 🐾) is more expensive but a bit classier, charging from £140-180 per double for B&B, either above the pub, in cottages out the back or in the new stylishly converted barn a short walk away.

Beck Hall (☎ 01729-830729, ☐ beckhallmalham.com; 16D/5D or T, all en suite; 🛏; 🐾; weekends min 2 nights) is a historic building in a charming setting at a ford in the river. They have a wide range of rooms costing £130-150 (no single rates). Packed lunches are not provided but you can order a sandwich from their menu the night before.

Where to eat & drink
Lister Arms (see Where to stay; food daily noon-9.30pm) has a great menu and a cosy setting: main courses such as steak & ale pie or wild mushroom risotto cost around £16. Reservations are recommended.

Simpler pub grub is also served at *The Buck Inn* (see Where to stay; food daily noon-8.30pm). The lunch menu is good value at £8 per main course

Beck Hall (see Where to stay; noon-9pm) has the village's most charming location, with romantic creekside seating. The food ranges from afternoon tapas to South

ROUTE GUIDE AND MAPS

Indian curries and Sunday roasts, with mains £14-19.

There's also *Old Barn Tea Room* (☎ 01729-830486, 🖥 oldbarnmalham.co.uk/cafe.html; early Feb to late Oct Mon-Fri 10am-5pm, Sat & Sun 9am-5pm; 🐾) near the National Park Centre. The all-day breakfasts, soups, sandwiches, coffee and cakes are all good, and great value with dishes around £4-5.

MALHAM TO HORTON-IN-RIBBLESDALE   MAPS 41-48

Route overview

Note that there aren't many options for getting food or snacks on this stage so **stock up before you go**. This probably won't feel like the shortest day on the

Distance	14½ miles (23.5km)
Ascent	2900ft (884m)
Time	6-8 hours

Pennine Way so far; it includes two tough climbs and some of the most exciting scenery to date, including one of the highlights of the whole walk at **Malham Cove** (Map 41). Malham's famous limestone amphitheatre, the site of an ancient waterfall to rival Niagara and home now to peregrine falcons and climbers, is encountered almost immediately on leaving the village. The ascent of the steps beside the Cove doesn't count as one of the two tough climbs, but it will have you breathing heavily, as will the climb out of **Watlowes** (Map 42), the impressive limestone valley beyond.

The Way passes **Malham Tarn**, an unusual lake in porous limestone country and a haven for waterfowl and more birdwatchers, before reaching **Tennant Gill Farm** (Map 43), and the foot of **Fountains Fell** (Map 44; see box p157). A mostly obvious path leads up this 900ft (274m) of ascent with incredible views all around, if the weather allows – note the complete lack of reservoirs, pylons and chimneys! As you reach the wall at the top of the climb, you'll get the first sight of Pen-y-ghent, meaning 'hill of the winds', one of the 'Yorkshire Three Peaks' and your next target.

Descending from Fountains Fell you follow a quiet country lane which provides a perfect panorama of the stepped profile of **Pen-y-ghent** (Map 46), which you will shortly be ascending. At its base the 600ft (183m) climb appears ferocious and quite daunting, but is actually much easier than it looks and the summit, with its trig point and shelter, is sublime.

The path down to **Horton-in-Ribblesdale** (Maps 46-48), on the other hand, can be quite jarring, hardened as it is to support the hundreds of thousands of 'Three Peakers' (see box p159) who use it every year. You may find you survived the ascent, only to be done in by the descent!

Navigation notes

The improved signage over Fountains Fell has removed the only lingering potential point of difficulty on this section of the Way. The path round Fountains Fell is clear, even in the thickest mist, and the signs point out any changes in direction.

Pen-y-ghent is so busy the path has to be industrial to cope with the footfall and as such is almost impossible to lose.)

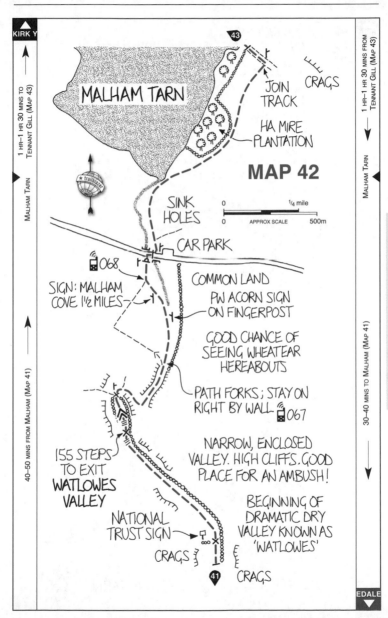

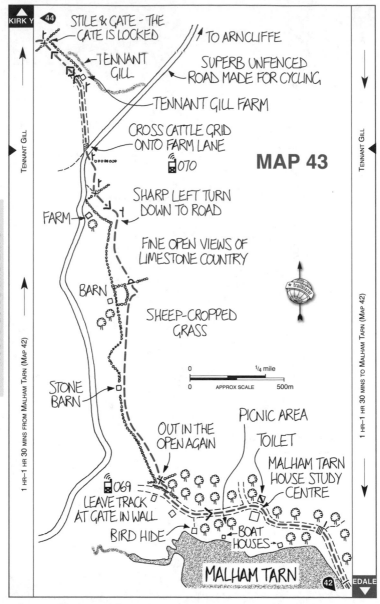

KIRK Y
44
STILE & GATE – THE GATE IS LOCKED
TENNANT GILL
TO ARNCLIFFE
SUPERB UNFENCED ROAD MADE FOR CYCLING
TENNANT GILL FARM
CROSS CATTLE GRID ONTO FARM LANE
070
MAP 43
SHARP LEFT TURN DOWN TO ROAD
FARM
FINE OPEN VIEWS OF LIMESTONE COUNTRY
BARN
SHEEP-CROPPED GRASS
STONE BARN
0   ¼ mile
0   500m
APPROX SCALE
PICNIC AREA
TOILET
OUT IN THE OPEN AGAIN
MALHAM TARN HOUSE STUDY CENTRE
069
LEAVE TRACK AT GATE IN WALL
BIRD HIDE
BOAT HOUSES
MALHAM TARN
42
EDALE

TENNANT GILL

1 HR–1 HR 30 MINS FROM MALHAM TARN (MAP 42)

TENNANT GILL

1 HR–1 HR 30 MINS TO MALHAM TARN (MAP 42)

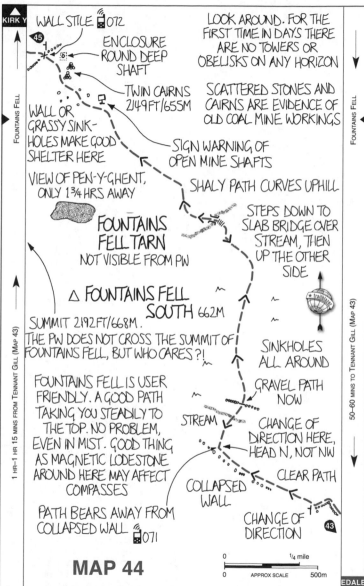

KIRK Y

WALL STILE 📶072

45

ENCLOSURE
ROUND DEEP
SHAFT

FOUNTAINS FELL

TWIN CAIRNS
2149FT/655M

WALL OR
GRASSY SINK-
HOLES MAKE GOOD
SHELTER HERE

SIGN WARNING OF
OPEN MINE SHAFTS

VIEW OF PEN-Y-GHENT,
ONLY 1¾ HRS AWAY

FOUNTAINS
FELL TARN
NOT VISIBLE FROM PW

△ FOUNTAINS FELL
SOUTH 662M

SUMMIT 2192FT/668M.
THE PW DOES NOT CROSS THE SUMMIT OF
FOUNTAINS FELL, BUT WHO CARES?!

FOUNTAINS FELL IS USER
FRIENDLY. A GOOD PATH
TAKING YOU STEADILY TO
THE TOP. NO PROBLEM,
EVEN IN MIST. GOOD THING
AS MAGNETIC LODESTONE
AROUND HERE MAY AFFECT
COMPASSES

PATH BEARS AWAY FROM
COLLAPSED WALL 📶071

LOOK AROUND. FOR THE
FIRST TIME IN DAYS THERE
ARE NO TOWERS OR
OBELISKS ON ANY HORIZON

SCATTERED STONES AND
CAIRNS ARE EVIDENCE OF
OLD COAL MINE WORKINGS

SHALY PATH CURVES UPHILL

STEPS DOWN TO
SLAB BRIDGE OVER
STREAM, THEN
UP THE OTHER
SIDE

SINKHOLES
ALL AROUND

GRAVEL PATH
NOW

STREAM

CHANGE OF
DIRECTION HERE,
HEAD N, NOT NW

CLEAR PATH

COLLAPSED
WALL

CHANGE OF
DIRECTION

43

FOUNTAINS FELL

1 HR–1 HR 15 MINS FROM TENNANT GILL (MAP 43)

50–60 MINS TO TENNANT GILL (MAP 43)

ROUTE GUIDE AND MAPS

MAP 44

0   ¼ mile
0   APPROX SCALE   500m

EDALE

ROUTE GUIDE AND MAPS

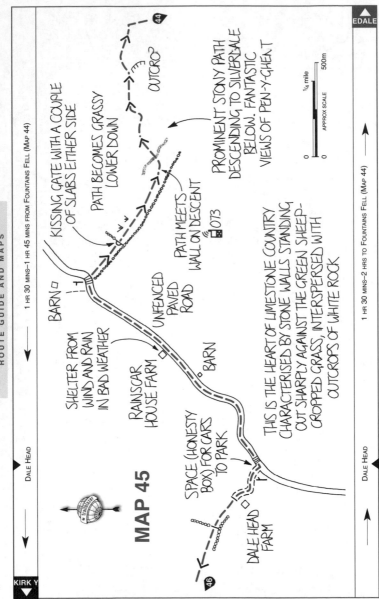

MAP 45

1 HR 30 MINS–1 HR 45 MINS FROM FOUNTAINS FELL (MAP 44)

1 HR 30 MINS–2 HRS TO FOUNTAINS FELL (MAP 44)

DALE HEAD

KIRK Y

EDALE

KISSING GATE WITH A COUPLE OF SLABS EITHER SIDE

PATH BECOMES GRASSY LOWER DOWN

OUTCROP

PROMINENT STONY PATH DESCENDING TO SILVERDALE BELOW. FANTASTIC VIEWS OF PEN-Y-GHENT

PATH MEETS WALL ON DESCENT

073

BARN

SHELTER FROM WIND AND RAIN IN BAD WEATHER

UNFENCED PAVED ROAD

RAINSCAR HOUSE FARM

BARN

THIS IS THE HEART OF LIMESTONE COUNTRY CHARACTERISED BY STONE WALLS STANDING OUT SHARPLY AGAINST THE GREEN SHEEP-CROPPED GRASS, INTERSPERSED WITH OUTCROPS OF WHITE ROCK

SPACE (HONESTY BOX) FOR CARS TO PARK

DALE HEAD FARM

44

46

APPROX SCALE
¼ mile
500m

DALE HEAD

KIRK Y

THIS INDUSTRIAL GRADE PATH NOW SUPPORTS THE PW & THE YORKSHIRE THREE PEAKS WALK AND SIGNPOSTS SHOW BOTH ROUTES

CRAGS

47

CAIRN

BEAR LEFT AT FINGERPOST

076

GATE WITH STONE STEP STILE IN WALL TO RIGHT OF GATE

STEEP BROAD STONY PATH, STEPPED IN PLACES. IF YOU'RE TIRED THIS LONG WINDING DESCENT WILL DO YOU IN!

PILE OF STONES

TWO STONE STILES

PEN-Y-GHENT
2283FT/696M

075

THOUGHTFULLY-DESIGNED CURVED WALL WIND BREAKS WITH BENCHES

PATH FLATTENS OUT; A CHANCE TO GET YOUR BREATH BACK

SLABS

LONG-DREADED ASCENT LOOKS GRUELLING BUT ONLY TAKES 15 MINS OF PANTING

MAP 46

074

SHOULDER OF PEN-Y-GHENT

PATH VIA BRACKEN-BOTTOM TO HORTON MAP 48 - TAKE IT IF YOU CAN'T FACE PEN-Y-GHENT

SOME SCRAMBLING INVOLVED AND LIMESTONE STEPS CAN BE SLIPPERY IN RAIN

DUCKBOARDS

THIS PATH GOES TO HELWITH BRIDGE & DUBCOTE FARM, MAP 48, FOR A SHORTCUT ESCAPE ROUTE

45

0   1/4 mile
0   APPROX SCALE   500m

2 HRS–2 HRS 30 MINS FROM DALE HEAD (MAP 45) TO HORTON-IN-RIBBLESDALE (MAP 48)

2 HRS–2 HRS 30 MINS FROM HORTON-IN-RIBBLESDALE (MAP 48) TO DALE HEAD (MAP 45)

ROUTE GUIDE AND MAPS

EDALE

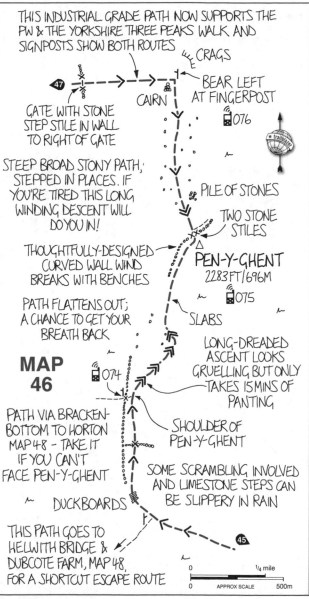

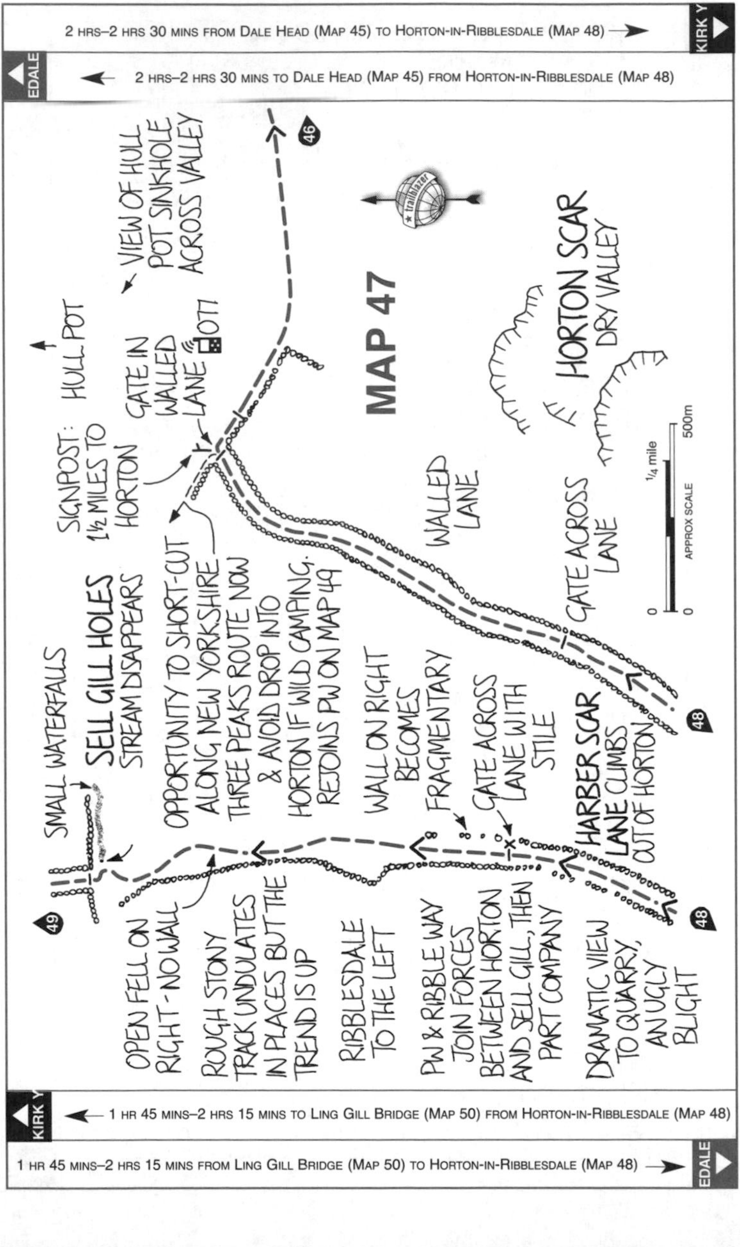

ROUTE GUIDE AND MAPS

46

↗ VIEW OF HULL POT SINKHOLE ACROSS VALLEY

HULL POT ↑

MAP 47

HORTON SCAR DRY VALLEY

SIGNPOST: 1½ MILES TO HORTON

GATE IN WALLED LANE

SELL GILL HOLES STREAM DISAPPEARS

SMALL WATERFALLS

WALLED LANE

GATE ACROSS LANE

¼ mile

500m

0   APPROX SCALE

0

OPPORTUNITY TO SHORT-CUT ALONG NEW YORKSHIRE THREE PEAKS ROUTE NOW & AVOID DROP INTO HORTON IF WILD CAMPING. RETAINS PW ON MAP 49

WALL ON RIGHT BECOMES FRAGMENTARY

GATE ACROSS LANE WITH STILE

HARBER SCAR LANE CLIMBS OUT OF HORTON

48

OPEN FELL ON RIGHT – NO WALL

ROUGH STONY TRACK UNDULATES IN PLACES BUT THE TREND IS UP

RIBBLESDALE TO THE LEFT

PW & RIBBLE WAY JOIN FORCES BETWEEN HORTON AND SELL GILL, THEN PART COMPANY

DRAMATIC VIEW TO QUARRY, AN UGLY BLIGHT

48

49

❏ **COAL MINING ON FOUNTAINS FELL** [Map 44, p153]

Named after its original owners, the Cistercian monks of Fountains Abbey near Ripon, Fountains Fell possessed substantial coal deposits beneath its cap of millstone grit. It probably still does, but not in sufficient quantity to make extraction economically viable. The most active period of coal extraction was the early 1800s when a road was constructed to the summit plateau where shafts were sunk. The remnants of this road now constitute the generally agreeable gradient of the Pennine Way. The output of coal was estimated at around 1000 tons a year which required some 10,000 packhorse loads to carry it away.

Very little now remains of the coal industry on Fountains Fell and the shafts have mostly been filled in. The ruins of the colliery building are in evidence but give no real idea of what was once a flourishing industry. Spare a thought for the miners who had to work in this inhospitable place, spending the week in makeshift accommodation (known as 'shops') within yards of their labours and getting up in the small hours to trudge to work in all weathers.

HORTON-IN-RIBBLESDALE
[Map 48]

There are no services along the route until you get to Horton, a famous landmark on the Pennine Way, but the rather glum village is sparse in terms of visitor services these days, especially with the closure of the **Pen-y-ghent Café**. For decades it played an invaluable role as information centre, shop and café but sadly it has been closed for the last couple of years. Their multi-volume Pennine Way visitors book was a wonderful record of everyone who passed along the Way over the years.

Limited **post office** services (Mon 3.30-6pm, Thur 9-11.30am) are provided in the Crown Hotel (see Where to stay).

Transport
[See also pp52-9] Horton is a stop on Northern Rail's Leeds–Carlisle line so **trains** are frequent, making it an ideal place to begin or end a walk along the Way. Dales Rail's seasonal Sunday service also calls here.

The only **bus** service to call here is NYCC's No 11 to and from Settle.

For a **taxi** call Settle Taxis (☎ 01729-822219).

Where to stay
In the centre of the village **camping** at *Holme Farm* (☎ 01729-860281, fb; 🐾) is £2 per tent plus £5pp; there are shower (£1)

and toilet facilities, as well as a few picnic benches. There's generally lots of space but booking is recommended as it's popular with people running or hiking the Three Peaks. It is open all year.

At the southern end of the village, through the car park behind the Golden Lion, is *3 Peaks Bunkroom* (☎ 07870 849419, 🖥 3peaksbunkroom.co.uk; 4 bunkrooms 6 en suite, 4 bunkrooms sleep 8 shared facilities), a converted barn with 56 beds in eight rooms. A kitchen, dining room and picnic benches are available to all. On weekends prices are set per room (£120/140 for a 6-/8-bed room), regardless of group size, but during the week walkers can book a room for S/D £40/75. Bedding costs an extra £10pp so bring a sleeping bag, pillow and towel.

Crown Hotel (☎ 01729-860209, 🖥 crown-hotel.co.uk; 1S/1Tr/1D or T shared facilities, 3D/2Tr/2Qd all en suite; 🛏; no wi-fi; ⓛ) is particularly convenient as it's right on the Way. They charge S/D £75/110 but generally require a two-day minimum stay on weekends.

The *Golden Lion Hotel* (☎ 01729-860206, 🖥 goldenlionhotel.co.uk; 1D/1D or T/2T/1Tr, all en suite; wi-fi downstairs only; ⓛ) charges D/Tr £95/135 for B&B (no sgl rates). They also have 15 beds in a **bunk room** (£15pp; bedding not included) with shower and toilet facilities.

ROUTE GUIDE AND MAPS

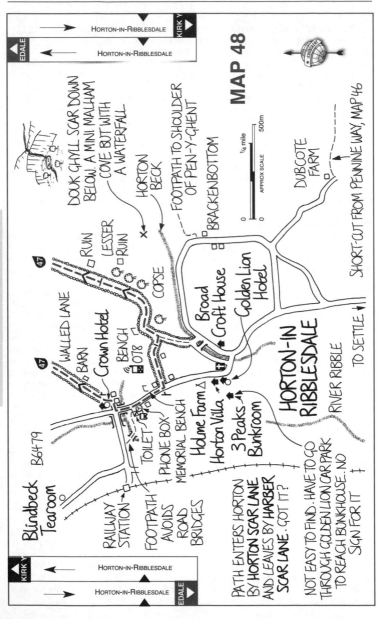

MAP 48

EDALE ◄ ← HORTON-IN-RIBBLESDALE

KIRK Y ▼ → HORTON-IN-RIBBLESDALE

DOUK GHYLL SCAR DOWN BELOW. A MINI MALHAM COVE BUT WITH A WATERFALL

HORTON BECK

FOOTPATH TO SHOULDER OF PEN-Y-GHENT

BRACKENBOTTOM

¼ mile
APPROX SCALE
500m

DUBCOTE FARM

SHORT-CUT FROM PENNINE WAY, MAP 46

RUIN
(LESSER RUIN)

COPSE

Broad Croft House

Golden Lion Hotel

47 WALLED LANE
BARN
Crown Hotel
BENCH

HORTON-IN-RIBBLESDALE

TO SETTLE ►

RIVER RIBBLE

B6479

Blindbeck Tearoom

RAILWAY STATION

FOOTPATH AVOIDS ROAD BRIDGES

TOILET
PHONE BOX
MEMORIAL BENCH

Holme Farm
Horton Villa

3 Peaks Bunkroom

PATH ENTERS HORTON BY HORTON SCAR LANE AND LEAVES BY HARBER SCAR LANE. GOT IT?

NOT EASY TO FIND. HAVE TO GO THROUGH GOLDEN LION CAR PARK TO REACH BUNKHOUSE. NO SIGN FOR IT

KIRK Y ◄ ← HORTON-IN-RIBBLESDALE

EDALE ▲ → HORTON-IN-RIBBLESDALE

Broad Croft House (☎ 01729-860419, 🖥 broadcrofthouse.co.uk; 1D/1D or T/1T, 2D in pods, all en suite; ⓛ; 🐾 in pods; summer weekends min 2 nights) charges S/D £82/95 B&B in the main house, or £98/115 in the two dog-friendly lodge-style pods.

Where to eat and drink
The town's two pubs are the only real choices, and neither is great.

The *Crown Hotel* (see Where to stay; food daily 6-8.15pm; winter times vary; mains £13-16), has a nice garden round the back but segregates walkers and residents into two bars.

The *Golden Lion Hotel* (see Where to stay; 🐾; food Mon-Thur 3-9pm, Fri & Sat noon-9pm, Sun noon-7pm) is more welcoming, with similar fare and prices, and offers breakfast (8.30-9.30am) if you book and pay for it the night before. Neither pub opens before 3pm during the week.

Just outside the northern end of the village is *Blindbeck Tea Room* (☎ 01729-860396, 🖥 blindbeck.co.uk; Mon-Tue & Thur-Fri 10am-6pm, Sat & Sun usually 9am-6pm; winter may close earlier) which serves home-made cakes and scones as well as hot and cold snacks. Check opening hours before setting off as it's a bit of a hike to get here.

HORTON-IN-RIBBLESDALE TO HAWES
MAP 48, MAP 47, MAPS 49-55

Route overview
For anyone who spent the night in Horton the day begins with the almost traditional climb out of the village; those who opted to do the Three Peaks short cut will avoid

Distance	13½ miles (21.5km)
Ascent	1700ft (518m)
Time	6¼-6¾ hours

this. The path ascends along the narrow **Harber Scar Lane** (Maps 47 & 48) with the views behind (if you ignore the scar of the quarry) being an easy excuse for a breather as you soak them in. A decent gap between your full English and this immediate climb out of the village may pay dividends here.

The day ahead consists of wall-enclosed stony tracks, old packhorse trails, used for centuries as thoroughfares over the wild limestone moors and a final descent across moorland and fields into Hawes. It has to be said that the ever-present walls on this section tend to mute the exhilaration of being out on the moors, but do make for easy navigation. With limestone comes pot holes and there are many examples within easy reach of the trail. At the one at **Sell Gill**

❏ FELL RUNNING
Whilst puffing steadily up the Cam High Road (see Maps 51 & 52), you may be igno-miniously overtaken by a wiry person in brief shorts, the scantiest of vests and strange-looking lightly studded shoes. He or she is a fell runner, a participant in a sport that is taken very seriously hereabouts. The routes involve the muddiest tracks and the steepest hills, the sort of terrain that most people would dismiss as un-runnable. It goes to extremes too, and the **Yorkshire Three Peaks Challenge** is one of them. On this event people have to run 26 miles (42km) from Pen-y-ghent Café up three peaks – Pen-y-ghent, Whernside and Ingleborough – which you can see around you, and back in less than 12 hours; the fastest time is less than three hours. See also p14.

ROUTE GUIDE AND MAPS

Holes (Map 47) the water from Sell Gill Beck disappears down into a gaping hole in the ground.

The Way now crosses **Jackdaw Hill** (Map 49; 1312ft/400m) on an old trading route. The landscape is known as 'karst'; a geographical term derived from an area of Slovenia and characterised by limestone scars, clints, ravines and dried river beds.

❏ **PACKHORSE BRIDGES**

What is a packhorse bridge? The simple answer is that it is a bridge that was built so that packhorses and their loads could cross an obstruction, usually a river or fast-flowing stream. Packhorse bridges had certain characteristics which separated them from other bridges; they are defined as being no more than six feet wide, built prior to 1800 and have known packhorse associations.

The use of packhorses to carry goods goes back to the transport of salt which was a very important product from early times. The main routes were from Cheshire but smaller salt pans existed down much of the east and south coast and some of these routes can still be followed on old Salters roads. Wool also became very important and in 1305 over 45,000 sacks of wool were carried and exported. The peak period for packhorses was between 1650 and 1800 when all manner of goods were carried, including fish to London as well as corn, coal, charcoal and, in the Pennines, lead and iron ores as well as wool and wool products.

Goods were carried in panniers which were slung on wooden pack frames on the side of the horse. To ensure that there was adequate clearance the parapets on packhorse bridges were very low or entirely absent. When the trade ceased, parapets were often added to the bridge for the safety of pedestrians. Over the years many routes have either disappeared or been upgraded to roads and in the latter case this usually meant that the bridge disappeared.

Old routes can often be traced by the names of the pubs en route such as the Packhorse Inn, beside the Pennine Way beyond Hebden Bridge. In Yorkshire, the term *Woolpack* indicates a packhorse route. The horses which carried the packs were known in Northern England either as *Galloways* or *Jaegers* which was a breed of packhorse from Germany. As well as pub names there are other words which indicate packhorse routes. A *badger* was a pedlar who was licensed to carry corn from an important market to smaller markets and several badger stones exist. *Stoops* were guide posts and *jagger*, which is a corruption of jaegar, is a name found on some routes.

The packhorse bridges on or near the Pennine Way include the following: **Edale** (at Ordnance Survey grid reference SK123 860 near the Old Nags Head, on Monks Road route); **Barber Booth** (SK088 861 at the foot of Jacob's Ladder on Monks Road route); **Standedge** (SE012 101, Thieves Bridge, close to where the Way crosses Thieves Clough); **Alcomden at Holme Ends** (SD956 321, 150 metres off the Way on the ascent to Walshaw Dean Lower Reservoir); **Beaumont Clough** (SD980 261, just off the Way at Edge End Farm descending from Stoodley Pike, on the path to Hebden Bridge); **Lower Strines** (SD959 285, near to Lower Strines Farm on Colden Water, visible from the Way); and **Ling Gill** (SD803 789, between Horton and Hawes).

Other packhorse bridges slightly further off the Way can be found at: **Hayfield** (SK050 870); **Marsden** (SE046 117 and SE029 121); **Hebden Bridge** (SD993 273 and SD992 278); **Haworth** (SE020 376 and SE015 375); and **Ravenseat** (NY862 034 after Keld, which is an alternative route to Tan Hill).   **William Gallon**

The reserve at **Ling Gill** (Map 50), with its deep ravine, protects important native tree species. Just beyond is the **packhorse bridge** (see box opposite), at **Ling Gill Bridge**, with its fading inscription, and the route continues out onto the open expanse of Cam Fell. Here the path meets the harsh logging road at **Cam End**, which provides immense views to all three of the Yorkshire Three Peaks as well as Ribblehead Viaduct and also carries the Pennine Way to **Cam High Road** (Maps 51 & 52), the route of an old Roman road.

Kidhow Gate (Map 53) has long been used by farmers to gather their sheep before driving them to market and it also marks the point at which the path leaves the tarmac to join **West Cam Road** (Map 53), another old drove route above the lush valley of Snaizeholme, hugging the lip of **Dodd Fell** on your right with the valley dropping away to the left.

Hills surround you, the sky is huge, the path unravels easily and the moorland walking is straightforward down **Rottenstone Hill** (Map 54) and into Hawes, which is visible long before you reach it, beckoning on down to its numerous pubs, cafés and shops. Make the most of the facilities in **Hawes** (Map 55) as they aren't replicated for another 35 miles (56km), until you reach Middleton-in-Teesdale.

Navigation notes

The only chance of going wrong on this section is the descent of Rottenstone Hill, where the path isn't always obvious on the ground and you may be dodging boggy sections if it's been raining recently. Even in bad visibility it would be hard to go too far wrong though. If in doubt aim for the half-size wooden gate at GPS 087 on Map 54.

ROUTE GUIDE AND MAPS

❑ BLACK (AND RED) GROUSE

Pennine Way walkers are unlikely to get as far as Bowes without seeing, or at least hearing, red grouse. Their distinctive nagging croak, which has been likened to the warning 'go-back, go-back, go-back', is a familiar sound on wild heather moors, as familiar as the lonely bubbling call of the curlew or the insistent pipe of the golden plover.

While the red grouse is the primary target of many a landowner's gun, the black grouse is a different matter altogether. Shot almost to extinction across most of Northern England, it is now only plentiful in the Scottish hills where the vast space and better cover have enabled it to survive in some numbers. In the Pennines only a few remain and these are carefully protected by gamekeepers and conservationists alike. Most keepers now appreciate the bird for its own sake and, like their changing attitudes to birds of prey, are simply glad it has survived.

In Baldersdale (Map 69) black grouse have been seen near the former YHA hostel where their curious courtship ritual was described to me by the warden. The hen birds line up on the branch of a tree like spectators grabbing the best seats in the stands to watch the cock birds perform their 'lek', a display acted out on a piece of prepared ground on which they parade, each trying to outdo the others in their strutting and posturing. Their lyre-shaped tail feathers are fanned out in a magnificent demonstration to win the hens' affections.

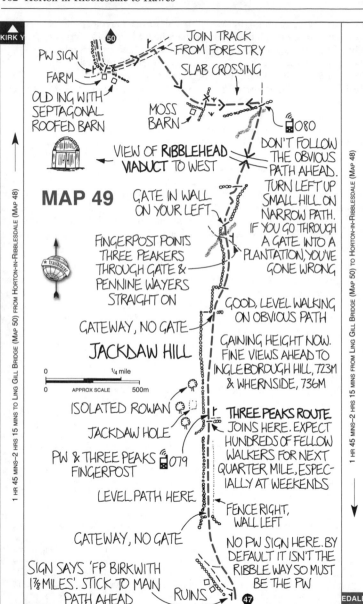

KIRK Y

1 HR 45 MINS–2 HRS 15 MINS TO LING GILL BRIDGE (MAP 50) FROM HORTON-IN-RIBBLESDALE (MAP 48)

50

PW SIGN

FARM

OLD ING WITH SEPTAGONAL ROOFED BARN

JOIN TRACK FROM FORESTRY

SLAB CROSSING

MOSS BARN

080

VIEW OF **RIBBLEHEAD VIADUCT** TO WEST

MAP 49

GATE IN WALL ON YOUR LEFT

DON'T FOLLOW THE OBVIOUS PATH AHEAD. TURN LEFT UP SMALL HILL ON NARROW PATH. IF YOU GO THROUGH A GATE INTO A PLANTATION, YOU'VE GONE WRONG

FINGERPOST POINTS THREE PEAKERS THROUGH GATE & PENNINE WAYERS STRAIGHT ON

GATEWAY, NO GATE

JACKDAW HILL

0   ¼ mile
0   APPROX SCALE   500m

ISOLATED ROWAN

JACKDAW HOLE

PW & THREE PEAKS FINGERPOST   079

LEVEL PATH HERE

GATEWAY, NO GATE

SIGN SAYS 'FP BIRKWITH 1⅞ MILES'. STICK TO MAIN PATH AHEAD

GOOD, LEVEL WALKING ON OBVIOUS PATH

GAINING HEIGHT NOW. FINE VIEWS AHEAD TO INGLEBOROUGH HILL, 723M & WHERNSIDE, 736M

THREE PEAKS ROUTE JOINS HERE. EXPECT HUNDREDS OF FELLOW WALKERS FOR NEXT QUARTER MILE, ESPEC-IALLY AT WEEKENDS

FENCE RIGHT, WALL LEFT

NO PW SIGN HERE. BY DEFAULT IT ISN'T THE RIBBLE WAY SO MUST BE THE PW

RUINS

47

1 HR 45 MINS–2 HRS 15 MINS FROM LING GILL BRIDGE (MAP 50) TO HORTON-IN-RIBBLESDALE (MAP 48)

EDALE

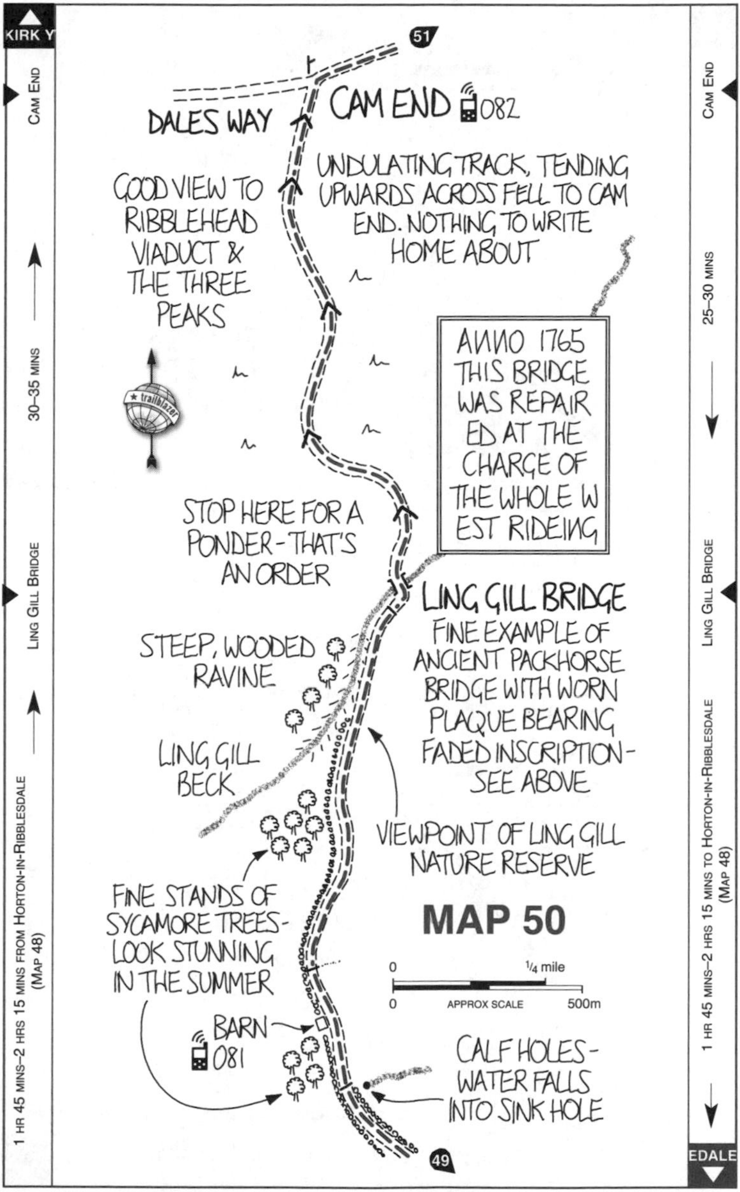

KIRK Y ▲

CAM END ◄

51

DALES WAY

CAM END 📱082

GOOD VIEW TO
RIBBLEHEAD
VIADUCT &
THE THREE
PEAKS

UNDULATING TRACK, TENDING
UPWARDS ACROSS FELL TO CAM
END. NOTHING TO WRITE
HOME ABOUT

★ trailblazer

ANNO 1765
THIS BRIDGE
WAS REPAIR
ED AT THE
CHARGE OF
THE WHOLE W
EST RIDEING

STOP HERE FOR A
PONDER - THAT'S
AN ORDER

LING GILL BRIDGE
FINE EXAMPLE OF
ANCIENT PACKHORSE
BRIDGE WITH WORN
PLAQUE BEARING
FADED INSCRIPTION -
SEE ABOVE

STEEP, WOODED
RAVINE

LING GILL
BECK

VIEWPOINT OF LING GILL
NATURE RESERVE

MAP 50

FINE STANDS OF
SYCAMORE TREES -
LOOK STUNNING
IN THE SUMMER

0   ¼ mile
0   APPROX SCALE   500m

📱 BARN
081

CALF HOLES -
WATER FALLS
INTO SINK HOLE

49

CAM END ▲
25-30 MINS ▼
LING GILL BRIDGE
1 HR 45 MINS-2 HRS 15 MINS TO HORTON-IN-RIBBLESDALE (MAP 48)
EDALE ▼

30-35 MINS
LING GILL BRIDGE
1 HR 45 MINS-2 HRS 15 MINS FROM HORTON-IN-RIBBLESDALE (MAP 48)

ROUTE GUIDE AND MAPS

ROUTE GUIDE AND MAPS

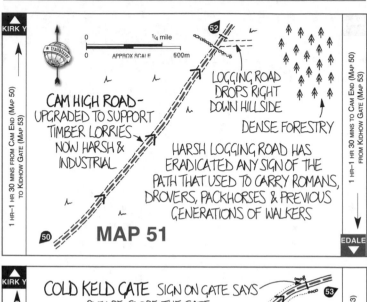

KIRK Y

1 HR–1 HR 30 MINS FROM CAM END (MAP 50) TO KIDHOW GATE (MAP 53)

1 HR–1 HR 30 MINS TO CAM END (MAP 50) FROM KIDHOW GATE (MAP 53)

52

LOGGING ROAD DROPS RIGHT DOWN HILLSIDE

DENSE FORESTRY

CAM HIGH ROAD – UPGRADED TO SUPPORT TIMBER LORRIES NOW HARSH & INDUSTRIAL

HARSH LOGGING ROAD HAS ERADICATED ANY SIGN OF THE PATH THAT USED TO CARRY ROMANS, DROVERS, PACKHORSES & PREVIOUS GENERATIONS OF WALKERS

50

MAP 51

EDALE

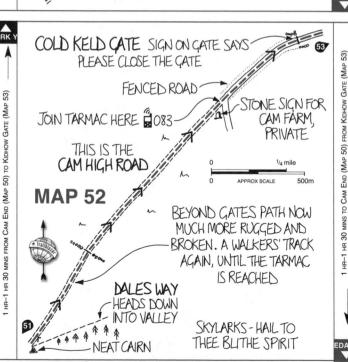

KIRK Y

1 HR–1 HR 30 MINS FROM CAM END (MAP 50) TO KIDHOW GATE (MAP 53)

1 HR–1 HR 30 MINS TO CAM END (MAP 50) FROM KIDHOW GATE (MAP 53)

53

COLD KELD GATE SIGN ON GATE SAYS PLEASE CLOSE THE GATE

FENCED ROAD

JOIN TARMAC HERE 083

STONE SIGN FOR CAM FARM, PRIVATE

THIS IS THE CAM HIGH ROAD

MAP 52

BEYOND GATES PATH NOW MUCH MORE RUGGED AND BROKEN. A WALKERS' TRACK AGAIN, UNTIL THE TARMAC IS REACHED

DALES WAY HEADS DOWN INTO VALLEY

51

NEAT CAIRN

SKYLARKS - HAIL TO THEE BLITHE SPIRIT

EDALE

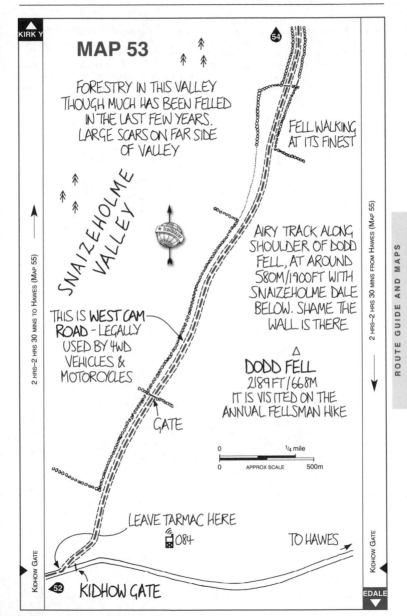

MAP 53

FORESTRY IN THIS VALLEY
THOUGH MUCH HAS BEEN FELLED
IN THE LAST FEW YEARS.
LARGE SCARS ON FAR SIDE
OF VALLEY

FELL WALKING
AT ITS FINEST

SNAIZEHOLME VALLEY

AIRY TRACK ALONG
SHOULDER OF DODD
FELL, AT AROUND
580M/1900FT WITH
SNAIZEHOLME DALE
BELOW. SHAME THE
WALL IS THERE

THIS IS **WEST CAM ROAD** – LEGALLY
USED BY 4WD
VEHICLES &
MOTORCYCLES

△
DODD FELL
2189FT/668M
IT IS VISITED ON THE
ANNUAL FELLSMAN HIKE

GATE

0   1/4 mile
0   APPROX SCALE   500m

LEAVE TARMAC HERE
📱 084

TO HAWES

KIDHOW GATE

52   KIDHOW GATE

KIRK Y

2 HRS–2 HRS 30 MINS TO HAWES (MAP 55)

54

2 HRS–2 HRS 30 MINS FROM HAWES (MAP 55)

ROUTE GUIDE AND MAPS

KIDHOW GATE

EDALE

HAWES [Map 55a, p169]

At 850ft (259m) above sea level, Hawes is the highest town in England that still holds a regular market. It's a down-to-earth Yorkshire town with a vibrant centre full of pubs and cafés. If you're in need of a break this could be the place to relax for a day or so. There's plenty to see: a good local museum, a traditional ropemaker – and this is the home of the world-famous Wensleydale cheese.

At the award-winning **Wensleydale Creamery** (☎ 01969-667664, 🖳 wensley-dale.co.uk; Easter to Oct daily 9am-5pm, winter hours vary) the 900-year-old art of

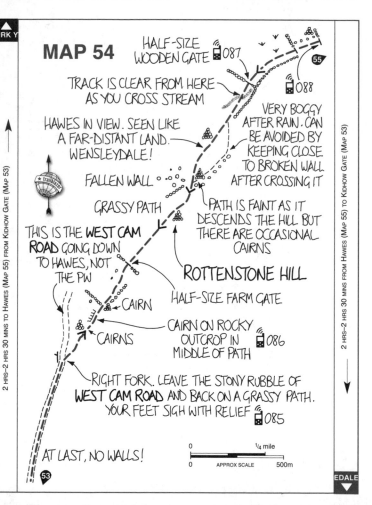

MAP 54

HALF-SIZE WOODEN GATE 🛰087

55

🛰088

TRACK IS CLEAR FROM HERE AS YOU CROSS STREAM

HAWES IN VIEW. SEEN LIKE A FAR-DISTANT LAND. WENSLEYDALE!

VERY BOGGY AFTER RAIN. CAN BE AVOIDED BY KEEPING CLOSE TO BROKEN WALL AFTER CROSSING IT

FALLEN WALL

GRASSY PATH

PATH IS FAINT AS IT DESCENDS THE HILL BUT THERE ARE OCCASIONAL CAIRNS

THIS IS THE **WEST CAM ROAD** GOING DOWN TO HAWES, NOT THE PW

ROTTENSTONE HILL

HALF-SIZE FARM GATE

CAIRN

CAIRNS

CAIRN ON ROCKY OUTCROP IN MIDDLE OF PATH 🛰086

RIGHT FORK. LEAVE THE STONY RUBBLE OF **WEST CAM ROAD** AND BACK ON A GRASSY PATH. YOUR FEET SIGH WITH RELIEF 🛰085

AT LAST, NO WALLS!

53

KIRK Y

2 HRS–2 HRS 30 MINS TO HAWES (MAP 55) FROM KIDHOW GATE (MAP 53)

2 HRS–2 HRS 30 MINS FROM HAWES (MAP 55) TO KIDHOW GATE (MAP 53)

ROUTE GUIDE AND MAPS

0   ¼ mile

0   500m
APPROX SCALE

EDALE

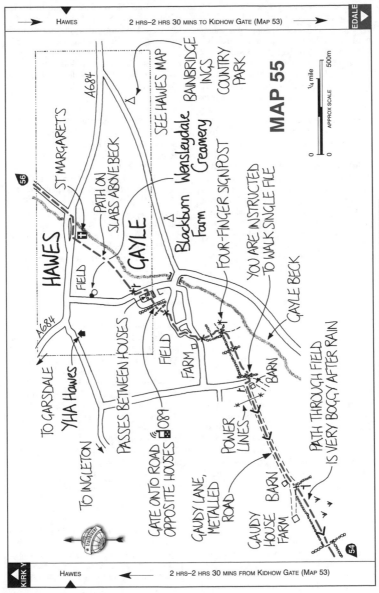

EDALE ►

MAP 55

¼ mile

APPROX SCALE

0   500m

56

HAWES

A684

ST MARGARET'S

PATH ON SLABS ABOVE BECK

SEE HAWES MAP

BAINBRIDGE INGS COUNTRY PARK

Blackburn Farm

Wensleydale Creamery

GAYLE

FIELD

FOUR-FINGER SIGNPOST

YOU ARE INSTRUCTED TO WALK SINGLE FILE

GAYLE BECK

A684

PASSES BETWEEN HOUSES

FIELD

FARM

BARN

TO GARSDALE
YHA HAWES

TO INGLETON

GATE ONTO ROAD
OPPOSITE HOUSES ☎ 089

POWER LINES

GAUDY LANE, METALLED ROAD

GAUDY HOUSE FARM

BARN

PATH THROUGH FIELD
IS VERY BOGGY AFTER RAIN

54

KIRK Y

ROUTE GUIDE AND MAPS

local cheese-making was nearly lost, only to be saved by the international popularity of Wensleydale-cheese-munching super-heroes Wallace & Gromit. Blending Wensleydale with cranberries soon became a best-seller, and now there's an array of Wensleydale cheeses with blends including apricot, pineapple, mango & ginger, and garlic & chives for the delectation of gourmet *fromageurs*. Don't miss the inner cheese shop where you can sample the various cheeses. There are also six **Cheese Experience Tours** (£5.95, last tour 3.30pm) per day, during which you learn about the history and science of cheese production, watch a demonstration, and view the factory floor (note that cheese is not made on weekends or after 2pm). The 2.30pm tour includes a tasting of cheese and chutney pairings. See also Where to eat.

Dales Countryside Museum (☎ 01969-666210, 🖥 dalescountrysidemuse um.org.uk; daily Feb-Oct 10am-5pm, Nov-Dec 10am-4pm; £4.80) is informative.

The Ropemaker (W R Outhwaite & Son; ☎ 01969-667487, 🖥 ropemakers.com), nearby, is not something you'll find in every town, though at the time of writing the shop and factory were closed to the public so check with them for reopening plans.

See p14 for details of events held here. On Tuesdays there's a street **market** as well as a livestock auction.

Transport

The nearest **railway station** is 13 miles away at Garsdale, on Northern Rail's Carlisle–Leeds services (see box p59 for details) and Dales Rail's (🖥 communityrail lancashire.co.uk/lines/dalesrail) seasonal (mid-May to early Sept) Blackpool–Carlisle service; the latter runs just once a day in each direction.

The best way to get there is by **taxi** (try Country Taxis ☎ 01539-739336, 🖥 country taxis.com), unless you are here at the right time to get Little White Bus's Garsdale Station Shuttle **bus**, which operates at scheduled times four times a day though is also a demand-responsive service so you can book it; see box pp54-9 for details. This company actually provides a vital transport

link between Hawes and the outside world, with their No 156 (Wensleydale Voyager: Gayle to Leyburn) being the town's most frequent service; for while Hawes is on a number of other **bus** routes, they seem to run on Sundays & Bank Hols only, including DalesBus's 856 and the seasonal 830, 831 & 875.

Services

In the Dales Countryside Museum you'll also find both Hawes National Park Centre and the **tourist information centre** (same phone & opening hours, 🖥 york-shiredales.org.uk). The website 🖥 wen sleydale.org also has useful information.

There's a Spar **supermarket** (Mon-Sat 7.30am-6pm, Sun 9am-3pm) while Elijah Allen & Sons (Mon-Sat 7.45am-5.30pm) is a classy old **grocery store** that shows how it used to be done and has been run by the same family since 1870.

For **outdoor gear** there's Three Peaks (Tue & Thur-Sat 10am-4.30pm), which has a selection of boots if yours have had it, or Cunningham's (Mon-Sat 9am-5.30pm, Sun 9.30am-4.30pm), which sells gas canisters.

The Upper Dales Community Office houses the **post office** (Mon-Fri 9am-5.30pm, Sat 9am-noon) and library with **internet access** (1 hour free; wi-fi) on Market Place, a small cul-de-sac just off the main street. There's also a **launderette** (Mon-Tue & Thur-Sat 9.30am-2pm, £6 per wash), J&E Hogg **chemist** (Mon-Sat 9am-5.30pm), and an **ATM** by the public toilets on Market Place.

Where to stay

There are a couple of places where you can **camp**.

Bainbridge Ings Country Park (☎ 01969-667354, 🖥 bainbridge-ings-coun trypark.co.uk; WI-FI; 🐾), three-quarters of a mile east of Market Place, is set in beautiful countryside. Backpackers pay £13pp and it's a good idea to book in advance as it's primarily a caravan/tourer park. Bring 20p coins for the shower. There's a pot washing area, a washing machine and phone charging in the office during working hours.

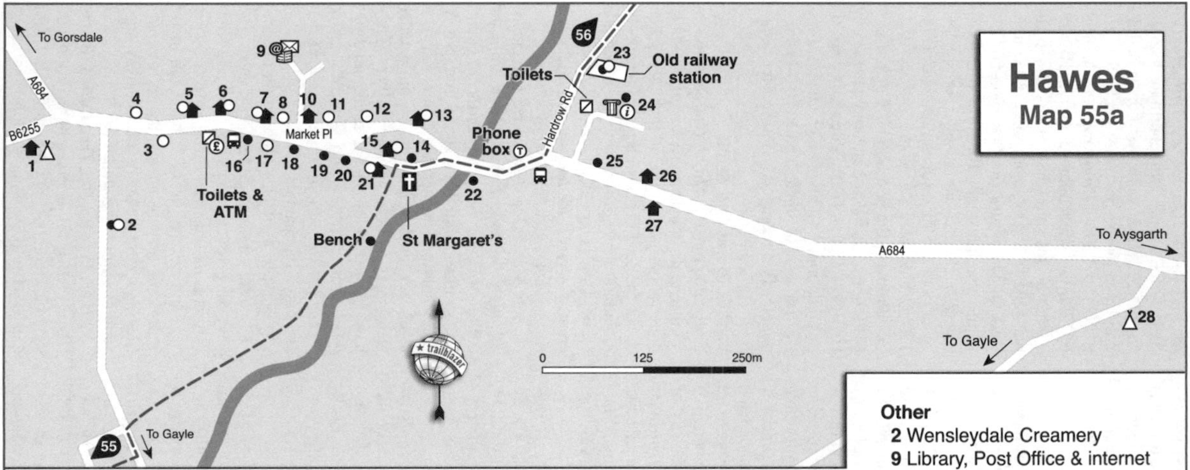

Hawes
Map 55a

To Aysgarth

△ 28

To Gayle

A684

Old railway station

Toilets

Hardrow Rd

56

23
24

25 26

27

Phone box ⓣ

22

13

St Margaret's

14
15

12

11
10
8
9 @⊠
7
6
5

Market Pl

16
17
18
19 20
21

Bench

Toilets & ATM

4

3

2

To Gayle

55

To Gorsdale

A684

B6255

△ 1

0   125   250m

Where to stay
1 YHA Hawes
5 Cockett's
6 The Board Inn
7 The Fountain
10 Dales House B&B
13 Laburnum House
15 White Hart
21 Herriot's
26 Wensleydale House

27 The House at Hawes
28 Bainbridge Ings Country Park

Where to eat and drink
2 Calvert's Restaurant &
  1897 Coffee Shop
3 The Chippie
4 Penny Garth Café
5 Cockett's
6 The Board Inn

7 The Fountain
8 Bay Tree Café & Bistro
11 The Folly
12 Caffe Curva
13 Laburnum House Tearoom
15 The White Hart
17 Wensleydale Pantry
21 Herriot's Café
23 Firebox Café

Other
2 Wensleydale Creamery
9 Library, Post Office & internet
14 Launderette
16 Spar
18 Cunningham's Outdoor Store
19 Elijah Allen & Son Grocers
20 Chemist
22 Three Peaks
23 Stage 1 Cycles
24 Dales Countryside Museum,
  Hawes National Park Centre
  & Tourist Info
25 The Ropemaker

Blackburn Farm (Map 55; ☎ 01969-667524; no wi-fi) is a simple place aimed at caravans but walkers can pitch a tent for £7pp. There are toilet and shower facilities. It's in Gayle, a 15-minute walk from Hawes.

A more convenient option is the privately-run *YHA Hawes* (reception ☎ 01969-667368 🖳 yha.org.uk/hostel/hawes; ⓛ; Mar/Apr-Oct); the comparatively bland exterior of this place belies the fact that it has all the trimmings inside, including 52 **beds** (2T en suite, mix of rooms sleep 1-8 shared facilities). Private double rooms cost £58-68 with shared bathrooms, or £71-81 en suite; check for dorm bed availability and prices. It opens at 5pm. Breakfast is available (£8) and there is a shop/bar, along with a self-catering kitchen, a comfortable lounge and a huge drying room. Laundry is a steal at £2.50 a load. **Camping** in the back garden costs £15 and includes access to all facilities – perfect during bad weather.

There's a clutch of **B&Bs** to the east of town which include *Wensleydale House* (☎ 01969-666020, 🖳 wensleydalehouse.co.uk; 2D or T/1D, all en suite; ➥; ⓛ; mid Mar-mid Oct), who offer comfortable B&B from S/D £80/100.

The House at Hawes (☎ 01969-667348, 🖳 thehouseathawes.co.uk; 4D, all en suite; ⓛ; Mar-mid Nov; usually min 2 nights) is another imposing Victorian property where B&B (adults only) costs from £115-140 for a room (no sgl rates).

Just off Market Place, is *Herriot's* (☎ 01969-667536, 🖳 herriotsinhawes.co.uk; 1S/2T/2D/1Tr, all en suite; ➥; ⓛ; 🐾) which charges from S/D £55/100 for B&B. At the time of writing their art gallery and café were both closed indefinitely – check with them for reopening plans.

Dales House B&B (☎ 01969-667437; 🖳 daleshousehawes.co.uk; 1 Qd private bathroom, 2D/1D or T/1Tr, all en suite; ➥; ⓛ; 🐾) has newly refurbished rooms from S/D £90/120.

Laburnum House (☎ 01969-667970, 🖳 laburnumhousehawes.co.uk; 1T/2D, all en suite; ➥; ⓛ; 🐾; Feb-Dec), The Holme, has B&B rooms costing from S/D £78/87 on weekdays and is just off Market Place.

Of the **pubs** offering accommodation,

the finest is the 16th-century *White Hart* (☎ 01969-667214, 🖳 whitehearthawes.co.uk, **fb**; 3D/2T, all en suite; ➥; ⓛ; 🐾; adults only), on Main St, with B&D for S/D £100/130. *The Fountain* (☎ 01969-667206, 🖳 fountainhawes.co.uk, **fb**; 2S/3T/6D all en suite) has rooms above the pub for £55-80 single or from £110 double. B&B at *The Board Inn* (☎ 01969-667223, 🖳 the boardinn.co.uk, **fb**; 1S private facilities, 2D/ 2D or T, all en suite; ➥; ⓛ; 🐾) costs from £65 for a smaller single or £100-130 for a double.

Probably the best **hotel** is *Cockett's* (☎ 01969-667312, 🖳 cockettshotelhawes.com, **fb**; 1S/7D/2D or T/1Tr, all en suite; ➥; ⓛ; usually min 2 nights), which charges from £70 for a small single, and £120-140 for a double. Two rooms have four-poster beds.

Where to eat and drink
The cafeteria-style *1897 Coffee Shop* at Wensleydale Creamery (see p166; daily 9am-4.30pm) offers mains such as chicken & bacon pie (£12) as well as lighter meals, including three different types of cheese scone. Don't come if you are lactose-intolerant. *Calvert's Restaurant*, on the same site, was closed at the time of writing.

On Market Place, at the western end of the high street, is *Penny Garth Café* (☎ 01969-667066, 🖳 pennygarthcafe.co.uk, **fb**; summer Mon-Thur 10am-3pm, Sat & Sun 9am-4pm, winter days/hours vary), a legendary lunch stop for bikers but equally welcoming to Pennine Way walkers. They have picnic tables on the street out front where you can tuck into sausage, egg & chips (£5), large English breakfasts (£6.50) and lunchtime paninis (£4).

Next to the Dales Museum in the former train station, **Stage 1 Cycles** (🖳 www.stage1cycles.co.uk) is a bicycle shop that rents mountain and e-bikes (£35-50 per day) and has the great *Firebox Café* (daily 9am-4pm) serving up quality coffee, pastries and sandwiches, with takeaway specials. It's worth the walk.

Back in town, *Bay Tree Café & Bistro* (**fb**; 10am-4pm) offers quiche, soup and sandwich combos. On the corner is *Caffe Curva* (**fb**; daily 9am-4.30pm); it has a small outside terrace and does wonderful filled rolls for £6.50, as well as breakfasts until 11am. Close by, *Laburnum House Tearoom* (see Where to stay; **fb**; Feb-Dec Fri-Tue 11am-4pm;) is a traditional tearoom that serves soups and sandwiches from noon to 2pm and then home-made scones and cakes. Book the blowout Wensleydale cream tea (May-Sept; £19pp) from 2pm.

None of the above allows dogs on their premises so if you're walking with man's best friend try *The Folly* (01969-666852; daily 10am-4pm, winter days/hours vary; ; cash only), a busy little place where you and your pooch are always greeted with a smile. Their toasties and soups are good and their cakes delicious too.

Evening meals are harder to come by in Hawes. *Wensleydale Pantry* (01969-667202, **fb**; Apr-Oct daily 8.30am-7.30pm) has a large menu for around £10-12, including roast dinner specials and liver and onion casserole, some available as half-portions, and uses locally-sourced ingredients (some from their own farm). It gets a lot of recom-

mendations from Pennine Way walkers.

A fine dinner in town is waiting for you at *Cockett's* (see Where to stay; summer Thur-Sat 6-8.30pm; winter closed) where slow-roasted Wensleydale lamb is £26. The good wine selection and nice outdoor café seating is also a plus. It's worth the slog from Horton, if not Edale itself!

The White Hart (see Where to stay; bar open all day; food served Tue-Sun noon-3.30pm & daily 5-8.30pm) is a welcoming locals' pub and it provides a square meal from around £12.95.

You can also get bar meals at *The Fountain* (see Where to stay; daily noon-2.30pm & 6-8pm) and *The Board Inn* (see Where to stay; food daily noon-2pm & 6-8pm, Sun noon-2pm only). The latter can stretch your bored taste buds with an aubergine tajine or chicken jalfrezi (£12).

Close to the YHA is *The Chippie* (thechippiehawes.co.uk; Tue-Sat 11.30am-2pm & 5-8.30pm, Sun 11.30am-6pm), a traditional English fish & chip takeaway (fish £6) with a sit-down restaurant attached.

HAWES TO TAN HILL   MAPS 55-64

Route overview

The limestone of the southern Dales is behind you now and the path will soon return, for a short while at least, to the peat landscapes encountered at the start of the

Distance	16 miles (25.5km)
Ascent	3300ft (1005m)
Time	8-10 hours

walk. First though you have a pleasant stroll through Wensleydale, out of Hawes, across hay meadows chock full of wild flowers in early summer but a delight to walk through at any time of year.

If you've been tormented by rain since leaving Edale you may get some compensation from a visit to **Hardraw Force** (waterfall), famous for a scene with Kevin Costner in the film *Robin Hood: Prince of Thieves*; access is around the side of the Green Dragon Inn in **Hardraw** (Map 56). This side excursion is only delaying the inevitable ascent of **Great Shunner Fell** (Map 59) though; standing at 2349ft (716m) this is Yorkshire's third highest mountain, but no ropes or helmets are required, just strong calf muscles to carry you along the 4½-mile (7.4km) track from the pub to the summit.

The long, gentle descent towards Swaledale and into **Thwaite** (Map 61) is rewarded with a slice of cake at the village *Tea Rooms* (see p176), where you can recharge your batteries before the next climb, out of the village, up the steep slopes of **Kisdon Hill**. In early September you may look down and see the mar-

ROUTE GUIDE AND MAPS

quees of the annual show held in the little village of Muker (see p176). The path around Kisdon is splendid, leading to the head of Swaledale along a narrow, rocky track with incredible views into Swinner Gill and onto East Stonesdale Moor.

All too soon the path forks and anyone staying in **Keld** (Map 62) needs to head straight on, while folk bound for Tan Hill turn right, over the footbridge. Keld has many more beds than Tan Hill, but most of them will have been booked months in advance by walkers doing Wainwright's Coast to Coast walk (another Trailblazer title that your bookshelf should not be without!). Both Keld and Muker are fine places to overnight.

Walkers aiming for Tan Hill still have work to do; four more miles (6.4km) and 800ft (244m) of ascent, first along a narrow lane between walls, reminis-

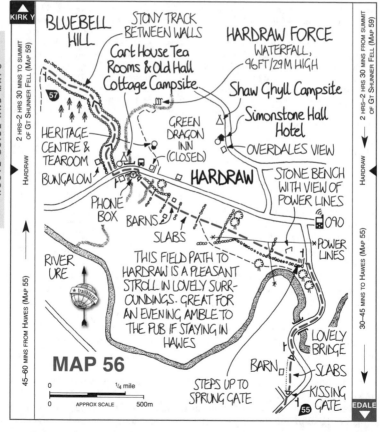

cent of the departure from Horton, and then along a wide, peat-cushioned path around the edge of **Stonesdale Moor** (Map 63) with *Tan Hill Inn* (Map 64 and see p180) soon appearing in the distance like a mirage.

Navigation notes

A close eye on the map between Hawes and Hardraw will avoid you getting lost in the fields and once you've found the lane out of Hardraw, the navigation over Great Shunner Fell and down into Thwaite is child's play, thanks mainly to the slabs. Things can get a little confusing between Thwaite and Keld though you shouldn't get lost for too long and you should be on an easy street all the way to the open fell beyond East Stonesdale Farm, the other side of Keld.

From here the path can be sketchy in places, especially on the open moorland sections and if night has beaten you, or the mist is down, this does need careful concentration. If you do lose the path, you always have the road, which is downhill to your left and that will take you all the way to Tan Hill Inn.

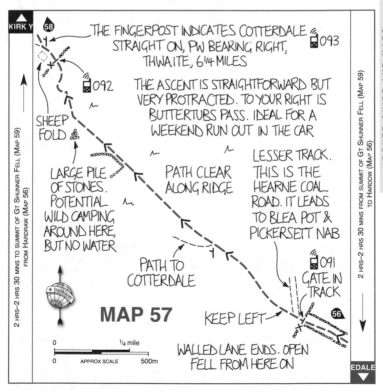

KIRK Y

58

THE FINGERPOST INDICATES COTTERDALE STRAIGHT ON, PW BEARING RIGHT, THWAITE, 6¼ MILES

093

092

THE ASCENT IS STRAIGHTFORWARD BUT VERY PROTRACTED. TO YOUR RIGHT IS BUTTERTUBS PASS. IDEAL FOR A WEEKEND RUN OUT IN THE CAR

SHEEP FOLD

LARGE PILE OF STONES. POTENTIAL WILD CAMPING AROUND HERE, BUT NO WATER

PATH CLEAR ALONG RIDGE

LESSER TRACK. THIS IS THE HEARNE COAL ROAD. IT LEADS TO BLEA POT & PICKERSETT NAB

091

GATE IN TRACK

PATH TO COTTERDALE

MAP 57

KEEP LEFT

56

WALLED LANE ENDS. OPEN FELL FROM HERE ON

0   ¼ mile

0   APPROX SCALE   500m

2 HRS–2 HRS 30 MINS TO SUMMIT OF GT SHUNNER FELL (MAP 59) FROM HARDRAW (MAP 56)

2 HRS–2 HRS 30 MINS FROM SUMMIT OF GT SHUNNER FELL (MAP 59) TO HARDROW (MAP 56)

ROUTE GUIDE AND MAPS

EDALE

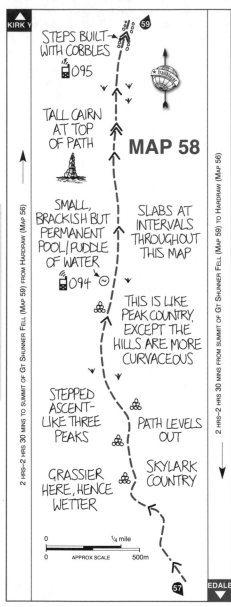

KIRK Y

STEPS BUILT WITH COBBLES
📱095

59

TALL CAIRN AT TOP OF PATH

MAP 58

2 HRS–2 HRS 30 MINS TO SUMMIT OF GT SHUNNER FELL (MAP 59) FROM HARDRAW (MAP 56)

SMALL, BRACKISH BUT PERMANENT POOL/PUDDLE OF WATER
📱094

SLABS AT INTERVALS THROUGHOUT THIS MAP

THIS IS LIKE PEAK COUNTRY, EXCEPT THE HILLS ARE MORE CURVACEOUS

STEPPED ASCENT- LIKE THREE PEAKS

PATH LEVELS OUT

GRASSIER HERE, HENCE WETTER

SKYLARK COUNTRY

0   ¼ mile
0   APPROX SCALE   500m

2 HRS–2 HRS 30 MINS FROM SUMMIT OF GT SHUNNER FELL (MAP 59) TO HARDRAW (MAP 56)

57

EDALE ▼

HARDRAW [Map 56, p172]
Hardraw's atmospheric **Green Dragon Inn** (☎ 01969-667392, 🖥 greendragonhardraw.com; 1D/6D or T/1Tr, all en suite, ✓; 🐕) has long been known for its fine ales. At the time of going to press it had recently announced its closure, due to high energy costs, though it's unclear if this is temporary – check with them for an update on reopening. Prior to closure, B&B was from £100. A bed in their bunkhouse (8 x 4-bed rooms share facilities) was from £25pp with bed linen (breakfast & towel hire extra). Food was served everyday in the main season. The pub provided the interior location for The Drovers Arms in the 2020 version of TV series *All Creatures Great and Small*.

You can visit the impressive **Hardraw Force** (🖥 hardrawforce.com; daily 10am-4pm; admission £4), said to be the highest waterfalls above ground in England, through the *Heritage Centre and Tearoom* (summer daily 9am-5pm), which serves coffee, cakes, toasties and soups.

Campers have two options. At *Old Hall Cottage Campsite* (☎ 01969-667691, 🖥 oldhallcottagecampsite.co.uk; Easter to end Oct) Pennine Way walkers can camp from £7pp (others pay £10). Shower (50p) and toilet facilities are available. They also manage *Cart House Tea Rooms* (🐕; Easter to end Oct Tue-Sun 10am-5pm) serving snacks, light lunches and afternoon teas.

To the east of the village the very quiet *Shaw Ghyll Campsite* (☎ 01969-667359, 🖥 shawghyll .co.uk; 🐕 on lead; Apr to end Oct) charges £20 for up to two walkers in a tent.

Booking is advised at all times. There are shower facilities (50p) and a toilet block.

If you feel like some luxury, treat yourself at *Simonstone Hall Hotel* (☎ 01969-667255, 🖳 simonstonehall.com; 5D or T/13D, all en suite; 🍴; ⓛ; 🐾). **B&B** costs up to £239-299 for a double in summer, dropping by up to 50% in June, when a sgl

costs £99; dinner bed & breakfast rates are also available. The **restaurant** (Mon-Sat noon-2pm & 6-8.45pm, Sun noon-2.30pm & 6-8pm) is open to non-residents; dinner costs £49/55 for two/three courses. You won't want to leave.

Hardraw is a stop on Little White Bus's No 113 **bus** service (see pp54-9).

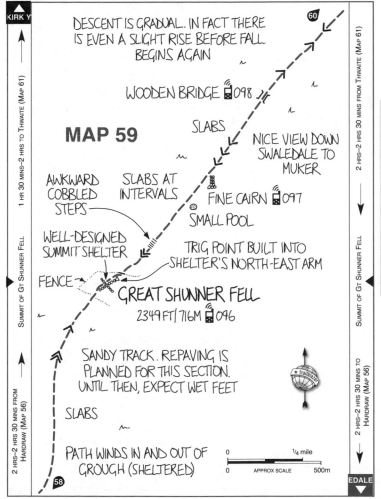

KIRK Y

↑ 1 HR 30 MINS–2 HRS TO THWAITE (MAP 61)

↑ SUMMIT OF GT SHUNNER FELL

↑ 2 HRS–2 HRS 30 MINS FROM HARDRAW (MAP 56)

60

↓ 2 HRS–2 HRS 30 MINS FROM THWAITE (MAP 61)

↓ SUMMIT OF GT SHUNNER FELL

↓ 2 HRS–2 HRS 30 MINS TO HARDRAW (MAP 56)

EDALE ▼

DESCENT IS GRADUAL. IN FACT THERE IS EVEN A SLIGHT RISE BEFORE FALL BEGINS AGAIN

WOODEN BRIDGE 📱098

SLABS

MAP 59

NICE VIEW DOWN SWALEDALE TO MUKER

AWKWARD COBBLED STEPS

SLABS AT INTERVALS

FINE CAIRN 📱097

SMALL POOL

WELL-DESIGNED SUMMIT SHELTER

TRIG POINT BUILT INTO SHELTER'S NORTH-EAST ARM

FENCE

GREAT SHUNNER FELL
2349 FT / 716 M 📱096

SANDY TRACK. REPAVING IS PLANNED FOR THIS SECTION. UNTIL THEN, EXPECT WET FEET

SLABS

PATH WINDS IN AND OUT OF GROUGH (SHELTERED)

0 ¼ mile
0 APPROX SCALE 500m

58

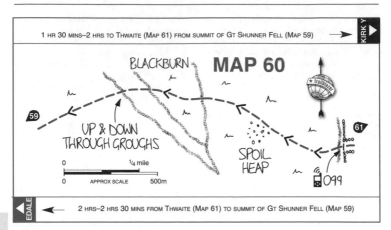

1 HR 30 MINS–2 HRS TO THWAITE (MAP 61) FROM SUMMIT OF GT SHUNNER FELL (MAP 59) → KIRK Y ▶

BLACKBURN

MAP 60

★ trailblazer

59

UP & DOWN THROUGH GROUGHS

0   ¼ mile
0   APPROX SCALE   500m

SPOIL HEAP

61

099

◀ EDALE ← 2 HRS–2 HRS 30 MINS FROM THWAITE (MAP 61) TO SUMMIT OF GT SHUNNER FELL (MAP 59)

THWAITE   [Map 61]

The village's former inn, the *Kearton Country Hotel* (☎ 01748-886277, 🖳 kear toncountryhotel.co.uk) has been reimagined as two self-catering **apartments**, one sleeping two (1D en suite; min 2 nights) and the other four (1D, 1D or T, both en suite; min 2 nights; 🐾) with hugely variable rates but starting from around £280 for two nights. The **tea rooms** (summer daily except Tue & Fri 10.30am-4pm; winter hours vary) are open for coffee, tea and home-made scones and the **bar** (same days to 11pm) for real ales.

Just over half a mile east through the meadows towards Muker brings you to the spacious **campsite** at *Usha Gap* (☎ 01748-886110, 🖳 ushagap.co.uk; 🐾; walkers £9pp), with lovely riverside pitches next to the road or more spacious grounds in the fields behind the farm. There are modern showers and toilets, along with a drying room, lockable phone-charging points, a kitchen area with fridge freezer and a useful shop at reception (open 8-10am, 3-6pm). *Ramsay's* (🖳 ramsaysfishandchips.co.uk) **fish & chip van** visits the site on Friday nights in summer.

Little White Bus's No 30 (Swaledale Shuttle) is the only **bus** service calling here (see pp54-9 for details).

MUKER   [off Map 61]

Another half a mile through the fields beyond Usha Gap and you reach Muker.

This is a very pleasant little place and a favourite of James Herriot (the Yorkshire vet who wrote *All Creatures Great and Small*). It has a church, a small **shop** and a pub, the warm and cosy *Farmers Arms* (☎ 01748-886297, 🖳 farmersarmsmuker.co.uk, **fb**; 🐾; food served Wed-Sun noon-2.30pm & 5.30-7.30pm), which serves a range of dishes from Yorkshire puddings with a selection of fillings (£8.85) to steak (from £13.75). You can book for food; if you just want a drink you may have to sit outside.

Muker Village Store and Teashop (☎ 01748-886409; **fb**) comprises the **village shop** (Easter to Oct Mon 10am-4pm, Wed-Sun to 5pm, Nov to Easter Thur-Sun 10am-noon), a **tearoom** (no WI-FI; 🐾; Easter to Oct Wed-Mon 10.30am-5pm) and they provide **B&B** (1D en suite; ①; from £80, sgl occ full room rate).

Another option for the night is *Stoneleigh B&B* (☎ 01748-886375, 🖳 stoneleighcottage.co.uk; 2D en suite, 1T private facilities; ①), which charges from £80 (sgl occ £50).

Feeling chilly? Then you'll be delight-

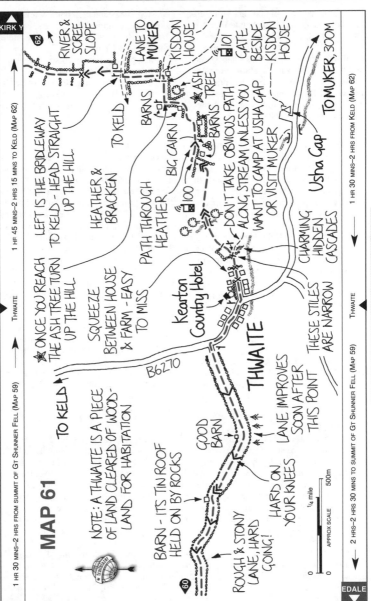

MAP 61

NOTE: A THWAITE IS A PIECE OF LAND CLEARED OF WOODLAND FOR HABITATION

TO KELD

BARN – ITS TIN ROOF HELD ON BY ROCKS

ROUGH & STONY LANE, HARD GOING!

HARD ON YOUR KNEES

GOOD BARN

LANE IMPROVES SOON AFTER THIS POINT

B6270

THWAITE

THESE STILES ARE NARROW

Keaton Country Hotel

SQUEEZE BETWEEN HOUSE & FARM – EASY TO MISS

★ ONCE YOU REACH THE ASH TREE TURN UP THE HILL

LEFT IS THE BRIDLEWAY TO KELD – HEAD STRAIGHT UP THE HILL

HEATHER & BRACKEN

PATH THROUGH HEATHER

BIG CAIRN

TO KELD

BARNS

ASH TREE

BARNS

RIVER & SCREE SLOPE

LANE TO MUKER

KISDON HOUSE

GATE BESIDE KISDON HOUSE

DON'T TAKE OBVIOUS PATH ALONG STREAM UNLESS YOU WANT TO CAMP AT USHA GAP OR VISIT MUKER

Usha Gap

CHARMING HIDDEN CASCADES

TO MUKER, 300M

KIRK Y

62

EDALE

100

101

100

APPROX SCALE

0   ¼ mile
0   500m

ed to learn that for over 30 years Muker has also been the home of **Swaledale Woollens** (☎ 01748-886251, 🖥 swaledalewoollens .co.uk), its products made from the yarn of Swaledale sheep as well as Wensleydale and Welsh Hill wool. The **shop** (daily Apr-Oct 10am-5pm, Nov-Mar 10am-4pm, Nov-Feb closed Tue & Thur) boasts that it actually saved the village following the depression caused by the collapse of the mining industry. Today about 30 home-workers are employed in knitting the jumpers, hats and many other items available in the store, which is near the pub.

See p14 for details about Swaledale's Arts Festival held here in May.

Little White Bus's No 30 (Swaledale Shuttle) and DalesBus seasonal No 830 (Sundays only) **bus** services call here (see pp54-9 for details).

KELD   [Map 62]

For a short while in Keld the Pennine Way and the popular Coast to Coast Path meet. Thus the town can be busy. Though the accommodation situation is not too bad, evening meal options are very limited so reserve in advance if you are not eating in your accommodation.

The unstaffed **Keld Countryside & Heritage Centre** (🖥 keld.org.uk; Apr-Oct 8am-9pm, Nov-Mar 8.30am-5pm) has displays and photographs of local history and farming heritage.

You can **camp** at *Rukin's Park Lodge Campsite* (☎ 01748-886274, 🖥 rukins-keld .co.uk; 🐾) from £8pp for walkers; pitches are next to the river or in an upper field, further from the toilets near Butt House. They don't take bookings but walkers will always be accepted. There are good toilet and shower facilities; there's also a **café** (Easter to end Sep daily 9am-6pm) with

snacks, cakes and bacon rolls, plus a sparsely provisioned **shop** (same hours) but no mobile phone reception.

Half a mile west of Keld is *Keld Bunk Barn & Swaledale Yurts* (☎ 01748 886549 or ☎ 01748 886159, 🖥 keldbunkbarnand yurts.com, **fb**; min 2 nights at weekends), now under new ownership. Some details (ⓛ; 🐾; Feb-end Nov) apply to both. Tea and coffee are available as is breakfast; options (from £4) are a hot breakfast baguette with bacon and egg, a bowl of porridge, two croissants and also cafetière coffee. Home-cooked evening meals (24hrs' notice required; menu on website) are served and they have an alcohol licence. There's even a hot tub for up to six people for hire (60 mins; £20 for two people plus £5pp). The site is a wonderful place to stay, with helpful hosts, excellent facilities and its very own fearsome waterfall – **Raiby**

❑ FIELD BARNS

As you pass through the Yorkshire Dales the prevalence of field barns will have been obvious. Swaledale is particularly noted for these isolated stone barns which are also known as laithes. It has been estimated that within a 1000-metre radius of the village of Muker there are 60 barns of this type. They were part and parcel of the traditional farming methods of the area which saw grazing land enclosed between stone walls, the cattle kept in the barns between October and May, fed on hay stored in the upper roof space of the barn. Cows were milked where they stood and their manure was spread on the surrounding fields. Typically, a field barn would house four or five cows, hence a farmer with a large herd would need plenty of barns to keep them in.

Today, field barns are largely redundant due to farmers making hay on a semi-industrial basis with automated machinery, the hay being baled and stored in huge modern barns close to the farm buildings for convenience. In some cases farmers have converted them into tourist accommodation, thanks to the availability of grants encouraging them to do so.

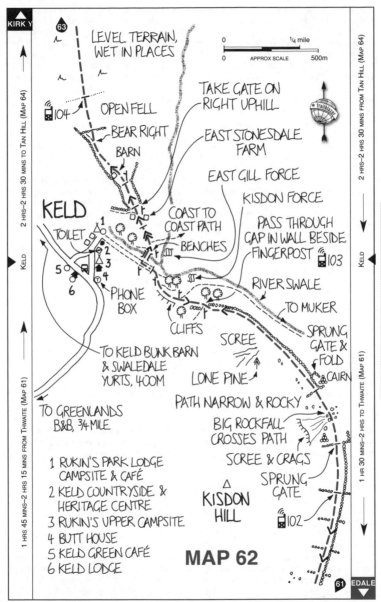

MAP 62

Force – gushing past the back door (you can swim in the pool beneath it in summer).

Rates (inc bedding and towel) in the **bunk barn** (1D/1Tr/1Qd) are from £79 for the en suite double room (sgl occ room rate) or from £90/120 in the triple/quad (shared facilities). As bunkhouses go it's about as comfortable as you can get with a kitchen, a small drying room, a dining area and a cosy lounge with a TV. Reserve in advance as it does get booked up by groups, especially on weekends.

Swaledale Yurts comprises five Mongolian yurts; (sleep 2-5, from £149 peak times, £109 off-peak, rates per night for two sharing plus £20 per additional person; sgl occ full rate). Incredibly cosy, bedding is provided and each has a wood-burning stove. Each yurt has a separate private shower, which has some kick to it, and washing facilities.

Keld Lodge (☎ 01748-886259, ⌨ keldlodge.com, **fb**; 3S/4D/3T/1Tr, all en suite, 2S share facilities; ⏾; 🐾; Feb-Oct) is a small licensed hotel with en suite rooms for S/D £57.50/115, and a couple of smaller rooms that share a bathroom for £45/90. They also have a **drying room**. Along with a **bar** (Mon-Thur 2.30-9.30pm, Fri-Sun noon-9.30pm) there's a **restaurant** (daily Apr-Oct 5.30-7.30pm, rest of year open only when they have guests; main courses £11-14) – **but booking is essential** in the high season as they get so busy.

Butt House (☎ 01748-886374, ⌨ butt housekeld.co.uk, **fb**; 1S/2T/1D/1Tr, all en suite; ☛; ⏾; Mar-Oct) has been a mainstay of the accommodation scene in Keld for many years and knows exactly what walkers want, including a bar. There is a boot room which can be used as a drying room, a laundry service (£10 per load) and if booked by 5pm they can provide an evening meal too. B&B costs S/D/Tr from £70/105/145, 15% higher in May and June.

Greenlands B&B (☎ 01748-886532, ⌨ greenlandskeld.co.uk; 2T; Apr-mid Oct; ⏾;) is another comfortable farmhouse option just under a mile south of the village. They have a drying room, laundry service (£8.50) and have a menu of evening meals (one/two/three courses £13.50/17.50/20) if booked four days in advance. They are licensed but don't have a guest lounge. B&B costs S/D £95/105.

Just over a mile from Keld itself but right on the Pennine Way, *Frith Lodge* (see Map 63; ☎ 01748-886489, ⌨ frithlodge keld.co.uk, **fb**; 3D/2T, all en suite; ⏾; May-end Sep) is as splendidly isolated as B&Bs get on the trail. It's a surprisingly stylish and modern place, with a lounge, bar and boot room and the owners are walkers themselves. Being so far from anywhere, thankfully they serve an evening meal for £17.95/21.95 for two/three courses, in one communal sitting. B&B costs from £117 for a double.

Keld Green Café (☎ 01748-898778, **fb**; daily 9am-5pm) is a new (in 2022) venture that offers take-away food and hot drinks that can be eaten on outdoor picnic tables. The menu is currently limited to burgers, sausage baps, soup, sandwiches and cakes but they plan to expand to evening meals if there is demand.

Little White Bus's No 30 (Swaledale Shuttle) and DalesBus seasonal No 830 and 831 (Sundays only) **bus** services call here (see pp54-9 for details).

TAN HILL   [Map 64, p182]

Tan Hill Inn (☎ 01833-628246, ⌨ tan-hillinn.com, **fb**; 3D/3T/1Tr, all en suite; ☛; ⏾; 🐾) prides itself on being the highest pub (1732ft/528m above sea level) in Britain. **B&B** costs £156-176 for a double (sgl occ less £10) or £190-220 for a deluxe room. There are also two **bunkrooms** (1 x 6-, 1 x 8-bunk-bed room; communal bathroom and mixed-sex dorms); a bed with breakfast, linens and towel costs a hefty £45pp. **Camping** round the back of the pub is possible but basic, with a tap, outside loo and some rocks for shelter, and you can use the staff shower – the £10 charge goes to charity. The pub itself is open all day year-round. **Food** (summer daily noon-3pm & 6.30-9pm, winter hours check website) is standard fare, with meals (£13-20) at the

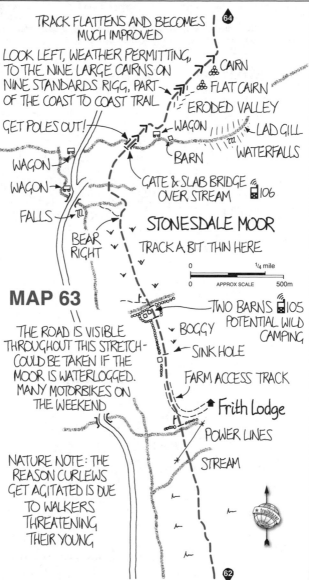

KIRK Y

TRACK FLATTENS AND BECOMES MUCH IMPROVED

64

LOOK LEFT, WEATHER PERMITTING, TO THE NINE LARGE CAIRNS ON NINE STANDARDS RIGG, PART OF THE COAST TO COAST TRAIL

CAIRN

FLAT CAIRN

ERODED VALLEY

GET POLES OUT!

WAGON

LAD GILL

WAGON

WATERFALLS

WAGON

BARN

FALLS

GATE & SLAB BRIDGE OVER STREAM 106

BEAR RIGHT

STONESDALE MOOR

TRACK A BIT THIN HERE

0   1/4 mile
0   APPROX SCALE   500m

MAP 63

THE ROAD IS VISIBLE THROUGHOUT THIS STRETCH—COULD BE TAKEN IF THE MOOR IS WATERLOGGED. MANY MOTORBIKES ON THE WEEKEND

TWO BARNS 105
POTENTIAL WILD CAMPING

BOGGY

SINK HOLE

FARM ACCESS TRACK

Frith Lodge

POWER LINES

NATURE NOTE: THE REASON CURLEWS GET AGITATED IS DUE TO WALKERS THREATENING THEIR YOUNG

STREAM

trailblazer

62

EDALE

2 HRS–2 HRS 30 MINS TO TAN HILL (MAP 64) FROM KELD (MAP 62)

2 HRS–2 HRS 30 MINS FROM TAN HILL (MAP 64) TO KELD (MAP 62)

ROUTE GUIDE AND MAPS

top end of pub grub rates. Book a table on the weekends.

By day the inn is a peaceful place for a cup of tea but on summer weekend evenings it can get much more raucous with live music and other events held most weeks. If you like a quiet pitch then avoid Saturdays.

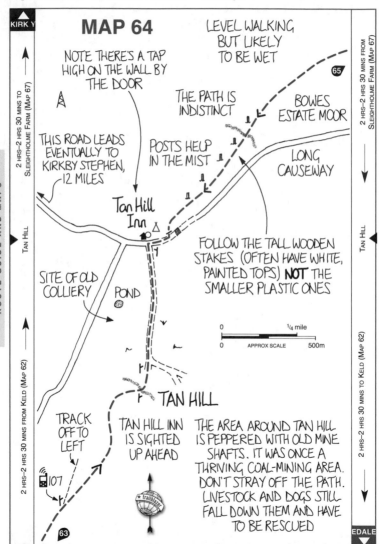

MAP 64

KIRK Y

2 HRS–2 HRS 30 MINS TO SLEIGHTHOLME FARM (MAP 67)

TAN HILL

2 HRS–2 HRS 30 MINS FROM KELD (MAP 62)

ROUTE GUIDE AND MAPS

LEVEL WALKING BUT LIKELY TO BE WET

NOTE THERE'S A TAP HIGH ON THE WALL BY THE DOOR

THE PATH IS INDISTINCT

BOWES ESTATE MOOR

65

THIS ROAD LEADS EVENTUALLY TO KIRKBY STEPHEN, 12 MILES

POSTS HELP IN THE MIST

LONG CAUSEWAY

Tan Hill Inn

FOLLOW THE TALL WOODEN STAKES (OFTEN HAVE WHITE, PAINTED TOPS) **NOT** THE SMALLER PLASTIC ONES

SITE OF OLD COLLIERY

POND

0   1/4 mile
0 APPROX SCALE 500m

TAN HILL

TRACK OFF TO LEFT

107

TAN HILL INN IS SIGHTED UP AHEAD

THE AREA AROUND TAN HILL IS PEPPERED WITH OLD MINE SHAFTS. IT WAS ONCE A THRIVING COAL-MINING AREA. DON'T STRAY OFF THE PATH. LIVESTOCK AND DOGS STILL FALL DOWN THEM AND HAVE TO BE RESCUED

63

2 HRS–2 HRS 30 MINS FROM SLEIGHTHOLME FARM (MAP 67)

TAN HILL

2 HRS–2 HRS 30 MINS TO KELD (MAP 62)

EDALE

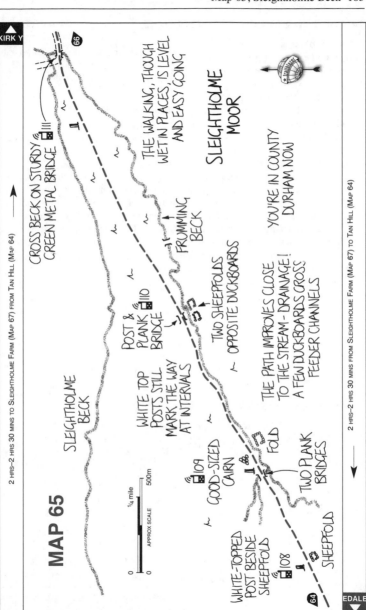

MAP 65

KIRK Y

66

CROSS BECK ON STURDY
GREEN METAL BRIDGE 111

2 HRS–2 HRS 30 MINS TO SLEIGHTHOLME FARM (MAP 67) FROM TAN HILL (MAP 64)

THE WALKING, THOUGH
WET IN PLACES, IS LEVEL
AND EASY GOING

SLEIGHTHOLME
MOOR

FRUMMING
BECK

YOU'RE IN COUNTY
DURHAM NOW

POST &
PLANK 110
BRIDGE

TWO SHEEPFOLDS
OPPOSITE DUCKBOARDS

THE PATH IMPROVES CLOSE
TO THE STREAM - DRAINAGE!
A FEW DUCKBOARDS CROSS
FEEDER CHANNELS

2 HRS–2 HRS 30 MINS FROM SLEIGHTHOLME FARM (MAP 67) TO TAN HILL (MAP 64)

SLEIGHTHOLME
BECK

WHITE TOP
POSTS STILL
MARK THE WAY
AT INTERVALS

FOLD

109
GOOD-SIZED
CAIRN

TWO PLANK
BRIDGES

¼ mile

500m

0
0   APPROX SCALE

WHITE-TOPPED
POST BESIDE
SHEEPFOLD 108

SHEEPFOLD

64

EDALE

TAN HILL TO MIDDLETON-IN-TEESDALE   MAPS 64-72

Route overview

You could be forgiven for thinking you're going in the wrong direction as you leave Tan Hill Inn the next morning – the route starts out downhill! This is hardly surpris-

Distance	16½ miles (26.5km)
Ascent	1700ft (518m)
Time	7¼-9¾ hours

ing, however, bearing in mind the pub's location and altitude. The route may be downhill, but the crossing of **Sleightholme Moor** (Map 65) could be the wettest section of the Pennine Way yet experienced. The peaty path becomes water-logged after prolonged rain and you may find yourself jumping across peat groughs in what will probably be a vain attempt to keep your boots dry.

Once you've crossed **Frumming Beck** (Map 65), however, things get eas-ier; a stony track, much cursed on the descent into Horton, is now hailed in equal measure and it brings you to **Sleightholme Farm** (Map 67) and beyond it a decision; the **Bowes Loop** (see below), or the direct route to Baldersdale? The Bowes Loop adds about four miles (6.4km). The Ancient Unicorn pub (see p189) and two new campsites now enable you to break the two long sections – between Hawes and Middleton-in-Teesdale – into three shorter ones. The Bowes Loop also takes a slightly drier path, avoiding Cotherstone Moor.

> ### Bowes Loop (alternative route)   [Maps 67a-c]
> The Bowes Loop (8½ miles/13.7km) came about as an alternative route for those seeking a bed, or a meal, in Bowes (see p189); it takes 1-1½hrs from the
> (cont'd on p188)

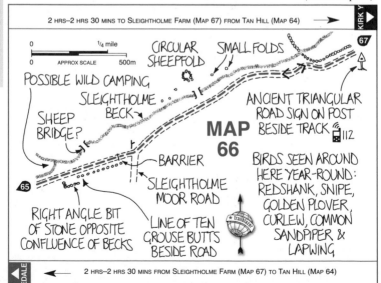

2 HRS–2 HRS 30 MINS TO SLEIGHTHOLME FARM (MAP 67) FROM TAN HILL (MAP 64) →

KIRK Y

0 ¼ mile
0 APPROX SCALE 500m

CIRCULAR SHEEPFOLD

SMALL FOLDS

67

POSSIBLE WILD CAMPING

SLEIGHTHOLME BECK

SHEEP BRIDGE?

ANCIENT TRIANGULAR ROAD SIGN ON POST BESIDE TRACK 112

MAP 66

BARRIER

SLEIGHTHOLME MOOR ROAD

BIRDS SEEN AROUND HERE YEAR-ROUND: REDSHANK, SNIPE, GOLDEN PLOVER, CURLEW, COMMON SANDPIPER & LAPWING

65

RIGHT ANGLE BIT OF STONE OPPOSITE CONFLUENCE OF BECKS

LINE OF TEN GROUSE BUTTS BESIDE ROAD

★ trailblazer

EDALE ◀ 2 HRS–2 HRS 30 MINS FROM SLEIGHTHOLME FARM (MAP 67) TO TAN HILL (MAP 64)

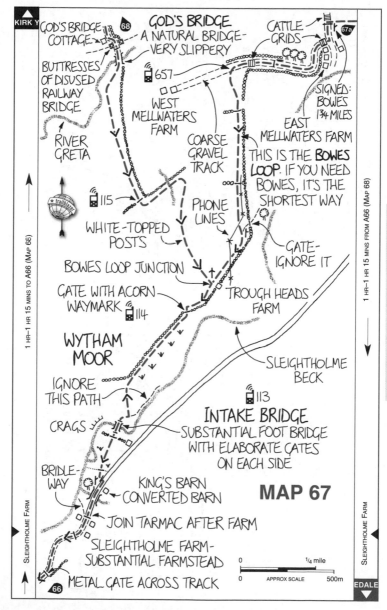

KIRK Y

GOD'S BRIDGE COTTAGE

68

GOD'S BRIDGE
A NATURAL BRIDGE- VERY SLIPPERY

CATTLE GRIDS

67a

BUTTRESSES OF DISUSED RAILWAY BRIDGE

657

SIGNED: BOWES 1¾ MILES

WEST MELLWATERS FARM

EAST MELLWATERS FARM

RIVER GRETA

COARSE GRAVEL TRACK

THIS IS THE BOWES LOOP. IF YOU NEED BOWES, IT'S THE SHORTEST WAY

trailblazer

115

PHONE LINES

WHITE-TOPPED POSTS

GATE- IGNORE IT

BOWES LOOP JUNCTION

GATE WITH ACORN WAYMARK

114

TROUGH HEADS FARM

WYTHAM MOOR

SLEIGHTHOLME BECK

IGNORE THIS PATH

113

CRAGS

INTAKE BRIDGE
SUBSTANTIAL FOOT BRIDGE WITH ELABORATE GATES ON EACH SIDE

BRIDLE- WAY

KING'S BARN CONVERTED BARN

MAP 67

JOIN TARMAC AFTER FARM

SLEIGHTHOLME FARM- SUBSTANTIAL FARMSTEAD

METAL GATE ACROSS TRACK

66

0   ¼ mile

0   APPROX SCALE   500m

1 HR-1 HR 15 MINS TO A66 (MAP 66)

1 HR-1 HR 15 MINS FROM A66 (MAP 68)

SLEIGHTHOLME FARM

SLEIGHTHOLME FARM

EDALE

ROUTE GUIDE AND MAPS

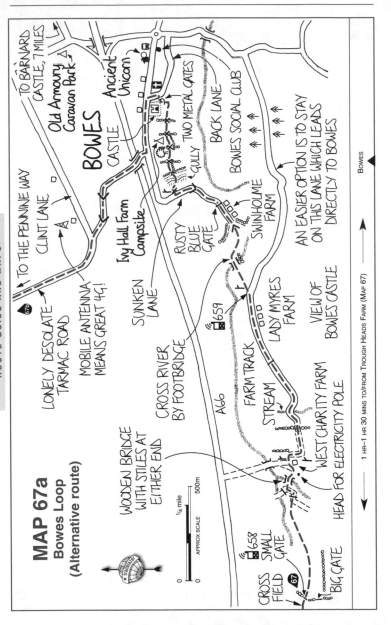

MAP 67a
Bowes Loop
(Alternative route)

WOODEN BRIDGE WITH STILES AT EITHER END

¼ mile

500m

APPROX SCALE

0

CROSS FIELD

SMALL GATE

658

BIG GATE

HEAD FOR ELECTRICITY POLE

WEST CHARITY FARM

A66

STREAM

FARM TRACK

LADY MYKES FARM

VIEW OF BOWES CASTLE

LONELY DESOLATE TARMAC ROAD

67b

TO THE PENNINE WAY

CLINT LANE

MOBILE ANTENNA MEANS GREAT 4G!

SUNKEN LANE

CROSS RIVER BY FOOTBRIDGE

659

Ivy Hall Farm Campsite

RUSTY BLUE GATE

SWINHOLME FARM

AN EASIER OPTION IS TO STAY ON THIS LANE WHICH LEADS DIRECTLY TO BOWES

BOWES

CASTLE

Ancient Unicorn

Old Armoury Caravan Park

TO BARNARD CASTLE, 7 MILES

GULLY TWO METAL GATES

BACK LANE

BOWES SOCIAL CLUB

1 HR–1 HR 30 MINS TO/FROM HEADS FARM (MAP 67)

BOWES

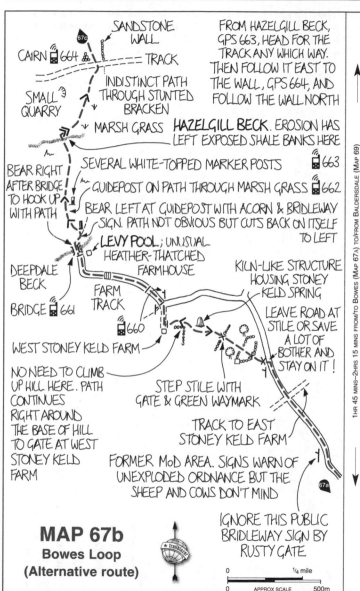

SANDSTONE WALL

CAIRN 664

TRACK

FROM HAZELGILL BECK, GPS 663, HEAD FOR THE TRACK ANY WHICH WAY. THEN FOLLOW IT EAST TO THE WALL, GPS 664, AND FOLLOW THE WALL NORTH

INDISTINCT PATH THROUGH STUNTED BRACKEN

SMALL QUARRY

MARSH GRASS

HAZELGILL BECK. EROSION HAS LEFT EXPOSED SHALE BANKS HERE

SEVERAL WHITE-TOPPED MARKER POSTS 663

BEAR RIGHT AFTER BRIDGE TO HOOK UP WITH PATH

GUIDEPOST ON PATH THROUGH MARSH GRASS 662

BEAR LEFT AT GUIDEPOST WITH ACORN & BRIDLEWAY SIGN. PATH NOT OBVIOUS BUT CUTS BACK ON ITSELF TO LEFT

LEVY POOL; UNUSUAL HEATHER-THATCHED FARMHOUSE

DEEPDALE BECK

KILN-LIKE STRUCTURE HOUSING STONEY KELD SPRING

FARM TRACK

BRIDGE 661

660

LEAVE ROAD AT STILE OR SAVE A LOT OF BOTHER AND STAY ON IT!

WEST STONEY KELD FARM

NO NEED TO CLIMB UP HILL HERE. PATH CONTINUES RIGHT AROUND THE BASE OF HILL TO GATE AT WEST STONEY KELD FARM

STEP STILE WITH GATE & GREEN WAYMARK

TRACK TO EAST STONEY KELD FARM

FORMER MoD AREA. SIGNS WARN OF UNEXPLODED ORDNANCE BUT THE SHEEP AND COWS DON'T MIND

67a

MAP 67b
Bowes Loop
(Alternative route)

IGNORE THIS PUBLIC BRIDLEWAY SIGN BY RUSTY GATE

0   1/4 mile
0   APPROX SCALE   500m

1HR 45 MINS–2HRS 15 MINS FROM/TO BOWES (MAP 67A) TO/FROM BALDERSDALE (MAP 69)

ROUTE GUIDE AND MAPS

(cont'd from p184) start of the branch route at **Trough Heads Farm** (Map 67, p185) to Bowes and about 2hrs from Bowes to the point where the paths converge at **Baldersdale** (Map 69, p192).

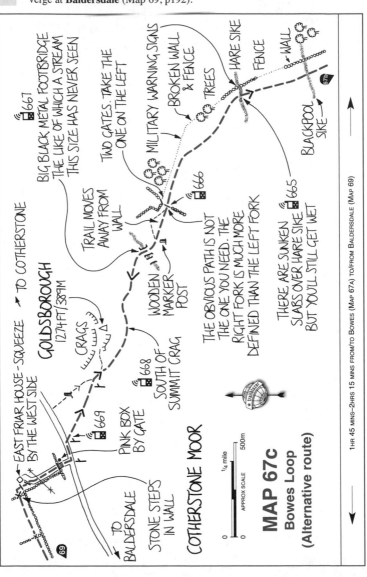

MAP 67c
Bowes Loop
(Alternative route)

1/4 mile

APPROX SCALE

500m

1HR 45 MINS–2HRS 15 MINS FROM/TO BOWES (MAP 67A) TO/FROM BALDERSDALE (MAP 69)

Facilities at **Bowes** (Map 67a) include camping (£6, cash only) at friendly *Ivy Hall Farm* (☎ 07776 491253, **fb**; Easter-Oct), right on the trail, with a toilet, shower and small honesty shop. A second camping option lies further from the trail on the north side of town, at the adults-only *Old Armoury Caravan Park* (☎ 07860 594999, 🖳 theoldarmourycampsite.com, **fb**; £6.) A new washroom was under construction at the time of writing.

For a bed and food in Bowes try the *Ancient Unicorn* (☎ 01833-628576, 🖳 ancientunicorn.com; 8D/1T/1Tr en suite, 1D/1T shared facilities; ✤; ⓛ; 🐾). **Room** rates are £85-110 B&B for a standard double (no sgl rates). You can get coffee and cake here during the day (9am-5pm) but you'll need a reservation for dinner (pies, curries and burgers around £13, with good vegetarian choices; 6-8.30pm) as it's the only place in town and residents get priority.

For a drink you are better off at the *Bowes Social Club* (**fb**; open from 7pm Mon, Tue, Thur & Fri, from 8pm Wed & Sun, from 5pm Sat, until around 10pm), a welcoming former working man's club and the de facto village pub and community centre.

Scarlet Band's **bus** No 72 goes to Barnard Castle (see pp54-9).

The only other reason to visit is to wander around the ruins of **Bowes Castle**. The castle is a Norman keep dating from around 1187, built upon the much earlier Roman fort of Lavatris, and it is managed by English Heritage; you are free to visit at any time. An information board at nearby St Giles Church describes how Charles Dickens' 1838 visit to Hawes inspired the characters of Wackford Squeers and Smike in *Nicholas Nickleby*, published the following year.

This longer route north to rejoin the main Pennine Way has noticeably **fewer ups and downs**, is generally drier and is a little more scenically appealing, although route finding can have **a few irritating moments**: care is needed after crossing the **bridge** at Levy Pool farmhouse (Map 67b). The Pennine Way guide post should point you on your way across the moor to Hazelgill Beck and the obvious path from the bridge leads you north-east towards the wall that can be seen ahead. Make sure to bear right for just a few yards after crossing the bridge, before turning left (north) to pick up the thin path through the tall grass. If you're using a GPS, aim for GPS Waypoint 662 after crossing the bridge. The Loop rejoins the Way near Blackton Reservoir at Baldersdale.

The main Pennine Way climbs up and over **Wytham Moor** and drops down to the natural stone span of **God's Bridge** (Map 67) after which it meets the **A66** trunk road (Map 68). For once you don't have to scurry across between the rushing vehicles as a thoughtful subway, unthoughtfully laid a couple of hundred yards off the direct line, takes you beneath the tarmac instead.

A long steady ascent follows, out of **Stainmore Gap**, past a scattering of rocks that glory in the name of **Ravock Castle**, and down to the possibly very welcome shelter of a shooting hut (Map 68) beside **Deepdale Beck**, before climbing again to the wall at **Race Yate** (Map 69) and the immense views ahead to Lunedale and the hills beyond Weardale.

Drop down the squelchy moorland to **Baldersdale** where the Way passes between two more reservoirs and, more significantly, reaches the halfway mark! Pat yourself on the back, many people don't make it this far, but you've obviously got the stuff that Pennine Wayfarers are made of; surely only injury can stop you from finishing now. The day's exertions haven't finished yet though, there are still 7 miles (11km) to Middleton-in-Teesdale and close to 1000ft (305m) of ascent over **Mickleton Moor** (Map 70) and **Harter Fell** (Map 71). You can arrange accommodation in Cotherstone (to the east off the Bowes Loop) or Lunedale but most people head for **Middleton-in-Teesdale** (Map 72) which offers many more options and sets you up nicely for the next (big) stage.

Navigation notes
Sleightholme Moor is vast and desolate, and at times the trail can be hard to find. Follow the white-topped posts that mark the trail but don't confuse them with the smaller, also white-tipped (!) stakes used by local gamekeepers. In really bad conditions a combination of the tarmac road from Tan Hill Inn and the Sleightholme Moor Road (track) could help you avoid the worst of the moor. The field boundaries around the lower slopes of Harter Fell (Map 71) can be confusing and somehow the route on the ground seems to be much longer than that shown on the map, so be patient and the waypoints marked on the map will come eventually.

COTHERSTONE   [off Map 67c]
If you happen to be here on a Tuesday after-noon there are **post office** services in the village hall between 2 and 4pm.

The Fox and Hounds (☎ 01833-650241, 🖳 cotherstonefox.co.uk; 2D/1T, all en suite; ☛; ⓛ; 🐾); has pleasant rooms, two with a spa bath, and they can pick you up from the trail and drop you off the next morning, a service which is includ-ed in the room rates of S/D £60/100.

However, note that a time needs to be pre-arranged as the phone signal is not good. They also serve **food** (Mon-Wed 6-8.30pm, Thur noon-2pm, 6-8.30pm, Fri & Sat noon-2pm, 5-8.30pm, Sun noon-4pm), including good fish & chips.

Scarlet Band No 95/96 **bus** services (see p59) regularly run through the village to Middleton and Barnard Castle.

❏ **HANNAH HAUXWELL**
Right on the edge of Blackton Reservoir beside the Pennine Way stands the farm of Low Birk Hat (see Map 69), home for many years to a remarkable woman. Hannah Hauxwell came to public attention through a number of television programmes and books (both formats are still available) telling the story of the life of someone living at subsistence level in Baldersdale in the 1970s. With a cow which had one calf a year, she allowed herself £250 a year for living expenses, without electricity or gas, surviving the harsh winters by the simple expedient of putting on another coat.

Later Hannah Hauxwell became famous for her courage and her natural under-standing of the world and its follies when she travelled for the cameras recording her impressions of cities around the world. Her curiosity and common-sense enabled her to put her finger on the unusual and get pleasure from the commonplace.

Hannah died in 2018 at the age of 81 but will be long remembered by those who followed her adventures. Her farm where at one time her father alone supported a family of seven, both sets of parents, himself, his wife and their daughter, has since been much modernised and a glimpse over the wall reveals merely an echo of the hard livelihood it once accommodated. See also box p195.

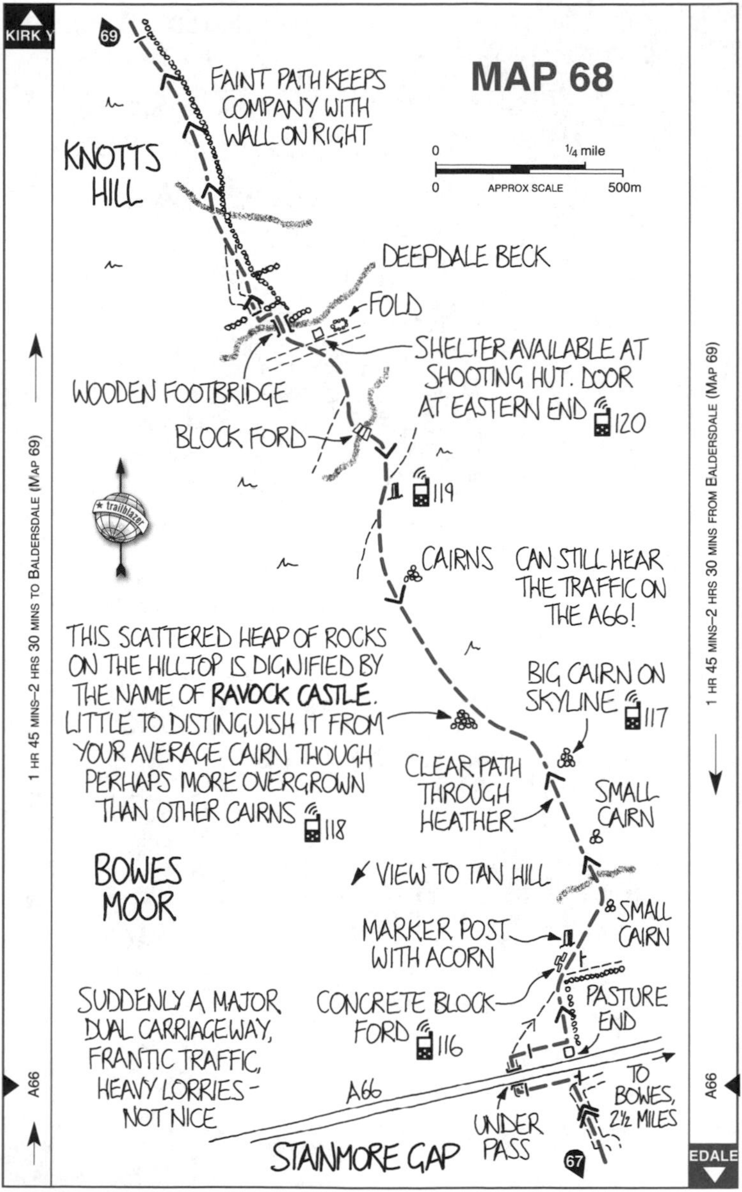

KIRK Y

69

FAINT PATH KEEPS
COMPANY WITH
WALL ON RIGHT

MAP 68

KNOTTS
HILL

0   1/4 mile

0   APPROX SCALE   500m

DEEPDALE BECK

FOLD

SHELTER AVAILABLE AT
SHOOTING HUT. DOOR
AT EASTERN END 📱120

WOODEN FOOTBRIDGE

BLOCK FORD

📱119

★ trailhaus

CAIRNS   CAN STILL HEAR
THE TRAFFIC ON
THE A66!

THIS SCATTERED HEAP OF ROCKS
ON THE HILLTOP IS DIGNIFIED BY
THE NAME OF **RAVOCK CASTLE**.
LITTLE TO DISTINGUISH IT FROM
YOUR AVERAGE CAIRN THOUGH
PERHAPS MORE OVERGROWN
THAN OTHER CAIRNS 📱118

BIG CAIRN ON
SKYLINE 📱117

CLEAR PATH
THROUGH
HEATHER

SMALL
CAIRN

**BOWES
MOOR**

↙ VIEW TO TAN HILL

SMALL
CAIRN

MARKER POST
WITH ACORN

CONCRETE BLOCK
FORD 📱116

PASTURE
END

SUDDENLY A MAJOR
DUAL CARRIAGEWAY,
FRANTIC TRAFFIC,
HEAVY LORRIES –
NOT NICE

A66

TO
BOWES,
2½ MILES

UNDER
PASS

67

STAINMORE GAP

A66

A66

EDALE

1 HR 45 MINS–2 HRS 30 MINS TO BALDERSDALE (MAP 69)

1 HR 45 MINS–2 HRS 30 MINS FROM BALDERSDALE (MAP 69)

ROUTE GUIDE AND MAPS

POTENTIAL WILD CAMP
BLACKTON NATURE
RESERVE SIGN

HANNAH'S MEADOW NATURE
RESERVE SIGN

THROUGH METAL
GATE

LOW BIRK
HAT

BLACKTON
RESERVE

BLACKTON
BRIDGE

BLACKTON
RESERVOIR

BALDERSDALE

671/124a

BIRD HIDE

RUIN

67c

BOWES LOOP
FINGERPOST

GOOD
TRACK

LONE ASH

BURNERS
SIKE

TINY
GATE
&
STILE

FROM
BOWES
LOOP

GATES

CP

670

124

WHITE PAINTED
MARKER POST WITH
GREEN WAYMARK ON IT

PATH DESCENDS,
FARMHOUSE AHEAD

123

DON'T CROSS THE
FOOTBRIDGE ON
YOUR RIGHT

EASY TO END UP ON
PARALLEL PATH BESIDE
BURNERS SIKE, BUT STILL
LEADS TO ROAD

COTHERSTONE
MOOR

POSTS AT RARE INTERVALS
MARK THE LINE

PEATBRIG
HILL

MAP 69

122
GUIDEPOST ON
PEATBRIG HILL

RACE
YATE

0   1/4 mile
0   APPROX SCALE   500m

121

RESERVOIR SEEN AHEAD,
10 O'CLOCK. THIS IS
BALDERHEAD RESERVOIR

68

KIRK Y

BALDERSDALE

1 HR 45 MINS – 2 HRS 30 MINS FROM A66 (MAP 68)

ROUTE GUIDE AND MAPS

BALDERSDALE

1 HR 45 MINS – 2 HRS 30 MINS TO A66 (MAP 68)

EDALE

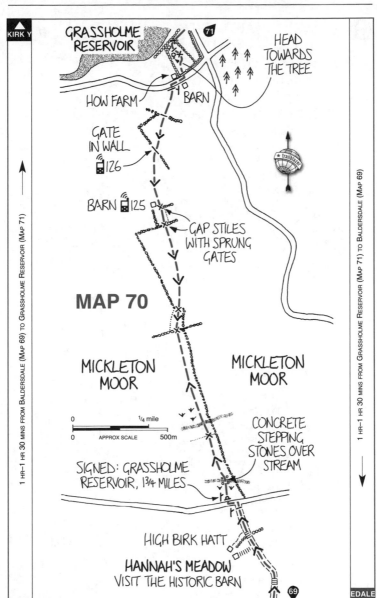

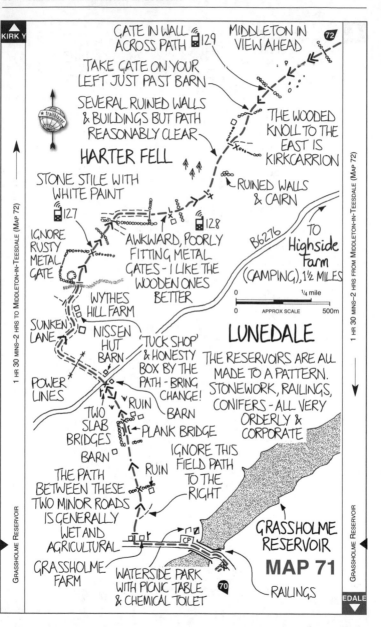

GATE IN WALL 📱129
ACROSS PATH

MIDDLETON IN
VIEW AHEAD

72

TAKE GATE ON YOUR
LEFT JUST PAST BARN

SEVERAL RUINED WALLS
& BUILDINGS BUT PATH
REASONABLY CLEAR

THE WOODED
KNOLL TO THE
EAST IS
KIRKCARRION

HARTER FELL

STONE STILE WITH
WHITE PAINT

📱127

RUINED WALLS
& CAIRN

📱128

IGNORE
RUSTY
METAL
GATE

AWKWARD, POORLY
FITTING METAL
GATES - I LIKE THE
WOODEN ONES
BETTER

B6276

TO
Highside
Farm
(CAMPING), 1½ MILES

0   ¼ mile
0   500m
APPROX SCALE

WYTHES
HILL FARM

LUNEDALE

SUNKEN
LANE

NISSEN
HUT
BARN

'TUCK SHOP'
& HONESTY
BOX BY THE
PATH - BRING
CHANGE!

THE RESERVOIRS ARE ALL
MADE TO A PATTERN.
STONEWORK, RAILINGS,
CONIFERS - ALL VERY
ORDERLY &
CORPORATE

POWER
LINES

RUIN

BARN

TWO
SLAB
BRIDGES

PLANK BRIDGE

BARN

RUIN

IGNORE THIS
FIELD PATH
TO THE
RIGHT

THE PATH
BETWEEN THESE
TWO MINOR ROADS
IS GENERALLY
WET AND
AGRICULTURAL

GRASSHOLME
FARM

CP

WATERSIDE PARK
WITH PICNIC TABLE
& CHEMICAL TOILET

70

GRASSHOLME
RESERVOIR

MAP 71

RAILINGS

KIRK Y

1 HR 30 MINS–2 HRS to MIDDLETON-IN-TEESDALE (MAP 72)

1 HR 30 MINS–2 HRS FROM MIDDLETON-IN-TEESDALE (MAP 72)

ROUTE GUIDE AND MAPS

GRASSHOLME RESERVOIR

GRASSHOLME RESERVOIR

EDALE ▼

LUNEDALE   [Map 71]

There's not much for walkers in Lunedale but two miles (3km) along the B6276 (and the same distance from Middleton by road) is the **campsite** at *Highside Farm* (off Map 71; ☎ 01833-640135, 🖥 highsidefarm-campingglamping.co.uk; £10, Apr-Sep;

🐏), Bow Bank. This small site (only five pitches) has showers, toilets and washing facilities. They also offer a secluded luxury glamping **pod** (1D, £120, usually min 2 nights) with a kitchen, sofa, TV, wi-fi, bathroom and small deck.

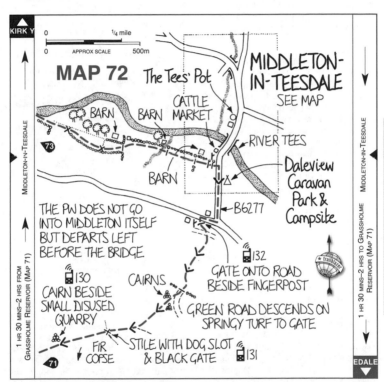

❑ HANNAH'S MEADOW   (see Map 70)

Part of the legacy of Hannah Hauxwell has been the preservation of her farmland which has been given the status of a study area for meadow grasses and wild flowers.

Purchased by Durham Wildlife Trust in 1988, the site was later designated a Site of Special Scientific Interest (see p61) qualifying by having 23 of the 47 species of rare and characteristic plants listed by Natural England. The meadows were never ploughed, being cut for hay in August and thereafter grazed by cows resulting in herb-rich meadows. Numerous varieties of birds are visitors to the meadows and no fewer than 16 kinds of dung-beetle have been identified.

MIDDLETON-IN-TEESDALE
[Map 72a]

On the banks of the River Tees, this small town thrived during the 19th century when the now defunct lead-mining industry was in its heyday. It's mostly laid out along one street, with handsome architecture interspersed with a few quirky buildings.

See p14 for details of Middleton Carnival held here in early August.

Services

The **tourist information centre** (TIC; ☎ 01833-641001; Tue 10am-1pm, other days 10am-1pm if volunteers are available), 10 Market Place, has limited opening hours but sells some interesting publications on the North Pennines and also has free information on the area. There's also useful information on ☐ visitmiddleton.co.uk.

For groceries there is a large, well-stocked Co-op **supermarket** (daily 7am-10pm). Next door in the UTASS centre is a **post office** (Tue 9.45am-12.45pm, Fri 1-3.30pm), and very near to that is G&J **newsagents**. There is also a Day Lewis **pharmacy** (Mon, Tue, Thur & Fri 9am-5.30pm, Wed & Sat 9am-1pm). J Raine & Son (**fb**; Mon, Tue, Thur & Fri 9am-5pm, Sat 9am-4pm) stocks some **outdoor gear** on the 2nd floor. The Barclays **Bank** (Mon, Tue & Fri 9.30am-2.30pm) here has an **ATM**. Early closing day for most of the town is Wednesday.

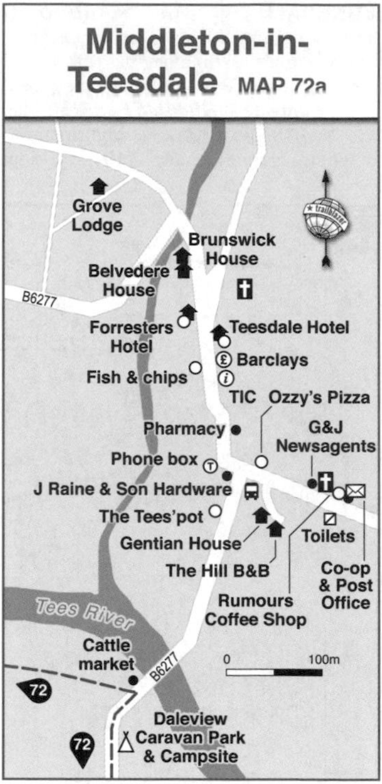

Transport

[See pp54-9] The nearest railway station is Darlington, 25 miles (40km) away and a stop on both LNER and TransPennine Express services. To get there take Scarlet Band's No 95 or 96 **bus** service to Barnard Castle and change there for the service to Darlington. Hodgsons No 73 calls here but only on a Wednesday.

Where to stay

Unless The Rolling Stones decide to play Middleton Village Hall, there is always going to be plenty of choice. The most convenient **campsite** is *Daleview Caravan Park and Camp Site* (☎ 01833-640233, 07788 245975, ☐ daleviewcaravanpark

Middleton-in-Teesdale MAP 72a

.com; 🐾; Mar-Oct) which you pass on your way into town. Hikers get their own area for £5pp including a shower. The friendly and unpretentious site boasts its own **pub** (Tue-Thur 5-9.30pm, Fri 5pm-midnight, Sat noon-midnight, Sun noon-9.30pm) and offers good-value food (Tue-Sun), with curry, rice and naan bread for £8, or lamb, rosemary and potato pie.

Don't be put off by the grand appearance of *Grove Lodge* (☎ 01833-640798, ☐ grovelodgemiddletoninteesdale.co.uk; 3T/3D, all en suite; ➍; ⏰; 🐾), a former Victorian shooting lodge just outside the far side of town and with great views back to Kirkcarrion and Harter Fell; they welcome walkers as long as you don't shake yourself off in the hallway like a wet dog. **B&B** costs S/D £70/90. The twin (with kitchen) and double in the garden rooms can be separate, or connected for a group of up to four people. They can provide an evening meal (from an à la carte menu) with dishes costing from £10. There's no online booking so you'll have to do it old school by phone.

Brunswick House (☎ 01833-640393, 🖳 brunswickhouse.net; 2T/3D, all en suite; ☛; Ⓛ) is more central and B&B costs £70/90 for S/D occupancy.

Forresters Hotel (☎ 01833-641435, 🖳 forrestersmiddleton.co.uk; 1S/3D/3D or T, all en suite; ☛; Ⓛ; clean 🐾) is a flashy place (all chrome fittings and shiny floors) with a modern bar and pool table. B&B costs £60-80 for a double (sgl occ £50-60).

For a change of style head over the road to ***The Teesdale Hotel*** (☎ 01833-640264, 🖳 teesdalehotel.co.uk, **fb**; 2S/2D or T/1T/7D/1Qd, all en suite; ☛; Ⓛ; 🐾), an old stone-built coaching inn, charging £88-98 for a classic double B&B (£10 less for sgl occ).

The central Victorian ***Belvedere House*** (☎ 01833-641277, 🖳 thebelvedere house.co.uk; 1S/1D/1T all en suite; ☛) charges S/D £60/75 for B&B. ***The Hill B&B*** (☎ 07881 812607, 🖳 thehillbandb.co.uk; 2D en suite, 1S private bathroom; ☛) has a central location, with modern bathrooms, and costs S/D £70/90 B&B, though the single room is quite small. Just a few doors down at No 5 is ***Gentian House*** (☎ 01833-640832, 🖳 gentianhouse.co.uk; 2D en suite), which has rooms for a similar price of £70-90 B&B depending on the season (no single rates).

Where to eat and drink
On a Sunday night your only option is the Teeside Hotel or a take-away pizza, so reserve a table in advance.

Closest to the Way is ***The Tees'pot*** (☎ 01833-640717, 🖳 the-teespot.business.site, **fb**; no wi-fi; 🐾; Thur-Tue 9am-4pm). Food is available to take away or eat in and you can get bacon, sausage or egg baps for £2.80; they also serve paninis, soups, meat pies and quiches for around £6-8.

There are a couple more cafés with outside terraces, including ***Rumours Coffee Shop*** (**fb**; Sat-Wed 10am-5pm).

Opposite the TIC is a cash-only **fish & chip** shop (Tue, Fri & Sat 11.30am-2pm & 4-8pm, Wed & Thur 4-7.30pm), or try ***Ozzy's Pizza*** (01833-640162, **fb**; Thur 4-9pm, Fri-Sat 4-10pm, Sun 4-9pm, Bank Holidays 4-10pm) for take away.

Food at ***Forresters*** (see Where to stay; food Wed-Sat noon-3pm, 5-8pm, Sun noon-2.30pm) is served at the somewhat brash bar (burgers or baguettes £10) and at the nicer restaurant which specialises in French-influenced food, including chicken Provencal (£13) and beef bourguignon.

Teesdale Hotel (see Where to stay; daily noon-2.30pm & 6-9pm) is a more attractive place for a beer or food; mains are around £14, including a fish pie or trout & prawn bubble & squeak.

MIDDLETON-IN-TEESDALE TO DUFTON   MAPS 72-83

Route overview
There are only two days that are longer than this on the Pennine Way (and only one if you're planning on breaking up the last section into Kirk Yetholm), but this is

Distance	20 miles (32km)
Ascent	2300ft (701m)
Time	9¾-10¾ hours

probably the best single day walk of the lot. The highlights get increasingly impressive as the day wears on, culminating in one of the best sights in England. If you like waterfalls, you're in for an extra-special treat!

For a linear, south to north walk, today is unusual in that it finishes further south than it started out, but this just goes to show how important the day is in terms of spectacle and how much the planners wanted to include this section of path.

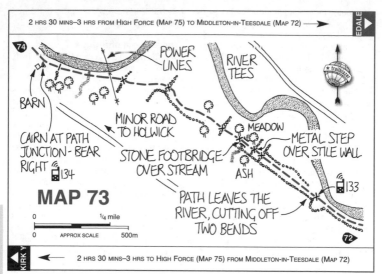

POWER LINES

RIVER TEES

BARN

MINOR ROAD TO HOLWICK

MEADOW

METAL STEP OVER STILE WALL

CAIRN AT PATH JUNCTION - BEAR RIGHT 134

STONE FOOTBRIDGE OVER STREAM

ASH

133

MAP 73

0   ¼ mile

0   APPROX SCALE   500m

PATH LEAVES THE RIVER, CUTTING OFF TWO BENDS

72

The first couple of miles out of Middleton may leave you wondering what all the fuss is about. The path is hampered with a tedious series of stiles and too many trees impair the long views, but the river is ever present on the right providing adequate compensation. Soon you arrive at **Low Force** (Map 75), an impressive double waterfall, quickly surpassed in magnitude by High Force. After Low Force the Tees river gets wider and runs faster and at **High Force** (see p202) it spills over 70ft (21m) in a magnificent display of power and white water. A short detour offers accommodation and food at the High Force Hotel (p202). Beyond High Force the scenery improves significantly and short excursions above the river provide views along its length and into the surrounding hills.

Soon you cross the Tees at **Cronkley Bridge** (Map 77) where your day can end in **Langdon Beck** (see p202). At **Widdy Bank Farm** the scene changes again and you are soon walking between rising cliffs, along the boulder-strewn, ankle-twisting margins of the river at **Falcon Clints** (Map 78).

The huge waterfall of **Cauldron Snout** is almost stumbled upon as you round a corner of cliff and without the knowledge that a path lay up the right side of the falls, you would wonder where to go next. A short scramble later and you'll stand beneath the concrete walls of **Cow Green Reservoir** which feeds the snout. The wilderness is temporarily muted as the Way scoots along the access road to the isolated farmstead of **Birkdale** (Map 79). But once through the farmyard it leads out on the open moors again, crossing **Grain Beck** and facing the only mildly noteworthy climb of the day to a crest alongside **Rasp Hill** and its long-abandoned mine workings.

CASCADES START

SLABS

STEPPING STONES OVER STREAM

NEWBIGGIN

★ trailblazer

75

COBBLY PATH HERE

📵135

B6277

MOOR HOUSE/ UPPER TEESDALE NATIONAL NATURE RESERVE SIGN

POWER LINES

GURGLING RIVER, MEADOWS AND BLUEBELLS

SEABERRY BRIDGE (WOODEN)

Low Way Farm→ Camping Barn

HOLWICK

RESCUE LIFEBELT

TO MIDDLETON

BACK TO RIVER LEVEL

FARMLAND

HOLWICK SCAR

STRATHMORE ARMS (CLOSED)

Farmhouse Kitchen

STEPPING STONES

LOW WAY FARM

CONCRETE BRIDGE

FENCE ENCLOSES PATH HERE

MAP 74

WILD GARLIC

PATH HIGH AGAIN

73

0   ¼ mile
0   APPROX SCALE   500m

TREES BETWEEN RIVER & PATH

The walk along the wide, open valley of **Maize Beck** (Maps 80 & 81) is a delight, but quickly becomes forgotten when you reach the highlight of the day, and possibly the whole walk; **High Cup** (also known as **High Cup Nick**; Map 81). Suddenly the land drops away in front of you in a textbook U-shaped demonstration of the aftermath of glacial erosion. The sides are rimmed with strata of hard rock, basalt or dolerite, interspersed with jumbled scree and twinkling rivulets, and from the head of the valley Maize Beck trickles down when it's not getting blown back in your face. This impressive scooped-out bowl of a valley is a genuine feast for the eyes. If the wind isn't howling up 'the Nick', sit and gawp as long as you can – you're only an hour or two from Dufton, four miles (6.4km) along an old miners' track and it's all downhill. Wild camping is

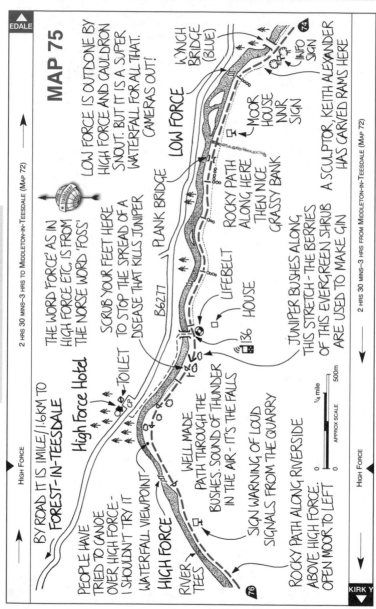

MAP 75

EDALE

LOW FORCE IS OUTDONE BY HIGH FORCE AND CAULDRON SNOUT. BUT IT IS A SUPER WATERFALL FOR ALL THAT. CAMERAS OUT!

THE WORD 'FORCE' AS IN HIGH FORCE ETC. IS FROM THE NORSE WORD 'FOSS'

WYNCH BRIDGE (BLUE)

74

INFO SIGN

MOOR HOUSE NNR SIGN

LOW FORCE

PLANK BRIDGE

ROCKY PATH ALONG HERE THEN NICE GRASSY BANK

2 HRS 30 MINS–3 HRS to Middleton-in-Teesdale (Map 72)

SCRUB YOUR FEET HERE TO STOP THE SPREAD OF A DISEASE THAT KILLS JUNIPER

B6277

LIFEBELT

136 HOUSE

JUNIPER BUSHES ALONG THIS STRETCH – THE BERRIES OF THIS EVERGREEN SHRUB ARE USED TO MAKE GIN

A SCULPTOR, KEITH ALEXANDER HAS CARVED RAMS HERE

2 HRS 30 MINS–3 HRS FROM MIDDLETON-IN-TEESDALE (MAP 72)

High Force

BY ROAD IT IS 1MILE / 1.6KM TO FOREST-IN-TEESDALE

High Force Hotel

TOILET
CP

PEOPLE HAVE TRIED TO CANOE OVER HIGH FORCE – I SHOULDN'T TRY IT

WATERFALL VIEWPOINT

HIGH FORCE

RIVER TEES

WELL MADE PATH THROUGH THE BUSHES. SOUND OF THUNDER IN THE AIR – IT'S THE FALLS

SIGN WARNING OF LOUD SIGNALS FROM THE QUARRY

ROCKY PATH ALONG RIVERSIDE ABOVE HIGH FORCE. OPEN MOOR TO LEFT

76

0   ¼ mile
0   500m
APPROX SCALE

High Force

KIRK Y

a possibility if the weather is amenable. **Dufton** (Map 83) has few services but is a lovely place to recharge your batteries and prepare for the ascent of the infamous Cross Fell.

Navigation notes
It would be hard to go wrong on this stage. The path is nearly always obvious and even when it isn't it follows a river.

HOLWICK [Map 74, p199]
Low Way Farm (☎ 01833-640506, 🖳 lowwayfarm.co.uk), a family-run Upper Teesdale working farm, offers **camping barn** accommodation in two barns (1 x 8-, 1 x 20- beds). The barns are open to groups only on the weekends (£10pp) but individual Pennine Way walkers can stay during the week (£14pp); booking is required. There are basic cooking facilities in the barns as well as toilets and showers, but there are no electric sockets or pans, nor is there crockery or cutlery; also lighting and the fridge are on a meter (£1 coins). The attached *Farmhouse Kitchen* (Easter-end Oct Sat & Sun 10.30am-5pm) at the farm

serves country café fare such as soups, sandwiches, pies and baked potatoes; Sunday lunch (£15) is available all year if prebooked. Beyond that you need to bring your own food. There is a sign from the trail and the barns are only about 200 metres off the route.

Just over half a mile from the Way, the **Strathmore Arms** was closed at time of research, but might conceivably reopen as a pub and B&B.

The only **bus** service is Hodgsons No 73 (see p57) on a Wednesday, but the bus stop is 20 minutes away in **Newbiggin**.

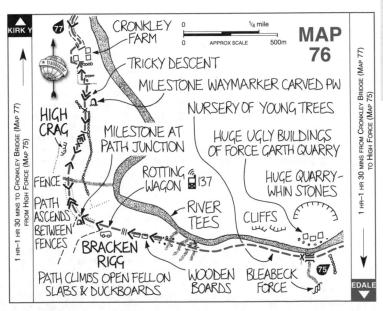

MAP 76

CRONKLEY FARM

TRICKY DESCENT

MILESTONE WAYMARKER CARVED PW

NURSERY OF YOUNG TREES

HIGH CRAG

MILESTONE AT PATH JUNCTION

HUGE UGLY BUILDINGS OF FORCE GARTH QUARRY

FENCE

ROTTING WAGON 137

HUGE QUARRY- WHIN STONES

PATH ASCENDS BETWEEN FENCES

RIVER TEES

CLIFFS

BRACKEN RIGG

PATH CLIMBS OPEN FELL ON SLABS & DUCKBOARDS

WOODEN BOARDS

BLEABECK FORCE

KIRK Y 77

EDALE

1 HR–1 HR 30 MINS TO CRONKLEY BRIDGE (MAP 77) FROM HIGH FORCE (MAP 75)

1 HR–1 HR 30 MINS FROM CRONKLEY BRIDGE (MAP 77) TO HIGH FORCE (MAP 75)

ROUTE GUIDE AND MAPS

HIGH FORCE [Map 75, p200]

High Force Hotel (☎ 01833-622336, 🖳 raby.co.uk/high-force/hotel; 1S/6D/3D or T, all en suite; ▼; Ⓛ; 🐕) charges £119-209 for a double **B&B** (smaller single £89). **Food** is served (Mon-Sat 8am-11am, noon-9pm, Sun 8am-11am, noon-6pm) and they have a specials board and also serve real ales in the bar. Reservations recommended. A coffee and ice cream stall by the car park caters to those passing through.

Hodgsons No 73 **bus** service calls here on a Wednesday; see p57.

❑ HIGH FORCE [Map 75, p200]

High Force is so big it has to claim some distinction over others. The highest? The biggest? These seem to belong elsewhere so what they say is it's the highest unbroken fall of water in England; the drop is 21 metres (70ft). It's certainly impressive, especially after rain when the water appears the colour of tea, tinged with the peat from the moors.

W A Poucher, the celebrated photographer and writer of a series of guides during the 1960s and '70s, said that it is a difficult subject to photograph well, facing north-east, hence having the wrong light conditions for effective photography. Its other problem, at least from the Pennine Way side of the river, is access for a good view. There are places where you can scramble through the undergrowth and cling on to the cliff edge but few where you can wield the camera effectively.

People have done some strange things here. Some have gone off the top, ending their lives in the torrent. Two boaters were stopped at the last minute from attempting to kayak off the top and a visitor from abroad slipped on the flat shelf at the lip and though saving himself, catapulted the infant on his back over the edge to its doom. There is an odd fascination about raging water which seems to compel some people to get just that little bit too close.

LANGDON BECK [Map 77]

YHA Langdon Beck (☎ 0345-371 9027, 🖳 yha.org.uk/hostel/langdon-beck; 1 x 5-bed room en suite, 2 x 2-, 4 x 4-, 1 x 8-bed room shared facilities; Ⓛ; Mar-end Oct) will be the chosen destination for many walkers, but note that the hostel gets booked up, particularly in the summer months. A dorm bed costs from £25pp and a private room from D/Qd £29/39, or £49 for a five-bed room with en suite bathroom; there are also laundry facilities and a drying room. Note that individuals can't book more than 60 days in advance. The warden is helpful and knowledgeable about the PW and local wildlife.

About a quarter of a mile north of the hostel is ***Langdon Beck Hotel*** (☎ 01833-622267, **fb**; 6D or T, all en suite; ▼; 🐕). The hotel was fully refurbished in 2022 and now has comfortable en suite **rooms** (£99-139, sgl occ from £79), some with impressive views. They serve **food** every day (daily 11am-9pm, winters hours vary) with everything home-made; mains such as their popular steak pie with chips and peas start from £10.95. They also do a Sunday carvery (£10.95).

Hodgsons No 73 **bus** runs from here to Middleton-in-Teesdale but only on a Wednesday; see p57.

DUFTON [Map 83, p209]

This quiet and attractive little village is a lovely place to stop after a great day's walking, whichever direction you're taking. There is an agricultural show here in August; see p14 for details.

YHA Dufton (bookings ☎ 0345-371 9734, 🖳 yha.org.uk/hostel/dufton; 1 x 2-bed room en suite, 1 x 2-, 4 x 4-, 2 x 6-bed rooms shared facilities; Ⓛ; Mar-end Oct), opposite the pub, is one of the best on the

(cont'd on p207)

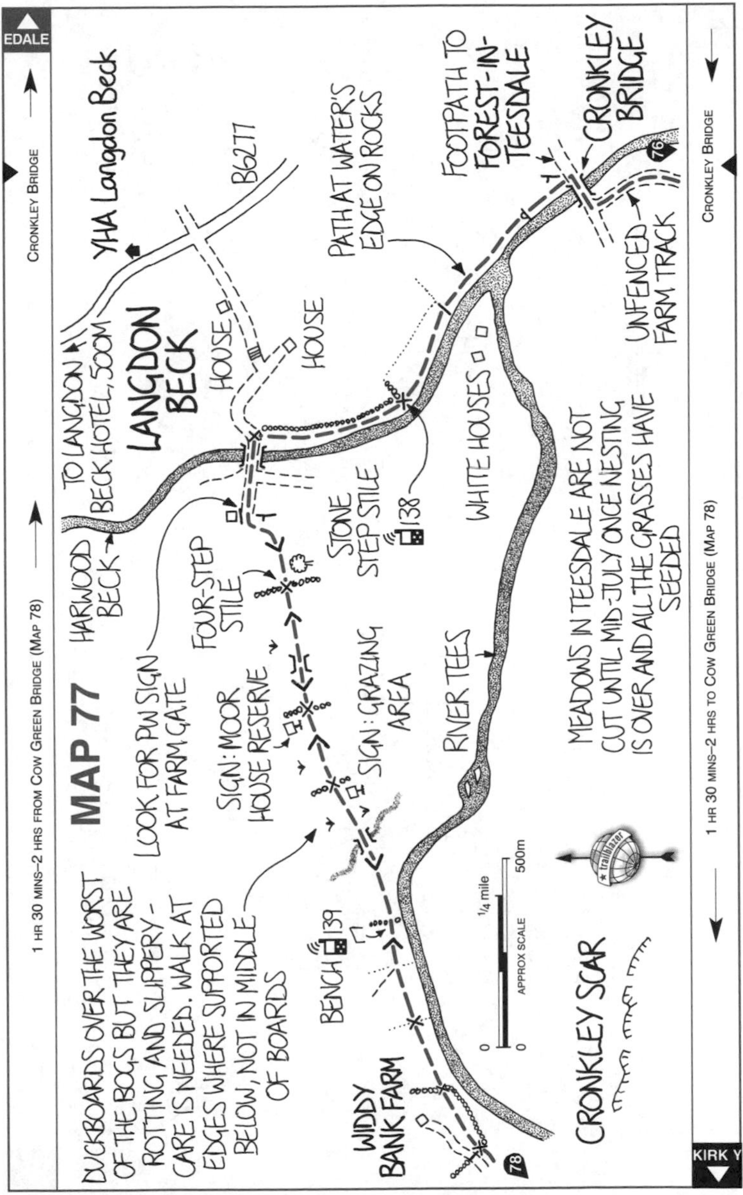

EDALE

CRONKLEY BRIDGE

1 HR 30 MINS–2 HRS FROM COW GREEN BRIDGE (MAP 78)

YHA Langdon Beck

B6277

MAP 77

HARWOOD BECK

TO LANGDON BECK HOTEL, 500m

LANGDON BECK

LOOK FOR PW SIGN AT FARM GATE

FOUR-STEP STILE

SIGN: MOOR HOUSE RESERVE

HOUSE

HOUSE

STONE STEP STILE

138

PATH AT WATER'S EDGE ON ROCKS

FOOTPATH TO FOREST-IN-TEESDALE

CRONKLEY BRIDGE

76

UNFENCED FARM TRACK

WHITE HOUSES

SIGN: GRAZING AREA

RIVER TEES

MEADOWS IN TEESDALE ARE NOT CUT UNTIL MID-JULY ONCE NESTING IS OVER, AND ALL THE GRASSES HAVE SEEDED

DUCKBOARDS OVER THE WORST OF THE BOGS BUT THEY ARE ROTTING AND SLIPPERY – CARE IS NEEDED. WALK AT EDGES WHERE SUPPORTED BELOW, NOT IN MIDDLE OF BOARDS

BENCH 139

WIDDY BANK FARM

78

CRONKLEY SCAR

trailblazer

APPROX SCALE

¼ mile

500m

0

0

CRONKLEY BRIDGE

KIRK Y

1 HR 30 MINS–2 HRS TO COW GREEN BRIDGE (MAP 78)

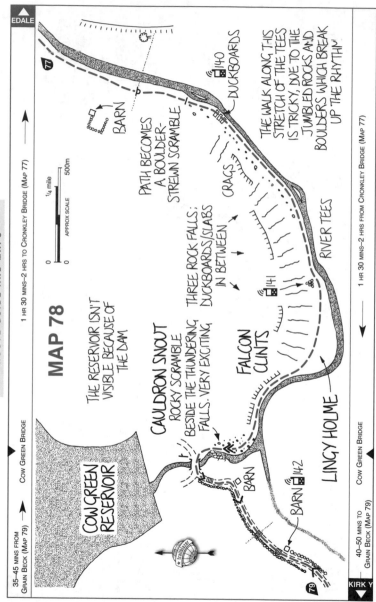

EDALE

77

DUCKBOARDS 140

THE WALK ALONG THIS STRETCH OF THE TEES IS TRICKY, DUE TO THE JUMBLED ROCKS AND BOULDERS WHICH BREAK UP THE RHYTHM.

BARN

P

PATH BECOMES A BOULDER-STREAM SCRAMBLE

CRAGS

MAP 78

1 HR 30 MINS–2 HRS TO CRONKLEY BRIDGE (MAP 77)

¼ mile

APPROX SCALE

0   500m

THE RESERVOIR ISN'T VISIBLE BECAUSE OF THE DAM

THREE ROCK FALLS; DUCKBOARDS/SLABS IN BETWEEN

141

RIVER TEES

CAULDRON SNOUT

ROCKY SCRAMBLE BESIDE THE THUNDERING FALLS. VERY EXCITING.

FALCON CLINTS

1 HR 30 MINS–2 HRS FROM CRONKLEY BRIDGE (MAP 77)

COW GREEN RESERVOIR

BARN

BARN 142

LINGY HOLME

COW GREEN BRIDGE

35–45 MINS FROM GRAIN BECK (MAP 79)

COW GREEN BRIDGE

40–50 MINS TO GRAIN BECK (MAP 79)

79

KIRK Y

True North

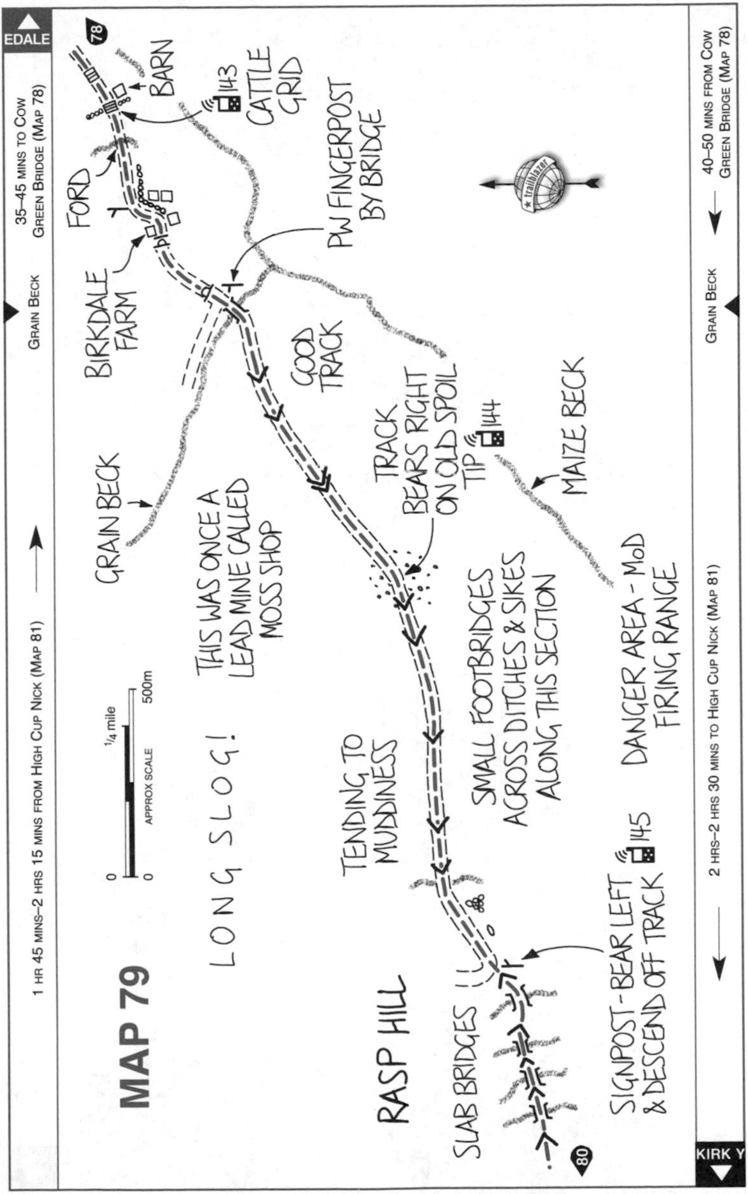

EDALE

78

BARN

📷143

CATTLE GRID

35–45 MINS TO COW GREEN BRIDGE (MAP 78)

GRAIN BECK

FORD

PW FINGERPOST BY BRIDGE

BIRKDALE FARM

GOOD TRACK

TRACK BEARS RIGHT ON OLD SPOIL TIP 📷144

MAIZE BECK

GRAIN BECK

40–50 MINS FROM COW GREEN BRIDGE (MAP 78)

MAP 79

1 HR 45 MINS–2 HRS 15 MINS FROM HIGH CUP NICK (MAP 81)

GRAIN BECK

THIS WAS ONCE A LEAD MINE CALLED MOSS SHOP

LONG SLOG!

¼ mile

500m

APPROX SCALE

TENDING TO MUDDINESS

SMALL FOOTBRIDGES ACROSS DITCHES & SIKES ALONG THIS SECTION

DANGER AREA – MoD FIRING RANGE

RASP HILL

SLAB BRIDGES

SIGNPOST – BEAR LEFT & DESCEND OFF TRACK 📷145

80

2 HRS–2 HRS 30 MINS TO HIGH CUP NICK (MAP 81)

KIRK Y

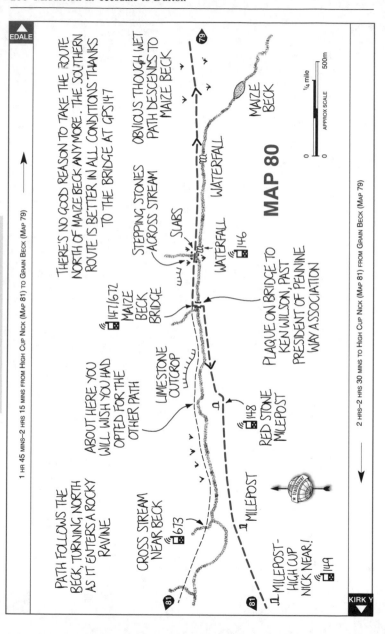

EDALE ▲

1 HR 45 MINS–2 HRS 15 MINS FROM HIGH CUP NICK (MAP 81) TO GRAIN BECK (MAP 79) →

THERE'S NO GOOD REASON TO TAKE THE ROUTE NORTH OF MAIZE BECK ANYMORE. THE SOUTHERN ROUTE IS BETTER IN ALL CONDITIONS THANKS TO THE BRIDGE AT GPS147

OBVIOUS THOUGH WET PATH DESCENDS TO MAIZE BECK

STEPPING STONES ACROSS STREAM

SLABS

147/672 MAIZE BECK BRIDGE

WATERFALL 146

WATERFALL

MAIZE BECK

MAP 80

0   ¼ mile
0   APPROX SCALE   500m

79

ABOUT HERE YOU WILL WISH YOU HAD OPTED FOR THE OTHER PATH

LIMESTONE OUTCROP

PLAQUE ON BRIDGE TO KEN WILSON, PAST PRESIDENT OF PENNINE WAY ASSOCIATION

148 RED STONE MILEPOST

PATH FOLLOWS THE BECK, TURNING NORTH AS IT ENTERS A ROCKY RAVINE

CROSS STREAM NEAR BECK

673

MILEPOST

MILEPOST – HIGH CUP NICK NEAR! 149

81

81

KIRK Y ▼

2 HRS–2 HRS 30 MINS TO HIGH CUP NICK (MAP 81) FROM GRAIN BECK (MAP 79) →

(cont'd from p202) Way. A dorm bed costs from £25pp, private rooms from D/Tr £29/39 (rising to £59/79 in high summer). The hostel is licensed and breakfast and dinner are available but there is also a self-catering kitchen. Note that the hostel is sometimes booked by groups so reservations are recommended.

Camping at *Grandie Caravan Park* (aka **Dufton Caravan Park**; ☎ 01768-353582, ☐ duftoncaravanpark.co.uk; 🐾; ⓛ; Apr-Oct) costs £8pp. There are two toilet/shower blocks. They also have three simple **Hobbit Huts** (2 x 2 single beds from £25, 1 x 4 bunk beds from £40, bedding extra or bring your own); booking is

particularly recommended at weekends for these. They also have a drying room and a wooden hut with seats and table where campers can escape the rain.

Dufton Barn Holidays (☎ 01768-352167, ☐ duftonbarnholidays.co.uk, 1Tr; 🐾) offer a 'Pennine Potting Shed' specifically designed for walkers. The compact but well-designed space includes bunk beds, a sofa, log burning stove, boot warmer, mini-kitchen and ensuite shower/toilet, as well as a private little patio. Rates are S/D/Tr £75/85/95, but three people would be a tight fit! A continental breakfast is available.

(cont'd on p210)

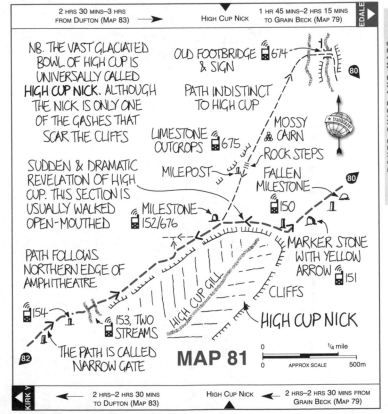

2 HRS 30 MINS–3 HRS FROM DUFTON (MAP 83) ➔

HIGH CUP NICK

1 HR 45 MINS–2 HRS 15 MINS TO GRAIN BECK (MAP 79)

TEESDALE ▶

ROUTE GUIDE AND MAPS

NB. THE VAST GLACIATED BOWL OF HIGH CUP IS UNIVERSALLY CALLED HIGH CUP NICK. ALTHOUGH THE NICK IS ONLY ONE OF THE GASHES THAT SCAR THE CLIFFS

OLD FOOTBRIDGE & SIGN 674

PATH INDISTINCT TO HIGH CUP

MOSSY & CAIRN

80

LIMESTONE OUTCROPS 675

ROCK STEPS

MILEPOST

FALLEN MILESTONE

SUDDEN & DRAMATIC REVELATION OF HIGH CUP. THIS SECTION IS USUALLY WALKED OPEN-MOUTHED

150

80

MILESTONE 152/676

PATH FOLLOWS NORTHERN EDGE OF AMPHITHEATRE

MARKER STONE WITH YELLOW ARROW 151

HIGH CUP GILL

CLIFFS

154

153, TWO STREAMS

HIGH CUP NICK

82

THE PATH IS CALLED NARROW GATE

MAP 81

0   ¼ mile

0   APPROX SCALE   500m

KIRKBY ◀

2 HRS–2 HRS 30 MINS TO DUFTON (MAP 83)

HIGH CUP NICK ◀

2 HRS–2 HRS 30 MINS FROM GRAIN BECK (MAP 79)

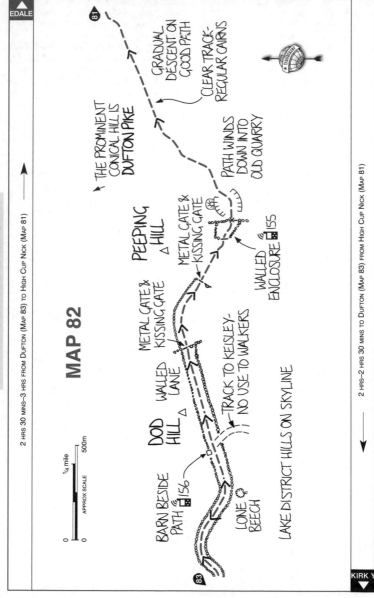

2 HRS 30 MINS–3 HRS FROM DUFTON (MAP 83) TO HIGH CUP NICK (MAP 81) →

MAP 82

¼ mile

500m

APPROX SCALE
0
0

BARN BESIDE
PATH 🏠156

DOD
HILL △

WALLED
LANE

METAL GATE &
KISSING GATE

PEEPING
HILL △

THE PROMINENT
CONICAL HILL IS
DUFTON PIKE

GRADUAL
DESCENT ON
GOOD PATH

CLEAR TRACK-
REGULAR CAIRNS

METAL GATE &
KISSING GATE

PATH WINDS
DOWN INTO
OLD QUARRY

WALLED
ENCLOSURE 🏠155

TRACK TO KEISLEY-
NO USE TO WALKERS

LONE
BEECH

LAKE DISTRICT HILLS ON SKYLINE

81

83

← 2 HRS 30 MINS TO DUFTON (MAP 83) FROM HIGH CUP NICK (MAP 81)

KIRK Y

SLAB BRIDGE

84

NOTE: THERE'S NO SIGNPOST BUT YOU NEED TO TAKE THE STILE OVER THE WALL ON YOUR LEFT HERE

COSCA HILL

157

HALSTEADS (RUIN)

ONCE THROUGH THIS GATE YOU'RE IN OPEN COUNTRY AGAIN

△ DUFTON PIKE 1578 FT / 481M

1 HR 30 MINS–2 HRS FROM KNOCK FELL (MAP 85)

trailblazer

IF IT HAS RAINED IN THE LAST SIX MONTHS THIS SECTION WILL HAVE MUD - LOTS OF MUD

MAP 83

1 HR 50 MINS–2 HRS 20 MINS TO KNOCK FELL (MAP 85)

NARROW HEDGED LANE

0   1/4 mile
0   APPROX SCALE   500m

☆ COATSYKE FARM SIGN & INFORMATION BOARD. THERE IS NO PW SIGN HERE AND IT CAN BE EASY TO GO TOO FAR. BEAR RIGHT ONTO FARM TRACK BESIDE WOODEN POST FOR COATSYKE FARM

COATSYKE FARM

BUNGALOW

SLAB BRIDGE

PW SIGN

PATH BETWEEN FENCES - FIELDS EITHER SIDE

PW SIGN

Dufton Barn Holidays

Post Box Pantry

Stag Inn

PW SIGN AGAINST WALL

PHONE

82

DUFTON

DUFTON

TO PENRITH & LONG MARTON

Grandie Caravan Park

RED STONE FARM

BILLYSBECK BRIDGE

EDALE

ROUTE GUIDE AND MAPS

(cont'd from p207)   The ***Post Box Pantry*** (☏ 07903-358081, 🖳 postbox pantry.co.uk, **fb**; 🐾; Easter-end Sep Mon-Wed & Fri 10am-4pm, Sat & Sun to 5pm), on the village green, is a gold mine, particularly if you're self-catering at the YHA hostel. They serve tea and coffee and a wide choice of snacks, sandwiches, breakfasts, cakes and ice-cream, as well as a small selection of useful items such as

bread, milk, canned foods and toiletries.

The Stag Inn (☏ 01768-351608, 🖳 thestagdufton.co.uk, **fb**; 🐾 in parts of the pub) is known for its substantial meals (**food** summer Tue-Fri 5.30-8pm, Sat & Sun noon-2pm & 5.30-9pm) in the £11-15 range. Note that the pub doesn't open until late afternoon on weekdays (Mon 6pm, Tue & Wed 5pm, Thur & Fri 6pm).

❏ **APPLEBY**

Appleby (🖳 visitcumbria.com/evnp/appleby), 3 miles south of Dufton, is an attractive country town on the Carlisle–Leeds railway (Northern Rail; see box p59) with banks, several pubs and a bakery or two, all settled around a bend in the River Eden. If you're due for a day off, you could do a lot worse than scheduling it around Dufton and Appleby. Be warned, however, that in June there's the annual week-long **horse fair** (🖳 applebyfair.org), the largest of its kind in the world and one that attracts a vast population of travellers, many arriving in their traditional gypsy caravans. It's quite a spectacle but can be very crowded and more than a little chaotic at this time. The fair ends on the second Wednesday in June.

DUFTON TO ALSTON   MAPS 83-94

Route overview

Today the challenge is tackling the highest point on the Pennine Way; Cross Fell stands at 2930ft (893m) above sea level and with Dufton standing at only 600ft

Distance	19½ miles (31.5km)
Ascent	3500ft (1066m)
Time	6½-8 hours

(183m), alas, there is quite a haul ahead. This is a serious mountain walk and it should not be undertaken lightly, not least because the very strong north-easterly **Helm Wind** (the UK's only named wind; see 🖳 metoffice.gov.uk) can be dangerous to unexpecting and ill-equipped walkers. Come prepared, and take care.

The Pennine Way may be a National Trail, but don't leave Dufton without proper waterproof clothing, compass and GPS as well as food and water to sustain you for the whole day – there is no re-supply option until Garrigill and possibly not there either depending on the day and time of arrival. Take heart though, you're a battle-scarred veteran of Kinder, Bleaklow and Pen-y-ghent; this is just another notch waiting to be cut into your walking pole.

The official route just skims the edge of Dufton, using a narrow path between fields on the village's south-eastern edge, but most will continue to use the 'unofficial' route through the village and along a quiet lane until both paths join before Coatsyke Farm. A muddy track leads to the old ruin of **Halsteads** and the final gate into open country. The ascent is gentle to begin with, but once beyond the ladder stile over the final access wall, the gradient increases significantly.

The next couple of miles up to **Knock Fell** (Map 85) account for almost 1500ft (457m) of today's total ascent, so be sure to turn and look across to the Lake District as you catch your breath. If the weather is in your favour the white golf-ball-like dome of the radar station on **Great Dun Fell** (Map 86) becomes your next goal, but in mist you may need to resort to compass or GPS to find the route off Knock Fell, though soon slabs and snow poles will act as a guide.

Two more ascents and another couple of miles will see you over the top of **Little Dun Fell** and standing on the summit of **Cross Fell** (Map 87) the roof of the Pennines, hopefully with a grand vista stretched before you. The route off the summit is not obvious in mist and a compass bearing may be needed from the trig point or shelter. A short, possibly boggy, descent takes you to the track that leads down to Garrigill.

You may feel a rush of relief at reaching the firm footing of **Corpse Road** (so called because in the past it was the route coffins had to be taken to reach consecrated ground as there was nowhere in Garrigill) and at being able to put away your map and compass, but this will be short lived as the miles into Garrigill begin to hammer at the soles of your feet and your knees begin to creak and groan under the constant descent. It's enough to make those who cross Cross cross. A brief respite can be found in **Greg's Hut** (see box p213); before you leave add your experiences to the visitors' book.

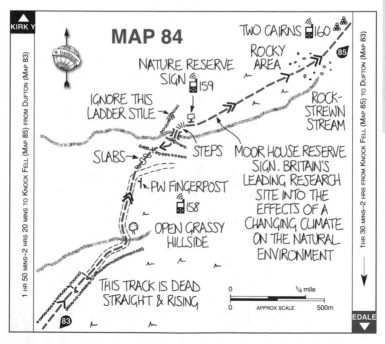

ROUTE GUIDE AND MAPS

KIRK Y

MAP 84

TWO CAIRNS 160

NATURE RESERVE
SIGN 159

ROCKY
AREA

85

IGNORE THIS
LADDER STILE

ROCK-
STREWN
STREAM

SLABS

STEPS

MOOR HOUSE RESERVE
SIGN. BRITAIN'S
LEADING RESEARCH
SITE INTO THE
EFFECTS OF A
CHANGING CLIMATE
ON THE NATURAL
ENVIRONMENT

PW FINGERPOST
158

OPEN GRASSY
HILLSIDE

THIS TRACK IS DEAD
STRAIGHT & RISING

0   ¼ mile

0   APPROX SCALE   500m

83

1 HR 50 MINS–2 HRS 20 MINS TO KNOCK FELL (MAP 85) FROM DUFTON (MAP 83)

1 HR 30 MINS–2 HRS FROM KNOCK FELL (MAP 85) TO DUFTON (MAP 83)

EDALE

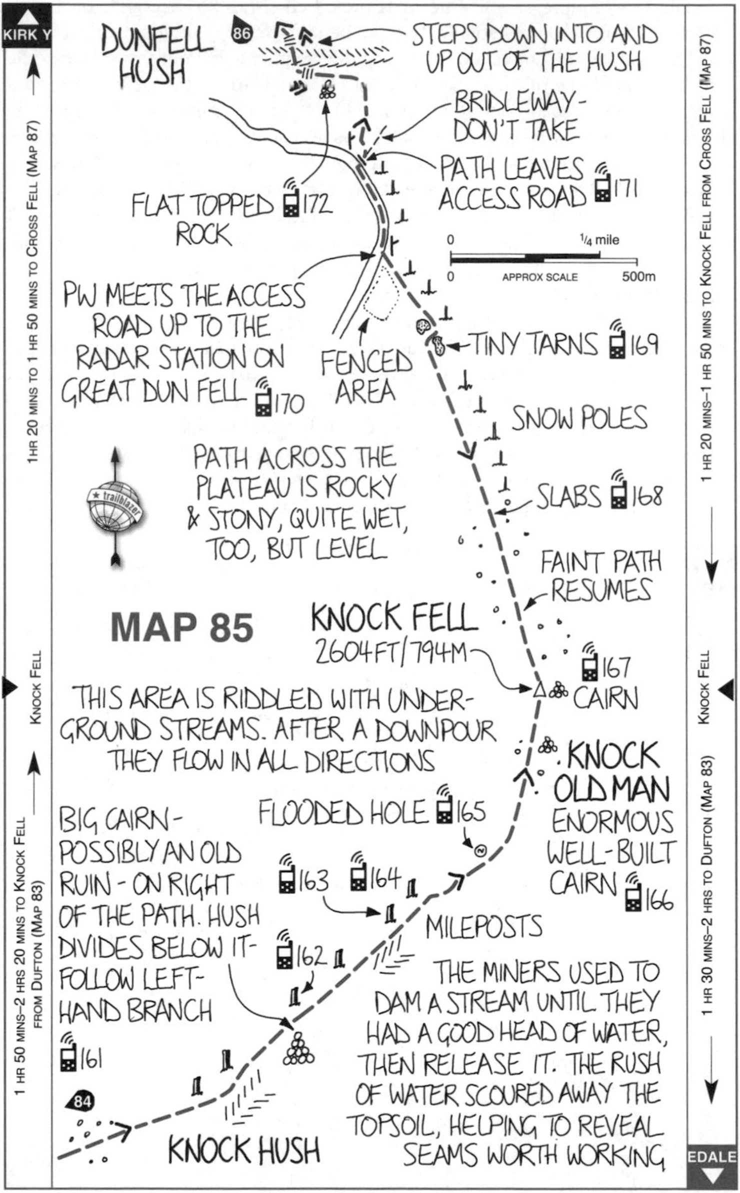

DUNFELL HUSH **86**

STEPS DOWN INTO AND UP OUT OF THE HUSH

BRIDLEWAY - DON'T TAKE

PATH LEAVES ACCESS ROAD 📱171

FLAT TOPPED ROCK 📱172

PW MEETS THE ACCESS ROAD UP TO THE RADAR STATION ON GREAT DUN FELL 📱170

FENCED AREA

TINY TARNS 📱169

SNOW POLES

SLABS 📱168

FAINT PATH RESUMES

PATH ACROSS THE PLATEAU IS ROCKY & STONY, QUITE WET, TOO, BUT LEVEL

0 .... ¼ mile
0 .... 500m
APPROX SCALE

MAP 85

KNOCK FELL 2604FT/794M

📱167 △ CAIRN

THIS AREA IS RIDDLED WITH UNDER-GROUND STREAMS. AFTER A DOWNPOUR THEY FLOW IN ALL DIRECTIONS

KNOCK OLD MAN ENORMOUS WELL-BUILT CAIRN 📱166

FLOODED HOLE 📱165

BIG CAIRN - POSSIBLY AN OLD RUIN - ON RIGHT OF THE PATH. HUSH DIVIDES BELOW IT- FOLLOW LEFT-HAND BRANCH

📱163 📱164

📱162

📱161

84

MILEPOSTS

THE MINERS USED TO DAM A STREAM UNTIL THEY HAD A GOOD HEAD OF WATER, THEN RELEASE IT. THE RUSH OF WATER SCOURED AWAY THE TOPSOIL, HELPING TO REVEAL SEAMS WORTH WORKING

KNOCK HUSH

KIRK Y ▲

1 HR 20 MINS to 1 HR 50 MINS TO CROSS FELL (MAP 87)

1 HR 20 MINS-1 HR 50 MINS TO KNOCK FELL FROM CROSS FELL (MAP 87)

ROUTE GUIDE AND MAPS

Knock Fell

Knock Fell

1 HR 50 MINS-2 HRS 20 MINS TO KNOCK FELL FROM DUFTON (MAP 83)

1 HR 30 MINS-2 HRS TO DUFTON (MAP 83)

EDALE ▼

ROUTE GUIDE AND MAPS

❑ GREG'S HUT   [Map 87]

Greg's Hut is a welcome and well-maintained bothy just over the summit of Cross Fell where walkers can take refuge from the elements or just pop in for a nose around. It holds a special place in the heart of many wayfarers. Originally it was used by lead miners whose tailing can be seen all around. They would stay here all week and walk home at the weekend. 'Greg' was actually John Gregory, a climber who died following an epic climbing accident in the Alps in 1968 in spite of the heroic efforts of his companion who held him on the rope and tended his injuries all night. Rescuers arrived too late.

Thanks to the efforts of the Mountain Bothies Association, the hut has been repaired and maintained, most recently in 2022. There are two rooms, the inner one has a raised sleeping platform with a stove, although fuel is scarce. Certainly you're unlikely to find any on the surrounding fell. This is a classic (though simple – no toilet) mountain bothy, unique along the Pennine Way, and it's hard to drag yourself out of it in horrible conditions. The visitors' book could be published as it stands, telling a multitude of stories, most of them epics of embellishment or endurance.

The descent continues and the sight of the road stretching ahead can be soul (and sole) destroying, but eventually Garrigill comes into sight and the worst is soon over. If you've timed it right the pub and shop in **Garrigill** (Map 91) may be open, but you're just as likely to find them both shuttered and silent. If you're pushing on to Alston the final few miles along the river may well be easier than Corpse Road, but they are no picnic; an obstacle course of stiles and sprung gates has been laid for you, but **Alston** (Map 94) is an oasis of refreshments and services galore.

Navigation notes

With good visibility, today's route poses no real problems, other than the lack of an obvious path off the summits of Knock Fell and, in particular, Cross Fell, both of which require a change of direction in order to keep on the Way. In mist

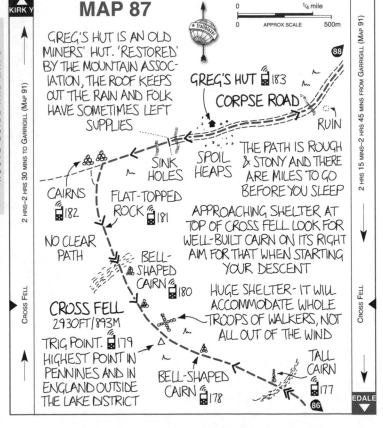

MAP 87

0 .... ¼ mile

0 .... 500m
APPROX SCALE

GREG'S HUT IS AN OLD MINERS' HUT. 'RESTORED' BY THE MOUNTAIN ASSOCIATION, THE ROOF KEEPS OUT THE RAIN AND FOLK HAVE SOMETIMES LEFT SUPPLIES

GREG'S HUT 📱183

CORPSE ROAD

RUIN

88

SINK HOLES

SPOIL HEAPS

THE PATH IS ROUGH & STONY AND THERE ARE MILES TO GO BEFORE YOU SLEEP

CAIRNS 📱182

FLAT-TOPPED ROCK 📱181

APPROACHING SHELTER AT TOP OF CROSS FELL LOOK FOR WELL-BUILT CAIRN ON ITS RIGHT AIM FOR THAT WHEN STARTING YOUR DESCENT

NO CLEAR PATH

BELL-SHAPED CAIRN 📱180

HUGE SHELTER- IT WILL ACCOMMODATE WHOLE TROOPS OF WALKERS, NOT ALL OUT OF THE WIND

CROSS FELL 2930FT/893M

TRIG POINT. 📱179 HIGHEST POINT IN PENNINES AND IN ENGLAND OUTSIDE THE LAKE DISTRICT

BELL-SHAPED CAIRN 📱178

TALL CAIRN 📱177

86

KIRK Y

ROUTE GUIDE AND MAPS

2 HRS–2 HRS 30 MINS TO GARRIGILL (MAP 91)

CROSS FELL

2 HRS 15 MINS–2 HRS 45 MINS FROM GARRIGILL (MAP 91)

CROSS FELL

EDALE

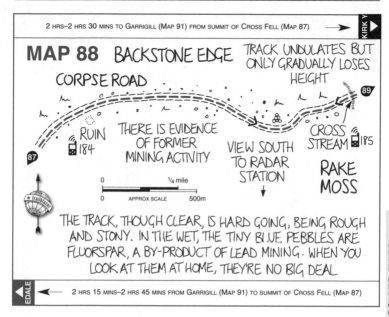

KIRK Y

MAP 88 BACKSTONE EDGE TRACK UNDULATES BUT ONLY GRADUALLY LOSES HEIGHT

CORPSE ROAD

89

RUIN 184

THERE IS EVIDENCE OF FORMER MINING ACTIVITY

VIEW SOUTH TO RADAR STATION ↓

CROSS STREAM 185

RAKE MOSS

87

0   ¼ mile
0   APPROX SCALE   500m

trailblazer

THE TRACK, THOUGH CLEAR, IS HARD GOING, BEING ROUGH AND STONY. IN THE WET, THE TINY BLUE PEBBLES ARE FLUORSPAR, A BY-PRODUCT OF LEAD MINING. WHEN YOU LOOK AT THEM AT HOME, THEY'RE NO BIG DEAL

EDALE

ROUTE GUIDE AND MAPS

or low cloud, however, the story changes significantly and the dome of the radar station cannot be relied on as a guide. The rock-strewn summit of Knock Fell does not hold a clear path, hence the proliferation of GPS waypoints along this section. Similarly on Cross Fell, the change in direction can be confusing, especially if you've rested in the shelter and lost your bearings. A line of small cairns leads north off Cross Fell, but more reliably, the GPS waypoints are there. Better still, a compass bearing can be taken from the trig point.

The path from Garrigill to Alston is never far from the river, except when it climbs to Bleagate (Map 93). Although it can be somewhat confusing at times, the signage is fairly good and there aren't too many alternative footpaths leading off the main path.

GARRIGILL   [Map 91, p218]

Don't be disturbed to find the shutters up on Garrigill's **post office**, these are to protect the antique windows when the shop is closed; when open (Mon & Wed-Fri 9am-4pm, Tue & Sat 9am-12.30pm) it transacts the usual business and includes a sparsely provisioned **shop** (same hours) as well as selling hot drinks.

If you want to **camp** at Garrigill, you can pitch up behind *Garrigill Village Hall* (bookings ☎ 01434-647516, 🖳 garrigillvh

.org.uk), on the border with the village green, using the nearby public toilets. The cost is £8, with use of the hall's drying facilities and shower an extra £2; put your payment in the postbox on the porch. Also here, above the hall, is an excellent community-run **bunkhouse** (1 x 8-bed room). Beds cost £18pp and give you access to a full kitchen, shower, drying room, charging ports and wi-fi; bedding hire is an extra £5, if you need it. You can book online.

At the time of research the village pub, the 17th century *George & Dragon* (☎ 01434-382691, 🖥 george-and-dragon.com;

4D or T/1Tr) was nearing the end of an extensive heritage restoration and was due to reopen its bar, restaurant and five en suite

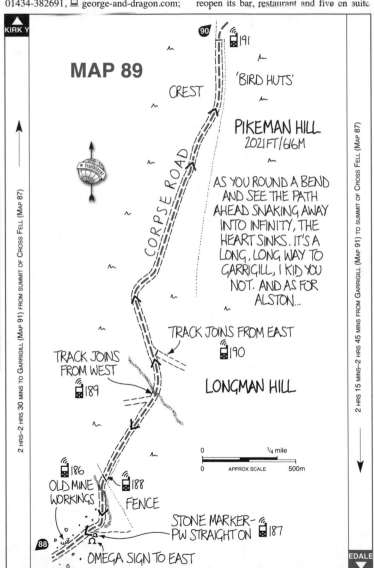

KIRK Y

MAP 89

90 📱191

CREST

'BIRD HUTS'

PIKEMAN HILL
2021FT/616M

CORPSE ROAD

AS YOU ROUND A BEND
AND SEE THE PATH
AHEAD SNAKING AWAY
INTO INFINITY, THE
HEART SINKS. IT'S A
LONG, LONG WAY TO
GARRIGILL, I KID YOU
NOT. AND AS FOR
ALSTON...

TRACK JOINS FROM EAST
📱190

TRACK JOINS
FROM WEST
📱189

LONGMAN HILL

0   ¼ mile
0   500m
APPROX SCALE

📱186
OLD MINE
WORKINGS

📱188

FENCE

STONE MARKER—
PW STRAIGHT ON 📱187

88

Ω

OMEGA SIGN TO EAST

ROUTE GUIDE AND MAPS

2 HRS–2 HRS 30 MINS TO GARRIGILL (MAP 91) FROM SUMMIT OF CROSS FELL (MAP 87)

2 HRS 15 MINS–2 HRS 45 MINS FROM GARRIGILL (MAP 91) TO SUMMIT OF CROSS FELL (MAP 87)

EDALE ▼

rooms in Spring 2023. A drying room, laundry and bike storage should be available. Great care is going into the restoration so it should once again be a great place to stop.

Nearby you'll also find cosy **East View** (☎ 01434-381561, 🖥 garrigillbedandbreakfast .co.uk; 1D private bathroom, 1Tr en suite; ◔; Ⓛ; 🐾) with B&B from S/D £55/70.

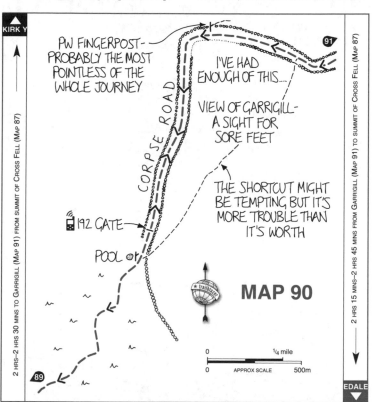

KIRK Y

PW FINGERPOST-
PROBABLY THE MOST
POINTLESS OF THE
WHOLE JOURNEY

I'VE HAD
ENOUGH OF THIS...

CORPSE ROAD

VIEW OF GARRIGILL-
A SIGHT FOR
SORE FEET

THE SHORTCUT MIGHT
BE TEMPTING BUT IT'S
MORE TROUBLE THAN
IT'S WORTH

192 GATE

POOL

MAP 90

2 HRS–2 HRS 30 MINS TO GARRIGILL (MAP 91) FROM SUMMIT OF CROSS FELL (MAP 87)

2 HRS 15 MINS–2 HRS 45 MINS FROM GARRIGILL (MAP 91) TO SUMMIT OF CROSS FELL (MAP 87)

0   ¼ mile
0   APPROX SCALE   500m

89

EDALE

ROUTE GUIDE AND MAPS

❑ SOUTH TYNEDALE RAILWAY

South Tynedale Railway (☎ 01434-382828, 🖥 south-tynedale-railway.org.uk; weekends Apr-Oct) operates trains from Alston to Slaggyford (35 mins, approx 5 miles) on 'England's highest narrow-gauge railway'. Steam locomotives are used on most services; visit the website for schedules and tickets. Return tickets start from £16.50, or you can buy single tickets at Alston station; Kirkhaugh and Lintley Halt stations are right on the Pennine Way. The line originally went to Haltwhistle and volunteers are now hoping to restore the line all the way there.

On weekends you may find the **Hub Museum** open (Sat 11am-4.30pm, Sun 9am-5pm, £2.50), by the station and full of nostalgia-inducing vintage vehicles.

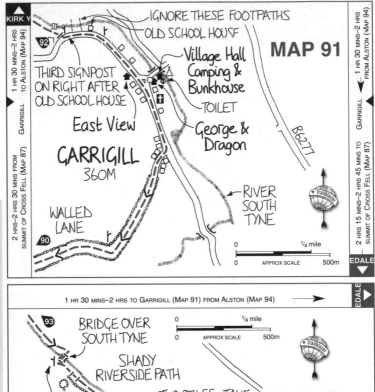

MAP 91

IGNORE THESE FOOTPATHS

OLD SCHOOL HOUSE

Village Hall Camping & Bunkhouse

THIRD SIGNPOST ON RIGHT AFTER OLD SCHOOL HOUSE

TOILET

East View

George & Dragon

GARRIGILL 360M

RIVER SOUTH TYNE

WALLED LANE

KIRK Y

1 HR 30 MINS–2 HRS TO ALSTON (MAP 94)

GARRIGILL

2 HRS–2 HRS 30 MINS FROM SUMMIT OF CROSS FELL (MAP 87)

1 HR 30 MINS–2 HRS FROM ALSTON (MAP 94)

GARRIGILL

2 HRS 15 MINS–2 HRS 45 MINS TO SUMMIT OF CROSS FELL (MAP 87)

EDALE

B6277

0   ¼ mile
0   500m
APPROX SCALE

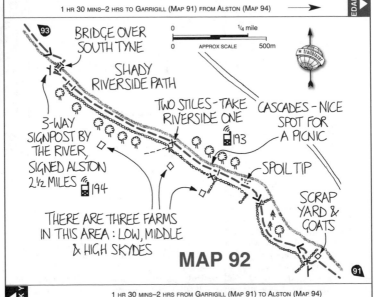

EDALE

1 HR 30 MINS–2 HRS TO GARRIGILL (MAP 91) FROM ALSTON (MAP 94)

BRIDGE OVER SOUTH TYNE

SHADY RIVERSIDE PATH

TWO STILES – TAKE RIVERSIDE ONE

CASCADES – NICE SPOT FOR A PICNIC

3-WAY SIGNPOST BY THE RIVER, SIGNED ALSTON 2½ MILES 📵194

📵193

SPOIL TIP

SCRAP YARD & GOATS

THERE ARE THREE FARMS IN THIS AREA: LOW, MIDDLE & HIGH SKYDES

MAP 92

0   ¼ mile
0   500m
APPROX SCALE

KIRK Y

1 HR 30 MINS–2 HRS FROM GARRIGILL (MAP 91) TO ALSTON (MAP 94)

ROUTE GUIDE AND MAPS

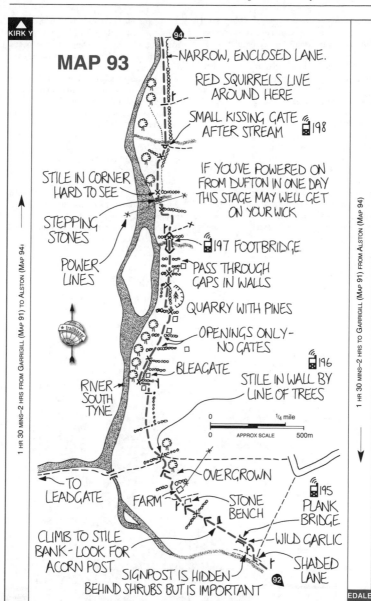

MAP 93

NARROW, ENCLOSED LANE.

RED SQUIRRELS LIVE AROUND HERE

SMALL KISSING GATE AFTER STREAM 📱198

IF YOU'VE POWERED ON FROM DUFTON IN ONE DAY THIS STAGE MAY WELL GET ON YOUR WICK

STILE IN CORNER HARD TO SEE

STEPPING STONES

POWER LINES

📱197 FOOTBRIDGE

PASS THROUGH GAPS IN WALLS

QUARRY WITH PINES

OPENINGS ONLY – NO GATES

BLEAGATE

📱196

STILE IN WALL BY LINE OF TREES

RIVER SOUTH TYNE

0   ¼ mile
0   500m
APPROX SCALE

TO LEADGATE

OVERGROWN

FARM

STONE BENCH

📱195 PLANK BRIDGE

WILD GARLIC

SHADED LANE

CLIMB TO STILE BANK – LOOK FOR ACORN POST

SIGNPOST IS HIDDEN BEHIND SHRUBS BUT IS IMPORTANT

92

KIRK Y

94

EDALE

1 HR 30 MINS–2 HRS FROM GARRIGILL (MAP 91) TO ALSTON (MAP 94)

1 HR 30 MINS–2 HRS TO GARRIGILL (MAP 91) FROM ALSTON (MAP 94)

ROUTE GUIDE AND MAPS

ALSTON   [Map 94a]

Alston is England's highest market town (although it no longer holds a regular weekly market) and its steep cobbled streets and 18th-century buildings give it a bit of character. It has an excellent range of services for walkers and is a welcome sight following two days of remote hiking.

Services

The **tourist information centre** (TIC; ☎ 01434-382244, 🖵 visiteden.co.uk; Mar to mid Oct Mon-Sat 10am-12.30pm, 1-4.30pm) is in the **library** at the Town Hall on Front St. Hi-Pennine Outdoor (☎ 01434-381389, **fb**; summer Mon-Sat 10am-4.30pm, Sun 11am-4pm), an **outdoor equipment shop**, is a good spot to restock worn-out socks, blister patches, gas canisters and the like.

Alston Wholefoods (🖵 alstonwhole foods.com; Mon-Sat 9am-5pm, except Wed from 10am; Sun noon-5pm) is a **grocery and deli** selling Fairtrade chocolate, over 40 varieties of local cheese and delicatessen items and responsibly sourced goods.

There are also two **supermarkets**; a Spar (daily 6am-10pm) at the Texaco petrol station, and a Co-op (daily 7am-10pm); both have an **ATM**. There is also a **chemist** (Mon & Wed-Fri 9am-5.30pm, Tue & Sat to 12.30pm) and a **post office** (Mon-Fri 9am-1pm & 2-5pm, Sat 9am-noon).

Transport

[See pp54-9] Go North East's 681 **bus** service heads from Alston to Birdoswald (twice a day). Wright Brothers' Coaches 889/889W service runs to Nenthead and Hexham (once a day), plus their seasonal

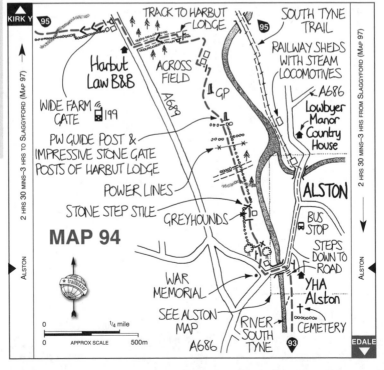

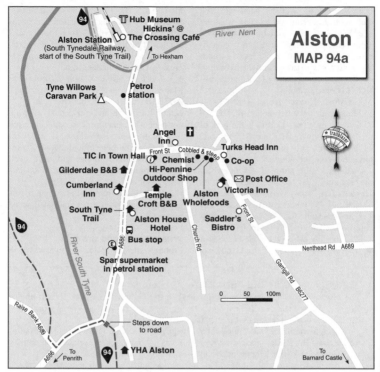

Alston
MAP 94a

Hub Museum
Hickins' @
The Crossing Café

Alston Station
(South Tynedale Railway,
start of the South Tyne Trail)

River Nent

To Hexham

Tyne Willows
Caravan Park

Petrol
station

Angel
Inn

TIC in Town Hall
Chemist
Hi-Pennine
Outdoor Shop

Gilderdale B&B

Cumberland
Inn

Temple
Croft B&B

South Tyne
Trail

Alston House
Hotel

Bus stop

Spar supermarket
in petrol station

Front St   Cobbled & steep

Turks Head Inn
Co-op

Post Office

Alston
Wholefoods

Victoria Inn

Saddler's
Bistro

Front St

Church Rd

Nenthead Rd   A689

Garrigill Rd   B6277

River South Tyne

Raise Bank A689

A686

Steps down
to road

To
Penrith

YHA Alston

To
Barnard Castle

0   50   100m

No 888 service stops between Newcastle and Keswick (summer weekends).

For a **taxi** try Alston Taxis (☎ 07990-593855).

Where to stay

Campers should make their way past the derelict cars behind Moredun garage to *Tyne Willows Caravan Park* (☎ 01434-382515; ﹐ Mar to end Oct). It costs from £5pp to **camp** on a bit of grass between the static caravans; there are basic toilet and shower facilities. The setup is a bit weird but it works, just.

YHA Alston (☎ 0345 260 2489, ☎ 01434-381509, 🖳 yha.org.uk/hostel/alston; Ⓛ) overlooks the South Tyne river. It has 30 beds (rooms sleep 2-6, shared facilities); a dorm bed costs from £25pp (private rooms from S/D £30/48). The hostel offers breakfasts and has laundry facilities, a kitchen and a drying room. Check-in is from 5pm.

There are several pubs, some past their prime; you may find traditional B&Bs a better bet.

Pubs with simple rooms include *Victoria Inn* (☎ 01434-381194; 4S/2D/2Tr, some en suite, others share facilities; Ⓛ; ﹐ bar only) which charges from £65/75 for a double with shared/en suite bathroom. *Cumberland Inn* (☎ 01434-381875, 🖳 cumberlandalston.com; 2D/3Tr all en suite; ⬤; Ⓛ; ﹐) charges from S/D £65/86.50 for a room above the pub.

Temple Croft B&B (☎ 01434-382660, 🖳 temple-croft.co.uk; 1D/1Tr/1Q all en suite; ⬤; Ⓛ) is a recommended place right in the centre of town. **B&B** rooms cost from S/D £70/95. Walkers' needs are well met with a drying room and washing machine. There is also a **bunkroom** with eight beds, lockers, a kettle and two dedicated bathrooms at £25-27pp, without breakfast but with towels and linens included. Evening meals (from £12.50) are available if booked by 6pm.

Alston House Hotel (☎ 01434-382200, 🖳 alstonhousehotel.co.uk, **fb**; 5D/2Tr, all en suite; ➥; ⓛ; 🛏) is the pick of the crop in town; B&B costs from S/D £100/120, with rates higher at weekends. It has great food (see Where to eat and drink).

About a mile north of Alston, where the Pennine Way crosses the A689, is *Harbut Law* (see Map 94; ☎ 01434-381950, 🖳 harbutlawcottages.co.uk; 1D/1Tr, both en suite; ⓛ; Mar-Oct) a comfortable B&B charging S/D/Tr from £45/80.

Gilderdale B&B (☎ 07460-177683, or ☎ 07410-598059, 🖳 jane.strickland@hot

mail.co.uk; 1D, T or Tr, private facilities; from £60 depending on season and occupancy; email to book), 3 Townfoot, is self-contained with a bed and sofa-bed (on request) and ingredients for a continental breakfast are left in the room.

Lowbyer Manor Country House (see Map 94; ☎ 01434-381230, 🖳 lowbyer.com; 2S/7D/2T, all en suite; ⓛ; 🛏) is an 18th-century Georgian house five minutes' walk north of Alston centre. Jim and Janice are welcoming hosts, breakfast is excellent (order the night before) and there's a comfortable communal lounge and bar, as well as outdoor seating in the sequoia-filled garden. Doubles cost around £95-110, with weekend rates a little higher. Single rooms are small but comfortable and good value from £65.

Where to eat and drink

Probably the best place in town is *Alston*

❑ LEAD MINING IN THE PENNINES

The history of digging in the earth for lead in the Pennine hills goes back to the Romans and probably earlier, evidence having been uncovered that Romans further exploited existing workings soon after they arrived.

The growth in the building of abbeys and castles increased the demand for lead for the roofs and stained-glass windows but it was not until the 19th century that mining assumed industrial proportions as the demand for lead increased.

The industry started to suffer when cheaper foreign sources threatened local production and by the early years of the 20th century mining was in decline. Today there is no lead mining in Britain although some of the old pits have been re-opened to exploit other minerals found there such as barytes and fluorspar. The ore, galena, also has a use in producing X-ray equipment.

The ruins evident around Alston, and around Keld in Swaledale, are a reminder of the extensive industry involved in lead mining at one time. Old spoil tips, ruined mine buildings and the occasional remains of a chimney are all that is left of this activity, now long discarded as uneconomic. Traces of bell pits are often to be seen as hollows in the ground. They used to sink a shaft to a certain level then widen the bottom of the hole until it was unsafe to go further. Everything dug out went to the surface in a bucket, firstly by hand and then by a winch, sometimes drawn up on a wheel by a horse walking in a circle. It was a primitive industry in the early days, reliant on the muscle power of the miners themselves. With the advent of engineering, ways were found to mechanise production and so multiply the output, increasing profits for the owners.

Around Middleton-in-Teesdale mining rights were held by the London Lead Mining Company, a Quaker concern, active from the latter part of the 1700s until early in the 1900s when they pulled out in the face of cheap imported ore from Europe.

House Hotel (see Where to stay) which serves food in its **café** (10.30am-3.30pm), bar and **restaurant** (daily noon-3pm, 5-8.30pm); the extensive menu includes pizzas, burgers and more ambitious dinner dishes such as lamb shoulder (£16.95) and Thai curry (£14.50).

Cumberland Inn (see Where to stay) is the most reliable place for a meal as it's open daily (noon-3pm & 6-9pm), with good value dishes ranging from fish pie to chicken tikka masala (£10.50), and a cheap lunch menu (£5-7.50) from 11am-3pm.

Saddler's Bakery & Bistro (☎ 07494-129845, 🖳 saddlers-bakery-bistro.business.site, **fb**; Tue-Sat 10am-3pm) serves up café-style breakfasts, stotties (filled rolls), soups, quiche and pies, with bread baked on the premises.

Hickins' @ The Crossing Café (☎ 07751-596469, **fb**; Wed-Sun 10am-3.30pm; 🐾) is a bright and buzzing café and lunch spot at Alston railway station. Breakfasts (until noon), paninis, coffee and cake are all good and things even stretch to a Thai noodle salad (all £6-8) and bottled beer.

Some of the pubs serve good food; try **the** *Victoria Inn* (see Where to stay; Tue-Sun 6-10pm) for curries and, under new management by the time you read this, *The Angel Inn*. The best place for a drink is *Turks Head Inn* (**fb**; daily from 3.30pm) which has a range of real ales.

If you need a break as you walk north of Alston, *The Nook Farm Shop* (see Map 95; 🖳 thenookfarmshop.com, **fb**; daily 9.30-4pm, last hot food order 3pm) at Whitley Castle is a shop and **café** that serves hot drinks, epic flapjacks (ours lasted three days), sandwiches, soups and light meals, including some daily specials and a wide range of farm-made chutneys. You can reach it by walking along the A689 from where the Way hits the road, or by taking a shortcut through the ruins of the Roman fort of Epiacum.

ALSTON TO GREENHEAD

MAPS 94-102

Route overview

It's hard to justify the allure of the Pennine Way over that of the South Tyne Trail (which runs between Garrigill and Haltwhistle) in the first part of today's

Distance	16½ miles (26.5km)
Ascent	2000ft (610m)
Time	7½-9½ hours

walk. The Pennine Way selects a bizarre, pedantic route through fields, farms and over countless stiles and gates whereas the South Tyne Trail meanders like an unbroken, gradient-free ribbon of contentment beside it. Admittedly when the planners laid down the Way, the South Tyne Trail didn't exist, but you now have a choice: traditionalist or pragmatist.

Today marks the end of the Pennine chain and the transition slowly to the Southern Upland range just beyond Hadrian's Wall; the hills are no less impressive though and there are many delights to come. This stage can be broken almost exactly in half by staying in Knarsdale but it's not particularly strenuous compared to the last couple of days, so push on to Greenhead and the Wall.

North of Alston you'll pass the unexcavated Roman fort of **Epiacum** (🖳 epiacumheritage.org), known popularly as **Whitley Castle** (Map 95). The lozenge-shaped fortifications housed around 500 Roman soldiers between the 2nd and 4th centuries who protected the nearby lead and silver mines. In this section between Alston and Kirkhaugh the Pennine Way shadows **Isaac's Tea Trail** (🖳 isaacs-tea-trail.co.uk), a 36-mile circular walking route celebrating itinerant tea merchant and philanthropist Isaac Holden.

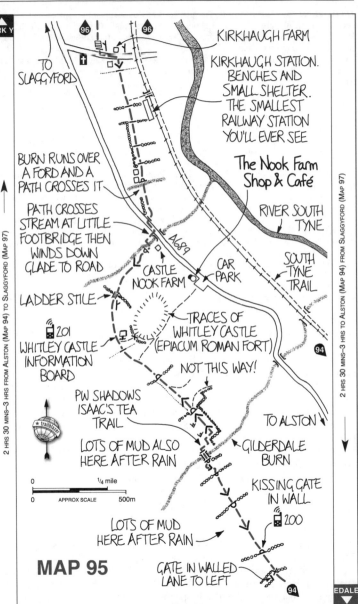

KIRK Y

TO
SLAGGYFORD

96   96   KIRKHAUGH FARM

KIRKHAUGH STATION.
BENCHES AND
SMALL SHELTER.
THE SMALLEST
RAILWAY STATION
YOU'LL EVER SEE

The Nook Farm
Shop & Café

BURN RUNS OVER
A FORD AND A
PATH CROSSES IT

RIVER SOUTH
TYNE

PATH CROSSES
STREAM AT LITTLE
FOOTBRIDGE THEN
WINDS DOWN
GLADE TO ROAD

A689

SOUTH
TYNE
TRAIL

CASTLE
NOOK FARM

CAR
PARK

LADDER STILE

201
WHITLEY CASTLE
INFORMATION
BOARD

TRACES OF
WHITLEY CASTLE
(EPIACUM ROMAN FORT)

NOT THIS WAY!

PW SHADOWS
ISAAC'S TEA
TRAIL

94

TO ALSTON

LOTS OF MUD ALSO
HERE AFTER RAIN

GILDERDALE
BURN

0   ¼ mile

0   APPROX SCALE   500m

KISSING GATE
IN WALL

200

LOTS OF MUD
HERE AFTER RAIN

MAP 95

GATE IN WALLED
LANE TO LEFT

94

trailblazer

2 HRS 30 MINS–3 HRS FROM ALSTON (MAP 94) TO SLAGGYFORD (MAP 97)

2 HRS 30 MINS–3 HRS TO ALSTON (MAP 94) FROM SLAGGYFORD (MAP 97)

EDALE

Whether you followed the Pennine Way or the South Tyne Trail, the first settlement is **Slaggyford** (see p226), a forgotten platform on a small, quiet railway line in a tiny hamlet of houses. A mile beyond Slaggyford both the Pennine Way and South Tyne Trail allow for a diversion to **Knarsdale** (see p231). Camping is available here and the village pub and restaurant should have reopened by the time you get here, should you want to break this day into two. Any pragmatists following the South Tyne Trail need to drop down to the left, off the far end of the viaduct by the farmhouse of Burnstones (Map 97), to meet the tarmac lane and take the Pennine Way up the hill and out of the valley.

The path has now joined the **Maiden Way** (Maps 97-98), an old Roman road that ferried troops and supplies between Epiacum and (Magna) Carvoran on Hadrian's Wall. There is a rare wild camp opportunity along this stretch by the idyllic **Glendue Burn** (Map 98), just beyond Knarsdale, though space is limited.

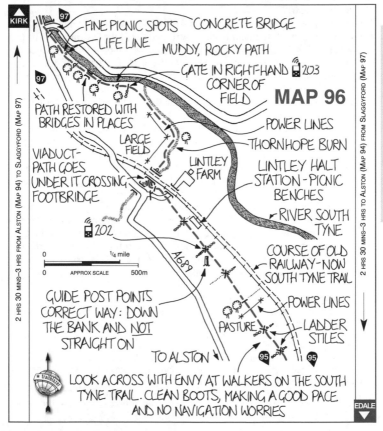

ROUTE GUIDE AND MAPS

KIRK

97

97

2 HRS 30 MINS–3 HRS FROM ALSTON (MAP 97) TO SLAGGYFORD (MAP 97)

FINE PICNIC SPOTS — CONCRETE BRIDGE
LIFE LINE — MUDDY, ROCKY PATH
GATE IN RIGHT-HAND 📱203
CORNER OF
FIELD — **MAP 96**

PATH RESTORED WITH
BRIDGES IN PLACES
POWER LINES
LARGE
FIELD
THORNHOPE BURN
VIADUCT–
PATH GOES
UNDER IT CROSSING
FOOTBRIDGE
LINTLEY
FARM
LINTLEY HALT
STATION – PICNIC
BENCHES
📱202
RIVER SOUTH
TYNE
COURSE OF OLD
RAILWAY – NOW
SOUTH TYNE TRAIL
POWER LINES
LADDER
STILES
PASTURE
A689
0   1/4 mile
0   APPROX SCALE   500m
GUIDE POST POINTS
CORRECT WAY: DOWN
THE BANK AND NOT
STRAIGHT ON
TO ALSTON
95   95
★ trailblazer
LOOK ACROSS WITH ENVY AT WALKERS ON THE SOUTH
TYNE TRAIL. CLEAN BOOTS, MAKING A GOOD PACE
AND NO NAVIGATION WORRIES

2 HRS 30 MINS–3 HRS TO ALSTON (MAP 94) FROM SLAGGYFORD (MAP 97)

EDALE

Make the most of the firm footing, because once you climb out of **Hartley Burn** (Map 99) and pass **Greenriggs Farm** (Map 100) you enter the quagmire that is **Blenkinsopp Common**. This is perhaps the wettest and boggiest section of the whole Way; even after a 12 week drought you're still going to get wet across here. You may breathe a sigh of relief as you reach the wall with its near-by trig point at **Black Hill**. It would be premature however; the Black Hill crossed on day two may have been tamed by slabs, but this one isn't and a squelchy crossing is almost a certainty.

Only when the track at GPS 228 (Map 101) is reached should you look for a stream to wash the mud off your boots, calves, thighs.... This track leads to the A69 where you need to scurry across between the trucks and then up the other side to walk beside the **golf course** down into Greenhead village. Here various places will feed, water and house you, in preparation for another big day!

Navigation notes

If you follow the South Tyne Trail from Alston to Burnstones there are no navigational issues at all, the path is clear, well laid (until the last mile or so) and impossible to lose. Traditionalists on the Pennine Way should be aware that signage isn't great along this section. The loop from Harbut Law B&B to Castle Nook Farm (Map 95) is a prime example of this; one eye on the map and the other on the ground is needed at all times.

The knot of tracks and footpaths at Knar Burn (Map 97), just after leaving Slaggyford, needs care too as the Pennine Way and the South Tyne Trail cross and diverge. The navigation through the back gardens at Merry Knowe can be disconcerting. At the ruin at High House (Map 99), just before you drop down to Hartley Burn, be sure to keep left as you descend. If anything err on the side of caution and bear too far left rather than stray right. Just a little further ahead, as you leave Ulpham Farm (Map 100), watch for the change of direction, through the gate, instead of along the very obvious lane.

The path beyond Greenriggs is almost non existent, a vast grassy swathe stretches ahead across Round Hill; soggy at best, down-right swampy the rest of the time. You won't keep your feet dry here no matter what line you take, so if in doubt, head for the fence line to the west and follow this due north. The path beside and across Greenhead Golf Course (Map 102) is easy enough and better signed than the previous few miles.

SLAGGYFORD   [Map 97]

Norma and Colin at *Fell View* (☎ 07714-190064; **fb**; 2D en suite; Apr-Oct; ①; ✖ by prior agreement) offer walkers comfortable **B&B** from £75, just 100m from the trail in Slaggyford. They have a guest lounge and, usefully, evening meals are available if booked in advance.

The Little Buffet Car (☎ 07810-540510; **fb**) at Slaggyford railway station offers hot drinks, cakes and snacks if you

manage to time your visit right. Opening hours change frequently, so check in advance, though you stand the best chance when the South Tynedale Railway (see box p217) service from Alston is running on summer weekends between 10.30am and 4pm.

Go North East's 681 **bus** service passes through between Alston and Birdoswald (twice a day); see p58.

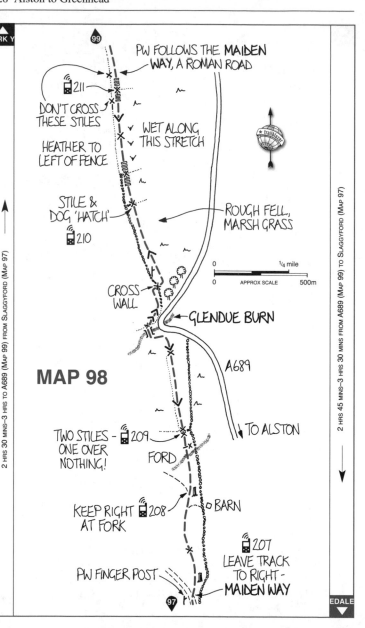

99

PW FOLLOWS THE **MAIDEN WAY**, A ROMAN ROAD

211

DON'T CROSS THESE STILES

HEATHER TO LEFT OF FENCE

WET ALONG THIS STRETCH

STILE & DOG 'HATCH'
210

ROUGH FELL, MARSH GRASS

0   ¼ mile
0   APPROX SCALE   500m

CROSS WALL

GLENDUE BURN

A689

MAP 98

TO ALSTON

TWO STILES – 209
ONE OVER NOTHING!

FORD

KEEP RIGHT 208
AT FORK

BARN

207
LEAVE TRACK TO RIGHT – **MAIDEN WAY**

PW FINGER POST

97

KIRK Y

EDALE

KIRK Y
▲

100

AIM FOR FARM BUILDINGS AHEAD

PASTURE

BIG DITCH

RATHER DULL COUNTRY, THIS. TOO AGRICULTURAL FOR MY LIKING

THROUGH GATE BESIDE FINGERPOST 218

DO NOT CROSS THIS STILE - IT SAYS 'NOT PENNINE WAY'

TOP OF WOODED BANK 217

216

FOOTBRIDGE OVER STREAM

TAKE CARE NOT TO BEAR AWAY RIGHT HERE

LOVELY WILD CAMPING SPOT

HARTLEY BURN

215

HIGH HOUSE RUIN

BANK

BANK

INTERMITTENT SLABS OVER BOGGY TERRAIN

ON A MOUND IN THE MARSH A STONE WITH AN ACORN & ARROW - LOOK FOR GUIDEPOSTS AHEAD

BANK

SOME MAY BE TEMPTED TO TURN LEFT ALONG THE WALL - DON'T EVEN THINK ABOUT IT

MAP 99

RUINED BARN

213

A689 ROAD CROSSING. THERE IS A NAME FOR THIS LONELY ROAD CROSSING - THE MIDDLE OF NOWHERE...

214

SLAB BRIDGE OVER STREAM

A689

TO LAMBLEY

IF YOU IGNORE ADVICE BELOW AND FOLLOW OBVIOUS PATH, THIS IS PROBABLY WHERE YOU'LL END UP

WHITE TOPPED MARKER POST

WHEN DESCENDING AIM FOR RUINED BARN BY A STONE WALL ON THE OTHER SIDE OF THE ROAD.

PATH VERY UNCLEAR

STONE MARKER

212

LEFT OVER FENCE AT STILE

98

0   1/4 mile

0   APPROX SCALE   500m

45-60 MINS TO KELLAH BURN (MAP 100)

A689

2 HRS 30 MINS-3 HRS FROM SLAGGYFORD (MAP 97)

1 HR 45 MINS-2 HRS 30 MINS FROM KELLAH BURN (MAP 100)

A689

2 HRS 45 MINS-3 HRS 30 MINS TO SLAGGYFORD (MAP 97)

ROUTE GUIDE AND MAPS

EDALE
▼

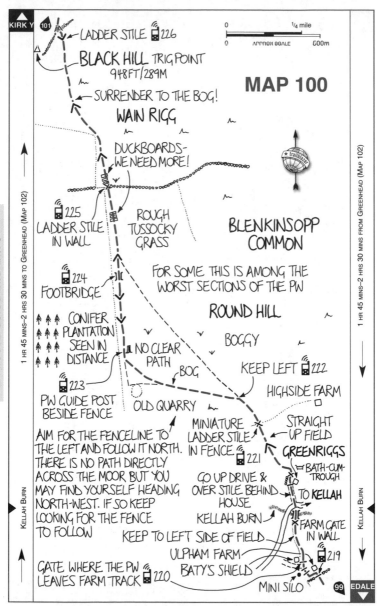

KIRK Y
101

LADDER STILE 📱226

BLACK HILL TRIG POINT
948FT/289M

SURRENDER TO THE BOG!

WAIN RIGG

0   ¼ mile
0   ᴀᴘᴘʀᴏx sᴄᴀʟᴇ   500m

MAP 100

DUCKBOARDS—
WE NEED MORE!

📱225
LADDER STILE
IN WALL

ROUGH
TUSSOCKY
GRASS

BLENKINSOPP
COMMON

📱224
FOOTBRIDGE

FOR SOME THIS IS AMONG THE
WORST SECTIONS OF THE PW

ROUND HILL

CONIFER
PLANTATION
SEEN IN
DISTANCE

BOGGY

NO CLEAR
PATH

📱223

BOG

KEEP LEFT 📱222

PW GUIDE POST
BESIDE FENCE

OLD QUARRY

HIGHSIDE FARM

AIM FOR THE FENCELINE TO
THE LEFT AND FOLLOW IT NORTH.
THERE IS NO PATH DIRECTLY
ACROSS THE MOOR BUT YOU
MAY FIND YOURSELF HEADING
NORTH-WEST. IF SO KEEP
LOOKING FOR THE FENCE
TO FOLLOW

MINIATURE
LADDER STILE
IN FENCE. 📱
221

STRAIGHT
UP FIELD

GREENRIGGS

GO UP DRIVE &
OVER STILE BEHIND
HOUSE

BATH-CUM-
TROUGH

TO KELLAH

KELLAH BURN

KEEP TO LEFT SIDE OF FIELD

FARM GATE
IN WALL

📱219

ULPHAM FARM
BATY'S SHIELD

GATE WHERE THE PW 📱
LEAVES FARM TRACK 📱220

MINI SILO

99

KELLAH BURN

KELLAH BURN

EDALE

KNARSDALE [Map 97]

Just a couple of hundred yards from the Pennine Way you can **camp** at *Stonehall Farm* (☎ 01434-381349; 🐾 on lead). At £5pp it's basic, with just an outside toilet, a cold water tap and a picnic table, but it's a pleasant, quiet place to camp. You'll need to be self-sufficient with food.

The **Kirkstyle Inn**, just 200 metres down the road, has long been a walker's favourite, and should reopen as a pub and restaurant in 2023 after major rebuilding and a change of management.

KELLAH [off Map 100]

Kellah Farm (☎ 01434-320816, 🖥 www.kellah.co.uk; 2D/2Tr, all en suite; 🛏; ⓛ) is about a third of a mile off the path, near Greenriggs. The accommodation is smart and the owners are helpful. Rates for **B&B** are from S/D/Tr £60/78/82. For an evening meal, you can either take a taxi to the closest pub (the Blenkinsop Castle near Greenhead) or to Haltwhistle, or order from the local takeaway (pizzas, fish & chips) that delivers to the farm, or enjoy one of the simple frozen meals made by the farm.

GREENHEAD [Map 102, p233]

Having arrived in the rather dispersed hamlet of Greenhead, you can take solace from the fact that you're very near Britain's geographical centre; a point equidistant from all shores. Not a lot of people know that.

Transport

The Newcastle to Carlisle railway line runs through Greenhead but services do not stop here. However, they do stop 3 miles away at Haltwhistle, (see Northern Rail, box p59).

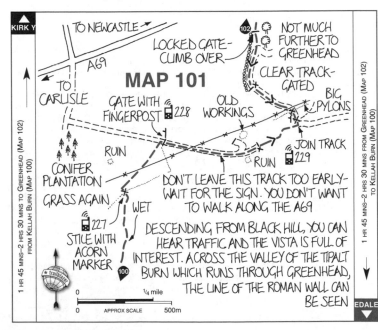

ROUTE GUIDE AND MAPS

However, Arriva's **bus** No 685 travels between Carlisle and Newcastle (and thus almost the entire length of the Wall too) via the A69 near Greenhead. Go North East operates the seasonal AD122 bus, which links Greenhead, the Milecastle Inn, The Sill, Vindolanda, Housesteads and Hexham in a circular route (the designated route 'AD122' is in honour of the Wall's inauguration by the Emperor Hadrian); see p58 for details.

Where to stay, eat & drink

A short ten-minute detour off the way, between Gisland and Greenhead, is *Chapel House Farm Campsite* (☎ 07717-700049, 🖥 chapelhousefarmgilsland.com; 🐾), with simple walker-only **camping** (toilets but no showers) for £10pp.

A converted Methodist chapel houses *Greenhead Hostel* (☎ 01697-747411; 🖥 greenheadhostel.co.uk; sleeps 47 in a mix of room sizes; no WI-FI; ①; 🐾; from £18pp), owned by Greenhead Hotel over the road. Meals are available in the hotel but there's a full kitchen in the hostel, as well as lounge, pool table and quiet room. The private rooms (2D/1Q shared bathroom; from £45) are in a self-contained flat.

Greenhead Hotel (☎ 01697-747411; 🖥 greenheadbrampton.co.uk; 4D/1T/2Tr, all en suite; ☛; ①; 🐾), in the middle of the village, offers **B&B** in recently refurbished doubles for £120-145 (sgl occ £10 discount). The hotel is currently your only option for an evening meal (**food** daily noon-8.30pm), served in both the bar and the restaurant, with options such as braised

ox cheek (£18) and pan-seared hake with mussels (£20). While hot meals are also available at lunchtimes, the afternoon menu is bar snacks or sandwiches only.

Right on the Way, half a mile north of the village, *Holmhead Guest House* (☎ 01697-747402, 🖥 bandb-hadrianswall.co .uk; 3D, all en suite; ①; 🐾 on lead and for campers/barn only) is a multiple accommodation complex for Wall-bound wayfarers. The pleasant walk there crosses a river, follows a track along the bank, through sheep fields and thence to the homestead. The **bunk barn** (from £30 solo walker, plus £10 per additional person) is currently only available on a pre-booked exclusive hire basis; it sleeps six and has a kitchenette and shower/toilet facilities; bring a sleeping bag. They also have a small garden where you can **camp** (£7pp; Mar-end Oct) but again you need to pre-book via email; basic toilet/shower facilities are available, with an outside tap, and it's cash only. Enquire whether the three **B&B** rooms are available, as they are often booked out by groups. Rooms cost £75-85 (sgl occ £70).

Nearby *Hadrian's Holidays* (☎ 01697-747972, 🖥 hadriansholidays.com; ①; 🐾) have two lovely, well-appointed pod-like **B&B lodges** (1T/1D, both en suite) costing S/D £85/105. Breakfast is served in your lodge.

Greenhead Tea Room (☎ 016977-47400, 🖥 greenheadtearoom.co.uk, **fb**; Mon-Sat 10am-4pm) is an efficient place serving up soup, toasted sandwiches (£6) on home-made bread and an all-day breakfast, with some outdoor seating.

❑ THIRLWALL CASTLE   [Map 102]

Thirlwall Castle was built in the 14th century by the powerful like-named family for protection and defence against border raiders. At that time the castle must have represented an impregnable stronghold to men armed only with spear and sword but by the 17th century these lawless times had passed and the Thirlwall family moved to more comfortable quarters in Hexham.

As a reminder of a time when the Borders were the scene of raids and struggles, Thirlwall serves a purpose but there are more absorbing antiquities than this to investigate. Ahead lies The Wall (from which the castle procured much of its building materials!).

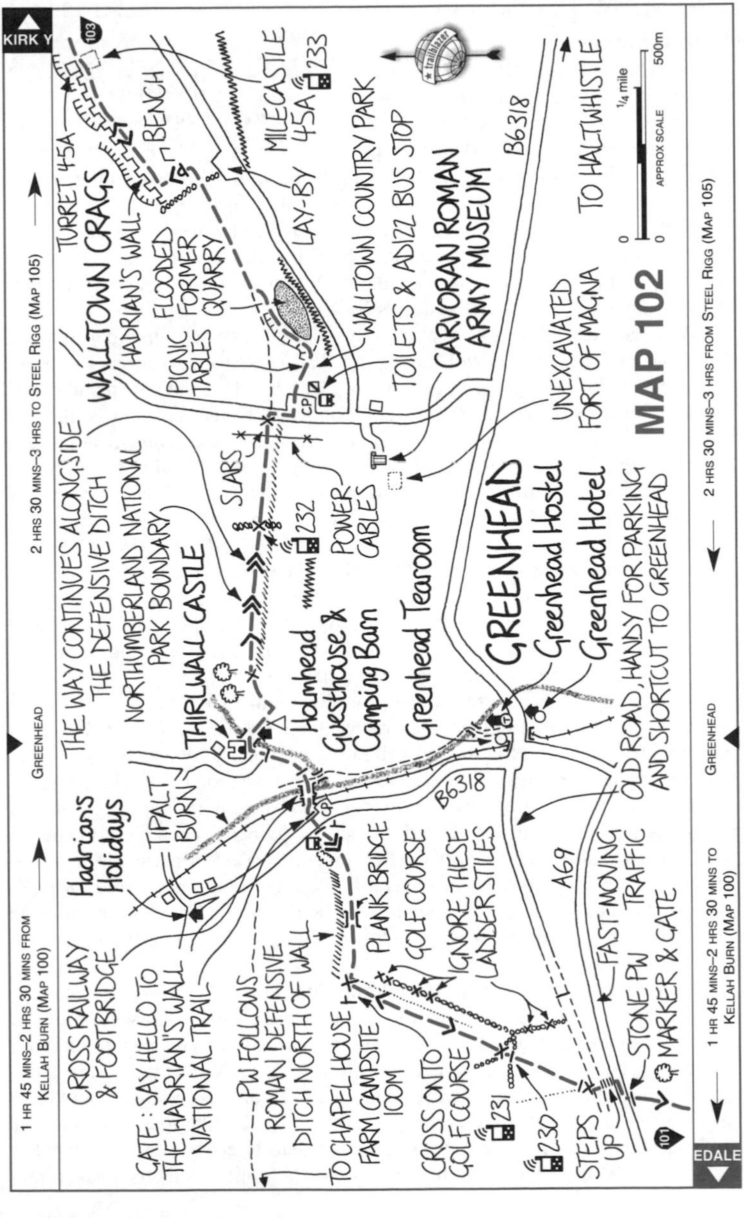

MAP 102

KIRK Y

103

TURRET 45A

WALLTOWN CRAGS

Hadrian's Wall

BENCH

MILECASTLE
45A 233

LAY-BY

FLOODED
FORMER
QUARRY

PICNIC
TABLES

WALLTOWN COUNTRY PARK

WALLTOWN CAR PARK BUS STOP

TOILETS & ADIZZ BUS STOP

CARVORAN ROMAN
ARMY MUSEUM

TO HALTWHISTLE

B6318

UNEXCAVATED
FORT OF MAGNA

THE WAY CONTINUES ALONGSIDE
THE DEFENSIVE DITCH
NORTHUMBERLAND NATIONAL
PARK BOUNDARY

THIRLWALL CASTLE

SLABS

Holmhead
Guesthouse &
Camping Barn

POWER
CABLES

232

Greenhead Tearoom

GREENHEAD

Greenhead Hostel
Greenhead Hotel

OLD ROAD, HANDY FOR PARKING
AND SHORTCUT TO GREENHEAD

2 HRS 30 MINS–3 HRS FROM STEEL RIGG (MAP 105)

1 HR 45 MINS–2 HRS 30 MINS FROM
KELLAH BURN (MAP 100)

2 HRS 30 MINS–3 HRS TO STEEL RIGG (MAP 105)

GREENHEAD

Hadrian's
Holidays

TIPALT
BURN

CROSS RAILWAY
& FOOTBRIDGE

GATE : SAY HELLO TO
THE HADRIAN'S WALL
NATIONAL TRAIL

PW FOLLOWS
ROMAN DEFENSIVE
DITCH NORTH OF WALL

TO CHAPEL HOUSE
FARM CAMPSITE
100M

231

230

STEPS
UP

101

EDALE

B6318

A69

PLANK BRIDGE

GOLF COURSE

IGNORE THESE
LADDER STILES

CROSS ONTO
GOLF COURSE

STONE PW
MARKER & GATE

FAST-MOVING
TRAFFIC

1 HR 45 MINS–2 HRS 30 MINS TO
KELLAH BURN (MAP 100)

GREENHEAD

0   APPROX SCALE 500m
0   ¼ mile

GREENHEAD TO BELLINGHAM   MAPS 102-112

Route overview

Fasten your *caligae* (Roman legionary
sandals) firmly, shoulder your *sarcina*
(marching pack) and thank the gods that
you're not carrying the 90-110lbs (40-

Distance	21½ miles (34.5km)
Ascent	3100ft (945m)
Time	9-10½ hours

50kg) of equipment regularly packed onto the back of a Roman soldier. Today
is a tough one if you intend to walk the full length from Greenhead to
Bellingham, having only slightly less ascent than the day over Cross Fell. If you
are interested in history then consider breaking this section into two days,
detouring to the fascinating Roman sites of Vindolanda and Housestead's Fort
and overnighting at Once Brewed or Stonehaugh.

At weekends and peak times you may want to leave early in order to avoid
the inevitable crowds that will throng the Wall close to the various car parks
along this section. This is the best-preserved length of Hadrian's Wall and draws
tens of thousands of visitors every year. You won't have seen crowds like this
since Hawes or Malham. Much of the day's ascent figures comprise steep little
climbs, as the Wall sticks to the edge of the escarpment. The first good section
of Wall is found at **Walltown Crags** (Map 102) and this is followed a couple of
miles later by the faint outline of **Great Chesters Fort** (Map 103), or Aesica as
the Romans would have called it. Those staying at *Hadrian's Wall Campsite*
(see p241) may want to turn off at **Caw Gap** (Map 104) and head south.

A more detailed exploration of the Wall and its associated archaeological
sites (see box p240) can be achieved by breaking this day at **Once Brewed**
(Map 105); this has the added benefit of reducing the remaining stretch to
Bellingham to a much more palatable 15 miles or so.

Keep an eye open for the iconic **lone Sycamore tree**, possibly the most
photographed tree in England, before reaching **Rapishaw Gap** (Map 106)
where you say farewell to the day-walking 'civilians' and other 'Wallkers' and
head north into the forest. If you're lucky the paths amongst the trees will be
dry and springy, a joy to walk on, but forestry paths are notorious for cutting up
easily and as the Way tries to avoid the harsh logging roads you could end up
with muddy boots here. Shortly after entering **Wark Forest** (Map 107),
campers can avail themselves of the sturdy walls of *Haughtongreen Bothy* (🏠
mountainbothies.org.uk), only a short diversion from the Way but pretty basic
(with unnerving police signs warning against criminal behaviour) and lacking
an obvious water source.

Leaving the trees to cross **Haughton Common** (Map 108) you may be
rewarded with a view of the Cheviots, now not so distant. This section of the
trail was heavily damaged in 2021 storm Arwen and subsequent tree clearing
has left a particularly desolate section of trail as far as Willowbog (Map 109).
The resulting temporary trail diversion along forestry roads should by now have
reverted to the original route described on the maps but the mess left by clear
cutting will remain for some time. At **Horneystead Farm** be sure to stop at the
Pit Stop (see Map 110, **fb** search Horneystead Pit Stop), a walkers' oasis offer-

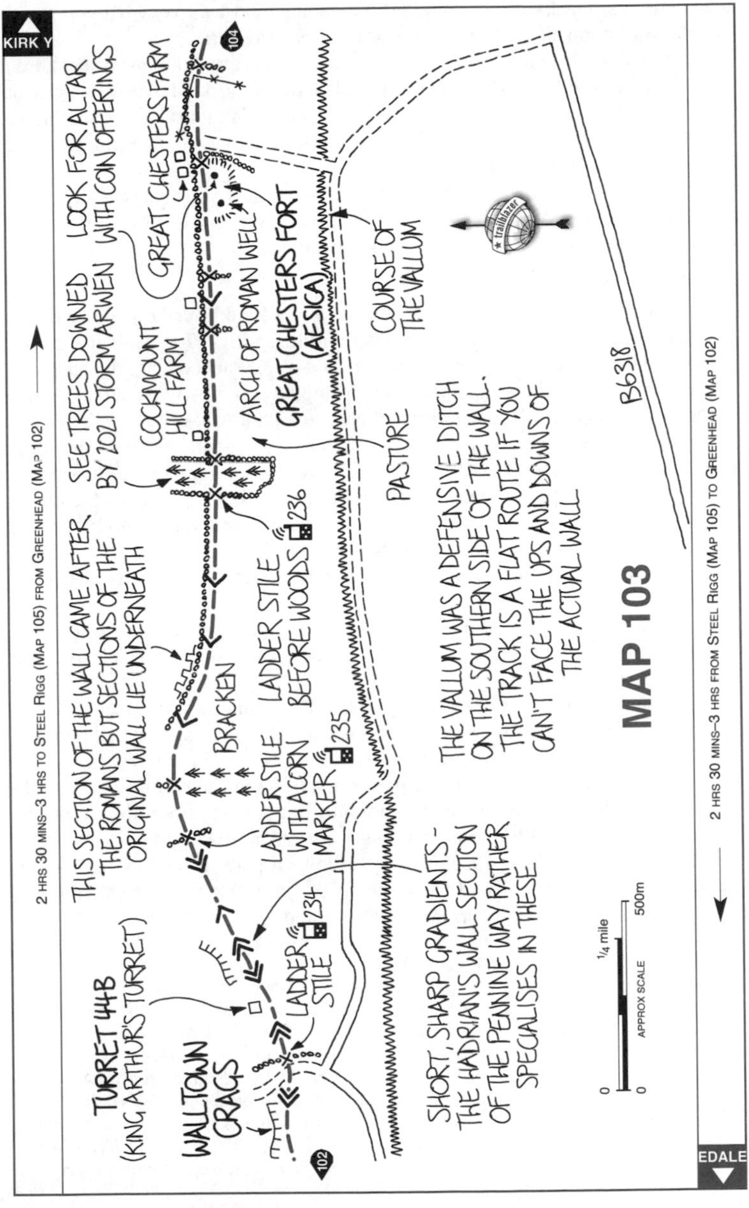

KIRK Y

2 HRS 30 MINS–3 HRS to STEEL RIGG (MAP 105) FROM GREENHEAD (MAP 102)

LOOK FOR ALTAR WITH COIN OFFERINGS

GREAT CHESTERS FARM

104

SEE TREES DOWNED BY 2021 STORM ARWEN

THIS SECTION OF THE WALL CAME AFTER THE ROMANS BUT SECTIONS OF THE ORIGINAL WALL LIE UNDERNEATH

COCKMOUNT HILL FARM

ARCH OF ROMAN WELL

GREAT CHESTERS FORT (AESICA)

COURSE OF THE VALLUM

BRACKEN

LADDER STILE BEFORE WOODS 📖 236

PASTURE

B6318

LADDER STILE WITH ACORN MARKER 📖 235

THE VALLUM WAS A DEFENSIVE DITCH ON THE SOUTHERN SIDE OF THE WALL. THE TRACK IS A FLAT ROUTE IF YOU CAN'T FACE THE UPS AND DOWNS OF THE ACTUAL WALL

MAP 103

TURRET 44B (KING ARTHUR'S TURRET)

LADDER STILE 📖 234

WALLTOWN CRAGS

102

SHORT, SHARP GRADIENTS – THE HADRIAN'S WALL SECTION OF THE PENNINE WAY RATHER SPECIALISES IN THESE

¼ mile

0 500m

0

APPROX SCALE

2 HRS 30 MINS–3 HRS FROM STEEL RIGG (MAP 105) TO GREENHEAD (MAP 102)

EDALE

ROUTE GUIDE AND MAPS

ing hot drinks, snacks, a fridge and even camping, under a 'pay what you want' system. If trail angels exist, they live at Horneystead Farm.

The next goal, visible from several miles away, is a radio transmitter station above **Shitlington Crag** (Map 111) which is reached through a mostly pleasant series of pasture, farmland and quiet country lanes. The mast can seem elusive but is eventually reached after a brief scramble up a rocky escarpment and a long steady climb across fields.

A final descent through more rough pasture brings you to a roadside walk into **Bellingham** (Map 112). Metaphorically (if not geographically) it's all downhill to the end from here; no-one gives up now!

Navigation notes

Despite the path through the forest and the many field boundaries later in the day, this section is mostly free of navigation difficulties. The Wall makes the perfect hand-rail for the first part of the day and once you head into the badlands of the former cattle-thieving barbarians the signage is mostly excellent thanks to the sterling work of Northumberland National Park Authority.

Hopefully new signage through Wark Forest will make the old way clear once again, even if the clear-cut landscape now looks completely different.

There are a couple of areas to be careful in, the first of which is the crossing of Warks Burn (Map 109). As you climb away from the tiny footbridge, be on the lookout for a right turn about halfway up the bank, marked by a large stone. If you miss this you will reach a wide farm gate at the top of the bank; turn sharp right through the gate, along the fence, to pick up the path again. Just beyond are the buildings at The Ash (Map 110); the number and position of gates can be confusing here, so try to keep the buildings to your left and you should keep to the path.

Complacency may set in as you approach Bellingham, so keep an eye open for the change in direction as you descend from the relay station. The natural course is to stay on the track beside the wall, but you need to cut left, across the rough pasture where the fingerpost points, even though the path may initially seem non-existent. A revision of the path into Bellingham, not reflected on the 2015 edition of the OS Explorer map, may also be confusing. In an attempt to avoid the busy B6320 the Pennine Way follows a path through Kings Wood, staying to the left of the road for around 500 yards before using a footpath beside the road. This is not currently well marked.

BURNHEAD [Map 104]

Ald White Craig Cottages (☎ 01434-321069, 💻 aldwhitecraig.co.uk; 4 cottages, 2x1D, 2 sleeps 5-6; ▼; 🐕) are self-catering cottages about halfway between Haltwhistle and the B6318, less than a mile south of the Milecastle Inn. The proprietors charge from £55-80 for a one-bed cottage, £125 for the larger cottages and will accept stays of only one night. If arranged in advance they can provide a continental breakfast and might be able to transfer guests to/from the PW.

Just off the B6318 across from Milecastle Inn, ***Bridge House*** (☎ 01434-320744, 💻 bridgehousecawfields.co.uk; 1D/1T en suite; Ⓛ) has two rooms offering B&B for £80, along with a drying room, laundry and a pick up/drop off service.

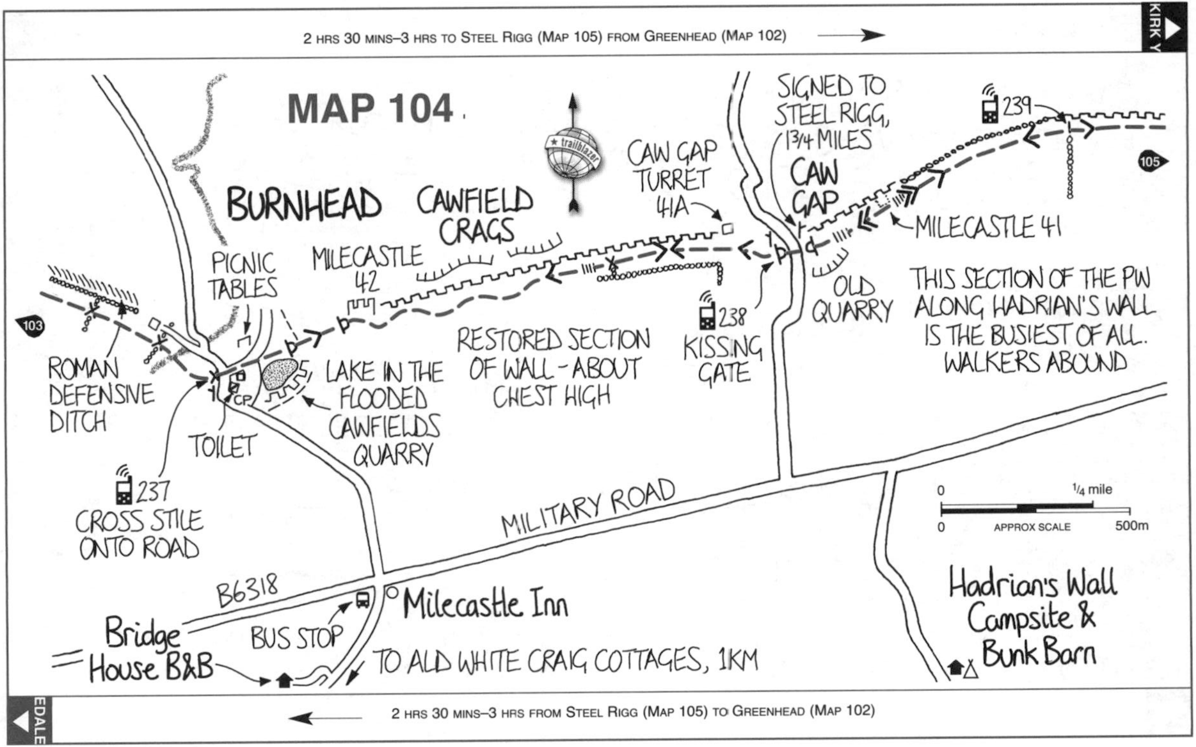
KIRK Y
2 HRS 30 MINS–3 HRS TO STEEL RIGG (MAP 105) FROM GREENHEAD (MAP 102)
MAP 104
trailblazer
BURNHEAD
CAWFIELD CRAGS
CAW GAP TURRET 41A
SIGNED TO STEEL RIGG, 1¾ MILES
CAW GAP
239
105
MILECASTLE 41
MILECASTLE 42
PICNIC TABLES
103
ROMAN DEFENSIVE DITCH
TOILET
CP
LAKE IN THE FLOODED CAWFIELDS QUARRY
RESTORED SECTION OF WALL - ABOUT CHEST HIGH
238
KISSING GATE
OLD QUARRY
THIS SECTION OF THE PW ALONG HADRIAN'S WALL IS THE BUSIEST OF ALL. WALKERS ABOUND
237
CROSS STILE ONTO ROAD
MILITARY ROAD
0 ¼ mile
0 APPROX SCALE 500m
B6318
Milecastle Inn
Bridge House B&B
BUS STOP
TO ALD WHITE CRAIG COTTAGES, 1KM
Hadrian's Wall Campsite & Bunk Barn
2 HRS 30 MINS–3 HRS FROM STEEL RIGG (MAP 105) TO GREENHEAD (MAP 102)
EDALE

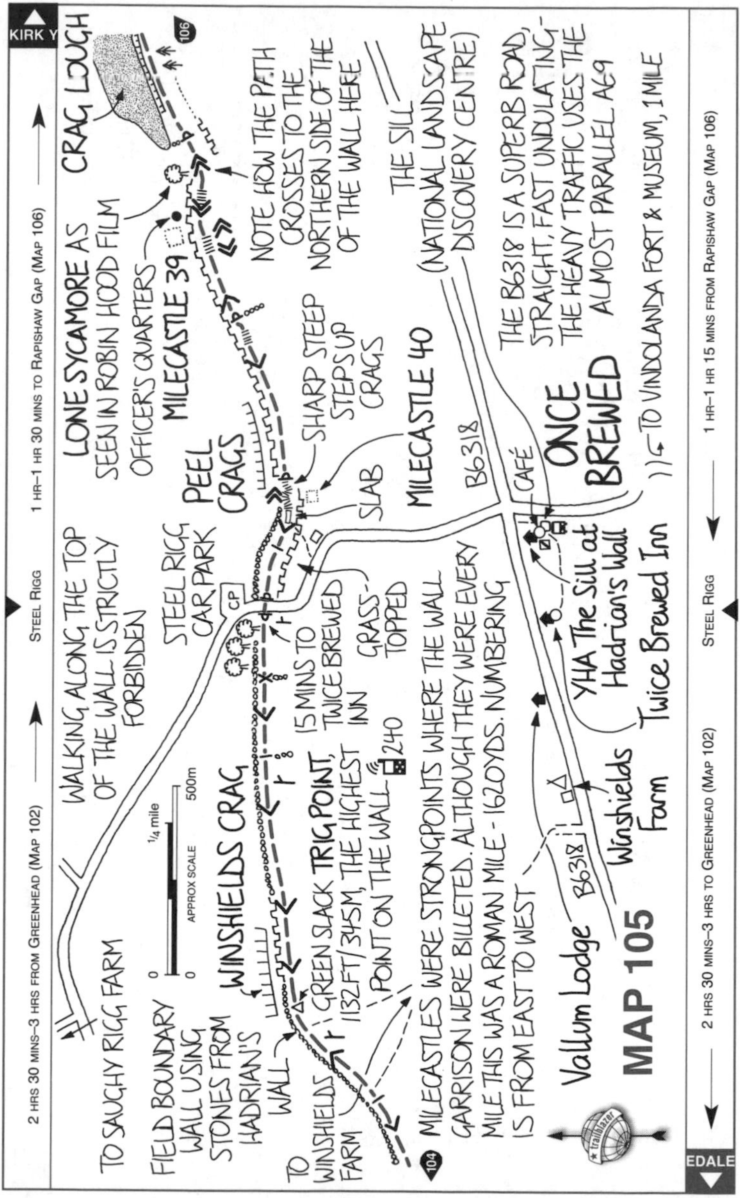

ROUTE GUIDE AND MAPS

KIRK Y ▲

CRAG LOUGH

106

LONE SYCAMORE AS
SEEN IN ROBIN HOOD FILM

OFFICER'S QUARTERS

MILECASTLE 39

NOTE HOW THE PATH
CROSSES TO THE
NORTHERN SIDE OF THE
OF THE WALL HERE

PEEL
CRAGS

SHARP STEEP
STEPS UP
CRAGS

THE SILL
(NATIONAL LANDSCAPE
DISCOVERY CENTRE)

WALKING ALONG THE TOP
OF THE WALL IS STRICTLY
FORBIDDEN

STEEL RIGG
CAR PARK

SLAB

MILECASTLE 40

B6318

THE B6318 IS A SUPERB ROAD,
STRAIGHT, FAST UNDULATING.
THE HEAVY TRAFFIC USES THE
ALMOST PARALLEL A69

CP

15 MINS TO
TWICE BREWED
INN

GRASS-
TOPPED

🏠240

CAFÉ

ONCE
BREWED

→ TO VINDOLANDA FORT & MUSEUM, 1 MILE

TO SAUCHY RIGG FARM

WINSHIELDS CRAG

GREEN SLACK TRIG POINT,
1132FT/345M, THE HIGHEST
POINT ON THE WALL

YHA The Sill at
Hadrian's Wall

Twice Brewed Inn

FIELD BOUNDARY
WALL USING
STONES FROM
HADRIAN'S
WALL

TO
WINSHIELDS
FARM

0   ¼ mile

0   500m

APPROX SCALE

MILECASTLES WERE STRONGPOINTS WHERE THE WALL
GARRISON WERE BILLETED. ALTHOUGH THEY WERE EVERY
MILE THIS WAS A ROMAN MILE - 1620YDS. NUMBERING
IS FROM EAST TO WEST

Vallum Lodge   B6318

Winshields
Farm

MAP 105

104

EDALE ▼

If you are desperate for some hot food, *Milecastle Inn* (☎ 01434-321372, 🖳 mile castle-inn.co.uk; **food** Easter-end Oct daily noon-2.30pm & 6-8.30pm) on Military Road, is just 10 minutes' walk down off the Way.

Go North East's seasonal AD122 **bus** service stops at the pub (see p58).

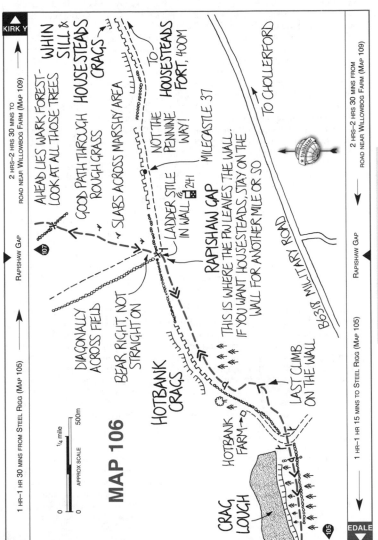

KIRK Y

2 HRS–2 HRS 30 MINS TO road near WILLOWBOG FARM (MAP 109)

WHIN SILL & HOUSESTEADS CRAGS

AHEAD LIES WARK FOREST – LOOK AT ALL THOSE TREES

GOOD PATH THROUGH ROUGH GRASS

TO HOUSESTEADS FORT, 400M

SLABS ACROSS MARSHY AREA

NOT THE PENNINE WAY!

MILECASTLE 37

LADDER STILE IN WALL 241

RAPISHAW GAP

TO CHOLLERFORD

2 HRS–2 HRS 30 MINS FROM road near WILLOWBOG FARM (MAP 109)

ROUTE GUIDE AND MAPS

RAPISHAW GAP

1 HR–1 HR 30 MINS FROM STEEL RIGG (MAP 105)

107

DIAGONALLY ACROSS FIELDS

BEAR RIGHT, NOT STRAIGHT ON

HOTBANK CRAGS

THIS IS WHERE THE PW LEAVES THE WALL. IF YOU WANT HOUSESTEADS, STAY ON THE WALL FOR ANOTHER MILE OR SO

B6318 MILITARY ROAD

LAST CLIMB ON THE WALL

HOTBANK FARM

MAP 106

¼ mile

500m

APPROX SCALE

0   0

CRAG LOUGH

105

1 HR–1 HR 15 MINS TO STEEL RIGG (MAP 105)

EDALE

❑ HADRIAN'S WALL

The Roman Emperor Hadrian first conceived the project after visiting Britain in AD122 and finding out for himself the extent of the difficulty faced by the occupying army in northern Britain. It was impossible to hold any kind of control over the lawless tribes in the area that is now called Scotland so, as the Chinese had done nearly 400 years earlier, it was decided to build a defensive wall. The line of the wall, drawn from the Solway to the Tyne, followed the fault-line of the Whin Sill, an 'escarpment' of resistant dolerite which acted as a natural east–west barrier.

The Wall ran for approximately 80 Roman miles (73 modern miles, or 117km) and had turrets or milecastles every (Roman) mile and larger forts at intervals along its length. In total around 20,000 soldiers from across the Roman Empire were garrisoned along the way; forts would have had a garrison of 500 cavalry or 1000 foot soldiers, and milecastles were manned by 50 men. The Wall was made of stone and turf and would have been five metres high and with a defensive ditch, the *vallum*, set between two mounds of earth, running the length of the southern side. Behind that ran a road to supply and provision the troops manning the wall. In addition to the vallum, they also dug a defensive ditch along the northern side of the Wall.

The construction of the Wall was supervised by the Imperial Legate, Aulus Platorius Nepos, and it took 10 years. The Wall remained in use for 200 years but as the Romans withdrew it fell into disuse and gradually the stones were plundered to build farmsteads and roads. **Thirlwall Castle** (see box p232 & Map 102) is among the many local buildings built with stones from the Roman Wall.

Today English Heritage, the National Trust and the National Park authorities preserve and protect what remains of the Wall, keeping it tidy and providing the information needed to help imagine what it was all for. It's well worth visiting **Housesteads Fort** (off Map 106; ☎ 01434-344363; daily Apr-Oct 10am-5pm, Nov-Mar 10am-4pm; £9; free to NT & English Heritage members), known to the Romans as Vercovicium, just before the Way heads north. You'll be pleased to know the communal latrines are particularly well preserved.

The other major site accessible from the Pennine Way is **Vindolanda** (🖥 vindolanda.com; off Map 105; ☎ 01434-344277; daily Apr-Sep 10am-6pm, Oct-Nov & mid Feb-Mar 10am-5pm, Dec & Jan variable; £9.25), considered the most important archaeological site along the wall. You can wander the fort foundations, including the cavalry barracks, bathhouse and the quarters used by Hadrian during his visit, and even watch archaeologists as they continue to excavate the site. The museum is particularly good and has multimedia examples of the site's famous tablets, which the British Museum voted as Britain's top national treasure. The ticket office will store your backpack while you wander the site and there's a reviving café at the museum. It's a 30-minute walk from the Sill, so budget a return trip of 3 hours.

Enthusiasts can also visit the **Carvoran Roman Army Museum**, just off the trail at Walltown (see Map 102), beside the site of the Roman fort of Magna; in that case buy the Saver ticket (£14) that covers both Carvoran and Vindolanda.

The information about the history of the Wall is fragmentary and circumstantial, historians having disputed for centuries over the finer details. What is certain is that the Wall is an extraordinary example of military might whilst demonstrating perhaps the futility of human endeavour. How can you hold back the tide of human expansion by anything so transient as a wall? Impressive, inspiring, unique, yes, but ultimately a failure. When you turn your back on it and head north into Wark Forest, the sight of the Whin Sill is like a breaking wave. The Wall blends into the landscape. The northern tribes had only to wait.

ONCE BREWED   [Map 105, p238]

Not really a village, Once Brewed is about half a mile south of the Way on the B6318, better known for nearly two millennia as the 'Military Road'. Doubtless the origins of this place's name torment your curiosity. The Twice Brewed Inn, a staging post between Carlisle and Newcastle, gained its name around 1710 when General Wade found the local ale so weak he advised that it be brewed again. When the hostel here was opened in the 1930s, the YHA's patron, Lady Trevelyan, remarked that she hoped her cup of tea would be brewed once, not twice like the General's ale, and so the name was born.

See p14 for details of the Roman Wall show held here in June.

Services

Here you'll find the enormously impressive **Sill National Landscape Discovery Centre** (☎ 01434-341200, 🖳 thesill.org.uk; Easter-Oct daily 10am-5pm, Nov-Easter 10am-4pm). As well as a *café* (see Where to stay & eat), shop and toilets, the centre also hosts child-friendly exhibitions on the local environment and staff are pretty knowledgeable about the area. Head up onto the grassed roof for views.

The website 🖳 visithadrianswall.co.uk also has lots of valuable advice on the area, including regional accommodation.

Transport

[See pp54-9] Go North East's seasonal AD122 **bus** service stops at the visitor centre. The service also stops at Haltwhistle railway station from where there are regular **train** services on the Carlisle–Newcastle line (Northern Rail).

For a **taxi**, call Sproul Taxis (☎ 07712-321064) in Haltwhistle.

Where to stay and eat

With multiple accommodation options, *Hadrian's Wall Campsite* (see Map 104; ☎ 01434-320495, 🖳 hadrianswallcampsite.co .uk; 🐾) is popular, though it's about a mile west of the pub and The Sill, at **Melkridge**, about 400m south of the B6318. Still, it's a friendly place with good facilities, including

centrally heated showers, laundry and drying room, a shop, a seasonal **café,** serving hot drinks and breakfast buns; and a hut with a microwave and kettle. **Camping** costs £11/20 for one/two hikers in a tent. They also have a **bunk barn** that sleeps up to 10 people (1 x 6-, 1x 4-bed room; booking recommended) for £16 per bunk (plus £5 bedding hire). Further options come in the form of four year-round **shepherd's huts** (4D; £65-95), each with a double bed, sofa and stove, and two glamping-style **bell tents** (sleep 2-4, £50-65, plus bedding fee) equipped with beds and a stove; both the huts and bell tents usually have a two-night minimum.

Another good option is *Winshields Farm Campsite* (☎ 07968-102780, 🖳 winshieldscampsite.co.uk), just west of Once Brewed and Vallum Lodge, where **camping** costs £10pp for backpackers and cyclists. A smart, modern **bunk barn** (1 x 5-bed room) with a separate lounge costs £22pp, plus £5 if you need bed linen and a towel. Reserve ahead as it's sometimes booked out by groups. The bunk barn and campsite share toilets and showers. A signed footpath leads here directly from the Pennine Way, just before the trig point at Winshields Crag.

YHA The Sill at Hadrian's Wall (☎ 0345-260 2702, 🖳 yha.org.uk/hostel/yha-the-sill-at-hadrians-wall; sleeps 88 in total in rooms with 2-4 beds, most en suite; Ⓛ) is a brand new purpose-built **hostel** on the site of the old one. A dorm bed costs £16-30 while rooms start at D/Qd £29/39, but rates can rise steeply on summer weekends to as high as S/D £69/119. Check-in is from 3pm and there is 24hr access; there are also laundry facilities and a drying room. The guest café (food daily 7.30-9am & 5-8pm) serves alcohol until 11pm.

Other accommodation in the area includes the superior *Vallum Lodge* (☎ 01434-344248, 🖳 vallum-lodge.co.uk; 2D/2T/1D or T/1D, T or F, all en suite; ▟; Ⓛ; Apr-Oct) charging £100 for double **B&B**. They also have a 'snug' (1D en suite; kitchen & lounge area) which costs from £110 per night including breakfast.

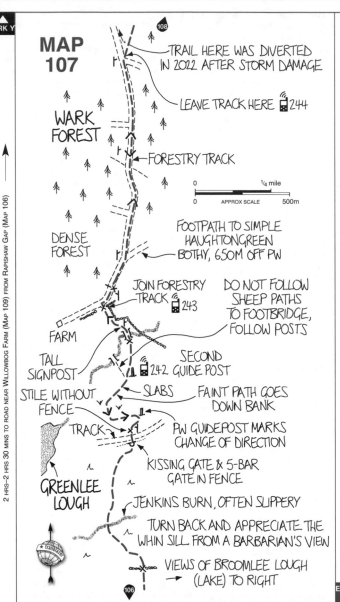

MAP 107

KIRK Y

108

TRAIL HERE WAS DIVERTED IN 2022 AFTER STORM DAMAGE

LEAVE TRACK HERE 📱244

WARK FOREST

FORESTRY TRACK

0   ¼ mile
0   APPROX SCALE   500m

DENSE FOREST

FOOTPATH TO SIMPLE HAUGHTONGREEN BOTHY, 6.50M OFF PW

JOIN FORESTRY TRACK 📱243

DO NOT FOLLOW SHEEP PATHS TO FOOTBRIDGE, FOLLOW POSTS

FARM

TALL SIGNPOST

📱242 SECOND GUIDE POST

STILE WITHOUT FENCE

SLABS   FAINT PATH GOES DOWN BANK

TRACK

PW GUIDEPOST MARKS CHANGE OF DIRECTION

GREENLEE LOUGH

KISSING GATE & 5-BAR GATE IN FENCE

JENKINS BURN, OFTEN SLIPPERY

TURN BACK AND APPRECIATE THE WHIN SILL FROM A BARBARIAN'S VIEW

VIEWS OF BROOMLEE LOUGH (LAKE) TO RIGHT

trailblazer

106

EDALE

Between the YHA hostel and Vallum Lodge is the *Twice Brewed Inn* (☎ 01434-344534, 🖳 twicebrewedinn.co.uk; 7D/11D or T/1Qd, all en suite; 🛏; Ⓛ; 🐾), whilst not *quite* so accommodating as to rebrew your beer, still does its best to please and provides many a happy hiker with a meal, a pint, and a bed for the night, with **B&B** from £120 (sgl occ £105). They serve good-quality pub **food** (daily noon-8.30pm; mains £11-14) and a decent selection of real ales, mainly from their own **brew house** next door. You can also book a tour of the brewery (£15pp; ☎ 01434-344534, 🖳 twice

brewedbrewhouse.co.uk); tours last 60-90 minutes and you get the chance to try three of their ales. They also regularly hold **Dark Skies stargazing nights** (from £30), using their own on-site observatory and local expert astronomers, taking advantage of their location in the Northumberland National Park.

At The Sill National Landscape Discovery Centre, their popular licensed *café* (daily summer 10am-5pm, last hot food orders 4.15pm, winter 10am-3pm) serves coffee, sandwiches, cakes, all-day breakfasts and some daily specials.

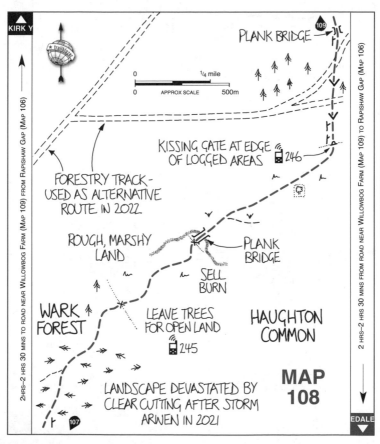

MAP 108

KIRK Y

PLANK BRIDGE

0   ¼ mile
0   APPROX SCALE   500m

KISSING GATE AT EDGE OF LOGGED AREAS 📱 246

FORESTRY TRACK - USED AS ALTERNATIVE ROUTE IN 2022

ROUGH, MARSHY LAND

PLANK BRIDGE

SELL BURN

WARK FOREST

LEAVE TREES FOR OPEN LAND 📱 245

HAUGHTON COMMON

LANDSCAPE DEVASTATED BY CLEAR CUTTING AFTER STORM ARWEN IN 2021

2HRS-2 HRS 30 MINS TO ROAD NEAR WILLOWBOG FARM (MAP 109) FROM RAPISHAW GAP (MAP 106)

2 HRS-2 HRS 30 MINS FROM ROAD NEAR WILLOWBOG FARM (MAP 109) TO RAPISHAW GAP (MAP 106)

ROUTE GUIDE AND MAPS

EDALE

ROUTE GUIDE AND MAPS

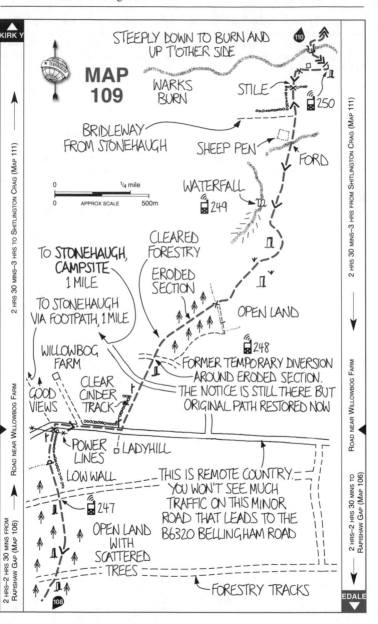

KIRK Y

MAP 109

STEEPLY DOWN TO BURN AND UP T'OTHER SIDE

110

WARKS BURN

STILE

250

BRIDLEWAY FROM STONEHAUGH

SHEEP PEN

FORD

WATERFALL
249

CLEARED FORESTRY

ERODED SECTION

TO **STONEHAUGH, CAMPSITE** 1 MILE

TO STONEHAUGH VIA FOOTPATH, 1 MILE

OPEN LAND

WILLOWBOG FARM

248

GOOD VIEWS

CLEAR CINDER TRACK

FORMER TEMPORARY DIVERSION AROUND ERODED SECTION. THE NOTICE IS STILL THERE BUT ORIGINAL PATH RESTORED NOW

POWER LINES

LADYHILL

LOW WALL

247

THIS IS REMOTE COUNTRY. YOU WON'T SEE MUCH TRAFFIC ON THIS MINOR ROAD THAT LEADS TO THE B6320 BELLINGHAM ROAD

OPEN LAND WITH SCATTERED TREES

FORESTRY TRACKS

108

EDALE

0   ¼ mile
APPROX SCALE   500m

2 HRS 30 MINS–3 HRS to SHITLINGTON CRAG (MAP 111)

ROAD near WILLOWBOG FARM

2 HRS–2 HRS 30 MINS from RAPISHAW GAP (MAP 106)

2 HRS 30 MINS–3 HRS FROM SHITLINGTON CRAG (MAP 111)

ROAD near WILLOWBOG FARM

2 HRS–2 HRS 30 MINS to RAPISHAW GAP (MAP 106)

STONEHAUGH [off Map 109]

Aside from licking dew off the grass, there are barely any refreshments on the route today except at the forestry outpost of Stonehaugh (pronounced 'Stone-hoff'), 8 miles from Bellingham. If you simply cannot walk any further, you could head for ***Stonehaugh Camp Site*** (☎ 01434-230798, 07415-759268, 🖳 stonehaughcampsite .com, **fb**; 🐾; 🕒; Easter to end Sep), which

charges £11pp (cash only), including use of the shower/toilet facilities. It's a mile off the route and there are no shops for 5 miles although you might be able to get a beer and WI-FI on the weekends at **Stonehaugh Community Hall** (Thur-Sun 8-11pm), just 300m away. Ask reception about the short cut back to the Pennine Way via bridleways.

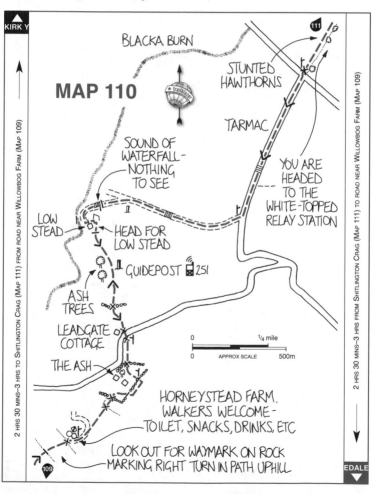

KIRK Y

BLACKA BURN

MAP 110

STUNTED HAWTHORNS

111

TARMAC

SOUND OF WATERFALL - NOTHING TO SEE

YOU ARE HEADED TO THE WHITE-TOPPED RELAY STATION

LOW STEAD

HEAD FOR LOW STEAD

GUIDEPOST 📱251

ASH TREES

LEADGATE COTTAGE

THE ASH

0 ¼ mile

0 APPROX SCALE 500m

HORNEYSTEAD FARM. WALKERS WELCOME - TOILET, SNACKS, DRINKS, ETC

LOOK OUT FOR WAYMARK ON ROCK MARKING RIGHT TURN IN PATH UPHILL

109

EDALE

2 HRS 30 MINS–3 HRS TO SHITLINGTON CRAG (MAP 111) FROM ROAD NEAR WILLOWBOG FARM (MAP 109)

2 HRS 30 MINS–3 HRS FROM SHITLINGTON CRAG (MAP 111) TO ROAD NEAR WILLOWBOG FARM (MAP 109)

ROUTE GUIDE AND MAPS

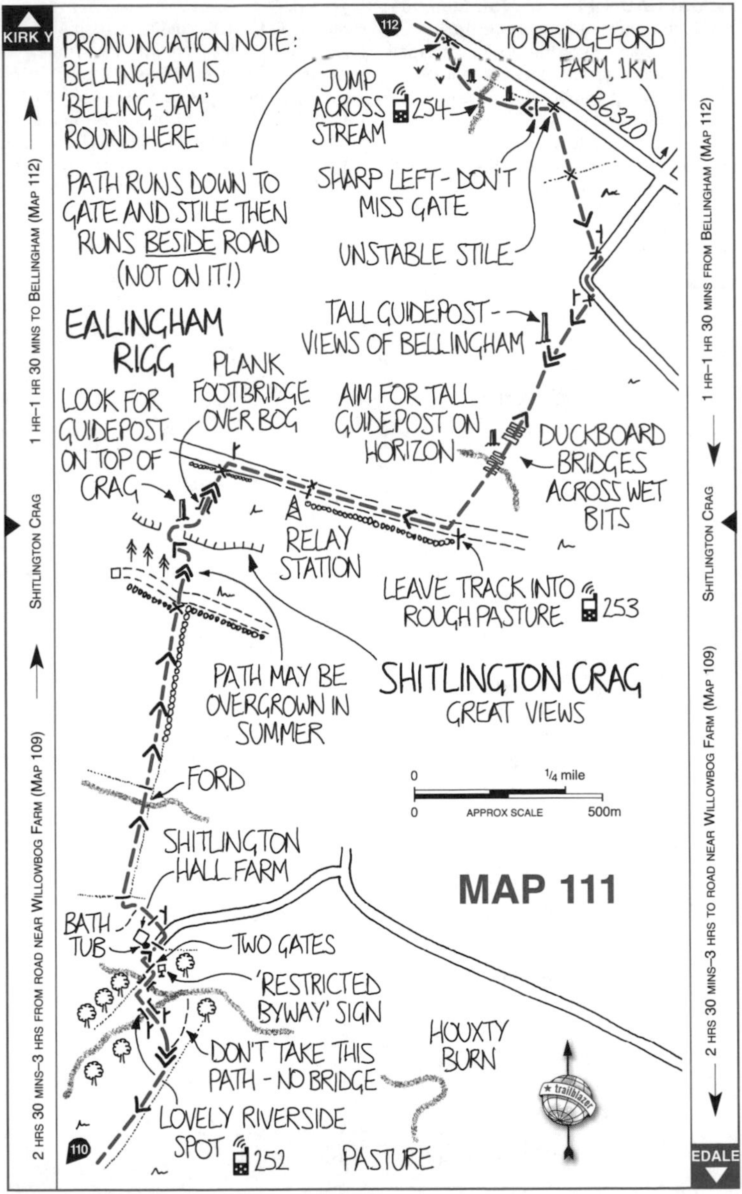

KIRK Y

1 HR–1 HR 30 MINS TO BELLINGHAM (MAP 112)

SHITLINGTON CRAG

2 HRS 30 MINS–3 HRS FROM ROAD NEAR WILLOWBOG FARM (MAP 109)

ROUTE GUIDE AND MAPS

112

PRONUNCIATION NOTE: BELLINGHAM IS 'BELLING-JAM' ROUND HERE

PATH RUNS DOWN TO GATE AND STILE THEN RUNS BESIDE ROAD (NOT ON IT!)

JUMP ACROSS STREAM

254

TO BRIDGEFORD FARM, 1KM

B6320

SHARP LEFT – DON'T MISS GATE

UNSTABLE STILE

EALINGHAM RIGG

TALL GUIDEPOST – VIEWS OF BELLINGHAM

LOOK FOR GUIDEPOST ON TOP OF CRAG

PLANK FOOTBRIDGE OVER BOG

AIM FOR TALL GUIDEPOST ON HORIZON

DUCKBOARD BRIDGES ACROSS WET BITS

RELAY STATION

LEAVE TRACK INTO ROUGH PASTURE 253

PATH MAY BE OVERGROWN IN SUMMER

SHITLINGTON CRAG GREAT VIEWS

FORD

SHITLINGTON HALL FARM

0   1/4 mile

0   APPROX SCALE   500m

MAP 111

BATH TUB

TWO GATES

'RESTRICTED BYWAY' SIGN

DON'T TAKE THIS PATH – NO BRIDGE

HOUXTY BURN

LOVELY RIVERSIDE SPOT 252

PASTURE

110

trailblazer

1 HR–1 HR 30 MINS FROM BELLINGHAM (MAP 112)

SHITLINGTON CRAG

2 HRS 30 MINS–3 HRS TO ROAD NEAR WILLOWBOG FARM (MAP 109)

EDALE

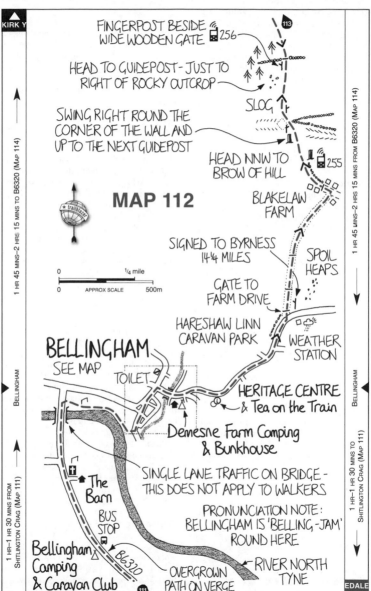

KIRK Y

FINGERPOST BESIDE
WIDE WOODEN GATE 📱256

HEAD TO GUIDEPOST - JUST TO
RIGHT OF ROCKY OUTCROP

SWING RIGHT ROUND THE
CORNER OF THE WALL AND
UP TO THE NEXT GUIDEPOST

SLOG

113

HEAD NNW TO
BROW OF HILL

📱255

MAP 112

BLAKELAW
FARM

SIGNED TO BYRNESS
14¼ MILES

SPOIL
HEAPS

0   ¼ mile
0   500m
APPROX SCALE

GATE TO
FARM DRIVE

HARESHAW LINN
CARAVAN PARK

WEATHER
STATION

BELLINGHAM
SEE MAP

TOILET

HERITAGE CENTRE
& Tea on the Train

Demesne Farm Camping
& Bunkhouse

The
Barn

SINGLE LANE TRAFFIC ON BRIDGE -
THIS DOES NOT APPLY TO WALKERS

BUS
STOP

PRONUNCIATION NOTE:
BELLINGHAM IS 'BELLING-JAM'
ROUND HERE

Bellingham
Camping
& Caravan Club

B6320

111

OVERGROWN
PATH ON VERGE

RIVER NORTH
TYNE

EDALE

1 HR 45 MINS–2 HRS 15 MINS TO B6320 (MAP 114)

1 HR 45 MINS–2 HRS 15 MINS FROM B6320 (MAP 114)

BELLINGHAM

BELLINGHAM

1 HR–1 HR 30 MINS FROM SHITLINGTON CRAG (MAP 111)

1 HR–1 HR 30 MINS TO SHITLINGTON CRAG (MAP 111)

ROUTE GUIDE AND MAPS

BELLINGHAM [Map 112a]
This old market town on the North Tyne is the last place on the Pennine Way offering most things you may need. Note Bellingham is pronounced 'Belling-jam'.

The **Heritage Centre** (Map 112; ☎ 01434-220050, 🖳 bellingham-heritage.org .uk; Easter-end Oct Wed-Sun 10am-4pm; £4), on Woodburn Rd out of town to the east, has displays on local history and can help with local information. There's also a **café** here (see Where to eat and drink).

See p14 for details of the country show held here in August.

Services
There's a **chemist** (Parkside Pharmacy; Mon-Fri 9am-12.30pm & 1.30-5.30pm, Sat 9am-12.30pm), **bakery** (see Where to eat), Thompson's **butcher**, and a Co-op **supermarket** (daily 7am-10pm), where you should stock up on food for the next three days. The Co-op **ATM** is the last on the route; that said, there aren't many places left on the route where you can actually spend money either! If that's not working you can try withdrawing money from the **post office** (Mon-Fri 6.30am-5.30pm, Sat 6.30am-4.30pm, Sun 8am-noon).

Bellingham Garage Services (Mon-Fri 8am-6pm, Sat & Sun 9am-5pm), on the way out of the village, sells Coleman fuel and gas canisters as well as general groceries.

Transport
[See also p54-9] Bellingham is a stop on Go North East's No 680 **bus** service (every couple of hours) heading to Hexham.

For a **taxi** call Bellingham Taxis ☎ 01434-220570.

Where to stay
Before the bridge on your way into town you'll pass *Bellingham Camping and Caravan Club* (see Map 112; ☎ 01434-220175, 🖳 campingandcaravanningclub.co .uk; 🐾; Mar-early Jan) which charges from £11 (members £9.35pp) for backpackers in high season and has four **wooden camping pods** (sleep 3; from £45; booking essential); the place has a wealth of facilities

including toilets and showers, a kitchen with fridge-freezer, a drying room, laundry room (£3.50 per load), shop and even a social area with a log-burning stove. Walkers will find it easier to book pods by phone than online.

Closer to the town centre, *Demesne Farm Campsite* (☎ 07967 396345, 01434-220258, 🖳 demesnefarmcampsite.co.uk) has **camping** (May-Oct; 🐾) for £10pp, with clean showers and toilets. No reservations are necessary.

Lyndale Guest House (☎ 01434-220361, 🖳 lyndaleguesthouse@hotmail .com; 1S/1T/2D, most en suite; ☛; Apr-Oct) is a bright and friendly place. B&B costs £100 for a double (sgl occ £90). They are happy to do washing/drying (£12 per bag) and also have a drying room for boots.

The Barn (see Map 112; ☎ 01434-220744, 🖳 thebarnbandbbellingham.co.uk; 1D or T en suite) has one room in a separate annexe, costing S/D £60/80 B&B. It's right on the Pennine Way, a 10-minute walk south-west of town.

If you'd like to stay in a pub *The Cheviot Hotel* (☎ 01434-220696, **fb**; 7D or T/1Tr, all en suite; ☛; ⓛ; 🐾) is the best choice with B&B from £65/110 S/D.

Bridgeford Farm (off Map 111; ☎ 01434-220940, 🖳 bridgefordfarmbandb.co .uk; 2D/1T, all en suite; ☛; ⓛ; 🐾) is about a mile before you get to Bellingham; however, if arranged in advance they provide a pick up and drop off service. For B&B they charge from £98 for a double.

Fountain Cottage B&B (☎ 01434-239224, 🖳 fountain-cottage.com; 4D, 2T, all en suite; ☛; ⓛ), at the northern end of the village and attached to the popular café, has comfortable B&B rooms from S/D £90/100. Superior rooms (S/D from £108/120) have a spa tub and bathroom TV.

Where to eat and drink
As you enter the village on the Way, the first place you will see serving food is the *Rocky Road Café* (☎ 01434-220510, 🖳 rockyroadcafe.co.uk, **fb**; summer daily 8.30am-4.30pm, winter hours vary) which does breakfasts, sandwiches, coffee and

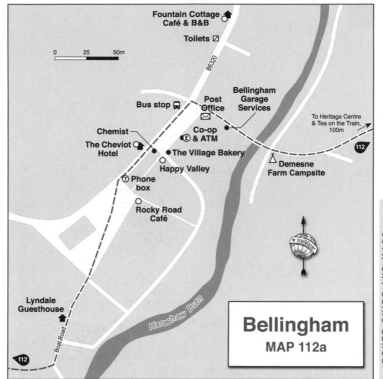

Fountain Cottage
Café & B&B

Toilets ☒

0   25   50m

B6320

Bus stop 🚏

Post
Office
✉

Bellingham
Garage
Services

To Heritage Centre
& Tea on the Train,
100m

112

Chemist

Co-op
£ & ATM

The Cheviot
Hotel

● The Village Bakery

Happy Valley

ℹ Phone
box

Demesne
Farm Campsite

Rocky Road
Café

Lyndale
Guesthouse

Boat Road

Hareshaw Burn

★ trailblazer

Bellingham
MAP 112a

112

cakes, as well as packed lunches. *Fountain Cottage Café* (see Where to Stay; summer Sun-Tue 9am-4pm, Wed-Sat 9am-8pm, winter daily 9am-4pm; 🐾) is a well-run place that covers all bases, with breakfasts, lunch sandwiches and evening burgers, pizza and fish & chips (£12.50), along with coffee, cakes and local bottled beers. The outdoor tables are popular on a sunny day. On Wednesday evenings in summer you can get two steaks for £20; Sunday lunches cost from £10.50.

Paninis, toasties and soups (£5-7.50) are also served in a fun converted railway carriage at *Tea on the Train* (☎ 01434-221151, 🖳 teaonthetrain.com; Apr-Oct 10am-4pm, Nov-Mar 10.30am-3.30pm), next to the Heritage Centre.

The Cheviot Hotel (see Where to stay; food daily noon-2.30pm & 6-9pm; takeaways available 6-10pm) is the best of the pubs. Pub favourites include steak & ale pie, or fish & chips (also available as takeaway). Starters cost £5-10 and mains are £10-20. Reservations recommended.

Next door to the Co-op, the *Village Bakery* (☎ 01434-220355; Mon-Fri 7am-5pm, Sat 8am-2.30pm) is a great place to stop as you set out in the morning, they open early enough to supply a snack for the road.

There's also a Chinese takeaway, *Happy Valley* (☎ 01434-221221; Mon & Wed-Sun 4.30-10pm), opposite, with an epic number of dish combinations, but payment is in cash only.

KIRK Y

GREEN ROAD –
FORMER COLLIERY
RAILWAY TRACK

114

ABBEY RIGG
△

SPOIL
TIPS

GUIDEPOST 📱259

OPEN FELL   HARESHAW HOUSE

IGNORE PATHS
TO LEFT AND
RIGHT. KEEP
STRAIGHT AHEAD

STILE ONTO
FARM TRACK
📱258

OLD
BARN

POWER LINES

HAZEL BURN

FOOTBRIDGE

MAP 113

BOGGY

THE DIRECTION IS NORTH
HEAD FOR HARESHAW
HOUSE AHEAD

CALLERHUES
CRAG

HEATHER

SKYLARKS ABOUND

DON'T DRIFT
TO THE
RIGHT

HEATHER

★ trailblazer

PATH OVER PIPE 📱257

SHEEP PATH

CIRCULAR STONE WALL

YOUNG TREES IN TUBES

HEATHER

OPEN FELL

0   ¼ mile
0   APPROX SCALE   500m

112

EDALE

1 HR 45 MINS–2 HRS 15 MINS to B6320 (MAP 114) FROM BELLINGHAM (MAP 112)

1 HR 30 MINS–2 HRS 15 MINS FROM B6320 (MAP 114) TO BELLINGHAM (MAP 112)

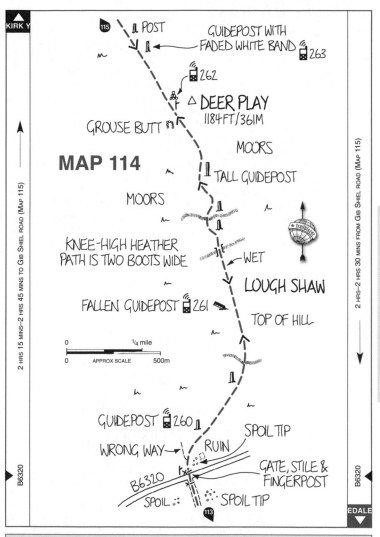

KIRK Y ▲

115 🔋 POST

GUIDEPOST WITH
FADED WHITE BAND 📱263

📱262

△ DEER PLAY
1184FT/361M

GROUSE BUTT 🔋

MAP 114

MOORS

🔋 TALL GUIDEPOST

MOORS

KNEE-HIGH HEATHER
PATH IS TWO BOOTS WIDE

WET

LOUGH SHAW

FALLEN GUIDEPOST 📱261

TOP OF HILL

trailblazer ★

0   ¼ mile
0   500m
APPROX SCALE

GUIDEPOST 📱260 🔋

WRONG WAY→   RUIN   SPOIL TIP

B6320   GATE, STILE &
FINGERPOST

SPOIL   SPOIL TIP

113

2 HRS 15 MINS–2 HRS 45 MINS TO GIB SHIEL ROAD (MAP 115)

B6320

2 HRS–2 HRS 30 MINS FROM GIB SHIEL ROAD (MAP 115)

ROUTE GUIDE AND MAPS

B6320

EDALE ▼

❑ **IMPORTANT NOTE – WALKING TIMES**
Unless otherwise specified, **all times in this book refer only to the time spent walking**. You will need to add 20-30% to allow for rests, photography, checking the map,
drinking water etc, not to mention time simply to stop and stare.

BELLINGHAM TO BYRNESS

MAPS 112-120

Route overview

A modest 15 miles, today's walk is some
thing of a warm-up for tomorrow's mountain marathon over the Cheviot range. Take
it easy and enjoy the relatively low-level

Distance	15 miles (24km)
Ascent	1800ft (549m)
Time	7¼-9 hours

route with its diverse scenery of green fields, heather moorland, forestry tracks
and riverside paths, for tomorrow is high, rolling hills and open skies all day.

The day starts, as usual, with a climb out of the village and into the green
fields around **Blakelaw Farm** (Map 112). This soon turns to rough pasture as
you approach **Hareshaw House** (Map 113) and beyond this last outpost of
civilisation you enter heather moorland; the track is little more than the width
of two boots and marked by occasional guide posts. The delightfully named
Deer Play (Map 114) gives glorious views, soon surpassed by those from
Whitley Pike (Map 115) and from the path around **Padon Hill** (Map 116).
Three hills are separated by patches of squelchy bog. The heather is left behind
as you begin the steep ascent of **Brownrigg Head**, using an old broken wall to
avoid the sodden edge of the forest.

It is with some relief that you reach the forestry road in **Redesdale Forest**
(Map 117). Unfortunately, where the Forestry Commission has cleared sections
of the forest the landscape is particularly harsh and bleak. It soon becomes appar-
ent that you've swapped one extreme for another, as the harsh stone surface

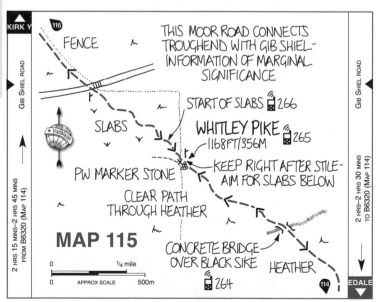

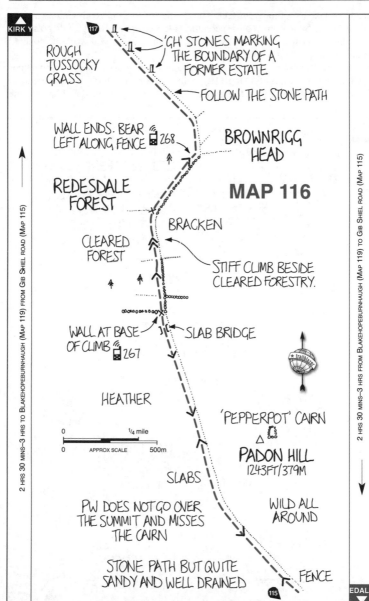

'GH' STONES MARKING THE BOUNDARY OF A FORMER ESTATE

FOLLOW THE STONE PATH

ROUGH TUSSOCKY GRASS

WALL ENDS. BEAR LEFT ALONG FENCE 268

BROWNRIGG HEAD

REDESDALE FOREST

MAP 116

BRACKEN

CLEARED FOREST

STIFF CLIMB BESIDE CLEARED FORESTRY.

WALL AT BASE OF CLIMB 267

SLAB BRIDGE

HEATHER

'PEPPERPOT' CAIRN

PADON HILL 1243FT/379M

0 ¼ mile
0 APPROX SCALE 500m

SLABS

WILD ALL AROUND

PW DOES NOT GO OVER THE SUMMIT AND MISSES THE CAIRN

STONE PATH BUT QUITE SANDY AND WELL DRAINED

FENCE

2 HRS 30 MINS–3 HRS TO BLAKEHOPEBURNHAUGH (MAP 119) FROM GIB SHIEL ROAD (MAP 115)

2 HRS 30 MINS–3 HRS FROM BLAKEHOPEBURNHAUGH (MAP 119) TO GIB SHIEL ROAD (MAP 115)

ROUTE GUIDE AND MAPS

KIRK Y

EDALE

begins to take its toll on your feet. Three miles of forestry road wind away into the distance, broken only by a pedantic side excursion through tall grass and bracken that most walkers rightly ignore. If you're lucky you won't be covered in dust by a speeding timber lorry!

You can finally wriggle your abused toes in the grass at the picnic benches at **Blakehopeburnhaugh** (Map 119), before continuing through storm-ravaged woodland beside the **River Rede** down to **Byrness village** (Map 120) and the

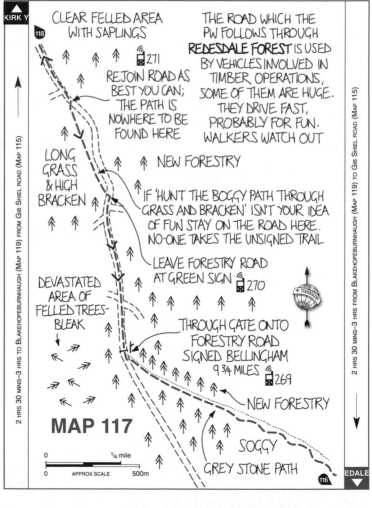

ROUTE GUIDE AND MAPS

▲ KIRK Y

118

CLEAR FELLED AREA WITH SAPLINGS

📱 271

REJOIN ROAD AS BEST YOU CAN; THE PATH IS NOWHERE TO BE FOUND HERE

LONG GRASS & HIGH BRACKEN

NEW FORESTRY

IF 'HUNT THE BOGGY PATH THROUGH GRASS AND BRACKEN' ISN'T YOUR IDEA OF FUN STAY ON THE ROAD HERE. NO-ONE TAKES THE UNSIGNED TRAIL

DEVASTATED AREA OF FELLED TREES- BLEAK

LEAVE FORESTRY ROAD AT GREEN SIGN 📱 270

THROUGH GATE ONTO FORESTRY ROAD SIGNED BELLINGHAM 9¾ MILES 📱 269

NEW FORESTRY

MAP 117

0   ¼ mile
0   APPROX SCALE   500m

SOGGY GREY STONE PATH

THE ROAD WHICH THE PW FOLLOWS THROUGH **REDESDALE FOREST** IS USED BY VEHICLES INVOLVED IN TIMBER OPERATIONS, SOME OF THEM ARE HUGE. THEY DRIVE FAST, PROBABLY FOR FUN. WALKERS WATCH OUT

2 HRS 30 MINS–3 HRS TO BLAKEHOPEBURNHAUGH (MAP 119) FROM GIB SHIEL ROAD (MAP 115)

2 HRS 30 MINS–3 HRS FROM BLAKEHOPEBURNHAUGH (MAP 119) TO GIB SHIEL ROAD (MAP 115)

116

EDALE ▼

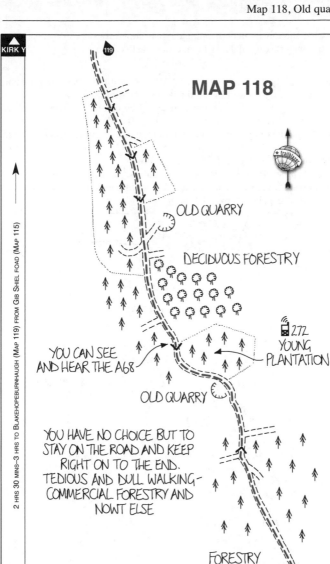

KIRK Y

119

MAP 118

OLD QUARRY

DECIDUOUS FORESTRY

272
YOUNG
PLANTATION

YOU CAN SEE
AND HEAR THE A68

OLD QUARRY

YOU HAVE NO CHOICE BUT TO
STAY ON THE ROAD AND KEEP
RIGHT ON TO THE END.
TEDIOUS AND DULL WALKING-
COMMERCIAL FORESTRY AND
NOWT ELSE

FORESTRY

0   ¼ mile
0   APPROX SCALE   500m

117

EDALE

2 HRS 30 MINS–3 HRS TO BLAKEHOPEBURNHAUGH (MAP 119) FROM GIB SHIEL ROAD (MAP 115)

2 HRS 30 MINS–3 HRS FROM BLAKEHOPEBURNHAUGH (MAP 119) TO GIB SHIEL ROAD (MAP 115)

A68. A varied and mostly undemanding day has hopefully set you up nicely for the immense undertaking of The Cheviot traverse that awaits.

Navigation notes

In very bad visibility the route may get a little thin as it branches around a bog below Callerhues Crag (Map 113) on the way to Hareshaw House, but a generally northern direction will bring you to the wall before Hazel Burn; head for the trees if they are visible. Soon after, at the B6320 a PW fingerpost helps you set off at the right bearing, NNW, to lock on to the line of guideposts leading to Deer Play hill (Map 114) then down and up again to Whitley Pike (Map 115). The path through the heather is fairly easy to follow.

Leaving Whitley Pike, be sure to bear right as you cross the fence, as an obvious path wants to draw you too far left. If in doubt, head for GPS 266 which marks the start of the slabs across the moor.

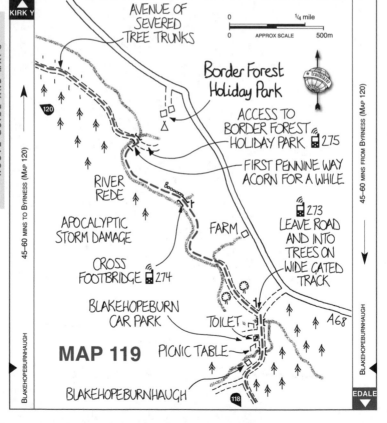

AVENUE OF
SEVERED
TREE TRUNKS

Border Forest
Holiday Park

ACCESS TO
BORDER FOREST
HOLIDAY PARK 📱 275

FIRST PENNINE WAY
ACORN FOR A WHILE

📱 273
LEAVE ROAD
AND INTO
TREES ON
WIDE GATED
TRACK

RIVER
REDE

APOCALYPTIC
STORM DAMAGE

FARM

CROSS
FOOTBRIDGE 📱 274

BLAKEHOPEBURN
CAR PARK

TOILET

A68

MAP 119

PICNIC TABLE

BLAKEHOPEBURNHAUGH

0 ____ ¼ mile
0 ____ APPROX SCALE ____ 500m

120

118

KIRK Y

ROUTE GUIDE AND MAPS

45–60 MINS TO BYRNESS (MAP 120)

BLAKEHOPEBURNHAUGH

45–60 MINS FROM BYRNESS (MAP 120)

BLAKEHOPEBURNHAUGH

EDALE

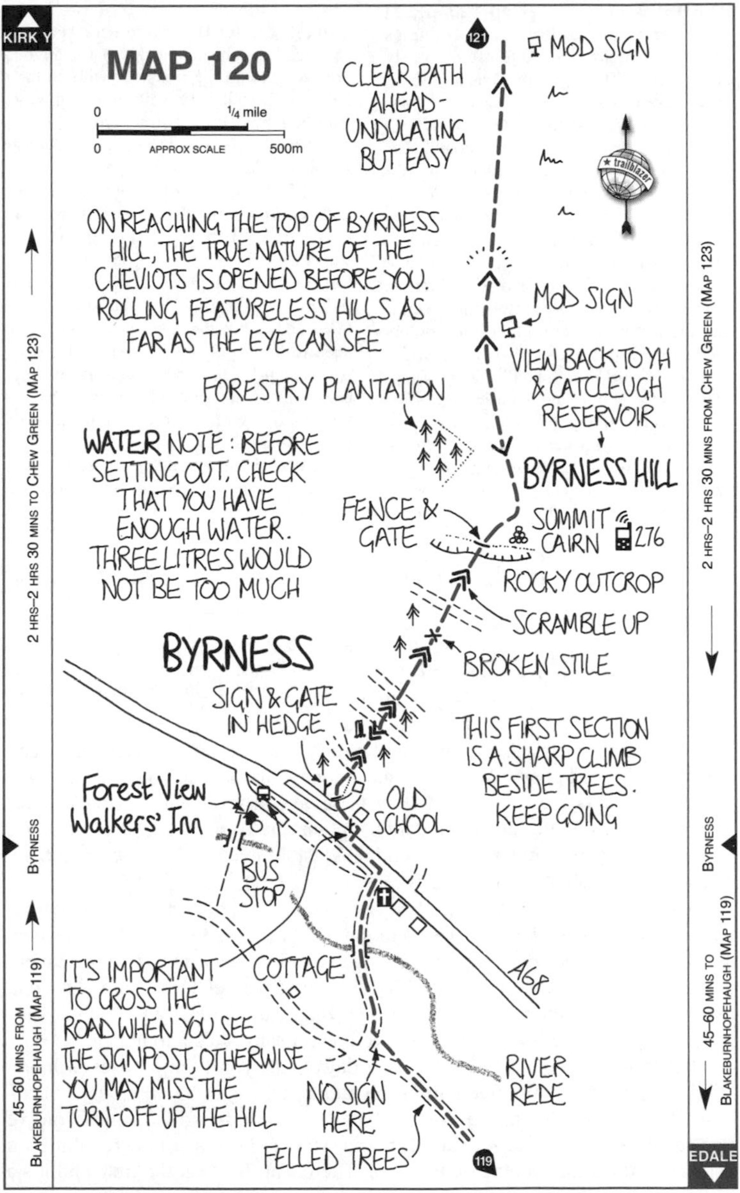

MAP 120

0 — 1/4 mile

0 — APPROX SCALE — 500m

CLEAR PATH AHEAD - UNDULATING BUT EASY

121

⚑ MOD SIGN

MOD SIGN

VIEW BACK TO YH & CATCLEUGH RESERVOIR

ON REACHING THE TOP OF BYRNESS HILL, THE TRUE NATURE OF THE CHEVIOTS IS OPENED BEFORE YOU. ROLLING, FEATURELESS HILLS AS FAR AS THE EYE CAN SEE

FORESTRY PLANTATION

BYRNESS HILL

SUMMIT CAIRN 276

WATER NOTE: BEFORE SETTING OUT, CHECK THAT YOU HAVE ENOUGH WATER. THREE LITRES WOULD NOT BE TOO MUCH

FENCE & GATE

ROCKY OUTCROP

SCRAMBLE UP

BROKEN STILE

BYRNESS

SIGN & GATE IN HEDGE

OLD SCHOOL

THIS FIRST SECTION IS A SHARP CLIMB BESIDE TREES. KEEP GOING

Forest View Walkers' Inn

BUS STOP

COTTAGE

IT'S IMPORTANT TO CROSS THE ROAD WHEN YOU SEE THE SIGNPOST, OTHERWISE YOU MAY MISS THE TURN-OFF UP THE HILL

NO SIGN HERE

FELLED TREES

A68

RIVER REDE

119

KIRK Y

2 HRS–2 HRS 30 MINS TO CHEW GREEN (MAP 123)

BYRNESS

45–60 MINS FROM BLAKEBURNHOPEHAUGH (MAP 119)

2 HRS–2 HRS 30 MINS FROM CHEW GREEN (MAP 123)

ROUTE GUIDE AND MAPS

BYRNESS

45–60 MINS TO BLAKEBURNHOPEHAUGH (MAP 119)

EDALE

BYRNESS [Map 120, p257]

These days this collection of buildings strung out along the A68 offers barely enough to fortify you for the final hurdle, so **arrive prepared**.

Forest View Walkers Inn (☎ 07928-376677, 🖳 forestviewbyrness.co.uk, **fb**; 2S private facilities, 2D/3Tr all en suite; Ⓛ, 🐾; Apr-Oct) is a fantastic place to stay, charging S/D from £58/116 for **B&B** (sgl occ £100). Booking is recommended. Limited **camping** (from £5pp) is available in the garden if arranged in advance; campers have access to shower/toilet facilities and a drying room. Make your orders for the *restaurant* (meals £9-11) by 5pm, as food is served communally at 7.30pm. There's also a **bar** and a basic **shop**. For any walker booking two nights they provide a free pick up service from and to the halfway point on the final section of the Way. They also provide a transfer service (£23 for up to two bags Bellingham to Byrness, £33 for Byrness to Kirk Yetholm; all bags must be under 20kg) for anyone preferring to do the last stage without their baggage. It's all very well organised. Note that the inn is closed before 4pm.

You'll pass round the back of *Border Forest Holiday Park* (see Map 119; ☎ 01830-520259, 🖳 borderforest.com; 🐾) with **camping** for Pennine Way walkers only from £10pp including use of shower/toilet facilities. They also offer three **pods** (£40 per pod); each pod has lighting and heating and can sleep up to three adults but there are no beds so you need to bring your own bedding. Booking is essential for the pods. There is no shop, bar or restaurant on site but they do have a kitchen area with a microwave oven and a fridge/freezer.

Peter Hogg of Jedburgh operate a **bus** service (No 131; Jedburgh–Newcastle) via here (see p58).

BYRNESS TO KIRK YETHOLM   MAPS 120-135

Route overview

This is possibly one of the longest single day walks you'll ever do, but you're ready; let's face it, you've been training for this for the last two weeks! It may be

Distance	25½ miles (41km)
Ascent	4800ft (1463m)
Time	10½-13 hours

almost as long as a marathon and have nearly a whole mile of vertical ascent, but thousands of Pennine Wayfarers have done it and so can you.

You would be advised to start early and give yourself plenty of time to complete this section; the accommodation options in Byrness are used to early departures. You may not get a cooked breakfast, or even a cheery wave at 5am, but you will be able to set out early.

Make sure you are carrying plenty of water when you set out, especially if warm weather is forecast, as there are almost no places to find running water, unless you're prepared to drop off the ridge and find a spring. The only exception is at **Chew Green** (marked on Map 123), though even here you will need to treat the water – there are a lot of sheep grazing nearby. Ideally you should also have enough food/snacks for at least two meal breaks – it's a long day.

For those who decide to make two days of it, you'll enjoy it even more. Wild camping offers the freedom of the hills but it might be necessary to drop down off the exposed plateau. Alternatively you could spend the night in one of two identical **refuge huts** (Map 125 and Map 131) with room for three on benches and another couple on the floor. There's no water at the first, and it's a

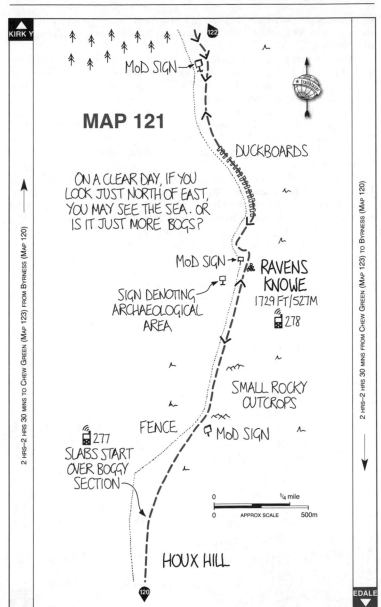

MoD SIGN

MAP 121

ON A CLEAR DAY, IF YOU
LOOK JUST NORTH OF EAST,
YOU MAY SEE THE SEA. OR
IS IT JUST MORE BOGS?

DUCKBOARDS

MoD SIGN

SIGN DENOTING
ARCHAEOLOGICAL
AREA

RAVENS
KNOWE
1729 FT/527M
278

SMALL ROCKY
OUTCROPS

FENCE

MoD SIGN

277
SLABS START
OVER BOGGY
SECTION

0   ¼ mile
0   APPROX SCALE   500m

HOUX HILL

2 HRS–2 HRS 30 MINS TO CHEW GREEN (MAP 123) FROM BYRNESS (MAP 120)

2 HRS–2 HRS 30 MINS FROM CHEW GREEN (MAP 123) TO BYRNESS (MAP 120)

15-minute walk away from the second. Just after the second refuge hut, about six or seven miles before Kirk Yetholm, a path leads down to *Mounthooly Bunkhouse* (see p262).

Also remember that there is one more option for those looking to stretch the walk over two days: if you have booked two nights at *Forest View Walkers' Inn* (see p258), they will pick you up and drop you off from the track at Trows, about two miles south of Windy Gyle.

Leaving Byrness you're faced with the inevitable steep climb up between trees to the airy summit of **Byrness Hill** (Map 120). Take a breather and enjoy the incredible views behind and ahead, but don't linger too long, there is a long way to go. Flanking you to the right are the military training grounds of the Otterburn Ranges.

Some slabs help you cross the previously appalling bog on **Houx Hill** (Map 121) and over **Ravens Knowe** to some anonymous grassy lines; all that remains of the Roman Camp at **Chew Green** (Map 123). The slabs are intermittent along the whole of the ridge; they help navigation, reduce the chances of being swallowed by the bogs and act as rhythm-maintaining tram rails.

The roller-coaster ridge can take its toll on your legs and you'll be pleased to arrive at the **Yearning Saddle Refuge Hut** at the foot of **Lamb Hill** (Map 125), about eight miles (12.9km) and four hours into the walk. A wonderful respite from wind and rain and a pleasant wooden bench to sit on in the sun.

The next eight miles are undoubtedly the hardest, with long ascent followed by long descent, seemingly ad infinitum. The trig point on **Windy Gyle** (Map 127) marks the approximate halfway point and the climb up **King's Seat** (Map 129) and up to the foot of **The Cheviot** (Map 130) will seem never-ending.

The optional diversion to The Cheviot's summit is skipped by most full-length walkers, for obvious reasons and you'll be wishing you could skip the

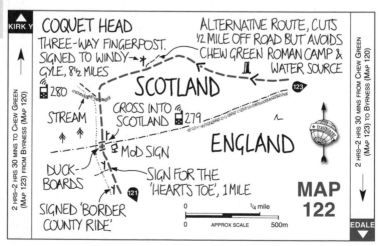

ROUTE GUIDE AND MAPS

KIRK Y

COQUET HEAD

THREE-WAY FINGERPOST.
SIGNED TO WINDY
GYLE, 8½ MILES

📶 280

STREAM

CROSS INTO
SCOTLAND 📶 279

SCOTLAND

ALTERNATIVE ROUTE, CUTS
½ MILE OFF ROAD BUT AVOIDS
CHEW GREEN ROMAN CAMP &
WATER SOURCE

123

ENGLAND

trailblazer

DUCK-
BOARDS

MoD SIGN

121

SIGN FOR THE
'HEARTS TOE', 1 MILE

SIGNED 'BORDER
COUNTY RIDE'

0   ¼ mile

0   APPROX SCALE   500m

MAP 122

2 HRS–2 HRS 30 MINS (MAP 123) FROM BYRNESS (MAP 120)

2 HRS–2 HRS 30 MINS FROM CHEW GREEN (MAP 123) TO BYRNESS (MAP 120)

EDALE

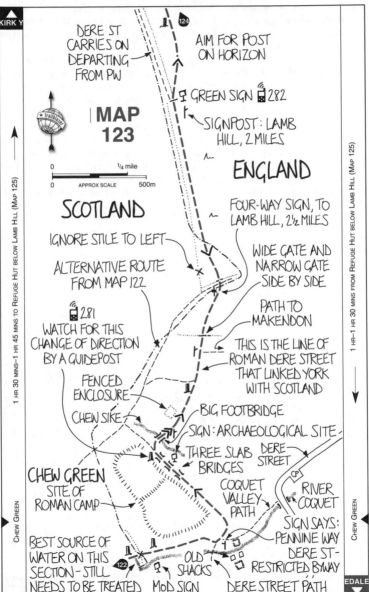

DERE ST CARRIES ON DEPARTING FROM PW

124

AIM FOR POST ON HORIZON

GREEN SIGN 282

SIGNPOST: LAMB HILL, 2 MILES

MAP 123

0   ¼ mile
0   APPROX SCALE   500m

ENGLAND

SCOTLAND

FOUR-WAY SIGN, TO LAMB HILL, 2½ MILES

IGNORE STILE TO LEFT

ALTERNATIVE ROUTE FROM MAP 122

WIDE GATE AND NARROW GATE SIDE BY SIDE

PATH TO MAKENDON

281
WATCH FOR THIS CHANGE OF DIRECTION BY A GUIDEPOST

THIS IS THE LINE OF ROMAN DERE STREET THAT LINKED YORK WITH SCOTLAND

FENCED ENCLOSURE

CHEW SIKE

BIG FOOTBRIDGE

SIGN: ARCHAEOLOGICAL SITE

THREE SLAB BRIDGES

DERE STREET

CHEW GREEN SITE OF ROMAN CAMP

COQUET VALLEY PATH

CP

RIVER COQUET

SIGN SAYS: PENNINE WAY DERE ST- RESTRICTED BYWAY

BEST SOURCE OF WATER ON THIS SECTION – STILL NEEDS TO BE TREATED

122

OLD SHACKS

MOD SIGN

DERE STREET PATH

knee-crunching descent from **Auchope Cairn** too. A short break in the **Auchope Refuge Hut** (Map 131) may recharge your batteries for the steepest ascent of the day, up to The Schil. A short descent from the hut takes you to water at the very scenic **Hen Hole**.

Just after the refuge hut a path leads down to ***Mounthooly Bunkhouse*** (off Map 131; ☎ 01668-216210, 🖥 www.college-valley.co.uk; 1 x 4-bed en suite, 1T & 2 x 9-bed rooms shared facilities; wi-fi; 🐕). Showers, cooking facilities, bedding, a log-burning stove and a drying room are provided, but you need to bring all your own food. A bed costs £20pp or the private 4-bed en suite room costs £70; book in advance particularly in the summer months. The bunkhouse is about 1½ miles from the Pennine Way and involves a steep descent of over 200 metres into College Valley and a steep climb back up the next day.

Just beyond **The Schil** (Map 131), you have to choose between more roller-coaster hills along the high route, or the more mundane, but easier, lower route (Map 132). The high route is the official path and is well worth the up-and-down effort it will require. It also offers the last wild camp options of the walk

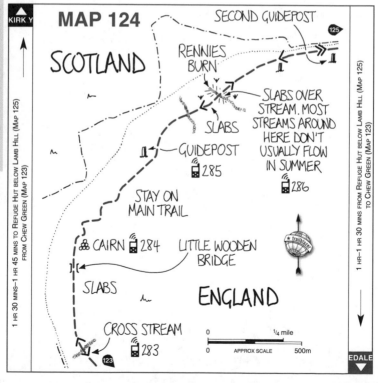

ROUTE GUIDE AND MAPS

KIRK Y

1 HR 30 MINS–1 HR 45 MINS TO REFUGE HUT BELOW LAMB HILL (MAP 125) FROM CHEW GREEN (MAP 123)

1 HR–1 HR 30 MINS FROM REFUGE HUT BELOW LAMB HILL (MAP 125) TO CHEW GREEN (MAP 123)

EDALE

MAP 124

SECOND GUIDEPOST

125

SCOTLAND

RENNIES BURN

SLABS OVER STREAM. MOST STREAMS AROUND HERE DON'T USUALLY FLOW IN SUMMER

SLABS

GUIDEPOST
285

286

STAY ON MAIN TRAIL

CAIRN 284 LITTLE WOODEN BRIDGE

SLABS

ENGLAND

CROSS STREAM
283

123

0   ¼ mile

0   APPROX SCALE   500m

and the opportunity to watch your final Pennine Way sunset, perhaps from the summit of White Law (Map 133). However, no-one will blame you if you head downhill.

At last you pull back your shoulders and pick up your dragging feet. There's no point in looking beaten. The villagers in **Kirk Yetholm** (Map 135) don't care one way or the other, but you have your pride. That said, given the number of Pennine Way walkers they must see, the Border Hotel extends a welcome to those that have completed the entire trail that is satisfyingly celebratory, with certificates and your free pint offered without quibble.

You should also sign their book, and you can read in there the comments of fellow lengthsmen and women, mostly nonchalant or triumphant, some philosophical. Add yours if you like: you have, after all, just completed what is arguably Britain's most challenging long-distance trail.

The last word, as always, is perhaps best left to Wainwright:

'Well, I'm glad that's finished, I must say.'

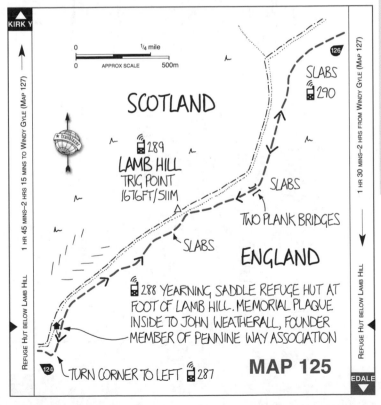

MAP 125

ROUTE GUIDE AND MAPS

1 HR 45 MINS–2 HRS 15 MINS TO WINDY GYLE (MAP 127)

REFUGE HUT BELOW LAMB HILL

1 HR 30 MINS–2 HRS FROM WINDY GYLE (MAP 127)

REFUGE HUT BELOW LAMB HILL

KIRK Y

EDALE

SCOTLAND

ENGLAND

SLABS
290

289
LAMB HILL
TRIG POINT
1676FT/511M

SLABS

TWO PLANK BRIDGES

SLABS

288 YEARNING SADDLE REFUGE HUT AT FOOT OF LAMB HILL. MEMORIAL PLAQUE INSIDE TO JOHN WEATHERALL, FOUNDER MEMBER OF PENNINE WAY ASSOCIATION

TURN CORNER TO LEFT 287

0   ¼ mile
0   APPROX SCALE   500m

Navigation notes

Leaving Byrness is the most likely cause for confusion today; the path runs straight as an arrow up the hill but the scramble up the final section isn't marked and you are left to follow the track on the ground until the cairn on Byrness Hill appears over the top. Even after here there is little indication that you are on the correct path until you reach the border with Scotland for the first time. Once the slabs appear, however, there's very little to distract you from the path. From Auchope Cairn (Map 30) the knee-popping descent to the second refuge hut is well trodden, as is the trail round and up to The Schil (Map 131) and down to

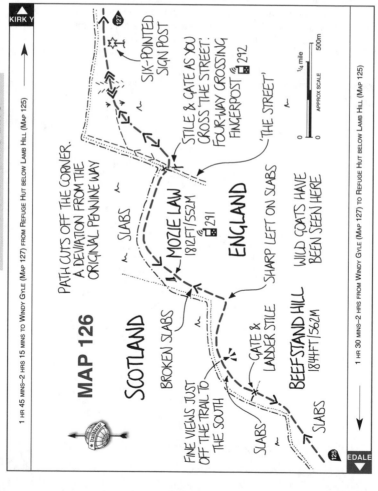

1 HR 45 MINS–2 HRS 15 MINS TO WINDY GYLE (MAP 127) FROM REFUGE HUT BELOW LAMB HILL (MAP 125)

KIRK Y

MAP 126

SCOTLAND

BROKEN SLABS

SLABS

FINE VIEWS JUST OFF THE TRAIL TO THE SOUTH

PATH CUTS OFF THE CORNER. A DEVIATION FROM THE ORIGINAL PENNINE WAY

SLABS

MOZIE LAW
1812FT/552M
291

GATE & LADDER STILE

SHARP LEFT ON SLABS

BEEFSTAND HILL
1844FT/562M

SLABS

WILD GOATS HAVE BEEN SEEN HERE

ENGLAND

127

SIX-POINTED SIGN POST

STILE & GATE AS YOU CROSS THE STREET. FOUR-WAY CROSSING FINGERPOST 292

'THE STREET'

¼ mile

APPROX SCALE

0   500m

EDALE

125

1 HR 30 MINS–2 HRS FROM WINDY GYLE (MAP 127) TO REFUGE HUT BELOW LAMB HILL (MAP 125)

the ladder stile leading to the high or low route divide, both of which roll unambiguously down to Kirk Yetholm.

All in all, even in poor visibility this very long day is made much easier by reasonable waymarking and orientation aids (aka 'slabs and fence lines'). All you have to do is last the distance.

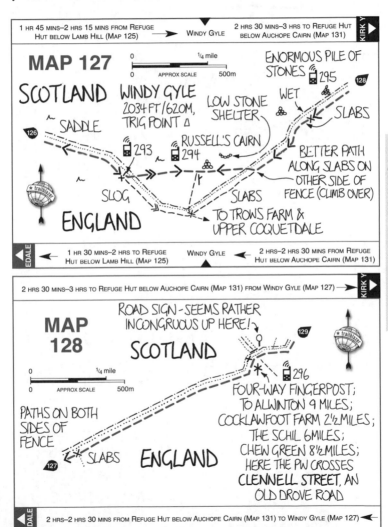

ROUTE GUIDE AND MAPS

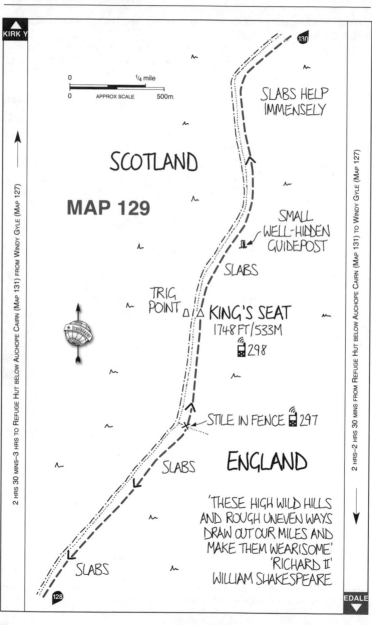

KIRK Y

2 HRS 30 MINS–3 HRS TO REFUGE HUT BELOW AUCHOPE CAIRN (MAP 131) FROM WINDY GYLE (MAP 127)

0   ¼ mile

0   APPROX SCALE   500m

SCOTLAND

MAP 129

130

SLABS HELP
IMMENSELY

SMALL
WELL-HIDDEN
GUIDEPOST

SLABS

TRIG
POINT

KING'S SEAT
1748 FT/533M
298

STILE IN FENCE 297

ENGLAND

SLABS

'THESE HIGH WILD HILLS
AND ROUGH UNEVEN WAYS
DRAW OUT OUR MILES AND
MAKE THEM WEARISOME'
'RICHARD II'
WILLIAM SHAKESPEARE

SLABS

128

2 HRS–2 HRS 30 MINS FROM REFUGE HUT BELOW AUCHOPE CAIRN (MAP 131) TO WINDY GYLE (MAP 127)

EDALE

Map 130, Auchope Cairn 267

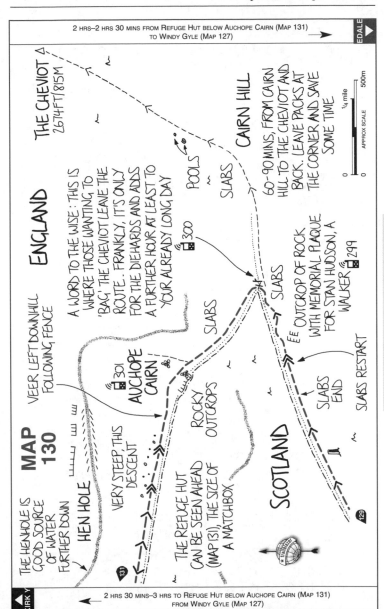

2 HRS–2 HRS 30 MINS from REFUGE HUT BELOW AUCHOPE CAIRN (MAP 131) to WINDY GYLE (MAP 127)

EDALE ▶

THE CHEVIOT 2674FT/815M

ENGLAND

A WORD TO THE WISE: THIS IS WHERE THOSE WANTING TO 'BAG' THE CHEVIOT LEAVE THE ROUTE. FRANKLY, IT'S ONLY FOR THE DIEHARDS AND ADDS A FURTHER HOUR AT LEAST TO YOUR ALREADY LONG DAY

POOLS

SLABS

CAIRN HILL

60–90 MINS, FROM CAIRN HILL TO THE CHEVIOT AND BACK. LEAVE PACKS AT THE CORNER AND SAVE SOME TIME

¼ mile

0   500m
0   APPROX SCALE

ROUTE GUIDE AND MAPS

THE HEN HOLE IS GOOD SOURCE OF WATER FURTHER DOWN

HEN HOLE

VEER LEFT DOWNHILL FOLLOWING FENCE

MAP 130

VERY STEEP, THIS DESCENT

301 AUCHOPE CAIRN

SLABS

300

SLABS

EE OUTCROP OF ROCK WITH MEMORIAL PLAQUE FOR STAN HUDSON, A WALKER 299

ROCKY OUTCROPS

SLABS END

SLABS RESTART

SCOTLAND

THE REFUGE HUT CAN BE SEEN AHEAD (MAP 131), THE SIZE OF A MATCHBOX

131

trailblazer

129

2 HRS 30 MINS–3 HRS to REFUGE HUT BELOW AUCHOPE CAIRN (MAP 131) from WINDY GYLE (MAP 127)

◀ KIRK Y

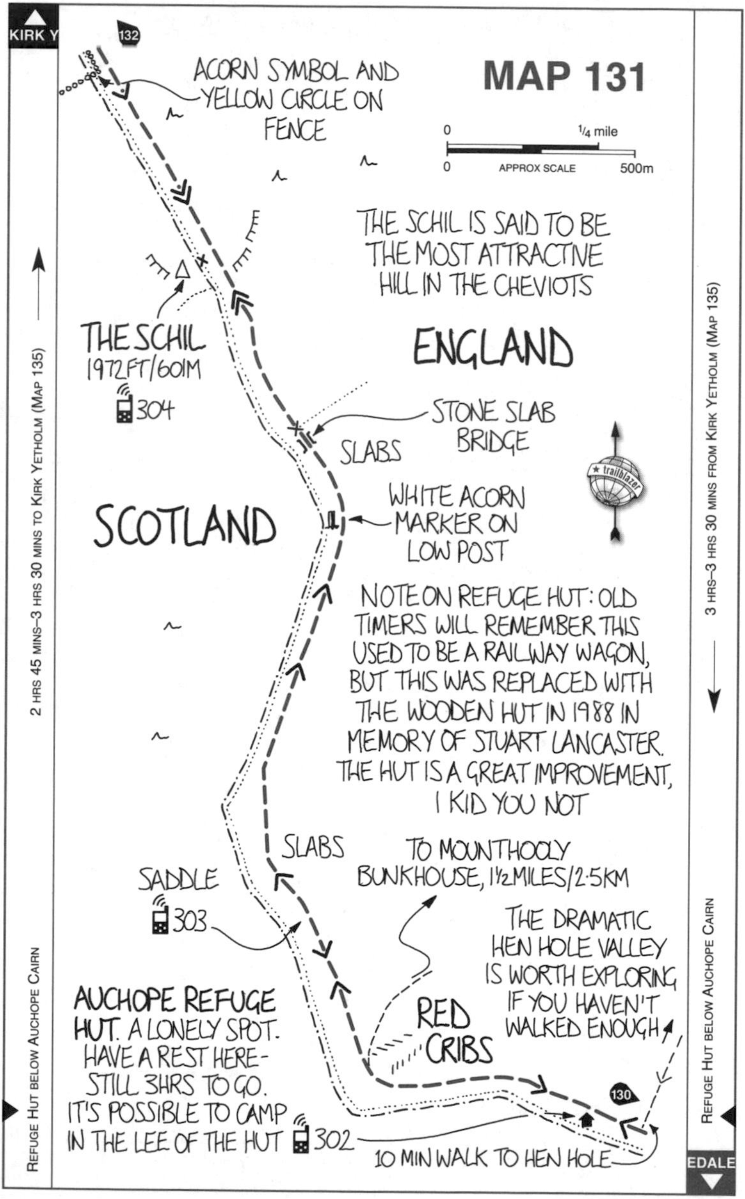

KIRK Y

132

ACORN SYMBOL AND
YELLOW CIRCLE ON
FENCE

MAP 131

0   ¼ mile
0   APPROX SCALE   500m

THE SCHIL IS SAID TO BE
THE MOST ATTRACTIVE
HILL IN THE CHEVIOTS

THE SCHIL
1972FT/601M
📱304

ENGLAND

STONE SLAB
BRIDGE

SLABS

WHITE ACORN
MARKER ON
LOW POST

SCOTLAND

NOTE ON REFUGE HUT: OLD
TIMERS WILL REMEMBER THIS
USED TO BE A RAILWAY WAGON,
BUT THIS WAS REPLACED WITH
THE WOODEN HUT IN 1988 IN
MEMORY OF STUART LANCASTER.
THE HUT IS A GREAT IMPROVEMENT,
I KID YOU NOT

SLABS

SADDLE
📱303

TO MOUNTHOOLY
BUNKHOUSE, 1½ MILES/2·5KM

THE DRAMATIC
HEN HOLE VALLEY
IS WORTH EXPLORING
IF YOU HAVEN'T
WALKED ENOUGH

AUCHOPE REFUGE
HUT. A LONELY SPOT.
HAVE A REST HERE-
STILL 3HRS TO GO.
IT'S POSSIBLE TO CAMP
IN THE LEE OF THE HUT 📱302

RED
CRIBS

130

10 MIN WALK TO HEN HOLE

EDALE

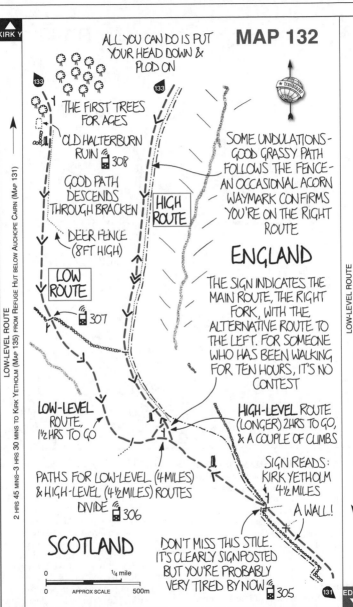

KIRK Y

MAP 132

ALL YOU CAN DO IS PUT
YOUR HEAD DOWN &
PLOD ON

THE FIRST TREES
FOR AGES

OLD HALTERBURN
RUIN 📱 308

GOOD PATH
DESCENDS
THROUGH BRACKEN

DEER FENCE
(8FT HIGH)

HIGH
ROUTE

SOME UNDULATIONS-
GOOD GRASSY PATH
FOLLOWS THE FENCE-
AN OCCASIONAL ACORN
WAYMARK CONFIRMS
YOU'RE ON THE RIGHT
ROUTE

ENGLAND

THE SIGN INDICATES THE
MAIN ROUTE, THE RIGHT
FORK, WITH THE
ALTERNATIVE ROUTE TO
THE LEFT. FOR SOMEONE
WHO HAS BEEN WALKING
FOR TEN HOURS, IT'S NO
CONTEST

LOW
ROUTE

📱 307

LOW-LEVEL
ROUTE,
1½ HRS TO GO

HIGH-LEVEL ROUTE
(LONGER) 2HRS TO GO,
& A COUPLE OF CLIMBS

PATHS FOR LOW-LEVEL (4 MILES)
& HIGH-LEVEL (4½ MILES) ROUTES
DIVIDE 📱 306

SIGN READS:
KIRK YETHOLM
4½ MILES

A WALL!

SCOTLAND

DON'T MISS THIS STILE.
IT'S CLEARLY SIGNPOSTED
BUT YOU'RE PROBABLY
VERY TIRED BY NOW 📱 305

0   ¼ mile
0   APPROX SCALE   500m

EDALE

LOW-LEVEL ROUTE
2 HRS 45 MINS–3 HRS 30 MINS TO KIRK YETHOLM (MAP 135) FROM REFUGE HUT BELOW AUCHOPE CAIRN (MAP 131)

LOW-LEVEL ROUTE
3 HRS–3 HRS 30 MINS FROM KIRK YETHOLM (MAP 135) TO REFUGE HUT BELOW AUCHOPE CAIRN (MAP 131)

ROUTE GUIDE AND MAPS

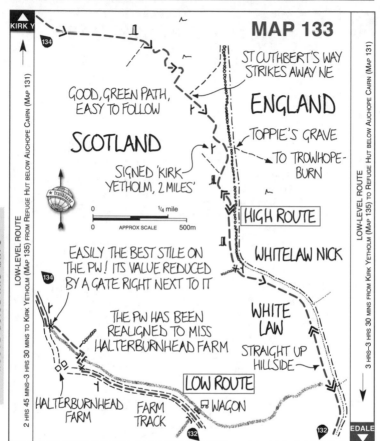

MAP 133

KIRK Y

134

ST CUTHBERT'S WAY
STRIKES AWAY NE

ENGLAND

GOOD, GREEN PATH,
EASY TO FOLLOW

SCOTLAND

TOPPIE'S GRAVE

TO TROWHOPE-
BURN

SIGNED 'KIRK
YETHOLM, 2 MILES'

HIGH ROUTE

WHITELAW NICK

* trailblazer

0   1/4 mile
0   APPROX SCALE   500m

EASILY THE BEST STILE ON
THE PW! ITS VALUE REDUCED
BY A GATE RIGHT NEXT TO IT

WHITE
LAW

134

STRAIGHT UP
HILLSIDE

THE PW HAS BEEN
REALIGNED TO MISS
HALTERBURNHEAD FARM

LOW ROUTE

HALTERBURNHEAD
FARM

FARM
TRACK

WAGON

132

132

EDALE

(left margin, top to bottom) LOW-LEVEL ROUTE (MAP 135) TO REFUGE HUT BELOW AUCHOPE CAIRN (MAP 131)

(left margin) ROUTE GUIDE AND MAPS

(left margin, bottom) 2 HRS 45 MINS–3 HRS 30 MINS TO KIRK YETHOLM (MAP 135) FROM REFUGE HUT BELOW AUCHOPE CAIRN (MAP 131)

(right margin, top to bottom) LOW-LEVEL ROUTE FROM KIRK YETHOLM (MAP 135) TO REFUGE HUT BELOW AUCHOPE CAIRN (MAP 131)

(right margin, bottom) 3 HRS–3 HRS 30 MINS FROM KIRK YETHOLM (MAP 135) TO REFUGE HUT BELOW AUCHOPE CAIRN

KIRK YETHOLM   [Map 135, p272]

It's probably fair to say that only a fraction of the people who have heard of this pleasant little village would have done so if the Pennine Way did not end here. As it is, it offers a perfect and well-appointed spot to wind down your big walk.

See p14 for details of Yetholm Festival week held in June; for general information visit 🖥 yetholmonline.org.

Transport

[See pp54-9] Peter Hogg of Jedburgh operates the No 81/81A **bus** services to Kelso (20-35 mins), from where you can catch Borders Buses' No 67 to Galashiels and Berwick-upon-Tweed's railway station or Peter Hogg's No 20 service to Hawick or their No 131 to Newcastle. There are no services to Kelso on a Sunday, so you'll need a taxi to connect with a bus there.

Taxis include **Hownam Taxis** (☎ 07768 070818), pronounced 'whonam', and **Border Villager Taxi** (☎ 01668-482888, or ☎ 07765-791348, 🖥 bordervill agertaxi.co.uk). A taxi from Kirk Yetholm to Berwick-upon-Tweed was around £42 at time of research; by bus around £9pp.

Places to stay, eat and drink

Campers should head to Town Yetholm (see p272) where there's a decent campsite.

As for **B&Bs**, *Mill House* (bookings ☎ 01573-420604, after booking ☎ 07721 463547, 🖥 millhouseyetholm.co.uk; 2D or T/2D/1Qd, all en suite; ▼; (Ⓛ) is well set up for walkers, with a laundry service (£5) and drying room for walking gear. B&B costs from £100-125 for double (sgl occ £80-105). They offer a pick-up and drop-off service (from £25 each way) for Pennine Way walkers from/to Cocklawfoot Farm (see Map 128; 2½ miles/4km off the PW), enabling you to divide the last stage across two days.

Border Hotel (☎ 01573-420237, 🖥 borderhotel.co.uk, **fb**; 2D/2D or T/1Tr, all cn suite; ▼; (Ⓛ; 🐾) has a welcoming bar (11.30am-midnight) where you can ask for the Pennine Way visitors book. Anyone who has finished the Pennine Way is offered a certificate and stood a free half-pint of Tyneside Blonde courtesy of Hadrian Border Brewery (there are plans to increase this to a full pint). **B&B** costs from £80-110 (sgl occ £10 discount). The menu (**food** summer Mon-Thur noon-2pm & 6-8.30pm, Fri & Sat noon-2.30pm & 6-8.30pm, Sun noon-8pm, winter hours vary) here offers a knee-weakening range of dishes to help pile back the calories burned up during the haul over from Byrness. You may need to book if you want to eat dinner in the restaurant. Non-residents can have breakfast here (daily 8-9am; £10).

Round the corner *Kirk Yetholm Friends of Nature House* (bookings ☎ 01573-420639, 🖥 thefriendsofnature.org.uk/houses/kirk-yetholm; sleeps 22 in 6

MAP 134

rooms; all shared facilities; Easter-end Oct) costs from £24pp in a single-sex dorm, or £48 for a double room. The hostel is self-

catering only, with no lockers, but bedding, coffee-making facilities and a drying room are provided.

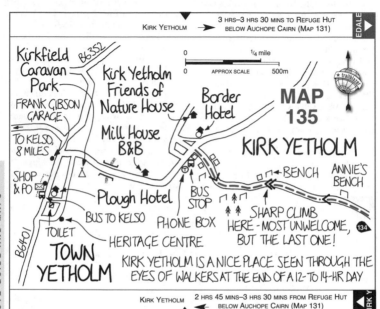

TOWN YETHOLM   [Map 135]

It could be one half mile too many but in Town Yetholm you'll find the newly refurbished **Yetholm community shop** (🖥 yetholmcommunityshop.co.uk, **fb**; Mon-Thur 8am-4pm, Fri to 5pm, Sat to 3pm, Sun 9am-1pm) and **post office** (Mon-Fri 9.30am-12.30pm, Sat 9am-noon).

If you have time to kill, you can learn about local history at the free **Yetholm Heritage Centre** (10am-4.30pm daily, end May to end Sep).

Kirkfield Caravan Park (☎ 07791-291956 or ☎ 01573-420346, 🖥 kirkfield caravanpark.co.uk; no wi-fi; 🐾; Apr-end Oct) is a peaceful place to pitch a tent (from £10pp) but reservations are required; you'll get a numbered site when you pay. Shower and toilet facilities are available. If in doubt contact Fiona on the phone numbers listed

or in person at nearby Frank Gibson's Garage during office hours.

There's also the *Plough Hotel* (☎ 01573-420215, 🖥 theploughhotelyetholm .co.uk **fb**; 1D/1T/1D or T/1Tr, all en suite; 🍷; 🄻; 🐾 £10) where **B&B** costs S/D from £75/95. The menu (**food** summer daily Mon-Sat noon-2.30pm & 5.30-8pm, Sun noon-7pm; mains £12-14) is similar to the Border Hotel in Kirk Yetholm, which they used to run. They also have a cheaper takeaway menu (daily noon-2.30pm & 5-7pm) and a morning coffe shop (daily except Wed, 10am-noon).

Peter Hogg of Jedburgh operate the No 81/81A **bus** services to Kelso (20-35 mins), some of which are school buses. As with Kirk Yetholm, there are no Sunday buses. See pp54-9.

APPENDIX A: WHAT3WORDS REFS ON MAPS

These what3words refs correspond to waypoints on maps and may be useful in an emergency; see p78

001 empire.swaps.newsreel	054 escalates.burden.dampen	107 configure.obligated.quitter
002 press.ever.detergent	055 gossip.sharpness.acclaimed	108 sifts.towers.goodnight
003 basics.also.resources	056 passwords.redeemed.tube	109 included.stretcher.blotchy
004 weeks.weeknight.renewals	057 limit.envisage.sublet	110 locator.senders.enhancement
005 rattler.quilt.topping	058 wider.improves.scrambles	111 hazelnuts.blurts.park
006 informal.captions.importing	059 perusing.toxic.deeper	112 unrealistic.agency.festivity
007 starring.aspect.caused	060 diverts.campsites.offices	113 warmers.villager.bride
008 doctors.palettes.crown	061 climate.invented.handbags	114 published.jigging.courts
009 suddenly.appointed.communal	062 nozzle.crumple.dignitary	115 loafing.strut.display
010 drifting.skidding.countries	063 snowy.niece.keys	116 advances.reporting.instead
011 wanting.dollar.relocated	064 combos.snored.concerned	117 rocks.misted.commoners
012 triads.living.earmarked	065 director.outbound.hops	118 stared.stocked.eyepieces
013 balconies.track.hazelnuts	066 swordfish.noted.waltz	119 canine.enthused.balance
014 pocketed.hang.shopping	067 assets.sardine.marathons	120 fits.drove.enchanted
015 browsers.pilots.downsize	068 voted.multiple.shadowed	121 cheat.powering.offstage
016 calms.operation.flamenco	069 waxing.nuptials.gives	122 wedding.shower.shrug
017 indicates.sampled.firelight	070 isolating.toxic.flaked	123 mammoth.uncle.moguls
018 sour.bins.pirates	071 stems.cluttered.innocence	124 coats.wiped.landlords
019 clutches.available.amazed	072 coached.ledge.ignore	124a gymnasium.snips.quit
020 fulfilled.snores.kneeled	073 novelist.surpassed.loudness	125 cement.wire.transmitted
021 monument.stems.banter	074 float.firework.pouting	126 stoppage.throwaway.changes
022 endlessly.weeds.sport	075 straying.grandest.conforms	127 bracing.revived.feuds
023 acrobatic.outfit.reservoir	076 consonant.noise.pigment	128 threaded.basis.dabbing
024 cushy.drips.beads	077 kiosk.fails.toffee	129 unlucky.asleep.romantics
025 acclaim.taskbar.bumps	078 hinders.unloading.abacus	130 flicked.beanbag.farmer
026 built.afternoon.sleeping	079 bloomers.revolts.ranks	131 bulletins.grocers.whiplash
027 submerged.rebounds.wasps	080 chiefs.suspends.flash	132 intestine.helpless.passions
028 protect.splashes.matchbox	081 sake.gazes.backyards	133 positions.hockey.allies
029 submitted.smiles.segregate	082 directs.outfitter.trip	134 aimed.inform.footsteps
030 juggled.wimp.piano	083 months.served.subjects	135 carpeted.green.contact
031 seatbelt.younger.loafing	084 divisible.circular.village	136 filled.funds.housework
032 cured.usages.boggles	085 laminated.imply.joked	137 enormous.clarifies.global
033 defensive.fond.canine	086 album.befitting.portfolio	138 flicked.unicorns.wooden
034 blank.professed.careful	087 balconies.scrubber.beeline	139 yachting.spending.hairpin
035 speared.firepower.shrub	088 disclose.palaces.browsers	140 harsh.searching.dove
036 spirit.foggy.jetted	089 edits.banquets.laces	141 shovels.veered.streaking
037 gazes.offhand.mugs	090 floating.immune.bats	142 overruns.aviators.tamed
038 brave.reverses.shell	091 pinks.polar.embellish	143 drips.satin.mush
039 tint.imparting.decently	092 televise.lousy.voice	144 napkins.bends.badly
040 haven.fires.following	093 heartburn.visual.insurance	145 idealist.streak.archduke
041 escapades.markets.tolerates	094 chapels.stupidly.betraying	146 hunk.waggled.punch
042 manifests.rich.swimsuits	095 comply.boarded.hologram	147 clarifies.verdict.matrons
043 repaying.breathing.rail	096 unite.remind.friday	148 responds.wasp.landscape
044 cucumber.hospitals.cocoons	097 level.heightens.clusters	149 elbowing.curiosity.ticket
045 mixture.whiplash.chapels	098 litters.royal.shortens	150 twitches.project.seated
046 silly.bouncing.equipment	099 awaited.cakewalk.stitch	151 outfitter.clothed.sprinter
047 mock.cups.worldwide	100 huddled.outs.physics	152 foot.modifies.wages
048 newsstand.basket.points	101 downs.pushing.reddish	153 included.variation.sprays
049 courier.steeped.lousy	102 goodbyes.perused.dabbing	154 pointed.watching.clockwork
050 jotting.rejoin.blink	103 alarm.resembles.setting	155 century.gains.gradually
051 skimmers.reddish.lottery	104 recur.overt.appealing	156 measuring.strategy.sleepers
052 campus.stages.fall	105 binders.bookings.tentacles	157 storyline.engine.coolest
053 amazed.retrieves.captures	106 majoring.registry.lentil	158 jumps.custodian.majors

159 tripods.slip.nipped	216 carriage.fairway.squaring	273 tolerable.inclined.zone
160 cushy.connects.rehearsed	217 manual.store.overheat	274 maps.scripted.harmlessly
161 stolen.dent.simulations	218 crawler.chill.shrugging	275 thumb.ferrying.recent
162 city.climate.baseless	219 commit.pictures.polishing	276 exposing.developed.library
163 magazines.tanks.climbing	220 tuxedos.strict.convey	277 singled.graph.water
164 uses.sprawls.intention	221 scale.older.ringside	278 horns.submerge.reacting
165 crumble.approve.shelving	222 seatbelt.disprove.sunk	279 formation.bunk.ironic
166 piglets.chuck.narrowest	223 rivals.perplexed.ambushes	280 embers.gasp.frostbite
167 swelling.altitude.searching	224 synthetic.river.trifling	281 quail.smallest.ribs
168 dynasties.basis.wiggles	225 helped.cutback.flitting	282 countries.eternity.ports
169 convey.swarm.props	226 innovate.bike.rival	283 handsets.handed.alas
170 goals.producers.assurance	227 lighters.causes.amicably	284 warms.riverbank.wipe
171 snore.billiard.duet	228 reliving.drag.care	285 pavilions.factor.establish
172 cheaply.pizzeria.chat	229 roadmap.saturate.popular	286 balloons.depending.packet
173 servers.followers.loom	230 visual.objective.champions	287 reflector.charmingly.beats
174 eager.forklift.clock	231 brittle.static.coveted	288 suspend.browsers.sprouting
175 tonal.stack.trinkets	232 pylon.birds.salmon	289 issued.outwards.chef
176 gobbles.reacting.managed	233 green.gems.bunch	290 jaunts.poses.magnum
177 footpath.scout.travel	234 kiosk.ants.dupe	291 wriggle.youths.wires
178 spike.composes.grandest	235 takes.skewing.camped	292 realm.logo.importers
179 shifting.estimates.isolating	236 renovated.headliner.sprinter	293 compiled.dreaming.helped
180 dragging.visa.adopters	237 clef.explained.silently	294 bookcases.glorified.reinstate
181 generally.commended.charts	238 blacken.become.dined	295 prefix.dialects.rival
182 sinkhole.scanty.pulses	239 monument.bands.rewrites	296 variously.newspaper.rams
183 unrated.benched.shirt	240 gurgling.gurgled.daffodils	297 restrict.glimmers.rafters
184 applauded.width.prices	241 says.ribcage.enjoyable	298 balancing.respects.impaled
185 universes.movie.puddles	242 surprises.fingernails.assist	299 fled.norms.demotion
186 universes.movie.puddles	243 trio.rubble.repeat	300 signature.create.blunders
187 series.cones.suffer	244 blush.policy.litigate	301 drifters.balloons.breath
188 orbited.diplomats.belief	245 query.superbly.spit	302 bounty.impressed.noises
189 eternity.clicker.probe	246 hologram.disbanded.teaspoons	303 onwards.whistling.skimmers
190 weeks.tender.newsreel	247 caskets.caged.widely	304 vandalism.modern.narrowest
191 inclines.froze.drank	248 regulates.vitals.animated	305 driven.jets.mush
192 surpasses.enter.inert	249 cries.staring.asking	306 screeches.showering.seasick
193 microfilm.vocals.rooftop	250 storeroom.sharpens.harnessed	307 clashes.squirts.struts
194 smallest.adopters.tripods	251 inversion.jaunts.raves	308 windows.outnumber.scavenger
195 ending.germinate.paddle	252 darts.haggis.drape	309 commented.toolbar.restores
196 threading.blindfold.kept	253 croutons.outreach.dramatic	657 kitten.soccer.bluffing
197 stream.surveyors.dream	254 admire.tagging.procured	658 plodding.joints.blankets
198 hired.costumed.inform	255 rehearsed.footsteps.baking	659 degrading.skylights.imposes
199 sway.wings.ripe	256 venue.cubed.beamed	660 locked.title.snooping
200 clearing.winner.amplified	257 emulated.rang.likening	661 firm.conned.something
201 beauty.snore.corrosive	258 budding.loving.unwound	662 stoppage.fake.speedily
202 idealist.tougher.hunches	259 struck.unloading.include	663 puzzled.twitching.clockwork
203 crunches.populate.skid	260 requests.currently.unique	664 mascots.jacket.subway
204 traps.sheds.spilling	261 directors.heckler.rejoined	665 freshest.fairly.guides
205 tastings.amuses.verifying	262 clocked.solved.appealing	666 haystack.chum.charm
206 voter.supple.threading	263 panthers.burglars.resolves	667 tightest.typist.remind
207 order.weary.aspect	264 dispose.ecologist.inhabited	668 sparrows.digested.paused
208 recover.upholding.passing	265 bond.slipped.easygoing	669 guess.emulating.organisms
209 mugs.schools.exits	266 careful.clearly.clincher	670 overused.smug.solid
210 bitters.insulated.smokers	267 adopting.clocks.lamenting	671 gymnasium.snips.quit
211 ambushes.magazines.dumps	268 sulk.synthetic.mouths	672 clarifies.verdict.matrons
212 honeybees.trial.utensil	269 laces.nylon.tribune	673 skinning.income.stared
213 gates.prouder.intelligible	270 deeds.shredder.policy	674 blotting.stapled.present
214 zones.cooked.wasps	271 remarried.troubles.hounded	675 bluff.taking.caged
215 bystander.empire.falters	272 encodes.trending.stray	676 foot.modifies.wages

These what3words refs correspond to waypoints on maps and may be useful in an emergency; see p78

APPENDIX B: GPS WAYPOINTS ON MAPS

Each GPS waypoint below was taken on the route at the reference number marked on the map as below. See opposite for the list of what3words refs that correspond to these waypoints. Gpx files for waypoints can be downloaded from 💻 trailblazer-guides.com.

Map	GPS	Lat	Long	OS Grid Ref	Description (what3words on p273)
Edale to Crowden (Maps 1-9)					
3	001	53.3753	-1.8818	SK 07860 86530	Bear left at cairn to Edale Rocks
3	002	53.3803	-1.8835	SK 07751 87079	Kinder Low trig point
4	003	53.3972	-1.8765	SK 08209 88962	Kinder Downfall
4	004	53.4077	-1.9047	SK 06433 90102	Straight ahead at guidepost
7	005	53.4613	-1.8597	SK 09311 96096	Bleaklow Head summit
7	006	53.4656	-1.8628	SK 09108 96582	Milestone
8	007	53.4753	-1.9060	SK 06237 97649	Gate in fence above Reaps Farm
Crowden to Standedge (Maps 9-15)					
10	008	53.5220	-1.9100	SE 05967 02849	Cross stream joining Crowden Great Brook
11	009	53.5299	-1.9035	SE 06396 03730	Cross stile in fence line
12	010	53.5387	-1.8836	SE 07711 04710	Black Hill summit
12	011	53.5505	-1.8772	SE 08138 06022	Path begins to bear left
13	012	53.5781	-1.9204	SE 05267 09084	Drop into valley, beside fingerpost
14	013	53.5756	-1.9485	SE 03412 08802	Cross bridge between reservoirs
15	014	53.5774	-1.9567	SE 02867 09000	Go through kissing gate in fence
15	015	53.5816	-1.9610	SE 02578 09470	Green PNFS signpost #357
Standedge to Calder Valley (Maps 15-22)					
15	016	53.5903	-1.9829	SE 01132 10434	Trig point (Millstone Edge)
16	017	53.5977	-1.9947	SE 00351 11264	Stone marker by Oldham Way
17	018	53.6151	-2.0157	SD 98960 13194	White Hill summit trig point
18	019	53.6408	-2.0417	SD 97242 16059	Shelter of sorts
18	020	53.6438	-2.0436	SD 97117 16394	Trig point (Blackstone Edge)
18	021	53.6500	-2.0418	SD 97240 17086	Aiggin Stone, turn left
18	022	53.6494	-2.0477	SD 96850 17018	Cross drainage ditch, then turn right, signed Rochdale Way
19	023	53.6684	-2.0555	SD 96335 19131	'Packhorse'-style bridge
20	024	53.6917	-2.0654	SD 95681 21727	Slabs start after Warland Reservoir
20	025	53.7047	-2.0515	SD 96597 23165	4-way marker on tall signpost
21	026	53.7192	-2.0314	SD 97927 24783	Straight on beside wall
Calder Valley to Ickornshaw (Maps 22-31)					
22	027	53.7389	-2.0480	SD 96833 26974	Signpost to Badger Fields Farm
23	028	53.7584	-2.0527	SD 96527 29141	Fingerpost by Mount Pleasant Farm
24	029	53.7639	-2.0579	SD 96183 29752	Path meets wall beside fingerpost
24	030	53.7736	-2.0822	SD 94582 30839	Pennine Bridleway sign; turn right
25	031	53.7871	-2.0820	SD 94600 32335	Layby; cut corner at fingerpost
26	032	53.7963	-2.0540	SD 96442 33356	Cross drain on metal bridge
26	033	53.8011	-2.0481	SD 96832 33895	Fingerpost points right up hill
27	034	53.8159	-2.0281	SD 98150 35536	Japanese fingerpost
28	035	53.8236	-2.0045	SD 99704 36395	At signpost turn left between walls
28	036	53.8267	-2.0040	SD 99735 36736	Switchback left at fingerpost
28	037	53.8312	-2.0188	SD 98762 37244	Leave tarmac onto green path before gate

Map	GPS	Lat	Long	OS Grid Ref	Description (what3words on p273)
Calder Valley to Ickornshaw (Maps 22-31) *(cont'd)*					
29	038	53.8362	-2.0187	SD 98769 37794	Leave track (turn left) at fingerpost
29	039	53.8465	-2.0324	SD 97867 38938	Guidepost beside path where wall ends abruptly, open moor ahead
29	040	53.8500	-2.0404	SD 97345 39331	Rank green pool beside path
29	041	53.8577	-2.0424	SD 97213 40191	Stone building
30	042	53.8579	-2.0440	SD 97109 40207	Stone shelter
30	043	53.8651	-2.0484	SD 96815 41013	Stone (shooting) hut
31	044	53.8707	-2.0457	SD 96995 41629	Door to garden and hut
31	045	53.8722	-2.0441	SD 97101 41798	Metal gate, change of direction
31	046	53.8859	-2.0546	SD 96412 43323	Spring; turn right through gate
Ickornshaw to Malham (Maps 31-41)					
32	047	53.8967	-2.0607	SD 96012 44527	Turn right onto road
32	048	53.9184	-2.0661	SD 95658 46938	Bench beside path
32	049	53.9202	-2.0739	SD 95149 47142	Two planks across ditch
33	050	53.9209	-2.0863	SD 94333 47225	Pinhaw Beacon trig point
33	051	53.9240	-2.1015	SD 93338 47565	Leave road bear left beside wall
33	052	53.9315	-2.1257	SD 91744 48402	PW fingerpost in farmyard
35	053	53.9415	-2.1406	SD 90774 49519	Leave lane, go through gate into field
35	054	53.9615	-2.1316	SD 91366 51737	Leave lane, go right into field through gate
36	055	53.9706	-2.1234	SD 91903 52753	Stone water tank
36	056	53.9739	-2.1188	SD 92211 53123	4-way fingerpost on Scaleber Hill
37	057	53.9791	-2.1137	SD 92546 53697	Right turn through gate into field by fingerpost
37	058	53.9911	-2.1166	SD 92358 55030	Stile in wall on right
38	059	54.0027	-2.1281	SD 91603 56330	Fingerpost by gate
38	060	54.0073	-2.1301	SD 91473 56832	Path between walls
38	061	54.0094	-2.1317	SD 91368 57072	Lone Pennine Way sign
38	062	54.0189	-2.1424	SD 90668 58132	Left off road after crossing bridge
39	063	54.0324	-2.1492	SD 90228 59627	Slab bridge over beck
39	064	54.0463	-2.1544	SD 89888 61174	Stone steps up to road
40	065	54.0510	-2.1529	SD 89991 61707	Fingerpost by wall corner
Malham to Horton-in-Ribblesdale (Maps 41-48)					
41	066	54.0732	-2.1584	SD 89633 64172	Bear left along wall
42	067	54.0816	-2.1670	SD 89076 65104	Bear right at fork, keep to wall
42	068	54.0869	-2.1644	SD 89245 65693	Paths meet
43	069	54.1018	-2.1721	SD 88745 67353	Leave track at gate in wall
43	070	54.1178	-2.1782	SD 88353 69140	Across cattle grid onto farm lane
44	071	54.1256	-2.1903	SD 87563 70005	Path bears right away from wall
44	072	54.1438	-2.2036	SD 86698 72030	Wall stile
45	073	54.1433	-2.2183	SD 85738 71977	Path meets wall on descent
46	074	54.1506	-2.2523	SD 83526 72800	Fingerpost shows way to Horton avoiding Pen-y-ghent
46	075	54.1560	-2.2486	SD 83766 73397	Summit of Pen-y-ghent
46	076	54.1634	-2.2505	SD 83648 74227	Bear left at fingerpost
47	077	54.1640	-2.2726	SD 82206 74300	Gate in walled lane
48	078	54.1484	-2.2907	SD 81011 72562	Bench beside track

Map	GPS	Lat	Long	OS Grid Ref	Description (what3words on p273)
Horton-in-Ribblesdale to Hawes (Maps 48-55)					
49	079	54.1694	-2.2923	SD 80919 74900	PW/3 Peaks fingerpost by gate in wall
49	080	54.1900	-2.2879	SD 81214 77189	Left after gate; not the obvious path ahead
50	081	54.1962	-2.3048	SD 80114 77889	Barn beside path
50	082	54.2193	-2.3057	SD 80069 80457	Cam End forestry road
52	083	54.2402	-2.2752	SD 82066 82779	Join tarmac here
53	084	54.2459	-2.2628	SD 82876 83409	Leave tarmac before Kidhow Gate
54	085	54.2772	-2.2426	SD 84205 86889	Leave West Cam Road for grassy path
54	086	54.2785	-2.2415	SD 84276 87032	Cairn on rocky outcrop on path
54	087	54.2857	-2.2326	SD 84861 87823	Half-size wooden gate
54	088	54.2915	-2.2231	SD 85478 88473	Gate after prominent cairn
55	089	54.2999	-2.2018	SD 86868 89403	Gate onto road opposite houses
Hawes to Tan Hill (Maps 55-64)					
56	090	54.3122	-2.1929	SD 87450 90766	Stone bench with view of powerlines
57	091	54.3242	-2.2203	SD 85676 92113	Gate in track
57	092	54.3341	-2.2359	SD 84662 93213	Gate next to stile
57	093	54.3344	-2.2355	SD 84691 93243	Fingerpost to Cotterdale
58	094	54.3496	-2.2409	SD 84344 94940	Permanent puddle to left of path
58	095	54.3653	-2.2394	SD 84445 96682	Steps built with cobbles
59	096	54.3708	-2.2346	SD 84763 97291	Great Shunner Fell summit
59	097	54.3769	-2.2271	SD 85252 97969	Fine cairn
59	098	54.3818	-2.2198	SD 85723 98520	Wooden bridge
60	099	54.3812	-2.1926	SD 87492 98444	Gate after stream
61	100	54.3811	-2.1612	SD 89533 98424	Gate beside barns
61	101	54.3824	-2.1515	SD 90160 98569	Gate beside Kisdon House
62	102	54.3908	-2.1483	SD 90373 99503	Wide gate in wall
62	103	54.4020	-2.1567	NY 89828 00752	Go through gap in wall by fingerpost
62	104	54.4138	-2.1678	NY 89111 02069	Gate in fence line
63	105	54.4279	-2.1731	NY 88768 03638	Two barns
63	106	54.4358	-2.1752	NY 88638 04520	Gate and slab bridge over stream
64	107	54.4430	-2.1674	NY 89147 05320	PW fingerpost
Tan Hill to Middleton-in-Teesdale (Maps 64-72)					
65	108	54.4662	-2.1378	NY 91070 07889	White-topped post beside sheepfold
65	109	54.4680	-2.1320	NY 91446 08094	Good-sized cairn
65	110	54.4718	-2.1216	NY 92120 08511	Post and plank bridge opp sheepfolds
65	111	54.4764	-2.1020	NY 93490 09013	Cross beck on sturdy metal bridge
66	112	54.4844	-2.0730	NY 95272 09913	Ancient triangular road sign by track
67	113	54.4913	-2.0680	NY 95596 10674	Intake Bridge
67	114	54.4956	-2.0628	NY 95930 11152	Gate with acorn waymark
67	115	54.5031	-2.0668	NY 95674 11986	Gate in wall
68	116	54.5129	-2.0707	NY 95426 13078	Concrete block ford
68	117	54.5197	-2.0733	NY 95258 13837	Big cairn on skyline
68	118	54.5222	-2.0771	NY 95010 14116	'Ravock Castle' (Rock cairn)
68	119	54.5264	-2.0782	NY 94939 14588	Marker post
68	120	54.5281	-2.0813	NY 94739 14775	Shelter in shooting hut
69	121	54.5402	-2.0910	NY 94116 16123	Gate in fence on Race Yate
69	122	54.5453	-2.0931	NY 93975 16686	Post on Peatbrig Hill
69	123	54.5486	-2.0961	NY 93785 17056	Guide post on left side of path
69	124	54.5538	-2.1006	NY 93494 17635	Path meets tarmac at fingerpost
69	124a	54.5582	-2.1040	NY 93275 18129	Bowes Loop fingerpost

Map	GPS	Lat	Long	OS Grid Ref	Description (what3words on p273)

Tan Hill to Middleton-in-Teesdale (Maps 64-72) *(cont'd)*

Map	GPS	Lat	Long	OS Grid Ref	Description
70	125	54.5813	-2.1116	NY 92883 20686	Barn by gap stile
70	126	54.5835	-2.1114	NY 92799 20945	Stile and metal gates
71	127	54.6025	-2.1207	NY 92204 23059	Stone stile with white paint
71	128	54.6048	-2.1156	NY 92535 23315	Gap in wall
71	129	54.6099	-2.1065	NY 93219 23862	Gate in wall across path
72	130	54.6117	-2.1028	NY 93358 24082	Cairn beside small disused quarry
72	131	54.6137	-2.0924	NY 94034 24304	Stile with dog slot and black gate
72	132	54.6187	-2.0854	NY 94486 24852	Gate onto road beside fingerpost

Bowes Loop Route (Map 67-69)

Map	GPS	Lat	Long	OS Grid Ref	Description
67	657	54.5079	-2.0586	NY 96202 12530	Bear right over cattle grid
67a	658	54.5101	-2.0491	NY 96820 12765	Small gate beside big gate
67a	659	54.5125	-2.0291	NY 98117 13032	Leave track and enter field
67b	660	54.5316	-2.0442	NY 97138 15160	Fingerposts beside gate
67b	661	54.5343	-2.0512	NY 96690 15460	Bridge over Deepdale Beck
67b	662	54.5354	-2.0514	NY 96675 15587	On path through marsh grass
67b	663	54.5392	-2.0528	NY 96582 16012	Splash through Hazelgill Beck
67b	664	54.5427	-2.0503	NY 96747 16397	Cairn marks path
67c	665	54.5477	-2.0533	NY 96554 16957	Sunken slabs over Hare Sike
67c	666	54.5497	-2.0552	NY 96427 17181	Through gate in wall
67c	667	54.5518	-2.0631	NY 95921 17413	Big black metal footbridge
67c	668	54.5532	-2.0720	NY 95342 17571	South of summit crag
67c	669	54.5561	-2.0816	NY 94725 17892	Meet road beside fingerpost
69	670	54.5575	-2.0920	NY 94054 18047	Tiny gate and stone stile
69	671	54.5582	-2.1040	NY 93275 18129	Bowes Loop fingerpost

Middleton-in-Teesdale to Dufton (Maps 72-83)

Map	GPS	Lat	Long	OS Grid Ref	Description
73	133	54.6249	-2.1030	NY 93350 25550	Step stile in wall
73	134	54.6309	-2.1236	NY 92022 26217	Cairn at path junction, bear right
74	135	54.6415	-2.1426	NY 90800 27399	Stepping stones over stream
75	136	54.6496	-2.1734	NY 88813 28300	Bridge, keep left
76	137	54.6488	-2.2135	NY 86223 28221	Rotting wagon at Bracken Rigg
77	138	54.6635	-2.2243	NY 85535 29864	Stone step stile in wall
77	139	54.6637	-2.2459	NY 84238 29870	Bench beside stile in wall
78	140	54.6519	-2.2623	NY 83078 28576	Duckboards
78	141	54.6478	-2.2742	NY 82307 28127	Large cairn
78	142	54.6494	-2.2985	NY 80743 28304	Barn beside path
79	143	54.6480	-2.3018	NY 80622 28138	Cattle grid
79	144	54.6405	-2.3175	NY 79606 27311	Old spoil tip on Moss Shop
79	145	54.6376	-2.3441	NY 77888 26997	Signpost: bear left; descend off track
80	146	54.6357	-2.3562	NY 77106 26792	Waterfall
80	147	54.6357	-2.3636	NY 76628 26791	Maize Beck Bridge
80	148	54.6347	-2.3724	NY 76059 26683	Red stone milepost
80	149	54.6333	-2.3865	NY 75148 26532	Milepost
81	150	54.6309	-2.3921	NY 74788 26264	Fallen milestone
81	151	54.6299	-2.3931	NY 74720 26156	Marker stone with yellow arrow
81	152	54.6298	-2.4012	NY 74197 26148	Milestone at junction of paths
81	153	54.6270	-2.4101	NY 73525 25858	Two streams
81	154	54.6259	-2.4122	NY 73388 25733	Way marker
82	155	54.6193	-2.4316	NY 72130 25008	Walled enclosure
82	156	54.6195	-2.4505	NY 70913 25038	Barn beside path

Map	GPS	Lat	Long	OS Grid Ref	Description (what3words on p273)
Maize Beck alternative route (Maps 80-81)					
80	672	54.6357	-2.3636	NY 76628 26791	Maize Beck Bridge
80	673	54.6351	-2.3832	NY 75265 26745	Cross stream near beck
81	674	54.6376	-2.3904	NY 74899 27012	Old footbridge
81	675	54.6327	-2.3970	NY 74375 26483	Limestone outcrops
81	676	54.6298	-2.4012	NY 74197 26148	Milestone at junction of paths
Dufton to Alston (Maps 83-94)					
83	157	54.6375	-2.4800	NY 69020 27051	Halsteads (ruin)
84	158	54.6485	-2.4693	NY 69722 28266	Pennine Way fingerpost
84	159	54.6516	-2.4654	NY 69977 28606	Nature reserve sign
84	160	54.6539	-2.4574	NY 70495 28861	Two cairns
85	161	54.6571	-2.4476	NY 71129 29213	Big cairn (possibly an old ruin)
85	162	54.6607	-2.4436	NY 71388 29611	Milepost
85	163	54.6621	-2.4402	NY 71610 29772	Milepost
85	164	54.6637	-2.4390	NY 71686 29943	Milepost
85	165	54.6640	-2.4389	NY 71691 29980	Flooded hole
85	166	54.6651	-2.4353	NY 71924 30096	Knock Old Man cairn
85	167	54.6665	-2.4334	NY 72046 30254	Knock Fell cairn
85	168	54.6695	-2.4349	NY 71956 30594	Slabs
85	169	54.6726	-2.4355	NY 71917 30934	Tiny tarns
85	170	54.6770	-2.4397	NY 71652 31423	PW meets access road
85	171	54.6787	-2.4414	NY 71542 31615	Path leaves access road
85	172	54.6803	-2.4453	NY 71289 31794	Flat-topped rock
86	173	54.6833	-2.4493	NY 71038 32129	Radar station on Great Dun Fell
86	174	54.6855	-2.4522	NY 70851 32379	Slabs start
86	175	54.6914	-2.4603	NY 70330 33042	Little Dun Fell summit
86	176	54.6974	-2.4695	NY 69745 33707	Nature reserve sign
87	177	54.7011	-2.4767	NY 69284 34123	Tall cairn
87	178	54.7022	-2.4816	NY 68968 34247	Bell-shaped cairn
87	179	54.7029	-2.4868	NY 68633 34329	Cross Fell summit
87	180	54.7048	-2.4873	NY 68604 34539	Bell-shaped cairn
87	181	54.7082	-2.4901	NY 68425 34923	Flat-topped rock
87	182	54.7108	-2.4921	NY 68300 35213	Cairn at track
87	183	54.7128	-2.4814	NY 68985 35429	Greg's Hut
88	184	54.7174	-2.4690	NY 69793 35929	Ruin
88	185	54.7168	-2.4498	NY 71025 35864	Cross stream
89	186	54.7181	-2.4457	NY 71290 35997	Old mine workings
89	187	54.7185	-2.4441	NY 71398 36048	Stone marker; PW straight on
89	188	54.7214	-2.4406	NY 71624 36366	Gate in fence
89	189	54.7255	-2.4369	NY 71864 36817	Track joins from west
89	190	54.7272	-2.4360	NY 71924 37009	Track joins from east
89	191	54.7420	-2.4310	NY 72254 38659	Gate
90	192	54.7513	-2.4210	NY 72903 39681	Gate between walls
92	193	54.7780	-2.4249	NY 72670 42663	Two stiles – take riverside one
92	194	54.7800	-2.4301	NY 72338 42883	3-way signpost by the river
93	195	54.7827	-2.4340	NY 72088 43190	Plank bridge
93	196	54.7848	-2.4388	NY 71783 43418	Stile in wall by line of trees
93	197	54.7976	-2.4411	NY 71642 44848	Footbridge
93	198	54.8033	-2.4418	NY 71600 45478	Small kissing gate after stream

Map	GPS	Lat	Long	OS Grid Ref	Description (what3words on p273)

Alston to Greenhead (Maps 94-102)

Map	GPS	Lat	Long	OS Grid Ref	Description
94	199	54.8205	-2.4566	NY 70662 47397	Wide farm gate
95	200	54.8211	-2.4651	NY 70116 47470	Kissing gate in the wall
95	201	54.8306	-2.4794	NY 69208 48531	Whitley Castle information board
96	202	54.8511	-2.4862	NY 68789 50813	Short ladder stile in wall
96	203	54.8574	-2.4899	NY 68551 51522	Gate in right-hand corner of field
97	204	54.8703	-2.5122	NY 67132 52968	Gate after tunnel under old railway
97	205	54.8735	-2.5146	NY 66981 53319	Wide gate beside fingerpost
97	206	54.8831	-2.5076	NY 67436 54384	Go under viaduct and turn left
98	207	54.8875	-2.5123	NY 67142 54876	Leave track to right (Maiden Way)
98	208	54.8914	-2.5120	NY 67160 55311	Keep right at fork
98	209	54.8937	-2.5116	NY 67192 55574	Two stiles
98	210	54.9049	-2.5158	NY 67024 56809	Stile and dog hatch
98	211	54.9159	-2.5195	NY 66704 58045	Duckboards either side of stile in fence
99	212	54.9187	-2.5208	NY 66621 58353	Left over fence at stile
99	213	54.9211	-2.5267	NY 66244 58620	A689 road crossing
99	214	54.9243	-2.5282	NY 66154 58981	Slab bridge over stream
99	215	54.9323	-2.5303	NY 66021 59871	High House ruin
99	216	54.9345	-2.5286	NY 66134 60122	Footbridge over stream
99	217	54.9357	-2.5292	NY 66098 60249	Top of wooded bank
99	218	54.9373	-2.5336	NY 65814 60435	Through gate beside fingerpost
100	219	54.9404	-2.5397	NY 65425 60775	Farm gate in wall
100	220	54.9409	-2.5411	NY 65342 60840	Gate where PW leaves farm track
100	221	54.9483	-2.5434	NY 65198 61655	Miniature ladder stile in fence
100	222	54.9495	-2.5461	NY 65029 61798	Keep left at faint fork in path
100	223	54.9513	-2.5558	NY 64409 61997	PW guide post beside fence
100	224	54.9539	-2.5559	NY 64400 62290	Footbridge
100	225	54.9580	-2.5563	NY 64378 62744	Ladder stile in wall
100	226	54.9656	-2.5600	NY 64148 63592	Ladder stile
101	227	54.9696	-2.5624	NY 64001 64044	Stile with acorn marker
101	228	54.9731	-2.5616	NY 64054 64428	Gate with fingerpost beside it
101	229	54.9731	-2.5451	NY 65110 64424	Join track at fingerpost
102	230	54.9824	-2.5459	NY 65066 65455	Gate in fence
102	231	54.9860	-2.5432	NY 65246 65850	Cross onto golf course

Greenhead to Bellingham (Maps 102-112)

Map	GPS	Lat	Long	OS Grid Ref	Description
102	232	54.9878	-2.5256	NY 66371 66048	Stile through wall
102	233	54.9906	-2.5094	NY 67412 66350	Milecastle 45a
103	234	54.9949	-2.4939	NY 68406 66824	Ladder stile
103	235	54.9933	-2.5010	NY 67951 66643	Ladder stile with acorn marker
103	236	54.9954	-2.4787	NY 69377 66872	Ladder stile before woods
104	237	54.9927	-2.4520	NY 71085 66556	Cross stile onto road
104	238	54.9957	-2.4281	NY 72615 66882	Kissing gate at road
104	239	54.9999	-2.4120	NY 73649 67339	Gate in wall
105	240	55.0020	-2.4046	NY 74120 67571	Winshield Crags trig point
106	241	55.0117	-2.3441	NY 77997 68633	Ladder stile in wall
107	242	55.0258	-2.3452	NY 77933 70207	Second guide post
107	243	55.0305	-2.3460	NY 77884 70731	Join forestry track
107	244	55.0411	-2.3443	NY 77999 71902	Leave track
108	245	55.0489	-2.3378	NY 78422 72773	Leave trees for open land
108	246	55.0566	-2.3197	NY 79581 73622	Kissing gate at edge of logged area
109	247	55.0648	-2.3166	NY 79781 74538	Cross forestry track

Map	GPS	Lat	Long	OS Grid Ref	Description (what3words on p273)
					Greenhead to Bellingham (Maps 102-112) *(cont'd)*
109	248	55.0746	-2.3089	NY 80281 75618	Start of old diversion
109	249	55.0813	-2.2983	NY 80959 76367	Waterfall
109	250	55.0873	-2.2949	NY 81176 77025	Left at guide post through gate
110	251	55.0978	-2.2888	NY 81573 78202	Guide post beside trees
111	252	55.1124	-2.2692	NY 82831 79815	Lovely riverside spot
111	253	55.1241	-2.2570	NY 83614 81114	Leave track into rough pasture
111	254	55.1344	-2.2555	NY 83713 82257	Jump across stream
					Bellingham to Byrness (Maps 112-120)
112	255	55.1542	-2.2415	NY 84611 84466	Guide post
112	256	55.1598	-2.2437	NY 84477 85088	Fingerpost by wide wooden gate
113	257	55.1677	-2.2431	NY 84518 85968	Path over pipe
113	258	55.1801	-2.2469	NY 84279 87343	Stile onto farm track
113	259	55.1852	-2.2516	NY 83981 87910	Guidepost
114	260	55.1914	-2.2495	NY 84120 88600	Guidepost beside path
114	261	55.1985	-2.2470	NY 84282 89387	Fallen guidepost
114	262	55.2063	2.2506	NY 84051 90257	Deer Play summit
114	263	55.2086	-2.2544	NY 83809 90514	Guidepost with white band
115	264	55.2129	-2.2609	NY 83402 91003	Concrete bridge over Black Sike
115	265	55.2151	-2.2698	NY 82833 91248	Whitley Pike summit
115	266	55.2164	-2.2724	NY 82672 91387	Slabs start
116	267	55.2351	-2.2935	NY 81338 93474	Wall at base of climb
116	268	55.2429	-2.2901	NY 81554 94340	Wall ends, bear left along fence
117	269	55.2542	-2.3182	NY 79773 95603	Through gate onto forestry road
117	270	55.2612	-2.3197	NY 79686 96389	Leave forestry road at green sign
117	271	55.2668	-2.3229	NY 79481 97009	Rejoin forestry road
118	272	55.2789	-2.3332	NY 78835 98366	Young plantation
119	273	55.2965	-2.3403	NT 78394 00326	Leave road and into trees
119	274	55.3019	-2.3466	NT 78000 00924	Cross footbridge
119	275	55.3051	-2.3506	NT 77745 01281	Access to Border Forest Holiday Park
					Byrness to Kirk Yetholm (Maps 120-135)
120	276	55.3231	-2.3570	NT 77347 03289	Byrness Hill summit cairn
121	277	55.3382	-2.3585	NT 77264 04968	Slabs start over boggy section
121	278	55.3495	-2.3483	NT 77916 06220	Ravens Knowe summit
122	279	55.3625	-2.3549	NT 77601 07673	Cross into Scotland
122	280	55.3671	-2.3506	NT 77782 08184	3-way (alternative route) fingerpost
123	281	55.3725	-2.3372	NT 78635 08782	Guide post, watch for change of direction
123	282	55.3887	-2.3351	NT 78771 10575	Green sign
124	283	55.3944	-2.3359	NT 78724 11209	Cross stream
124	284	55.3992	-2.3347	NT 78807 11746	Cairn
124	285	55.4021	-2.3308	NT 79056 12072	Guide post
124	286	55.4054	-2.3254	NT 79398 12437	Slabs over stream
125	287	55.4067	-2.3133	NT 80163 12579	Turn corner to left
125	288	55.4095	-2.3109	NT 80314 12892	Refuge hut at foot of Lamb Hill
125	289	55.4135	-2.3007	NT 80961 13334	Lamb Hill trig point
125	290	55.4198	-2.2939	NT 81399 14031	Slabs again
126	291	55.4286	-2.2721	NT 82780 15003	Mozzie Law summit
126	292	55.4285	-2.2624	NT 83394 14985	Stile & gate by 4-way fingerpost
127	293	55.4307	-2.2359	NT 85076 15232	Gate and stile in fence
127	294	55.4306	-2.2300	NT 85446 15212	Russell's Cairn
127	295	55.4335	-2.2207	NT 86036 15534	Enormous pile of stones

MAP	GPS	LAT	LONG	OS GRID REF	DESCRIPTION (WHAT3WORDS ON P273)
Byrness to Kirk Yetholm (Maps 120-135) *(cont'd)*					
128	296	55.4380	-2.2049	NT 87035 16030	4-way fingerpost at Clennell Street
129	297	55.4454	-2.1941	NT 87722 16850	Stile in fence
129	298	55.4498	-2.1930	NT 87793 17344	King's Seat trig point
130	299	55.4666	-2.1709	NT 89192 19216	Outcrop of rock with memorial plaque
130	300	55.4680	-2.1662	NT 89495 19364	Corner of path to summit
130	301	55.4724	-2.1741	NT 88998 19859	Auchope Cairn
131	302	55.4752	-2.1961	NT 87608 20169	Auchope Hill refuge hut
131	303	55.4839	-2.2052	NT 87036 21139	Saddle
131	304	55.4949	-2.2082	NT 86848 22371	Access to The Schil summit
132	305	55.5033	-2.2174	NT 86271 23301	Stile over wall
132	306	55.5053	-2.2243	NT 85835 23524	Low- & high-level routes divide
132	307	55.5122	-2.2365	NT 85063 24301	Gate in wall
132	308	55.5206	-2.2360	NT 85103 25228	Old Halterburn ruin
134	309	55.5424	-2.2559	NT 83854 27665	High route rejoins from right

APPENDIX C: TAKING A DOG

Many are the rewards that await those prepared to make the extra effort required to bring their best friend along the trail. You shouldn't underestimate the amount of work involved, though. Indeed, just about every decision you make will be influenced by the fact that you've got a dog. If you're also sure your dog can cope with (and will enjoy) walking 12 miles or (significantly) more a day for several days in a row, you need to start preparing accordingly. You also need to be sure that your dog will be able to negotiate the many stiles on the path – or that you'll be able to lift them over if they can't! Extra thought also needs to go into your itinerary. Study the village facilities table on pp34-7 (and the advice on p32).

Looking after your dog
To begin with, you need to make sure that your own dog is fully **inoculated** against the usual doggy illnesses, and also up to date with regard to **worm pills** (eg Drontal) and **flea preventatives** such as Frontline. **Pet insurance** is also a very good idea; if you've already got insurance, do check that it will cover a trip such as this. Perhaps the most important implement you can take with you is the **plastic tick remover**. While fiddly to use, these do help you to remove the tick safely (ie without leaving its head behind buried under the dog's skin).

Being in unfamiliar territory makes it more likely that you and your dog could become separated. All dogs in the UK must, by law, be microchipped, but you should also make sure your dog has a **tag with your contact details on it** (your mobile phone number is best).

When to keep your dog on a lead
● **When crossing farmland**, particularly in the lambing season (March to May) when your dog can scare the sheep, causing them to lose their young. Farmers are allowed by law to shoot at and kill any dogs that they consider are worrying their sheep. During lambing, most farmers would prefer it if you didn't take your dog at all. The exception is if your dog is being attacked by cows (see box opposite).

● **On National Trust land**, where it is compulsory to keep your dog on a lead.

● **Around ground-nesting birds** It's important to keep your dog under control when crossing an area where certain species of birds nest on the ground. Most dogs love foraging around in the woods but make sure you have permission to do so; some woods are used as 'nurseries' for game birds and dogs are only allowed through them if they are on a lead.

❏ WALKING THROUGH FIELDS OF CATTLE

The Pennine Wayfarer will meet cattle almost every day of the walk; there will be dozens of encounters with these large, mostly docile creatures and the vast majority of people will complete the walk without any adverse incident at all. However, there are very rare cases of walkers being attacked by cattle. Cows are most nervous when they see a dog in their field and this can be heightened significantly if they have calves with them. In some cases cows will approach you, or follow you, through curiosity or in the expectation of food, but they usually keep a respectable distance from you. Ramblers (see box p50) offer the following guidelines:

● Try not to get between cows and their calves
● Be prepared for cattle to react to your presence, especially if a dog is with you
● Move quickly and quietly, and if possible walk around the herd
● Keep your dog close and under effective control, ideally on a lead
● If you are threatened by cattle, let your dog go as the cattle will chase the dog
● Don't put yourself at risk, find another way round the cattle and rejoin the footpath as soon as possible
● Don't panic or run, most cattle will stop before they reach you, if they follow just walk on quietly.

● **On hill and mountain tops** It's a sad fact that, every year, a few dogs lose their lives falling over the edge of steep slopes. It usually occurs when they are chasing rabbits (which know where the edge is and are able, unlike your poor pooch, to stop in time).

What to pack

● **Food/water bowl** Foldable cloth bowls are popular with walkers, being light and taking up little room in the rucksack. You can get also get a water-bottle-and-bowl combination, where the bottle folds into a 'trough' from which the dog can drink.
● **Lead and collar** An extendable one is probably preferable for this sort of trip. Make sure both lead and collar are in good condition – you don't want either to snap on the trail, or you may end up carrying your dog through sheep fields until a replacement can be found.
● **Bedding** A simple blanket may suffice
● **Food/water** Bring treats as well as regular food to keep up your mutt's morale
● **Medication** You'll know if you need to bring any lotions or potions.
● **Tick remover** See opposite.   ● **Poo bags** Essential   ● **Raingear & old towel**
● **Hygiene wipes** For cleaning your dog after it's rolled in stuff.
● **A favourite toy** Helps prevent your dog from pining for the entire walk.
● **Corkscrew stake** Available from camping or pet shops, this will help you to keep your dog secure in one place while you set up camp/doze.

When packing, I always leave an exterior pocket of my rucksack empty so I can put used poo bags in there (for deposit at the first bin reached). I like to keep all the dog's kit together and separate from the other luggage (usually inside a plastic bag inside my rucksack). I have also seen several dogs sporting their own 'doggy rucksack', so they can carry their own food, water, poo etc – which certainly reduces the burden on their owner!

Cleaning up after your dog

It is extremely important that dog owners behave in a responsible way when walking the path. Dog excrement should be cleaned up. In towns, villages and fields where animals graze or which will be cut for silage, hay etc, you need to pick up and bag the excrement.

Staying (and eating) with your dog

In this guide we have used the symbol 🐕 to denote where a place welcomes dogs. However, this must always be arranged in advance. Many B&B-style places have only one or two rooms suitable for people with dogs; hostels do not usually permit them unless they are an assistance (guide) dog; smaller campsites tend to accept them, but some of the larger holiday parks do not – however, in either case it is likely the dog will have to be on a lead. Before you turn up always double check whether the place you would like to stay accepts dogs and whether there is space for them.

When it comes to **eating**, some cafés accept dogs and most landlords allow dogs in at least a section of their pubs, though few restaurants do. Make sure you always ask first and ensure your dog is on a lead and secured to your table or a radiator so it doesn't run around.

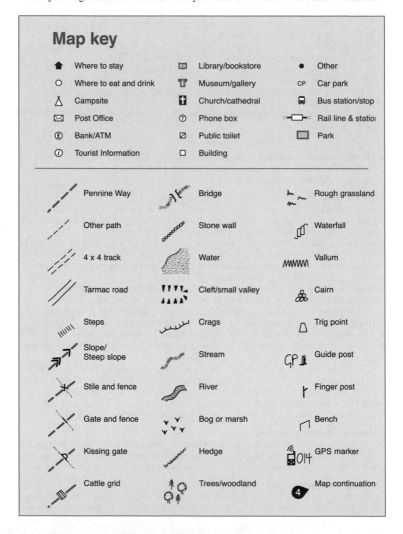

Map key

♠ Where to stay	📖 Library/bookstore	● Other
○ Where to eat and drink	🏛 Museum/gallery	CP Car park
Λ Campsite	🕇 Church/cathedral	🚌 Bus station/stop
⊠ Post Office	☉ Phone box	—■— Rail line & station
ⓔ Bank/ATM	☑ Public toilet	▭ Park
ⓘ Tourist Information	▢ Building	

Pennine Way	Bridge	Rough grassland
Other path	Stone wall	Waterfall
4 x 4 track	Water	Vallum
Tarmac road	Cleft/small valley	Cairn
Steps	Crags	Trig point
Slope/Steep slope	Stream	Guide post
Stile and fence	River	Finger post
Gate and fence	Bog or marsh	Bench
Kissing gate	Hedge	GPS marker
Cattle grid	Trees/woodland	Map continuation

INDEX

Page references in red refer to maps

Opposite: The last two days of the Pennine Way (see pp258-70) wind through some of the wildest and least populated sections of the trail. After reaching the safe haven of Byrness it's a two-day (or extremely long single day) push over the magnificently empty Cheviot Hills, along the border with Scotland. **Above**: View down into Carlcroft Burn from Mozie Law. **Below, left**: Yearning Saddle Refuge Hut on Lamb Hill (p263). **Below, right**: Descending to Auchope Refuge Hut in the wild and woolly Cheviots: just seven miles to go!

	Edale	Upper Booth	Torside	Crowden	Standedge	Blackstone Edge	Mankinholes	Calder Valley	Blackshaw Head	Colden	Widdop	Ponden/Stanbury	Ickornshaw	Lothersdale	East Marton	Gargrave	Airton	Kirkby Malham
Edale	0																	
Upper Booth	1.5																	
Torside	15	13.5																
Crowden	16	14.5	1															
Standedge	27	25.5	12	11														
Blackstone Edge	32.5	31	17.5	16.5	5.5													
Mankinholes	38.5	37	23.5	22.5	11.5	6												
Calder Valley	41.5	40	26.5	25.5	14.5	9	3											
Blackshaw Head	43	41.5	28	27	16	10.5	4.5	1.5										
Colden	43.5	42	28.5	27.5	16.5	11	5	2	0.5									
Widdop	46	44.5	31	30	19	13.5	7.5	4.5	3	2.5								
Ponden/Stanbury	52	50.5	37	36	25	19.5	13.5	10.5	9	8.5	6							
Ickornshaw	57	55.5	42	41	30	24.5	18.5	15.5	14	13.5	11	5						
Lothersdale	59.5	58	44.5	43.5	32.5	27	21	18	16.5	16	13.5	7.5	2.5					
East Marton	65.5	64	50.5	49.5	38.5	33	27	24	22.5	22	19.5	13.5	8.5	6				
Gargrave	68	66.5	53	52	41	35.5	29.5	26.5	25	24.5	22	16	11	8.5	2.5			
Airton	72	70.5	57	56	45	39.5	33.5	30.5	29	28.5	26	20	15	12.5	6.5	4		
Kirkby Malham	73.5	72	58.5	57.5	46.5	41	35	32	30.5	30	27.5	21.5	16.5	14	8	5.5	1.5	
Malham	74.5	73	59.5	58.5	47.5	42	36	33	31.5	31	28.5	22.5	17.5	15	9	6.5	2.5	1
Horton-in-R'dle	89	87.5	74	73	62	56.5	50.5	47.5	46	45.5	43	37	32	29.5	23.5	21	17	15.5
Hawes	102.5	101	87.5	86.5	75.5	70	64	61	59.5	59	56.5	50.5	45.5	43	37	34.5	30.5	29
Hardraw	104	102.5	89	88	77	71.5	65.5	62.5	61	60.5	58	52	47	44.5	38.5	36	32	30.5
Thwaite	112	110.5	97	96	85	79.5	73.5	70.5	69	68.5	66	60	55	52.5	46.5	44	40	38.5
Keld	115	113.5	100	99	88	82.5	76.5	73.5	72	71.5	69	63	58	55.5	49.5	47	43	41.5
Tan Hill	119	117.5	104	103	92	86.5	80.5	77.5	76	75.5	73	67	62	59.5	53.5	51	47	45.5
Baldersdale	129	127.5	114	113	102	96.5	90.5	87.5	86	85.5	83	77	72	69.5	63.5	61	57	55.5
Lunedale	132	130.5	117	116	105	99.5	93.5	90.5	89	88.5	86	80	75	72.5	66.5	64	60	58.5
Middleton-in-T	135.5	134	120.5	119.5	108.5	103	97	94	92.5	92	89.5	83.5	78.5	76	70	67.5	63.5	62
Holwick	138	136.5	123	122	111	105.5	99.5	96.5	95	94.5	92	86	81	78.5	72.5	70	66	64.5
High Force	140.5	139	125.5	124.5	113.5	108	102	99	97.5	97	94.5	88.5	83.5	81	75	72.5	68.5	67
Dufton	155	153.5	140	139	128	122.5	116.5	113.5	112	111.5	109	103	98	95.5	89.5	87	83	81.5
Garrigill	170.5	169	155.5	154.5	143.5	138	132	129	127.5	127	124.5	118.5	113.5	111	105	102.5	98.5	97
Alston	174.5	173	159.5	158.5	147.5	142	136	133	131.5	131	128.5	122.5	117.5	115	109	106.5	102.5	101
Knarsdale	181.5	180	166.5	165.5	154.5	149	143	140	138.5	138	135.5	129.5	124.5	122	116	113.5	109.5	108
Greenhead	191	189.5	176	175	164	158.5	152.5	149.5	148	147.5	145	139	134	131.5	125.5	123	119	117.5
Burnhead	195	193.5	180	179	168	162.5	156.5	153.5	152	151.5	149	143	138	135.5	129.5	127	123	121.5
Once Brewed	197.5	196	182.5	181.5	170.5	165	159	156	154.5	154	151.5	145.5	140.5	138	132	129.5	125.5	124
Hetherington	208	206.5	193	192	181	175.5	169.5	166.5	165	164.5	162	156	151	148.5	142.5	140	136	134.5
Bellingham	212.5	211	197.5	196.5	185.5	180	174	171	169.5	169	166.5	160.5	155.5	153	147	144.5	140.5	139
Byrness	227.5	226	212.5	211.5	200.5	195	189	186	184.5	184	181.5	175.5	170.5	168	162	159.5	155.5	154
Kirk Yetholm	253	251.5	238	237	226	220.5	214.5	211.5	210	209.5	207	201	196	193.5	187.5	185	181	179.5

Pennine Way
DISTANCE CHART

miles (approx)

	Malham	Horton-in-Ribblesdale	Hawes	Hardraw	Thwaite	Keld	Tan Hill	Baldersdale	Lunedale	Middleton-in-Teesdale	Holwick	High Force	Dufton	Garrigill	Alston	Knarsdale	Greenhead	Burnhead	Once Brewed	Hetherington	Bellingham	Byrness
Horton-in-Ribblesdale	14.5																					
Hawes	28	13.5																				
Hardraw	29.5	15	1.5																			
Thwaite	37.5	23	9.5	8																		
Keld	40.5	26	12.5	11	3																	
Tan Hill	44.5	30	16.5	15	7	4																
Baldersdale	54.5	40	26.5	25	17	14	10															
Lunedale	57.5	43	29.5	28	20	17	13	3														
Middleton-in-Teesdale	61	46.5	33	31.5	23.5	20.5	16.5	6.5	3.5													
Holwick	63.5	49	35.5	34	26	23	19	9	6	2.5												
High Force	66	51.5	38	36.5	28.5	25.5	21.5	11.5	8.5	5	2.5											
Dufton	80.5	66	52.5	51	43	40	36	26	23	19.5	17	14.5										
Garrigill	96	81.5	68	66.5	58.5	55.5	51.5	41.5	38.5	35	32.5	30	15.5									
Alston	100	85.5	72	70.5	62.5	59.5	55.5	45.5	42.5	39	36.5	34	19.5	4								
Knarsdale	107	92.5	79	77.5	69.5	66.5	62.5	52.5	49.5	46	43.5	41	26.5	11	7							
Greenhead	116.5	102	88.5	87	79	76	72	62	59	55.5	53	50.5	36	20.5	16.5	9.5						
Burnhead	120.5	106	92.5	91	83	80	76	66	63	59.5	57	54.5	40	24.5	20.5	13.5	4					
Once Brewed	123	108.5	95	93.5	85.5	82.5	78.5	68.5	65.5	62	59.5	57	42.5	27	23	16	6.5	2.5				
Hetherington	133.5	119	105.5	104	96	93	89	79	76	72.5	70	67.5	53	37.5	33.5	26.5	17	13	10.5			
Bellingham	138	123.5	110	108.5	100.5	97.5	93.5	83.5	80.5	77	74.5	72	57.5	42	38	31	21.5	17.5	15	4.5		
Byrness	153	138.5	125	123.5	115.5	112.5	108.5	98.5	95.5	92	89.5	87	72.5	57	53	46	36.5	32.5	30	19.5	15	
Kirk Yetholm	178.5	164	150.5	149	141	138	134	124	121	117.5	115	112.5	98	82.5	78.5	71.5	62	58	55.5	45	40.5	25.5

TRAILBLAZER'S BRITISH WALKING GUIDES

We've applied to destinations which are closer to home Trailblazer's proven formula for publishing definitive practical route guides for adventurous travellers. Britain's network of long-distance trails enables the walker to explore some of the finest landscapes in the country's best walking areas. These are guides that are user-friendly, practical, informative and environmentally sensitive.

● **Unique mapping features** In many walking guidebooks the reader has to read a route description then try to relate it to the map. Our guides are much easier to use because walking directions, tricky junctions, places to stay and eat, points of interest and walking times are all written onto the maps themselves in the places to which they apply. With their un-cluttered clarity, these are not general-purpose maps but fully edited maps drawn by walkers for walkers.

'The same attention to detail that distinguishes its other guides has been brought to bear here'.

THE
SUNDAY TIMES

● **Largest-scale walking maps** At a scale of just under 1:20,000 (8cm or 3⅛ inches to one mile) the maps in these guides are bigger than even the most detailed British walking maps currently available in the shops.

● **Not just a trail guide – includes where to stay, where to eat and public transport** Our guidebooks cover the complete walking experience, not just the route. Accommodation options for all budgets are provided (pubs, hotels, B&Bs, campsites, bunkhouses, hostels) as well as places to eat. Detailed public transport information for all access points to each trail means that there are itineraries for all walkers, for hiking the entire route as well as for day or weekend walks.

Cleveland Way *Henry Stedman*, 1st edn, ISBN 978-1-905864-91-1, 240pp, 98 maps

Coast to Coast *Henry Stedman*, 10th edn, ISBN 978-1-912716-25-8, 268pp, 109 maps

Cornwall Coast Path (SW Coast Path Pt 2) *Stedman & Newton*, 7th edn, ISBN 978-1-912716-26-5, 352pp, 142 maps

Cotswold Way *Tricia & Bob Hayne*, 4th edn, ISBN 978-1-912716-04-3, 204pp, 53 maps

Dales Way *Henry Stedman*, 2nd edn, ISBN 978-1-912716-30-2, 192pp, 50 maps

Dorset & South Devon (SW Coast Path Pt 3) *Stedman & Newton*, 3rd edn, ISBN 978-1-912716-34-0, 340pp, 97 maps

Exmoor & North Devon (SW Coast Path Pt I) *Stedman & Newton*, 3rd edn, ISBN 978-1-9912716-24-1, 224pp, 68 maps

Glyndŵr's Way *Chris Scott,* 1st edn, ISBN 978-1-912716-32-6, 220pp, 70 maps (**mid 2023**)

Great Glen Way *Jim Manthorpe*, 2nd edn, ISBN 978-1-912716-10-4, 184pp, 50 maps

Hadrian's Wall Path *Henry Stedman*, 7th edn, ISBN 978-1-912716-37-1, 250pp, 60 maps

London LOOP *Henry Stedman*, 1st edn, ISBN 978-1-912716-21-0, 236pp, 60 maps

Norfolk Coast Path & Peddars Way *Alexander Stewart*, 1st edn, ISBN 978-1-905864-98-0, 224pp, 75 maps

North Downs Way *Henry Stedman*, 2nd edn, ISBN 978-1-905864-90-4, 240pp, 98 maps

Offa's Dyke Path *Keith Carter*, 5th edn, ISBN 978-1-912716-03-6, 268pp, 98 maps

Pembrokeshire Coast Path *Jim Manthorpe*, 6th edn, 978-1-912716-13-5, 236pp, 96 maps

Pennine Way *Stuart Greig & Bradley Mayhew*, 6th edn, 978-1-912716-33-3, 272pp, 138 maps

The Ridgeway *Nick Hill*, 5th edn, ISBN 978-1-912716-20-3, 208pp, 53 maps

South Downs Way *Jim Manthorpe*, 7th edn, ISBN 978-1-912716-23-4, 204pp, 60 maps

Thames Path *Joel Newton*, 3rd edn, ISBN 978-1-912716-27-2, 256pp, 99 maps

West Highland Way *Charlie Loram*, 8th edn, ISBN 978-1-912716-29-6, 224pp, 60 maps

'The Trailblazer series stands head, shoulders, waist and ankles above the rest.
They are particularly strong on mapping ...'
THE SUNDAY TIMES

TRAILBLAZER
British Walking Guides
SEE OPPOSITE FOR FULL TITLE LIST

West Highland WAY

Hadrian's Wall PATH

Coast to Coast PATH

Glyndŵr's WAY

EXMOOR & North Devon COAST PATH

Cornwall COAST PATH

Scottish Highlands Hillwalking Guide

Great Glen Way

Thurso

Orkney

Stornoway

Skye

Inverness

Aberdeen

Fort William

SCOTLAND

Mull

West Highland Way

Milngavie

Glasgow

Edinburgh

Berwick upon Tweed

Kirk Yetholm

Arran

Pennine Way

Bowness-on-Solway

Carlisle

Hadrian's Wall Path

Wallsend

Newcastle upon Tyne

N. IRELAND

Belfast

Coast to Coast

St Bees

Bowness-on-Windermere

Dales Way

Robin Hood's Bay

Filey

Helmsley

Cleveland Way

REP. OF IRELAND

Dublin

Isle of Man

Ilkley

York

Hull

Pennine Way

Leeds

Liverpool

Manchester

Edale

Prestatyn

Bangor

Lincoln

Offa's Dyke Path

Anglesey

Nottingham

ENGLAND

Norfolk Coast Path & Peddars Way

Cromer

Norwich

Great Yarmouth

Knettishall Heath

Glyndŵr's Way

Welshpool

Knighton

Birmingham

Cotswold Way

Chipping Campden

The Ridgeway

Ivinghoe Beacon

London LOOP

Cardigan

WALES

Pembrokeshire Coast Path

Amroth

Chepstow

Kemble

Cardiff

Bristol

Bath

Overton Hill

London

Thames Path

Canterbury

Exmoor & N Devon Coast Path

Minehead

Winchester

Salisbury

Farnham

Dover

North Downs Way

Bude

Exeter

Poole

Portsmouth

Brighton

Eastbourne

Cornwall Coast Path

Plymouth

Isle of Wight

South Downs Way

Isles of Scilly

Dorset & S Devon Coast Path

ENGLISH CHANNEL

IRISH SEA

trailblazer

0   50   100km
0   25   50 miles

TRAILBLAZER TITLE LIST

Adventure Cycle-Touring Handbook
Adventure Motorcycling Handbook
Australia by Rail
Cleveland Way (British Walking Guide)
Coast to Coast (British Walking Guide)
Cornwall Coast Path (British Walking Guide)
Cotswold Way (British Walking Guide)
The Cyclist's Anthology
Dales Way (British Walking Guide)
Dorset & Sth Devon Coast Path (British Walking Gde)
Exmoor & Nth Devon Coast Path (British Walking Gde)
Glyndŵr's Way (British Walking Guide)
Great Glen Way (British Walking Guide)
Hadrian's Wall Path (British Walking Guide)
Himalaya by Bike – a route and planning guide
Iceland Hiking – with Reykjavik City Guide
Inca Trail, Cusco & Machu Picchu
Japan by Rail
Kilimanjaro – the trekking guide (includes Mt Meru)
London Loop (British Walking Guide)
London to Walsingham Camino
Madeira Walks – 37 selected day walks
Moroccan Atlas – The Trekking Guide
Morocco Overland (4x4/motorcycle/mountainbike)
Nepal Trekking & The Great Himalaya Trail
Norfolk Coast Path & Peddars Way (British Walking Gde)
North Downs Way (British Walking Guide)
Offa's Dyke Path (British Walking Guide)
Overlanders' Handbook – worldwide driving guide
Pembrokeshire Coast Path (British Walking Guide)
Pennine Way (British Walking Guide)
Peru's Cordilleras Blanca & Huayhuash – Hiking/Biking
Pilgrim Pathways: 1-2 day walks on Britain's sacred ways
The Railway Anthology
The Ridgeway (British Walking Guide)
Scottish Highlands – Hillwalking Guide
Siberian BAM Guide – rail, rivers & road
The Silk Roads – a route and planning guide
Sinai – the trekking guide
South Downs Way (British Walking Guide)
Thames Path (British Walking Guide)
Tour du Mont Blanc
Trans-Canada Rail Guide
Trans-Siberian Handbook
Trekking in the Everest Region
The Walker's Anthology
The Walker's Anthology – further tales
West Highland Way (British Walking Guide)

For more information about Trailblazer and our
expanding range of guides, for guidebook updates or
for credit card mail order sales visit our website:

trailblazer-guides.com

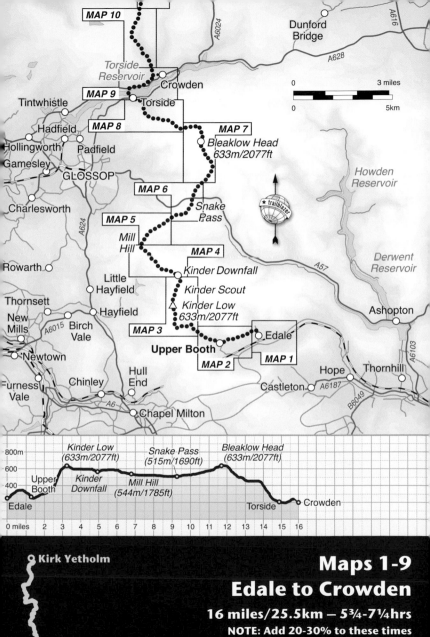

MAP 10

MAP 9

MAP 8

MAP 7

MAP 6

MAP 5

MAP 4

MAP 3

MAP 2

MAP 1

Torside
Reservoir
Crowden
Torside

Dunford
Bridge

A6024

A628

A616

Tintwhistle
Hadfield
Hollingworth
Gamesley
GLOSSOP
Padfield

Charlesworth

Rowarth

Little
Hayfield

Thornsett
New
Mills
Newtown

Birch
Vale

Hayfield

A6015

A624

Bleaklow Head
633m/2077ft

Howden
Reservoir

★ trailblazer

Snake
Pass

Mill
Hill

Kinder Downfall

Kinder Scout

Kinder Low
633m/2077ft

A57

Derwent
Reservoir

Ashopton

Upper Booth

Edale

Hull
End

Chinley

Furness
Vale

A6

Chapel Milton

Hope

Castleton

A6187

Thornhill

A6103

B6049

0   3 miles

0   5km

Elevation profile:

800m

600

400

Kinder Low
(633m/2077ft)

Snake Pass
(515m/1690ft)

Bleaklow Head
(633m/2077ft)

Upper
Booth

Kinder
Downfall

Mill Hill
(544m/1785ft)

Torside

Crowden

Edale

0 miles 2   3   4   5   6   7   8   9   10   11   12   13   14   15   16

Kirk Yetholm

Crowden

Edale

Maps 1-9
Edale to Crowden

16 miles/25.5km – 5¾-7¼hrs
NOTE: Add 20-30% to these times
to allow for stops

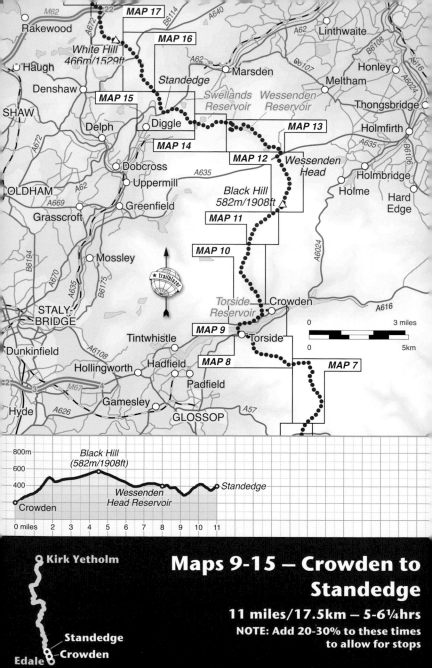

Maps 9-15 – Crowden to Standedge

11 miles/17.5km – 5-6¼hrs

NOTE: Add 20-30% to these times to allow for stops

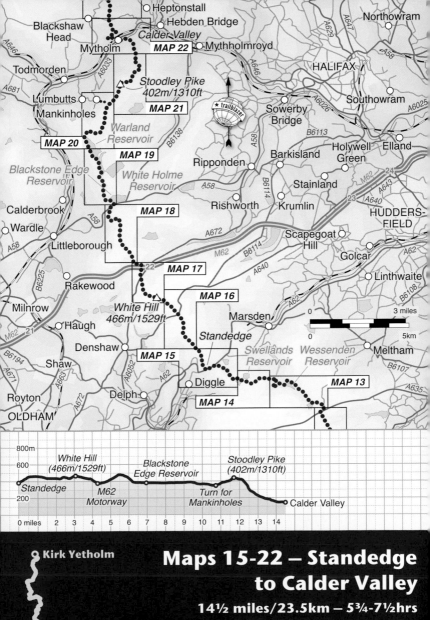

Maps 15-22 – Standedge to Calder Valley

14½ miles/23.5km – 5¾-7½hrs

NOTE: Add 20-30% to these times to allow for stops

Kirk Yetholm

Calder Valley
Standedge

Edale

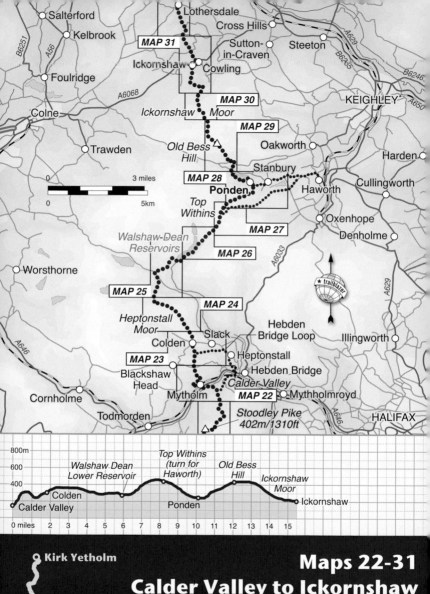

MAP 31

Salterford
Kelbrook
Foulridge
Colne
Trawden
Worsthorne

Lothersdale
Cross Hills
Sutton-in-Craven
Steeton
Cowling
Ickornshaw
KEIGHLEY

MAP 30
Ickornshaw Moor

MAP 29
Oakworth
Harden

Old Bess Hill
Stanbury
Cullingworth

MAP 28
Ponden
Haworth

Top Withins
Oxenhope
Denholme

Walshaw-Dean Reservoirs

MAP 27

MAP 26

★ trailblazer

MAP 25
Heptonstall Moor

MAP 24
Slack
Colden
Heptonstall
Hebden Bridge Loop
Illingworth

MAP 23
Blackshaw Head
Hebden Bridge
Calder Valley
Mytholm
MAP 22
Mytholmroyd

Cornholme
Todmorden
Stoodley Pike 402m/1310ft
HALIFAX

Elevation profile:
800m — 600 — 400 — 200

Top Withins (turn for Haworth)
Walshaw Dean Lower Reservoir
Old Bess Hill
Ickornshaw Moor
Colden
Calder Valley
Ponden
Ickornshaw

0 miles 2 3 4 5 6 7 8 9 10 11 12 13 14 15

Kirk Yetholm

Ickornshaw
Calder Valley

Edale

Maps 22-31
Calder Valley to Ickornshaw
15½ miles/25km – 5½-7½hrs
NOTE: Add 20-30% to these times to allow for stops

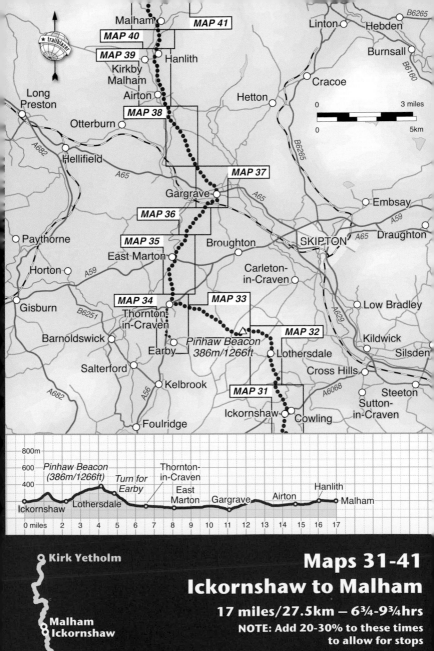

MAP 41

Malham

MAP 40

MAP 39

Hanlith

Kirkby
Malham

Airton

MAP 38

Otterburn

Linton   Hebden

B6265

Burnsall

B6160

Cracoe

Hetton

0   3 miles

0   5km

Long
Preston

Hellifield

A682

A65

MAP 37

Gargrave

A65

Embsay

A59

Draughton

Paythorne

MAP 36

SKIPTON

A65

East Marton

MAP 35

Broughton

Carleton-
in-Craven

Horton

A59

MAP 34

MAP 33

Thornton-
in-Craven

Pinhaw Beacon
386m/1266ft

Low Bradley

A629

Gisburn

B6251

Earby

Kildwick

Silsden

Barnoldswick

Salterford

Kelbrook

MAP 32

Lothersdale

Cross Hills

A6068

Steeton

Sutton-
in-Craven

MAP 31

A56

A682

Foulridge

Ickornshaw   Cowling

800m

600

Pinhaw Beacon
(386m/1266ft)

400

Thornton-
in-Craven

Turn for
Earby

Hanlith

East
Marton

Gargrave

Airton

Ickornshaw   Lothersdale   Malham

0 miles   2   3   4   5   6   7   8   9   10   11   12   13   14   15   16   17

Kirk Yetholm

Malham
Ickornshaw

Edale

Maps 31-41
Ickornshaw to Malham

17 miles/27.5km — 6¾-9¾hrs

**NOTE: Add 20-30% to these times
to allow for stops**

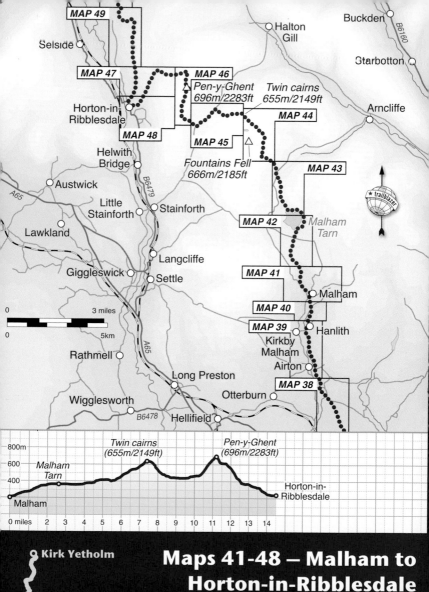

MAP 49

Buckden

Halton Gill

Selside

MAP 47

MAP 46

Pen-y-Ghent
696m/2283ft

Twin cairns
655m/2149ft

Starbotton

Horton-in-
Ribblesdale

MAP 48

MAP 45

Arncliffe

MAP 44

Helwith
Bridge

Fountains Fell
666m/2185ft

MAP 43

Austwick

A65

Little
Stainforth

Stainforth

Lawkland

★ trailblazer

MAP 42

Malham
Tarn

Langcliffe

Giggleswick

Settle

MAP 41

MAP 40

MAP 39

Malham

Hanlith

3 miles

Kirkby
Malham

0

5km

Rathmell

A65

Long Preston

Airton

MAP 38

Wigglesworth

Otterburn

B6478

Hellifield

800m
600
400

Twin cairns
(655m/2149ft)

Malham
Tarn

Pen-y-Ghent
(696m/2283ft)

Malham

Horton-in-
Ribblesdale

0 miles   2   3   4   5   6   7   8   9   10   11   12   13   14

Maps 41-48 – Malham to
Horton-in-Ribblesdale

14½ miles/23.5km – 6-8hrs

**NOTE: Add 20-30% to these times
to allow for stops**

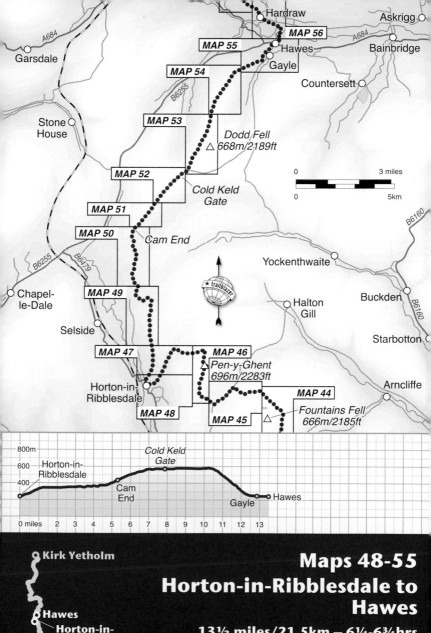

Hardraw

Askrigg

MAP 56

A684

MAP 55

Hawes

Bainbridge

Gayle

MAP 54

Countersett

A684

Garsdale

B6255

Stone
House

MAP 53

Dodd Fell
△ 668m/2189ft

B6160

MAP 52

Cold Keld
Gate

MAP 51

Yockenthwaite

Buckden

MAP 50

Cam End

B6255

B6479

Halton
Gill

Starbotton

B6160

Chapel-
le-Dale

MAP 49

Selside

MAP 47

MAP 46

Pen-y-Ghent
△ 696m/2283ft

Arncliffe

MAP 44

Horton-in-
Ribblesdale

MAP 48

MAP 45

△

Fountains Fell
666m/2185ft

★ trailblazer

800m

600

400

Horton-in-
Ribblesdale

*Cold Keld
Gate*

Cam
End

Gayle

Hawes

0 miles 2 3 4 5 6 7 8 9 10 11 12 13

0 ────── 3 miles
0 ────── 5km

Kirk Yetholm

Hawes
Horton-in-
Ribblesdale

Edale

Maps 48-55
Horton-in-Ribblesdale to
Hawes

13½ miles/21.5km – 6¼-6¾hrs

**NOTE: Add 20-30% to these times
to allow for stops**

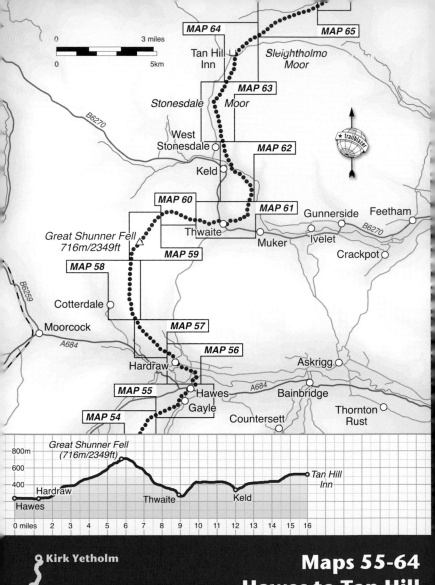

MAP 64

MAP 65

MAP 63

MAP 62

MAP 60

MAP 61

MAP 59

MAP 58

MAP 57

MAP 56

MAP 55

MAP 54

Tan Hill
Inn

*Sleightholmo
Moor*

Stonesdale Moor

West
Stonesdale

Keld

Great Shunner Fell
716m/2349ft

Gunnerside   Feetham

Thwaite

Muker   Ivelet

Crackpot

Cotterdale

Moorcock

Hardraw

Askrigg

Bainbridge

Hawes
Gayle

Countersett

Thornton
Rust

B6270

B6259

A684

0   3 miles

0   5km

Great Shunner Fell
(716m/2349ft)

800m

600

400

Hardraw   Tan Hill
                                                  Inn

Hawes   Thwaite   Keld

0 miles 2 3 4 5 6 7 8 9 10 11 12 13 14 15 16

Kirk Yetholm

Tan Hill
Hawes

Edale

Maps 55-64
Hawes to Tan Hill

16 miles/25.5km – 8-10hrs
NOTE: Add 20-30% to these times
to allow for stops

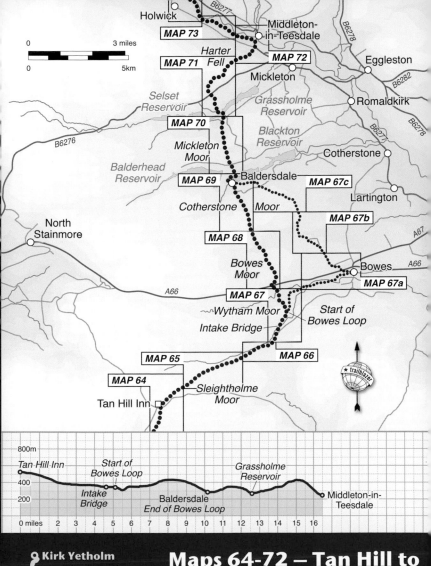

Holwick

B6277

MAP 73

Middleton-in-Teesdale

MAP 72

B6278

Harter Fell

MAP 71

Mickleton

Eggleston

B6282

Selset Reservoir

Grassholme Reservoir

Romaldkirk

B6276

MAP 70

Blackton Reservoir

B6277

B6278

Mickleton Moor

Balderhead Reservoir

MAP 69

Baldersdale

MAP 67c

Cotherstone

Lartington

Cotherstone Moor

MAP 67b

North Stainmore

MAP 68

A67

Bowes Moor

Bowes

A66

A66

MAP 67

MAP 67a

Wytham Moor

Start of Bowes Loop

Intake Bridge

MAP 65

MAP 66

★ trailblazer

MAP 64

Sleightholme Moor

Tan Hill Inn

0 miles   3 miles
0   5km

800m

Tan Hill Inn

Start of Bowes Loop

Grassholme Reservoir

400

Intake Bridge

Baldersdale End of Bowes Loop

Middleton-in-Teesdale

200

0 miles 2 3 4 5 6 7 8 9 10 11 12 13 14 15 16

○ **Kirk Yetholm**

○ **Middleton-in-Teesdale**

○ **Tan Hill**

○ **Edale**

Maps 64-72 – Tan Hill to Middleton-in-Teesdale

16½ miles/26.5km – 7¼-9¾hrs

Maps 67, 67a-67c & 69

Bowes Loop 8½ miles/13.7km – 3-3½hrs

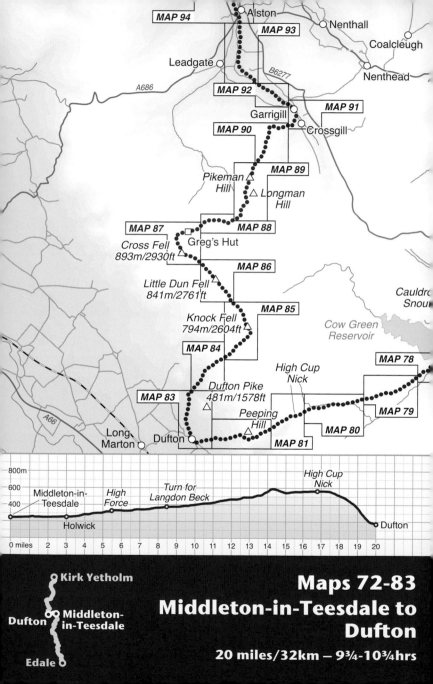

MAP 94
Alston
Nenthall
Coalcleugh
MAP 93
Leadgate
B6277
Nenthead
A686
MAP 92
Garrigill
MAP 91
MAP 90
Crossgill
MAP 89
Pikeman
Hill
Longman
Hill
MAP 87
MAP 88
Cross Fell
893m/2930ft
Greg's Hut
MAP 86
Little Dun Fell
841m/2761ft
MAP 85
Cauldro
Snou
Knock Fell
794m/2604ft
Cow Green
Reservoir
MAP 84
MAP 78
High Cup
Nick
MAP 83
Dufton Pike
481m/1578ft
MAP 79
A66
Peeping
Hill
MAP 80
Long
Marton
Dufton
MAP 81

800m
600
400
High Cup
Nick
Middleton-in-
Teesdale
High
Force
Turn for
Langdon Beck
Dufton
Holwick

0 miles 2   3   4   5   6   7   8   9   10 11 12 13 14 15 16 17 18 19 20

Kirk Yetholm

Dufton Middleton-
in-Teesdale

Edale

Maps 72-83
Middleton-in-Teesdale to Dufton
20 miles/32km – 9¾-10¾hrs

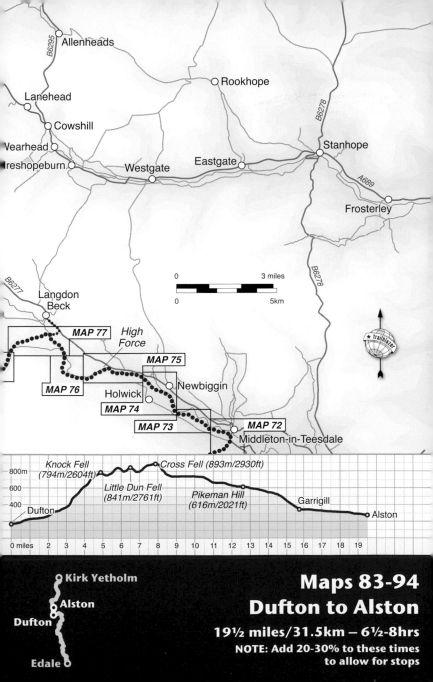

Allenheads

Rookhope

Lanehead

Cowshill

Stanhope

Vearhead

eshopeburn

Westgate

Eastgate

Frosterley

Langdon Beck

MAP 77

High Force

MAP 75

MAP 76

Holwick

Newbiggin

MAP 74

MAP 73

MAP 72

Middleton-in-Teesdale

Knock Fell
(794m/2604ft)

Cross Fell (893m/2930ft)

800m

Little Dun Fell
(841m/2761ft)

Pikeman Hill
(616m/2021ft)

Garrigill

600

Dufton

400

Alston

0 miles 2 3 4 5 6 7 8 9 10 11 12 13 14 15 16 17 18 19

Kirk Yetholm

Alston

Dufton

Edale

Maps 83-94
Dufton to Alston
19½ miles/31.5km – 6½-8hrs
NOTE: Add 20-30% to these times
to allow for stops

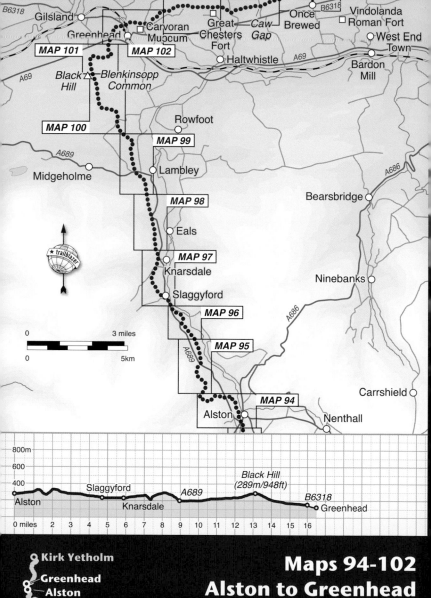

Gilsland
B6318
Once
Brewed
Vindolanda
Roman Fort
Great
Chesters
Fort
Caw
Gap
West End
Town
Carvoran
Museum
Greenhead
MAP 101
MAP 102
Haltwhistle
A69
Bardon
Mill
A69
Black
Hill
Blenkinsopp
Common
MAP 100
Rowfoot
MAP 99
A689
Bearsbridge
Midgeholme
Lambley
A686
MAP 98
★trailblazer
Eals
MAP 97
Knarsdale
Ninebanks
Slaggyford
0   3 miles
MAP 96
A686
0   5km
MAP 95
A689
Carrshield
MAP 94
Alston
Nenthall

800m
600
400
Black Hill
(289m/948ft)
Slaggyford
A689
B6318
Greenhead
Alston
Knarsdale

0 miles 2   3   4   5   6   7   8   9   10 11 12 13 14 15 16

Kirk Yetholm
Greenhead
Alston

Edale

Maps 94-102
Alston to Greenhead
16½ miles/26.5km – 7½-9½hrs
**NOTE: Add 20-30% to these times
to allow for stops**

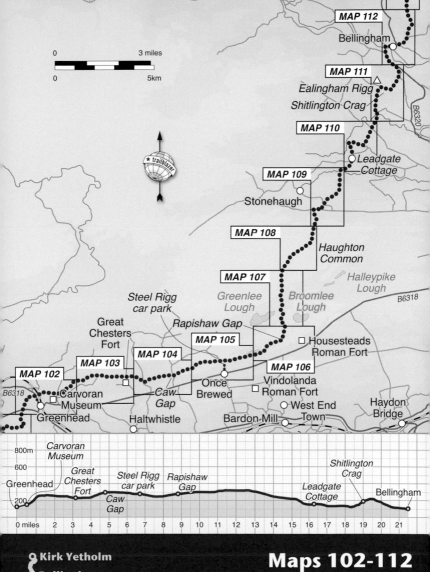

MAP 112

Bellingham

MAP 111

Ealingham Rigg

Shitlington Crag

B6320

MAP 110

Leadgate
Cottage

MAP 109

Stonehaugh

MAP 108

Haughton
Common

Halleypike
Lough

MAP 107

Greenlee
Lough

Broomlee
Lough

B6318

Steel Rigg
car park

Rapishaw Gap

Great
Chesters
Fort

MAP 105

Housesteads
Roman Fort

MAP 104

MAP 103

Caw
Gap

Once
Brewed

MAP 106

Vindolanda
Roman Fort

MAP 102

B6318

Carvoran
Museum

Greenhead

Haltwhistle

Bardon Mill

West End
Town

Haydon
Bridge

0   3 miles

0   5km

★ trailblazer

800m

600

200

Carvoran
Museum

Great
Chesters
Fort

Steel Rigg
car park

Rapishaw
Gap

Shitlington
Crag

Greenhead

Caw
Gap

Leadgate
Cottage

Bellingham

0 miles 2   3   4   5   6   7   8   9   10   11   12   13   14   15   16   17   18   19   20   21

Kirk Yetholm

Bellingham

Greenhead

Edale

Maps 102-112
Greenhead to Bellingham

21½ miles/34.5km – 9-10½hrs

**NOTE: Add 20-30% to these times
to allow for stops**

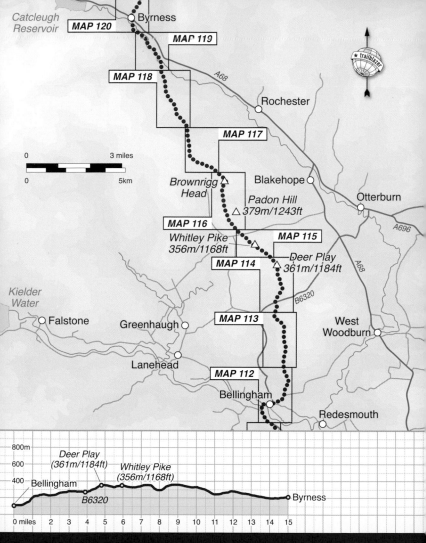

Catcleugh
Reservoir

Byrness
MAP 120

MAP 119

A68

MAP 118

Rochester

0   3 miles

0   5km

Blakehope

Otterburn

MAP 117

A696

Brownrigg
Head △

Padon Hill
△ 379m/1243ft

MAP 116

Whitley Pike
356m/1168ft △

MAP 115

Deer Play
△ 361m/1184ft

MAP 114

A68

Kielder
Water

B6320

Falstone

Greenhaugh

MAP 113

West
Woodburn

Lanehead

MAP 112

Bellingham

Redesmouth

800m
600
400

Deer Play
(361m/1184ft)

Whitley Pike
(356m/1168ft)

Bellingham

B6320

Byrness

0 miles 2   3   4   5   6   7   8   9   10 11 12 13 14 15

Kirk Yetholm
Byrness
Bellingham

Edale

Maps 112-120
Bellingham to Byrness

15 miles/24km – 7¼-9hrs
NOTE: Add 20-30% to these times
to allow for stops

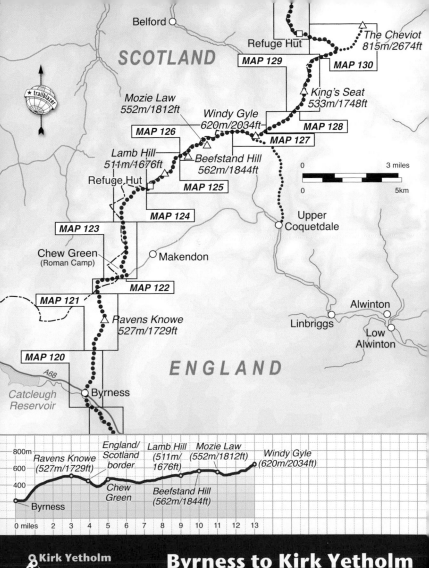

Belford

SCOTLAND

Refuge Hut

The Cheviot
815m/2674ft

MAP 129

MAP 130

Mozie Law
552m/1812ft

King's Seat
533m/1748ft

Windy Gyle
620m/2034ft

MAP 126

MAP 128

Lamb Hill
511m/1676ft

Beefstand Hill
562m/1844ft

MAP 127

Refuge Hut

MAP 125

MAP 124

0   3 miles

MAP 123

0   5km

Upper
Coquetdale

Chew Green
(Roman Camp)

Makendon

MAP 122

Alwinton

MAP 121

Linbriggs

Low
Alwinton

Ravens Knowe
527m/1729ft

MAP 120

ENGLAND

A68

Catcleugh
Reservoir

Byrness

800m

England/
Scotland
border

Lamb Hill
(511m/
1676ft)

Mozie Law
(552m/1812ft)

Windy Gyle
(620m/2034ft)

Ravens Knowe
(527m/1729ft)

600

400

Chew
Green

Beefstand Hill
(562m/1844ft)

Byrness

0 miles   2   3   4   5   6   7   8   9   10   11   12   13

Kirk Yetholm
Windy Gyle
Byrness

Byrness to Kirk Yetholm

Maps 120-127 – Byrness to Windy Gyle

13 miles/21km – 5¼-6½hrs

**NOTE: Add 20-30% to these times
to allow for stops**

Edale

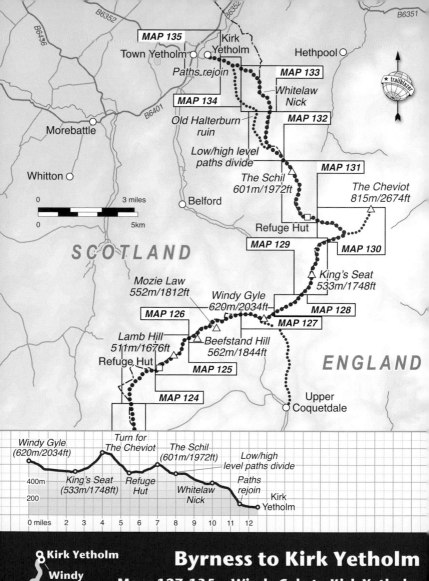

MAP 135
MAP 134
MAP 133
MAP 132
MAP 131
MAP 129
MAP 130
MAP 126
MAP 127
MAP 128
MAP 125
MAP 124

Town Yetholm
Kirk Yetholm
Hethpool
Paths rejoin
Whitelaw Nick
Morebattle
Old Halterburn ruin
Low/high level paths divide
Whitton
The Schil 601m/1972ft
The Cheviot 815m/2674ft
Belford
Refuge Hut

SCOTLAND

King's Seat 533m/1748ft
Mozie Law 552m/1812ft
Windy Gyle 620m/2034ft
Lamb Hill 511m/1676ft
Beefstand Hill 562m/1844ft
Refuge Hut

ENGLAND

Upper Coquetdale

0   3 miles
0   5km

Windy Gyle (620m/2034ft)
Turn for The Cheviot
The Schil (601m/1972ft)
Low/high level paths divide
King's Seat (533m/1748ft)
Refuge Hut
Whitelaw Nick
Paths rejoin
Kirk Yetholm
400m
200
0 miles 2 3 4 5 6 7 8 9 10 11 12

Kirk Yetholm
Windy Gyle
Edale

Byrness to Kirk Yetholm
Maps 127-135 – Windy Gyle to Kirk Yetholm
12½ miles/20km – 5¼-6½hrs
NOTE: Add 20-30% to these times to allow for stops

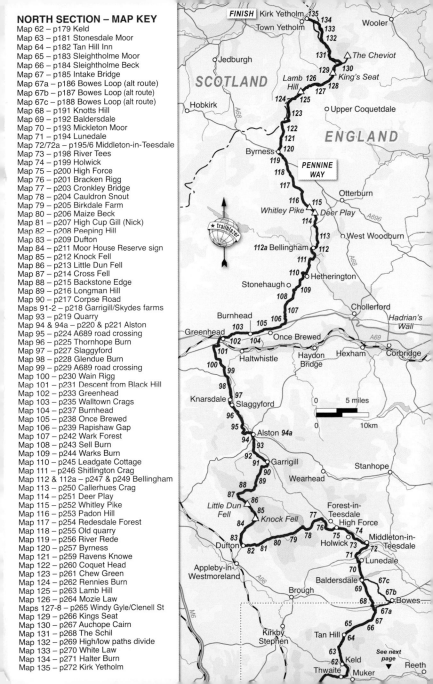

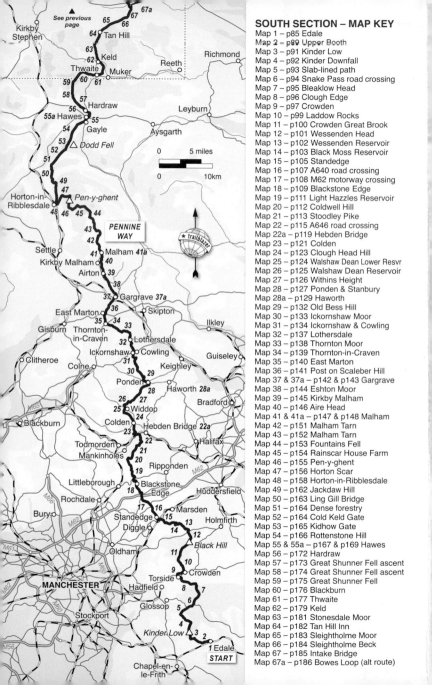